MR. CARR  The Car Hire Man	**MRS. CARR**  The Car Hire Man's Wife	**MISS CARR**  The Car Hire Man's Daughter	**MASTER CARR**  The Car Hire Man's Son

JOHN GILLO
ANDRAS KALDOR

Printed by Tozer & Co.
Dartmouth

CW00549774

HAPPY FAMILIES
Familiæ Felices
DARTMOUTH HAPPY FAMILIES

MASTER CRISP  The Greengrocer's Son	**MISS CRISP**  The Greengrocer's Daughter	**MR. CUTMORE**  The Butcher	**MRS. CUTMORE**  The Butcher's Wife	**MASTER CUTMORE**  The Butcher's Son	**MISS CUTMORE**  The Butcher's Daughter
MASTER HAIR  The Vet's Son	**MISS HAIR**  The Vet's Daughter	**MR. KAIN**  The Fruit Grower Man	**MRS. KAIN**  The Fruit Grower's Wife	**MASTER KAIN**  The Fruit Grower's Son	**MISS KAIN**  The Fruit Grower's Daughter
MASTER LEGGE  The Athlete's Son	**MISS LEGGE**  The Athlete's Daughter	**MR. MEASURES**  The Pharmacist	**MRS. MEASURES**  The Pharmacist's Wife	**MASTER MEASURES**  The Pharmacist's Son	**MISS MEASURES**  The Pharmacist's Daughter
MASTER PILLAR  The Builder's Son	**MISS PILLAR**  The Builder's Daughter	**MR. PRICE**  The Bank Manager	**MRS. PRICE**  The Bank Manager's Wife	**MASTER PRICE**  The Bank Manager's Son	**MISS PRICE**  The Bank Manager's Daughter

MASTER SLEEP The B & B Lady's Son	**MISS SLEEP** The B & B Lady's Daughter	**MR. SWINDELL** The Banker	**MRS. SWINDELL** The Banker's Wife	**MASTER SWINDELL** The Banker's Son	**MISS SWINDELL** The Banker's Daughter

The
Chronicles
of
Dartmouth

AN HISTORICAL YEARLY LOG
1955 – 2010

The superyacht Eos *sails out of Dartmouth after her first visit in 2007.* PHIL SCOBLE

The Chronicles *of* Dartmouth

AN HISTORICAL YEARLY LOG
1955 – 2010

Phil Scoble

in association with
The Dartmouth Chronicle

Foreword by Simon Drew

Richard Webb

DEDICATION

AUTHOR'S DEDICATION

To Lesley, my incredible, beautiful lady, without whose love, support, patience and strength
I would not be published today – thank you.
Phil Scoble

PUBLISHER'S DEDICATION

To Gilly, my wife for her love and loyalty and to mark 20 years of happy marriage in 2012.
Richard Webb

IN LOVING MEMORY

1907 – 1988

LT COLONEL RICHARD WEBB, Royal Signals
Officer Brother of the Order of St.John
President of Dartmouth St.John Ambulance
Co-founder of the Dartmouth & Kingswear Society

1909 – 1996

MRS IRIS K WEBB, RHS Gold Medallist
Author of *The Complete Guide to Flower & Foliage Arrangement*
President of the National Association of Flower Arrangement Societies
Founder of the Dartmouth Flower Club, President of the Old Dartmothians' Ladies Section

———◆◆◆———

First published in the United Kingdom in 2012 by Richard Webb, Publisher
First impression April 2012

Designed by Laurence Daeche, Anon Design Co, Christchurch, Dorset
Pre-edited by Richard Webb and Lynne Belt
Edited and indexed by Michael Forder

ACKNOWLEDGMENT

Full and grateful acknowledgement is given to the directors of the *Dartmouth Chronicle* and
South Hams Newspapers Limited for the use of source material and extracts from their archives.

A CIP catalogue record for this book is available from the British Library
ISBN 978-0-9568464-2-6

Typesetting: Titling: New Aster Semi Bold Body copy: New Aster

• 300 pages including colour endpapers • 627 illustrations including over 400 in colour
• 130,000 words including comprehensive index • 6 chapters plus 3 appendices

Printed and bound in China: Lion Production Ltd./Hanway Press Ltd.

Richard Webb, Publisher
Dartmouth, Devon, England

www.dartmouthbooks.co.uk

CONTENTS

SIMON DREW – half artist: half wit

Simon Drew has exhibited his work in his own gallery in Foss Street, Dartmouth since 1981. From the start he has produced prints and greetings cards which can be found around the world: some of these images have found their way onto other things such as mugs and aprons.

Diana Steel of the Antique Collectors Club became Simon's publisher and in 1983 his first book was published by ACC and since then there has been a new book published every year.

Simon's humour is sometimes surreal: he has described his illustrations as 'ideal for those who suffer from a deranged sense of humour and an urgent need to make fun of the world'. His original work often depicts still lives with a difference, juxtaposing the ordinary with the bizarre.

In the 1980s and 1990s Simon was part of a local group called 'The Dartmouth Artists' with John Donaldson, John Gillo, Andras Kaldor and Paul Riley. They held exhibitions together and, for a number of years, performed mind-boggling sketches together at Coombe Farm Studios' Christmas concerts.

Since 1988, Simon has had original artwork on show in the Chris Beetles Gallery in St James', London and each November his work is included in Chris's famous Illustrators' Exhibition.

FOREWORD

Over the years, I have moved around a little but in 1980, I settled in Dartmouth with my wife Caroline: the important word in that sentence is 'settled'. Dartmouth is a town that grabs you and makes you put down roots. I had never lived anywhere before where I wanted to stay: I was born and brought up in Reading so I know what boring towns are like.

For a while, I didn't notice how Dartmouth was seducing me, but it gradually dawned on me that I was completely besotted. I've tried to work out why and I've slowly realised that there are many reasons. First of all you notice the people, many of whom are featured in this book. Then you see how important the History is: to live and walk and trade in a town that is steeped in the past engenders a feeling of being somewhere significant. It's not just the Crusades, the Civil War and Chaucer that give perspective to a place: it's also the more recent history chronicled here. All this has coloured what Dartmouth is today.

It isn't coincidence that a natural deep harbour, so useful to ships and boats for centuries, happens to be beautiful as well as exciting.

A hundred years ago the town hit a low point in its prosperity: the days of wealthy merchants had passed and the twentieth century hadn't properly arrived. In some ways the lack of progress meant that some of the more ancient buildings were never demolished leaving us to enjoy them. Gradually since the Second World War Dartmouth has found new friends and its evolution is continuing. Interesting people have always lived here and interesting people have joined them. We're still preoccupied with parking and swimming pools and mad town councillors but Dartmouth has so much that other towns don't have. I think of it as a place full of stories and fascinating inhabitants with the added dimension of being by the sea.

Having a shop is a good way to meet people. It might be an American ('Was Dartmouth famous for pigs? No? Oh! I assumed that's why it's called the South Hams.') or a Dutchman ('We like your pictures. Have you ever exposed yourself in Holland?') or Elizabeth Cooper ('I've decided you're going to do some pictures for this pack of cards') or locals dropping by for a gossip about the carpark/ seagull nests/ art galleries/ vanishing police stations.

This town never stands still and generally gets better despite how councils try to stop progress. The Flavel Centre is the best thing that's happened to the town in my time; but there are no end of other great improvements like the Music Festival, the Food Festival and the Comedy Festival to add to the brilliant Regatta. Having lived in another similarly-sized south coast town, where nothing happened. I know what a gem we have.

Anyone who has had anything to do with Dartmouth in the last fifty years will recognise stories and people in this book. Some will have happy memories and some will remember incidents that worried them at the time. However, whatever you find, Phil Scoble has written a wonderful book complete with fascinating photographs. This book will take you on a nostalgic journey and you will look forward to finding what's round the next corner.

Simon Drew
Dartmouth, 2012

INTRODUCTION

It seemed a simple thing: write about what's happened in Dartmouth since 1955, based on what was in the *Dartmouth Chronicle*. But it quickly dawned on me, as I opened my first copy of the paper, what my problem was: What stories are important enough to be included? That is no simple puzzler. My strength as a local reporter was to listen and appreciate people's points of view. I fought hard to get the coverage people wanted and, in most cases, deserved. I loved to write about fishing festivals, Brownie outings, school achievements and council arguments. I loved being the man who could 'speak for the community'.

I didn't always get it right in my professional life, and Dartmouth is littered with people who I have disappointed or let down in some way, but I did my best. Trying to make sure everything got an equal chance of coverage, I wrote 3,000 words for every edition, and double that for the two Regatta editions. That's 162,000 words about Dartmouth, every year. So in my five years at the *Chronicle*, I wrote, give or take, 800,000 words. Or eight times what I have in this book to sum up 55 years.

So: not everything will be mentioned. And for that, I'm sorry. The question will always be what I found interesting and, frankly, I probably have completely missed out the thing you remember. However, if that's the case, why did I spend nearly 1,000 hours over two and a half years reading *Chronicles*, making 344,000 words of notes in the process? Because the town of Dartmouth deserves a history of the last five decades which highlights the transformation it has gone through. The changes the town has undergone, both socially and physically, have been some of the most profound it has faced. New developments have altered the face of the town in ways unimaginable in 1955, but the differences in attitudes and lifestyle would have, perhaps, seemed even more outlandish.

The people of Dartmouth however, retain a strength of character all their own.

Since taking on the task of trying to sum up fifty five years of Dartmouth's history in 100,000 words, I have done many things. Read 2,986 *Dartmouth Chronicles*, in a wide range of designs and configurations; Marvelled at the regularity of some types of stories; Realised how cold rooms in newspaper offices get after everyone has gone home; Got an aching neck sitting at a microfiche reader in a public library and come to appreciate the fantastic work of generations of journalists at the *Chronicle*. This has been the biggest learning experience of my life and I am incredibly thankful for the opportunity to do it.

It has been a wonderful, fun and exciting adventure to discover all of these things about Dartmouth – I hope you enjoy them all.

Phil Scoble
Dartmouth, 2012

From left to right: *Simon Drew, artist, Phil Scoble, author and journalist, and Richard Webb, publisher.*

HILARY BASTONE

CHAPTER I

A New Century for the *Chronicle*
1950s
1955 – 1959

DECADE OF DECORUM

The *Dartmouth Chronicle*, as it entered its second century, was at the centre of the life of Dartmouth. It was the first port of call for anyone wanting to know what was happening in the town, where to buy a house, car or any other item and even get advice on what to wear.

The town had come through the huge changes, challenges and traumas thrown up by the Second World War, and was, when 1955 came around, looking to the future.

The whole country was beginning to become more positive thanks to the coronation of Queen Elizabeth II. The event had a huge impact on the whole nation, being one of the first widely-televised events in the country's history and Dartmouth was rightly proud of its strong Royal connections as the Queen and Prince Philip had met at Britannia Royal Naval College.

The *Chronicle* reflected this with its usual frank assurance during the 1950s. Its touching and gentle way of reporting events had no hint of the journalistic cynicism which would later characterise much of the press.

It was truly the voice of the town at this time, reflecting the shifts and changes in the public view during the decade, showing reserve, tact and decency in the way it dealt with sensitive and traumatic tales.

The other element which is so in contrast with later periods in the *Chronicle* is the decorum and politeness of its politics. The 1950s seems to have been a time in Dartmouth where those representing the people of the town on its borough council conducted themselves in a respectful and refined way towards their council colleagues, whatever their views on them in private.

The decade can be categorised by an inherent optimism in the *Chronicle*, though it marked the beginning of long running debates and the first occurrences of issues which would dominate the town's *Chronicle* for decades – not least parking issues and the need for a swimming pool.

A time capsule of 1956 when Dartmouth had a thriving ship building industry, showing Philip & Son Ltd floating dock (1924–1961) off Sandquay with a Trinity House lightship The Bar *docked for repairs with HMS* Venus *of the Dartmouth Training Squadron in the background. Painted by Harold Ing.*
DARTMOUTH MUSEUM

The Regatta edition of the Chronicle *welcomes Dartmouth's most popular annual event.*

ESTABLISHED 1854

CASTLE BAKERY
NEWCOMEN ROAD
Phone 2140
Specialists in Cakes and almond goods
Bread deliveries Daily

Dartmouth Chronicle

CIRCULATING IN DARTMOUTH, BRIXHAM, KINGSBRIDGE AND THE SOUTH HAMS

[Telephone: Dartmouth 24]   [Telegrams: "Chronicle," Dartmouth]

No. 6018   AUGUST 26, 1955   Price 2d.

Parkham Hote...

Welcome to Dartmouth Regatta!

GAY CROWDS SEE MAYOR HAND OVER SILVER OAR

By JOHN DOCKERTY, Chronicle Staff Reporter

DARTMOUTH crowds in gay holiday moods lined Victoria Road and the Royal Avenue Gardens on Wednesday evening to

"WHAT A LOVELY PLACE"

VISITORS TELL MAYOR

Through the courtesy of the Editor of the Dartmouth Chronicle I am privileged to send to all inhabitants of Dartmouth my greetings on this our great reunion, the 110th Royal Regatta.

I do not usually indulge in prophecies, but last year I told you that I felt certain that Dartmouth would once deserved—and look at us now in this marvellous summer of 1955. What splendid events we have witnessed—the Annual British Legion Rally which

THE BISHOP OF PLYMO... COMES TO KINGSWEA... TO INDUCT NEW VICA...

ST. THOMAS of Canterbury Church, Kingswear, lavishly ... with flowers, was crowded on Wednesday evening fo... stitution and induction of the new Vicar, Rev. A. W. G. Du... the Bishop of Plymouth, The Rt. Rev. Norman Clarke).

Rev. Mr. Duffield succeeds the Rev. F. H. Keyworth signed recently after more than 20 years at Kingswear, d health.

The new Vicar of Kingswear who ... before coming to the Devon parish, was ... Vicar of St. John the Baptist, Chester. He ... was a graduate of the University of ...

1955 There was some economic good news for Dartmouth for the first time since the war. The town saw a boom in the summer of 1955 with the country only just coming through the effects of the Second World War.

1954 had seen 'the first normal Christmas for fifteen years' according to the *Chronicle*, as the 1950s started to become what they later were categorised as – a time of optimism and growth.

Hotels and Bed & Breakfast businesses were fully booked and café's saw 'record business' throughout a summer so hot there were a series of fires in fields around the area too. However the August 19 edition of the *Chronicle* featured the ominous headline, 'Holiday boom is bringing car parking problems'.

CARS BRING MONEY AND CHAOS

Motorists seemed to be getting fined left right and centre for causing obstructions around the town as desperation saw them park wherever they could.

Chairman of the town's Magistrates Court, Dr JH Smith said that 'it [is] impossible to rely on the common sense of motorists who were visiting the town for the first time' and suggested no waiting signs be erected.

Another problem was the rubbish left by free-spending tourists with road sweepers starting earlier and finishing later. The tourists also caused more damage to roads, steps and other amenities. Councillors were constantly annoyed by the extra engineers needed to make repairs.

The visitors brought money and a need for the town's oldest event to be put under the microscope.

Regatta should have been a time of celebration, but instead faced a stern examination of its values from one of its staunchest supporters, Les Prout.

The stalwart of the event bemoaned the lack of former traditions held dear by the populace. These included: the coal conveyor off the North Embankment which use to hide 'her ugly framework in a proud panoply of festive colour' and serve as the starting point for many race; the 'Regatta Ham' used by families as an easy alternative to fixing meals at irregular times they instead had a large ham in the larder which they could take from at any time; 'Phil Strong' who used to be part of the 'Cheap Jacks' and show off his amazing physique and challenge bystanders to a bet to see if they could use his famous 'five-strand' chest expander as easily as he did. He apparently always promised to wrestle his female assistant and break a chain across his chest, but 'never did'.

Mr Prout also complained that the 'tricksters' which now frequented the fair were not interested in entertainment, or even wholesome family fun, but in simply getting 'every last penny' from revellers.

Despite his protestations the *Chronicle* proclaimed the Regatta created 'a post-war record' for visitor numbers, with 45,000 crossing the river Dart in the *SS Mew* passenger ferry alone.

Dartmouth found itself dealing with one of the most horrible stories to grace the *Chronicle*'s pages in a generation.

Howard Koppenhagen (centre) next to Christopher Milne and Dartmouth Pottery employees before his fateful 'brainstorm' which apparently caused him to kill his wife, daughter, dog and himself.
COURTESY OF HARRY NORTON

The town reeled after Dartmouth Pottery Managing Director Howard Koppenhagen shot his wife Patricia and daughter Christine.

Koppenhagen, 36, shot his wife, who was also 36, at close range before killing their 12 year old daughter and the loyal family Newfoundland dog Rusty on October 11. He then turned the gun on himself in a downstairs armchair at the family home at Weeke Hill. The tragedy seemed worse because there was seemingly no motive, the man's business was well in order and the family was thought to be blissfully happy.

The coroner put the incident down to a 'brainstorm' caused by long-term effects of having meningitis during the Second World War.

The grisly scene had met the family's housekeeper as she arrived to do her job on a Tuesday morning. She found the front door open and the lights on and wondered why Rusty had not bounded up to meet her in his usual enthusiastic manner. She went to answer a ringing phone in the sitting room and discovered Mr Koppenhagen sitting upright in an armchair with a shotgun resting on his thigh, having fired the gun at his own head, killing himself instantly.

Despite the coroner's assertion that the mans 'balance of mind was disturbed', he had taken exactly the right amount of shotgun cartridges from his office at the pottery – not one was left in the house – and each killing had taken only one shot.

Mr Koppenhagen had come to Dartmouth in the late forties and helped found the pottery in the derelict brewery at Warfleet Creek. He was described as having a nervous energy, never settling or seeming at ease, and was prone to bouts of sleepiness and severe, debilitating headaches. Despite this his pottery was thriving and a new site had been acquired for the company in Townstal soon after the company started. It was said at the time to be in a very healthy financial position.

RATES SHOOT UP TO UNIVERSAL ALARM

The businesses in the town reeled for a different reason – when the rates more than doubled. The huge hike came about because the rateable values of the properties had not been reviewed since the outbreak of the war, so more than fifteen years had gone by since anyone had looked at them. Not surprisingly they jumped considerably.

Mr Ralph Foster – the *Chronicle* never reported who he was – spoke to the town's Chamber of Trade and gave a gloomy picture.

The arrival of the new British Rail passenger ferry, the Humphrey Gilbert.
SOUTH HAMS NEWSPAPERS

'I am not over-estimating when I give that rough forecast,' he told them. 'I know towns where they are having to face an increase of three or four times. It is a prospect of the utmost gravity.'

He told traders that the only hope they had of escaping a big increase was if they lived in the premises they worked in, where the residential part of the property would be judged on 1939 values and the 1955 values would be confined to the business property.

The councillors of Kingswear voted to buy Waterhead Creek by just one vote, securing a beautiful site for the good of the village, even though they wanted originally to use it for landfill.

The British Transport Commission had offered to sell the land to the people of Kingswear so it could be filled in and used to build public amenities for the people of the village. However, detailed negotiations over ten years saw these conditions changed and the creek was secured for the now mind-boggling sum of £175 as a 'public open space'. Cllr Harry Aaron repeatedly opposed the scheme but was defeated by a single vote and the purchase went through. It was pointed out that the purchase and subsequent contract would allow the later filling-in of the creek at the council's leisure, but Cllr Aaron said that the £20,000 costs of such an undertaking would cripple the village.

BOROUGH BAND LOSING TIME DUE TO STICK WAGGLER

The Dartmouth Borough Band came under threat in November. Only twelve members of the band remained, although it had boasted more than twice that figure in the past. Only a small and dedicated band came along to a special meeting to discuss the crisis at the Guildhall.

More than twenty players had left the band and in 1954 it had brought in only a third of the revenue it had in 1922. After 70 years of musical history the Borough Band seemed to be on its last legs.

The reason seemed to be money with many experienced players knowing they would be paid if they joined one of the many bands touring the country offering big band dance music at the time – all they got in Dartmouth was the thanks and appreciation of the town's people. This had resulted in fewer experienced musicians getting involved and the troupe using young players who were prone to mistakes and slips. At Regatta that year the band had lost its time as it marched past the market. They then stopped playing entirely later on in the march.

The performance was a huge embarrassment. The band leader J Govett, said he had no explanation for the stop. However he must have keenly felt the criticism as he offered to step down 'gladly' and said 'I would rather play an instrument than waggle a stick.'

Offers of advice were given to the band members, with one far reaching thought being 'playing less complicated' music so that all members of the band were capable of joining in for the whole piece. The band continued but its future remained uncertain.

A new Woolworths store was opened in the town making its debut on Victoria Road.

Opening on November 10, the store was mobbed by housewives and children on their way to school. The *Chronicle* reported the first three customers received a free bone china tea set 'with the compliments' of Manager William Pell. All three agreed that the store was a good thing for Dartmouth and hoped that the cheap prices of products would mean all prices would drop across the borough.

It certainly seemed to encourage shopping as the post-war malaise was finally shaken off and people flexed the power of their wallets, especially at Christmas.

Tellingly the *Chronicle* told its readers that shoppers had been 'dipping into their savings like never before' and had 'beaten all records' for the town's traders.

'Window displays are more lavish than ever,' it said in its December 23 edition, perhaps heralding the new 'consumer culture' which defined much of the late 20th century. 'Toy shops are showing all the old favourites – the dolls and scooters – and a host of new ideas to delight the children on Christmas morning.'

SHIP SLIPS SIDEWAYS BUT AVOIDS SINKING

1956 Philip & Son at Noss on Dart saw their biggest success to date nearly become their biggest disaster.

The *Syyid Khalifa* was built for the Sultan of Zanzibar, and had the ability to carry more than 1,000 tons of cargo in two cargo holds, while also carrying nine passengers in first class, and extremely luxurious, accommodation.

The vessel was 200 *feet* long and had a gross tonnage of 1,650. She was the largest vessel built on the river Dart up to that point and was part of the shipyard's great renaissance during the mid to late 1950s, which saw it produce more than twenty five lightships and countless tugs and other vessels for clients all over the world.

She was launched in 1955 and moved to the large floating dock which was moored off Sandquay to be fitted out by the highly-skilled and proud workmen of Philip & Son. The workmanship of the yard was so renowned the Sultan had personally chosen the yard to build his ship.

On February 1, during one of the coldest snaps in the South Hams in many years, the whole of the dock and ship keeled over and the whole lot would have sunk had it not keeled onto the shipyard pontoon.

Men were forced to run and jump for their lives during the incident. The ship had slipped off the blocks it sat on inside the dock as water was pumped out to allow work to be carried out.

Remarkably the ship was not badly damaged by the incident and left dock with only one hinge on the cargo doors showing any sign it had not had a trouble-free construction. The good name of Philip & Son continued.

The town's naval training establishment was shown how good a name it had in February. After fifty one years Dartmouth acknowledged the importance of the Britannia Royal Naval College to the area by granting its officers and cadets the 'freedom of the town' in a special ceremony.

The day was a joyous one in February as church bells rang and the town celebrated its connection with the best sailors in the world, and the world's greatest naval training establishment. Three hundred of the College's cadets marched through the town and were met by crowds cheering and waving Union Flags wherever they went. The *Chronicle* made no bones about the pride with which the town regarded the College.

The Philip & Son Floating Dock before its near disastrous capsizing whilst holding the Syyid Khalifa *in 1956.*
DARTMOUTH MUSEUM

Dartmouth Schools – Fighting for Investment

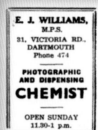

ESTABLISHED 1854

Dartmouth Chronicle

CIRCULATING IN DARTMOUTH, BRIXHAM, KINGSBRIDGE AND THE SOUTH HAMS

[Telephone: Dartmouth 21]

[Telegrams "Chronicle," Dartmouth]

No. 6041.

OCTOBER 25, 1957

Price 2d.

Churston School is first to be built in Devon for 30 years

Dartmouth's education has, for most of the last fifty five years, been seen to be in a precarious position. Parents, teachers, pupils, students and councillors have had to periodically fight for the right to see their children educated in their own town.

The first problems came in 1957 – when the grammar school was shut and Churston Ferrers Grammar School was opened.

'No one who saw the opening of the new grammar school at Churston Ferrers on Tuesday October 22, 1957 can doubt that the children of Dartmouth will, in the long run gain much more than they have lost by the change over' said the *Chronicle* in its front page story showing happy teachers and pupils in the new building.

Despite the positive tone the closure of the grammar school shook the town – it was too

small to sustain such a school, and too far away from the population centres of the area to ever be the site of major investment in education.

Secondary education has always been a numbers game – numbers of students. The economic model which British education has used for most of the last sixty years, the infamous comprehensive system, is based on schools having more than 800 students to be viable. Economies of scale mean that the costs per student only become affordable across the country if they are grouped in sufficient numbers.

Dartmouth has for many years boasted the country's second-smallest secondary school in a non-island community in the British Isles.

This has been championed by many of the school's Headteachers, stating that smaller class

Staff and pupils at Dartmouth Grammar School in the Fifties. DARTMOUTH MUSEUM

sizes will aid education. But with small size comes great challenges, namely trying to make the meagre funding you get stretch to fulfil all the needs of the school.

Several times during the last fifty five years the secondary school has looked closure full in the face – most notably when Devon County Council stalled on putting new buildings at the Milton Road site in the early 1980s. It emerged that the council was planning for a future without Dartmouth Community College because it was 'not viable'.

Politics won out over long-term planning on that day, because despite the officers at the council clearly believing closing Dartmouth was the only way, their political pay-masters looked at the angry faces of parents gathered at countless public meetings and decided that closing the school would be a very painful process and more trouble than it was worth. It remained open.

The school became a Community College – in one of those government-driven name changes no one but people working in education seem to understand or care about.

But there have always been fears for not only the school's future, but also whether its lack of money was affecting the quality of its educational standards.

Falling student numbers again put the school's future in question throughout the Nineties and the new Millennium.

It then gained 'Arts Status' securing extra funding for arts activities thanks to the stellar reputation of its art department and its hard-working staff. But this was not something that secured its future.

In 2007 it was announced that a new, £800,000 children's centre would be built on the Milton Lane Campus, meaning children up to the age of nineteen and beyond would be educated there. It heralded the start of a period of re-birth for the area's schools.

In 2008 the College announced it was to become 'Federated' with Dartmouth Primary School. This meant that the two organisations would have one board of governors, and the site which both occupied was renamed the 'Dartmouth Learning Campus'. It was the first such federation in Devon and one of only a handful in the country.

The secondary school takes shape on the Milton Lane campus. TOTNES IMAGE BANK

A creative writing class at Dartmouth Community College in the 21st century. PHIL SCOBLE

Hopes of a new – or at least significantly re-built – school for the site were announced at the end of the year, by the county council, perhaps at last acknowledging the need for a permanent secondary school in Dartmouth. Using funds from the Government's Building Schools for the Future scheme, it was hoped up to £9 million would become available for the revamp/rebuild.

Then in September 2009, before the decision on the rebuild money was made by central government, a bid for the campus to become an Academy was made. This would mean the school would 'partner' with a commercial organisation that would put educational expertise and funding into the school. The academy would also be separated from the local education authority – Devon County Council – and have more freedom in how it structured its classes and the way it taught its students.

Academies were a controversial and difficult subject for many in education. The National Union of Teachers was bitterly opposed to them. The academies, it claimed, moved the education system into the open market, with the trials and tribulations that brought with it.

In the middle of what was clearly a difficult and bitter fight – the good news came through that the Building Schools for the Future bid had been successful, and the school would have a three-quarter rebuild by 2013.

No one seemed to doubt that the Academy would be implemented, an idea reinforced when the school ordered the new Academy uniform before the end of the official consultation period.

The decision was duly taken to close the school officially in July and re-open in September 2010 as an Academy for 3 – 16 year olds.

A new start for education in Dartmouth? Finally the investment needed for the young people of this community? Only time will tell.

'For more than eight hundred years the fortunes of maritime Dartmouth has been linked with the Royal Navy and on Wednesday February 22 the people of this ancient port made this age-old association stronger by granting Britannia Royal Naval College the Freedom of the Borough of Dartmouth,' it proclaimed. 'At noon on that day nearly 300 cadets exercised for the first time their privilege of marching through the town with bayonets fixed, drums beating and bands playing. One hour earlier Mayor Dorothy Holwill surrounded by distinguished guests from all three services was handed a portfolio granting the Freedom to the Captain of the College, Capt WG Crawford. There were moving scenes as a great crowd watched and cheered the naval cadets marching through the snow-covered streets of Dartmouth. Despite the intense cold there were many children among the hundreds who lined the flag decked streets.'

TOWN PROUD OF THE MAYOR'S TV PERFORMANCE

The town also got 'worked up' when it moved into the new exciting future of broadcasting as Dartmouth's TV Aerial Service was started.

The new service was to have been premiered at the Chamber of Trade Exhibition in November the previous year. The exhibition was hailed as a great success by most traders who took part but the initial demonstration by the company's owner John Pullen was a damp squib because parts had not arrived. His second attempt on February 6, 1956, drew a big crowd because the town's Mayor, Dorothy Holwill was appearing on *'What's My Line?'* and everyone wanted to see her.

The show was huge news at the time: contestants had to do a mime of what they did for a living and then answer questions from the panel about their occupation as the panel tried to guess what they did. Cllr Holwill gave, to all appearances, a peerless performance. She 'baffled' the experts trying to work out what in hen's teeth she did.

The *Chronicle* gave two reactions to it; one from the editor said simply: 'Fortunate Dartmouth – to have a Mayor like Mrs Dorothy Holwill, there she was on Monday evening on TV for the whole country to see. How the panel and its Chairman Eamonn Andrews responded to her friendliness. No pomposity with the Mayor of Dartmouth. It is not surprising that many Londoners who had looked in at the programme recognised and greeted her in the streets and shops of London the following morning.'

The other, in the Around the Town section, said: 'I think everyone will agree that our Mayor, Mrs Dorothy Holwill, did a splendid job for us on *'What's My Line?'* on Monday evening. I was among the crowd gathered outside the HQ of the TV Aerial Service in Market Square and when the Mayor defeated the panel there was spontaneous outburst of clapping.'

The TV service seems to have benefited from the Mayor's success and 'circuits' of cable were soon running along Foss Street, Church Close, Higher Street and Newcomen Road as more people signed up. The new service allowed subscribers to receive television through wires connected to a temporary mast rigged up on the hills above the town.

The first customer to be connected was Mr DH Mason who told the *Chronicle*: 'reception is perfect and entirely free of interference. It's much better than I'd hoped for and I am very satisfied indeed.'

As satisfying was the support shown to Dartmouth's 'Cottage' hospital when it acquired a League of Friends.

More than 100 people turned out for a meeting at the end of March to form the group.

The Mayor Dorothy Holwill chaired the meeting and commented: 'A friend is a person who is willing to help in any way required and it is very encouraging to see so many present.'

The feeling was that despite the love and affection felt for the hospital, since the inception of the NHS, any money given to the hospital might be diverted to the larger state – but the Friends group meant all money given to it had to be used in the local hospital.

The love and affection were well earned as in an average year more than 5 per cent of the town's population passed through its doors as a patient, so helping the hospital, according to the Mayor, was simply a case of 'helping your neighbour' and even 'helping yourself' because chances were if you fell ill you'd be in there.

GOODBYE DOLLY

In May, Dartmouth saw the end of the tenure of its first female Mayor since the role was created by Edward the Black Prince more than 600 years before – Dorothy Holwill.

As she stepped down gracefully from the role, her friend Bob Middleton said: 'When I first heard of Mrs Holwill's election as Mayor I wondered what the general public's reaction would be. For centuries it has been a male preserve, but Mrs Holwill has shown us she can come up to and even surpass the men in energy, tact and initiative.'

The town also gained something of a novelty – the youngest Mayoress in the country.

Doreen Lavers was Bertie's daughter, and as he was installed at the history-laden Mayor-making Ceremony at the Guildhall in the 616th Mayoral year, she was just 17. Doreen took up the role as her mother had tragically died and became something of a national celebratory.

It became normal to see pictures of her, pigtails swinging, helping her father to ceremonially plant a tree, or attend a function at the Britannia Royal Naval College in the pages of the *Chronicle* and even those of the *Daily Mail*. She became very well loved and the town's residents became fiercely proud and protective of her and her father for inviting her into the role.

Less successful was the town's carnival, which turned into a damp squib and the organisers knew what to blame...tall ships and the weather.

The tall ships were big news as they sailed into the harbour before racing to Lisbon. It was the first Tall Ships Race of its kind and was billed as the 'greatest fleet of sailing ships ever assembled'. The race was founded to give young sailors the chance of high adventure on the high seas, and more than a thousand cadets were involved in sailing the twenty two vessels from eleven countries all the way from Torbay to Spain. A special 'inshore' Regatta was held involving sailing, swimming, rowing and other races, and special social events were also organised.

The *Chronicle* gave the event huge coverage, and tried to sell the carnival in the same excited manner, under the headline '...and there's a Carnival on too!' but, perhaps inevitably, the carnival events suffered, especially as the June

weather deteriorated and many events, including the fascinating 'dog parade and crazy sports day', were cancelled or seriously curtailed. Also many events had fewer entrants because all the town's employers, especially the hotels, pubs and restaurants were at full stretch dealing with the huge influx of visitors.

The carnival was such a failure even its failure couldn't budge the Tall Ships from the front page lead story.

The Tall Ships brought a huge amount of trade to the town, one hotelier said: 'It was an absolute tragedy having to turn so many people away; it was our busiest week for years.'

The race itself was won by the British ship *Moyana*, crewed by fifteen young cadets from the University of Southampton. The ship took the gleam off its victory by sinking on its way back in heavy seas, thankfully after the whole crew had been taken off by a Royal Navy frigate.

The Regatta, in contrast to the carnival, seemed to be heading for great success. How could it fail to be, with the Queen as its official patron?

The Queen 'graciously' accepted the role of patron of the event, which had become the 'Royal Regatta' in 1856 after Queen Victoria granted her patronage whilst visiting the waterborne event.

Queen Elizabeth II, in only the third year of her reign, sent a letter which was read out at the Opening Ceremony by Chairman Gilbert White, wishing good luck to the Regatta. It didn't bring much luck.

The sailing and local rowing were described as descending into 'chaos' because of violent and bitter gales which swept in from the Atlantic.

Many yachts were capsized, one was dismasted and another split her mainsail, giving the safety boat crews a nightmare few days. The storms created what was described by the chairman as 'the coldest Regatta in history'.

'May I express my thanks to the many competitors who so nobly carried on in spite of the weather and also to the committee and other helpers who stuck to their work and did such an excellent job,' he said after the event. 'Financially, we shall be down, but personally I am sure the committee also went to bed on Saturday night with a feeling of elation rather than depression because never have I had so many good wishes from so many people.'

THE AMAZING MR SMITH AND MR BATTERSBY

The town became the centre of an international event when two men from Toronto sailed 3,700 miles to Dartmouth in a 27 foot ketch called *Orenda*.

The two men were Arthur Smith, a second generation Canadian of British descent and Alan Battersby a Brit from Poulton Le Flyde near Blackpool.

The pair had decided to take up the challenge of sailing across the seas as a way of earning money and starting a business. They left Toronto and braved rapids and the loss of most of the mainmast before they reached the open sea.

They ran out of food and had to deal with immensely rough seas before they reached their goal – and had to be towed into harbour when they did.

They sailed across the Atlantic through October, a famously rough month for the weather, and yet seemed to come through it none-the-worse-for-wear.

They then got a shock as two reporters were dropped into the sea next to the boat from a helicopter to interview them and get a 'scoop'. One of these reporters was then promptly taken ill, so they had to stop in at Salcombe and then the wind dropped.

They received a tow into Dartmouth following their detour, but no one seemed to care. They received a salute from submarine HMS *Trespasser* and were greeted by hundreds of boats who followed them to the Hospital Steps where the huge crowds saw that Smith wasn't wearing any boots.

Smith said: 'It's great to be on solid ground again and to see so many welcoming faces.'

Battersby said: 'We expected a welcome but this exceeds our wildest dreams. We know we are among friends.'

Their boat was taken to London and put on display at the National Boat Show, the pair returned to Canada and Smith wrote a book he hoped would raise funds for him to start his own business.

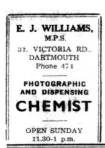

E. J. WILLIAMS,
M.P.S.
3t. VICTORIA RD.,
DARTMOUTH
Phone 474

PHOTOGRAPHIC
AND DISPENSING
CHEMIST

OPEN SUNDAY
11.30-1 p.m.

ESTABLISHED 1854

Dartmouth Ch

CIRCULATING IN DARTMOUTH, BRIXHAM, KINGSBRIDGE

[Telephone: Dartmouth 21]

No. 6105   APRIL 26, 1957

MEMORABLE SCENE AT MAYFLOWER ARRIVAL

*Mayor and Mayoress received by
Commander Alan Villiers*

I am anxious to sail as early as possible. It looks as though we might be stuck here for some while and I might have to get an ocean-going tug, possibly from Plymouth."

Brixham was caught unawares last Wednesday when Mayflower

The tug, Englishman, a frequent

The Chronicle acknowledges the arrival of Mayflower II.

1957

The town started to feel the heat of petrol rationing which was caused by issues connected to the Suez crisis in 1956.

The rationing came in on December 17, 1956, but the effects were being felt mainly in 1957 because a lot of motorists had stocked up on fuel, even though most petrol stations tried to put measures in to stop it. Panic buying brought local reserves to breaking point and the emergency services were forced to bring in their own supply. It affected every walk of life for more than seven months before the Chancellor ended the scheme in June.

BAKER JUMPS FROM OVEN INTO FIRE

A baker from Slapton was sent to gaol for three years after setting fire to his bakery. He was convicted of setting the fire and of attempting to gain an insurance payout. Mr William Powlesland pleaded not guilty to the charge because he claimed he didn't think he was insured when he set the fire.

Mr Powelsland had debts of more than £3,675 at the time he tipped his waste paper bin up on the floor and put a match to it.

'I never thought of it before,' he said. 'It was just a sudden impulse. I didn't want my customers to think it was through my fault the business had failed. I wanted them to think the fire was the cause of the failure.'

He told a tale of spiralling debt concluding with him being a desperate man out of his depth with too many creditors. The jury took a rather dimmer view and concluded he had wanted to claim the thousands on insurance to pay off the debt – he was found guilty on all counts in less than twenty minutes.

The Mayflower II sails out of Dartmouth.
Dartmouth Museum

JULY 12, 1957   THE CHRONICLE

Introducing

Mister Carnival

DARTMOUTH Carnival claims, with all due modesty, to be "The best in the West." There is some justification for this categorical statement, too, as a trip round other carnivals will show.

Larger towns with more advan-

Top: *The Chronicle declares George Perring 'Mr Carnival'.*

Above left: *The Carnival Queen 1957.*
SOUTH HAMS NEWSPAPERS

Above middle: *Carnival Baby Valerie Collins looks perplexed by the attention paid to her.*
SOUTH HAMS NEWSPAPERS

Above right: *Dartmouth Carnival Association's Pantomime.*
SOUTH HAMS NEWSPAPERS

The *Mayflower II* – the replica of the famous vessel – visited Dartmouth before sailing from Brixham to its new home in America in April.

The vessel was the victim of scandalous rumours stating it was un-seaworthy, despite being based on the vessel which had actually sailed across the Atlantic in 1620.

The vessels Captain, ex-Britannia Royal Naval College instructor Captain Allan Villiers said: 'Those who have been asking me if the *Mayflower* will arrive are talking nonsense. What do they think the explorers used and how do they think the world was opened up – with jet aeroplanes? Every discovery worth making was by means of little sailing ships.'

The ship's visit – though brief – was a major event for the town and many dignitaries turned out as it sailed into port for less than twelve hours. The next day hundreds of school children were disappointed after walking to the Castle to watch it leave only to find it had already gone: it sailed early to catch the tide.

ACKNOWLEDGING OUR CONNECTION TO AMERICA – AFTER 337 YEARS

The town decided to make something of its connection with the birth of the richest nation on earth, with the unveiling of a commemorative stone to the Pilgrim Fathers in May.

The US Ambassador sent a representative – the wonderfully named Brewster H Morris – to attend the ceremony. The stone and bronze plaque was donated by the General Society of *Mayflower* descendents, of which Brewster was one, it turned out.

He distanced the society from the visit of the *Mayflower II* which seemed, as a private enterprise, something of an embarrassment to the proud organisation.

A minor outbreak of Foot and Mouth disease in the summer in South Brent, resulting in restrictions of movement for animals around the area, highlighted the increasing importance of tourism to the town just when thousands poured into the region.

The August Bank Holiday was a boom time with many taking advantage of the good weather – and the fact that petrol rationing had not been re-introduced as feared – to visit South Devon. The *Chronicle* summed up the mood of the times.

'The bank holiday brought an influx of visitors which has not been seen for many a long day,' it said. 'Inflation, deflation, strikes, lock outs, H-Bombs, taxes – all were forgotten for a while and the crowds just swarmed in by car, coach or train to this, the most beautiful corner of England, bent on enjoying themselves.'

But it was not all sunny – many went away complaining there was a scarcity of 'attractions', and one visitor had his letter on the front of the *Chronicle* complaining the charges at cafes in the area were exorbitant:

'The town and the setting were still as charming, the people still as friendly… but the prices…!

Our shock came on the first day when we discovered the 'one and six-penny sausage'. Egg and chips at one café was 3s but the addition of a sausage made it 4s 6d! This was only a start, however. Cups of coffee at 10d, sandwiches at 9d and 1s each (one round of bread sliced in half and folded) and hot water- yes ordinary hot water for the baby's bottle cost us as much as 3d and 6d a jug. Avarice is the same the world over but it is a great pity that these café proprietors cannot see the sense of charging only a reasonable profit and increasing the custom. We live only twenty minutes from London and often have a day there. But we have never yet encountered such downright profiteering.'

The increasing need to publicise the town was strongly in the minds of traders – and they demanded a bigger budget for publicity from the council, but failed to give as big a donation themselves.

Cllr Lee-Palin, chairman of Dartmouth Borough Council's Publicity Committee which organised the marketing of the town, urged the traders to reach into their pockets to make them deeper next time round.

'It is a growing thing,' he told them, 'and you won't necessarily get the benefit the first year. To talk about a publicity fund of only £200 is ridiculous, but the council's contribution is limited by what we can ourselves collect. The hotels and boarding houses in general have contributed less than the ordinary traders to this fund, and the Licensed Victuallers have given nothing for this year's campaign, though they receive the first and most direct benefit from it.'

However the traders hit back that the publicity scheme run by the council had not been very effective and was a waste of money.

GLORIOUS REGATTA IN GLORIOUS WEATHER

The Regatta benefited from all the good weather its immediate predecessor had prayed for. The gales, storms and overturned yachts of 1956 were replaced by competitive and popular racing in all events.

The fairground reported good business, especially for the 'boxing booths' which featured punters going up against seasoned fighters for cash prizes.

The *Chronicle* painted the picture well: 'The boxing booths were well patronised, as always, and the 'Golden Terror' came in for his usual round of booing. He managed to bear this with fortitude, and casually combed his hair between rounds, to the great delight of the crowds.'

Dartmouth Territorials pleased after winning the Travers Cup for the Best First Aid Team.
SOUTH HAMS NEWSPAPERS

Dartmouth's Senior and Junior Crews – both WEARA champions in 1957.
SOUTH HAMS NEWSPAPERS

Her Majesty's Band of the Royal Marines, BRNC Dartmouth, march out of the Royal Avenue Gardens for the last time after being disbanded in May 2009. PHIL SCOBLE

'Our Band': Dartmouth's 53 year association with Her Majesty's Band of the Royal Marines

(See years 2004 and 2009)

The farewell performance on Coronation Park. PHIL SCOBLE

Dartmouth's 'Ship on the Hill' was home to Her Majesty's Band of the Royal Marines, Dartmouth for fifty three years – and its presence was a source of pride for the town.

A standard fixture at Mayoral Parades, Regatta events and important funerals, the band gave a sense of significance to every occasion they graced.

From the first moment the Marines arrived in the town, it seemed as though Dartmouth took the band and its members to its heart and never let go.

They were referred to as 'our' band.

For fifty years 'bandies' came to Dartmouth and were welcomed with open arms, moved to the town and made their lives here, in the most beautiful town in the county of Devon.

But economics and the changing political situation meant that fears began to circulate in the late 1960s and early 1970s that the Naval College would shut – taking the band with it.

During every round of spending cuts the town held its collective breath waiting for the axe to fall on its beloved band, and heaved a huge sigh of relief when nothing was cut, or cuts were in line with the rest of the services.

Marching out of the College Gates for the last time.
PHIL SCOBLE

Marching down Duke Street. PHIL SCOBLE

Her Majesty's Band of the Royal Marines, Dartmouth became the first and only Marines band to receive the 'Freedom' of a town or borough in 2004. They were presented with a special scroll declaring their right to march through the town with bayonets fixed and drums playing. They had a special event to celebrate the honour, and people began to relax about the future of the Naval College and its band.

But then in February 2008 it was announced that the band would be 'suspended' for eight months as members of the band were redeployed to provide 'strategic support' for troops in Afghanistan.

The MoD pointedly refused to answer questions on whether the band would return.

It didn't.

As details of the 'redeployment' came to light it became clear this was a permanent move: most of the band members were in fact being shared between the other Marine bands around the country.

Of the thirty six band members, only six were being sent to Afghanistan initially, and in total only sixteen were to be sent there.

It came as no surprise when the MoD finally announced that the Dartmouth band would 'disband' in November 2008. It was the long-dreaded end of the town's proud musical group.

But there was to be a last hurrah. In the same press release the MoD announced there would be a 'proper goodbye' in May 2009.

The day came round and careful planning seemed destined to be washed out by terrible weather. The forecast was for torrential downpours, and everyone prayed the day would not be ruined.

Someone must have been listening.

The special day of events on Wednesday May 20, 2009 was bathed in glorious sunshine which lent a special lustre to a terribly sad day for the town. Everywhere the band marched they were clapped and cheered.

The sun shone down as the band marched out under the College gates for the last time, and switched to play 'Colonel Bogey' as it passed the Ship in Dock Pub – in memory of its former landlord Bob Downes.

More than a thousand people watched them Beat Retreat on Coronation Park. The band gave a performance to be proud of as they marched in perfect time. All of them had called Dartmouth their home at some time or another, including Capt Jon Ridley, RM Band Officer who was married in the Britannia Royal Naval College Chapel in 2006.

They performed faultlessly under blue skies, under the gaze of the College's clock tower, and in front of the town's residents who had taken the band to their hearts for more than half a century.

Capt Ridley then asked the town's Mayor, Debbie Morris, for permission to march around the town, as per their right given in the Freedom Declaration.

Sid Davis, ex-Bandmaster and Dartmouth resident, carried the scroll ahead as they marched around the town one last time, and into the Royal Avenue Gardens. There the scroll was handed back to the town and then immediately given to the official museum of the Royal Marines for posterity.

'A terrible loss – but what wonderful goodbye' was how the Mayor summed up the day, and few would have contradicted her. The route the band followed was packed: people fell over each other to catch a final glimpse of the group.

As the band marched out of the Royal Avenue Gardens and down Duke Street, into Victoria Road and up to the Guildhall, every person felt the tide of history rolling past, and onwards.

As the Mayor led three cheers for the band, and they were told to finally stand at ease, there was not one person among the crowd who didn't feel the emotion of the moment, and more than one person had tears in their eyes.

It was the end, but what a glorious end to have.

The Scroll giving the Freedom of the Town to Her Majesty's Band of the Royal Marines, Dartmouth, is carried around the town by former Bandmaster, and Dartmouth resident, Sid Davies. PHIL SCOBLE

Left: *Dartmouth's Les Anstey turns professional footballer.*
SOUTH HAMS
NEWSPAPERS

Right: *Mayor N Hewson putting up bills for a road safety campaign.*
SOUTH HAMS
NEWSPAPERS

A Slapton farmer was killed – crushed beneath his own combine harvester. Michael McCoy, 31, a married man with three children, was taking a farm-hand through how best to drive the tractor and harvester on the steep incline of one of his fields.

However the demonstration went badly wrong as Mr McCoy neared the turn at the bottom of the field it slipped too fast and tipped over. Mr McCoy tried to jump clear but ended up in the way of the harvester as it tipped over and was crushed.

The farmhand and his younger brother managed to jump clear of the heavy equipment and ran through the September sunshine to get help. Desperate attempts to lift the harvester off Mr McCoy failed and he was declared dead at the scene.

A shake up of education in the borough began with the opening of Churston Grammar School and the end of grammar education in Dartmouth.

The *Chronicle* gave the opening big coverage and a picture of dignitaries and school boys outside the new building adorned the front of the *Chronicle* on October 25. Getting a picture into the paper was a complex and difficult process saved only for the most important subjects, and this showed how much the change affected the children of the town.

The Headmaster of the new school, Dr DW Carter, had also been Headmaster at Dartmouth and for many the change was a positive one – getting a better education in a newer building with better facilities, but it was felt the change could only be to the detriment of Dartmouth as a community, if not for the individuals getting the education.

The *Chronicle* was unequivocal: 'Dartmouth no longer has its own grammar school within the bounds of the borough, and this is a matter for regret, on practical as well as sentimental grounds. But no one who saw the opening of the new grammar school at Churston Ferrers on Tuesday October 22, 1957 can doubt that the children of Dartmouth will, in the long run gain much more than they have lost by the change over.'

The opening of the new Churston Grammar School spelled the end for Dartmouth Grammar.
SOUTH HAMS
NEWSPAPERS

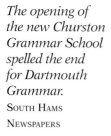

Dartmouth Chronicle

CIRCULATING IN DARTMOUTH, BRIXHAM, KINGSBRIDGE AND THE SOUTH HAMS

[Telephone: Dartmouth 24]   [Telegrams: "Chronicle," Dartmouth]

No. 6068   FRIDAY, MAY 2, 1958   Price 2d.

SHERRELLS
PAY HIGH PRICES
FOR FURNITURE.
Single Items to
Housefulls
45, NEWCOMEN
ROAD,
DARTMOUTH

POOL PROJECT GETS £14 SEND-OFF

GUILDHALL PACKED TO THE DOORS FOR PUBLIC MEETING

BY AN OVERWHELMING MAJOR-
ITY—THERE WAS ONLY ONE DIS-
SENTING VOICE—THE AUDIENCE
WHICH FILLED THE GUILDHALL
TO CAPACITY ON MONDAY NIGHT,
INDICATED IN NO UNCERTAIN

asked? That depended on the site and
the type of pool. There must be a
proper cleansing system and a chlor-
ination plant, and a pool of the same
size as that to be built at Totnes would
cost between 12 and 15 thousand

SGT. BARNES LEAVING

Sgt. H. W. Barnes, who has been
sergeant in charge at Dartmouth
since October 1 1954 will be leav-

1958 saw a rebirth of the campaign for a swimming pool in Dartmouth.

DON'T LOSE INTEREST IN REGATTA

1958 Regatta Chairman Mr H White slammed lack of interest in Regatta. At the annual meeting in February Mr White looked around a room with hardly anyone in it – certainly nobody new to help re-invigorate the event – and seemed to snap.

'It is pathetic that the greatest event in the town should be so poorly supported,' he raged. 'This meeting has been called by the Mayor, not the Regatta committee and there is only one councillor present. I have to wonder whether Dartmouth wants a Regatta. The man in the street supports it but I am worried about the lack of money in the event. Two or three bad years could see our spare funds vanish.'

But the carnival organiser George Perring spoke up, obviously the veteran of many a badly attended meeting.

'There is no need for Mr White to panic,' he said. 'I have served on the Regatta committee since before he came to Dartmouth, and we have never had big attendances at meetings. Yet the Regatta carries on. It would still carry on even if Mr White left the committee. We old Dartmothians will never let the Regatta fail.'

Treasurer F Burwood gave his financial report and revealed that the balance of the Regatta account had gone up by £28 13s 9d to £101 12s 7d.

In a year described as 'tough' by many for finance of all kinds, the increased figure was to be applauded. The borough council put up its rates from 19s 4d in the pound to one pound and sixpence – but the decision met with no passionate debate in chamber, it was just considered the way things were, you had to put the rates up just to keep 'at a standstill'.

Chairman of the Finance Committee Alderman H Wheatley said: 'Another difficult year has gone by and the year ahead promises to be no less difficult because wages and salaries have once again risen with adverse effects on the cost of services. These increases are likely to be a permanent recurring charge and will have to be met by all ratepayers – falling more heavily on those not now in employment. No council can stem these repercussions without rate increases – even temporary relief can only be maintained if considerable working balances are available and we have no such golden nest egg. All councils have been asked by the Ministry of Housing and Local Government to exercise the strictest economy and to observe a standstill period for new and non-essential work.'

JOBLESS FIGURES GIVE CAUSE FOR CONCERN

The perception that the town had so quickly fallen on hard times after a brief boom in '55 and '56 seemed to be supported in the jobless statistics released in June as they were 50 per cent higher than a year before. Forty seven men, sixteen women, six boys and four girls were out of work in June, seventy three in total, twenty three more than a year before, but down sixteen on the previous month. However this was simply put down to more seasonal employment.

However the 1957 unemployment figures represented a record low for the town, so perhaps the large headline the story attracted caused more alarm than actually indicated a terrible situation.

The town mourned the death of a former Mayor – Dr James Henry Smith, OBE, who died aged 74 in February.

1958 World Events
● Seven Manchester United footballers are among the twenty one people killed in the Munich air disaster in West Germany
● Bertrand Russell launches the Campaign for Nuclear Disarmament (CND)
● Subscriber Trunk Dialling (STD) introduced for the first time
● BBC TV series *Blue Peter* started

Mr Smith seemed to be one of those remarkable men who quietly achieve an incredible amount in their lives, all without much fuss or bother.

After his name, Dr Smith could have displayed the letters: MPS, BSc, FBOA (hon) FS MC, FNAO, D.Opt, BSc(Econ), PhD, FRAS, FICA, FRSA, FR Econ S.

He was also chairman of the Dartmouth Bench of Magistrates. He served a total of fifteen years on the council and became Mayor in 1932. His tenure was marked by his own support of a scheme to bridge the river Dart during 1932, which was defeated by a single vote and never came about.

He was also, in no particular order of importance, Freeman and Liveryman of the City of London, Chairman of the Dartmouth Commercial Association, Chairman of the Torbay Pharmaceutical Society and the Torbay branch of the Optical Practitioners Association and was a fellow of the Royal Astronomical Society for his research in the early development of the Spectroscope for spectral analysis.

So just to recap: he was an economist, a chemist, a Justice of the Peace, an optician and a Doctor of Philosophy. He also helped develop one of the main tools used by astronomers all over the world before he was out of his teens.

He achieved his final degree in economics at the age of 66 as he got bored after retiring, perhaps not surprisingly.

The town was not even remotely bored of discussing a possible swimming pool.

The pool attracted more fevered discussion and the later-famous 'sixpence a week' scheme was started.

SWIMMING POOL PLANS PERSIST TO SHOW PROMISE

In May, after nearly ten years of campaigning to get a pool, a public meeting was called jointly by the borough council and the town's swimming club. The catalyst for this was that the swimming club used Castle Cove which had sustained heavy damage after gales throughout the previous winter. Repairs were not thought to be forthcoming due to the tight finances of both the borough council and the swimming club. Add to this a recent scare that polio had returned to the town through contaminated river water, putting the normal back-up for the club – the Boatfloat – out of bounds and the need for a pool seemed obvious to most residents.

The problem was the borough council were not well off and had a large amount of outgoings already and the Mayor N Hewson, was concerned that any pool project did not impact on the finances of good council practice.

Hence the payment scheme.

An overwhelming majority at the meeting voted for the scheme, which it was hoped would bring in £1,300 in two years to use to get a bid going for a pool, hopefully somewhere around the lower town.

A committee was formed and the decision made for everyone to give 6d per week towards the pool. It was believed that if everyone contributed, there would soon be enough for a pool.

The economic well-being of the town hung on the fortunes of a few large organisations, and the continued success of one of them was celebrated by the *Chronicle*.

PHILIP & SON CELEBRATE 100 YEARS

Dartmouth's biggest employer, Philip & Son, turned 100.

The *Chronicle* rightfully hailed the shipyard which gave a number of generations an apprenticeship in a useful trade and put some of the finest ships ever to be built on the river Dart in the water. Its 100th anniversary came in the year it had completed its 27th lightship for Trinity House – at a rate of more than one per year – and its order books were full.

The coverage – front page story plus a page of pictures, at the time an expensive and complicated process – showed how relevant the firm was.

'Just a hundred years ago,' the *Chronicle* wrote, 'in 1858 Mr George Philip, a Scot from Aberdeen, after four years as a foreman shipbuilder with Mr Kelly of Dartmouth, took the plunge and bought the yard at Sandquay when Mr Kelly retired. From being an employee he became a Master-Man and founded the firm which today, as Philip & Son Ltd., is the biggest employer of labour in

Flags and sirens welcome the Duke to Dartmouth

QUEEN'S SWORD GOES TO BRIXHAM CADET

AFTER A SOMEWHAT STORMY PASSAGE FROM THE SCILLY ISLES ON MONDAY, THE ROYAL YACHT BRITANNIA BEARING H.R.H. THE DUKE OF EDINBURGH SAILED SERENELY INTO CALM WATERS OF DARTMOUTH HARBOUR TO BE GREETED BY A WELCOMING PEAL FROM THE BELLS OF ST. SAV-IOURS.

She moored up at the buoys opposite the South Embankment and was followed by the escorting ships of the Dartmouth Squadron. The skies were overcast warning of rain to come.

Promptly at 9:30 a.m. the Royal Barge came alongside the B.R. pontoon which had been beautifully decorated in blue and white. As the Duke step-ped onto the red carpet he was greeted

Back on the dais the Mayor asked His Royal Highness to accept as a gift from the Corporation, an oil painting of the Britannia entering Dartmouth harbour on the occasion of the Duke's previous visit in 1954.

With the civic part of the Duke's visit over, the Royal party entered the official cars which moved off to the Royal Naval College. As the band played the National Anthem, the sun broke through the clouds and the child-ren cheered and waved to the smiling Duke. H.M.S. Orwell fired a Royal salute and the Duke's personal stand-ard was broken at the College mast-head.

As the Duke entered the grounds of the College he was received by the C-in-C Plymouth. Vice Admiral Sir

Rev. Urwin to be Priest-in-charge of St. Barnabas

In his Parish Magazine the Vicar of Dartmouth, the Rev. Roger T. Urwin, says that he has been told by the Arch-deacon that he is to be appointed Priest-in-charge of St. Petrox with St. Barnabas when the present incum-bent, the Rev. W. A. Roberton resigns. He adds "I was also instructed to take steps to secure the services of a second assistant priest.

"The Rev. G. Hilton Nicholson is the name of this new man. He has been at

Dartmouth. The story of the firm is one of steady expansion always under the control of the direct descendents of the same George Philip. Today John Alexander Philip, his great-grandson, is managing director and his son, George Alexander Philip in turn is the most recent recruit to the board. Such a proud centenary could not be allowed to pass unnoticed and on Friday evening more than 200 guests were entertained by the company to a sumptuous dinner at the Grand Hotel in Torquay.'

George however, did not have a happy summer. Returning home from a night out in Paignton with friends his boat turned over in heavy seas in August, and although he and most of his friends survived, a gentleman named G Sharpe of Romford, with whom George was friendly, died following the group's rescue by the Royal Navy.

The town was disappointed when the Queen failed to visit in July due to illness. She was instead represented by her husband the Duke of Edinburgh, and the town made a very good show of 'not being disappointed'. The borough council even sent a get well message to the Monarch giving her the best wishes from the whole of Dartmouth. She replied almost instantly, giving her personal apology and expressing extreme disappointment at not being able to visit the town where she met her husband nearly twenty years before.

The Prince's visit was covered extensively with the whole of the August 1 edition's front page dedicated to photos of the event including the Royal Yacht *Britannia* in the harbour and Prince Philip meeting people from the town in a walkabout. He must have been glad for the solid ground after a stormy journey from the Scilly Isles on this extensive tour of Wales and the southwest.

Accompanied by his uncle the First Sea Lord Earl Mountbatten he went to a reception on Coronation Park, and planted a commemorative tree next to the Old Dartmothians' hut there. According to the *Chronicle* the Greek Prince was 'an expert tree-planter'.

The town mourned the death of racing driver Peter Collins, who was killed racing for Ferrari at the Nurburgring in Germany in August.

Collins kept his boat *Genie Maris* at Kingswear and spent many happy days around the area and was notoriously good fun. He was a tragic figure who inspired huge love and respect among all he met. His crowning achievement was when having the chance to take the drivers championship from his team leader Fangio in the final race of the season when the 'greatest driver ever' had steering column failure, he pulled into the pits and handed over his car so the Argentinean could continue racing and win the championship, dropping to third in the drivers standings in the process. This won the respect and love of Enzo Ferrari, the company's notoriously hard-to-please owner and leader, and the pair were said to be like father and son from then on. Collins was killed whilst pushing for the lead on the banked tracks of the legendary tough German circuit. Losing control, he was thrown clear of his car and hit a tree, sustaining head injuries from which he later died in hospital.

A member of both the Royal Dart and Dartmouth Yacht Club, he was mourned as perhaps the most honourable and fun driver of his generation, who never achieved his full potential.

Left: *Prince Philip presents Sub Lt G Booth – the outstanding Cadet of his class – with the Queen's Sword.*
SOUTH HAMS
NEWSPAPERS

Right: *The Prince created lots of positive headlines during his visit.*

A SOCIETY BEGINS

1959 In January a wall falling down started a chain of events which would result with the Flavel Arts Centre being built in 2005.

The long wall on the road above Warfleet Creek collapsed on January 18 thanks to a combination of very heavy rain and frosts over the previous few months.

The wall was later replaced with a castellated concrete construction, totally different from the native stone wall which had been there before. Its bright blank façade angered many people; especially when they found out no one had been consulted about its suitability.

Three men in particular got very angry: Robert Smith, Christopher Milne and Lt Col Richard Webb. The men decided to form a group which would fight for sensible and sensitive development of the town of Dartmouth and the surrounding villages of Kingswear, Dittisham, Stoke Fleming and Strete, and to preserve and enhance the beauty of the area. The Dartmouth & Kingswear Society was formed in October. One of its first successes was to persuade shops around the Boatfloat to tidy up with a lick of paint.

Dartmouth's Mayor managed to fulfil a promise and secure a place for those over a certain age to have somewhere to go to meet friends, chat about the world and enjoy a cup of tea. The cinematically named Harold Lloyd, Mayor of the town, had promised to provide a place for the retired folk of the town to go. This 'Rest Room' needed a secure and solid funding base and the Mayor was determined to see it brought to fruition.

'This scheme has been a long cherished idea of both the Mayoress and myself,' said Cllr Lloyd. 'I included it in my address on becoming Mayor. But I realise that the project is one which will have to start off in a small way and expand as and when possible. I would like to see a rest room in a level part of the town and centrally situated. A place where they can take shelter in inclement weather, rest between shopping or just call and have a chat with friends, whom they may not otherwise have an opportunity of meeting, and also where they can not only find a warm and comfortable spot for their rest but also partake in the inevitable cup of tea at a small charge. Companionship is something which many of the town's older folk are sadly missing and in addition such a rest room may allow these folk to remain in the town for a few more hours rather than hurry back to a midday meal and not able to make a second journey.'

The founders of the Dartmouth & Kingswear Society from left to right Lt Col Richard Webb, John Smith and Christopher Milne.
RICHARD WEBB/MICHAEL SMITH/DARTMOUTH & KINGSWEAR SOCIETY

RATEPAYERS CAN'T AGREE

The town's Ratepayers' Association disbanded in April – and went out with a particularly stormy meeting. The association was formed to help give the views of the electorate to the borough council, and to raise funds for town projects. However, it had been inactive since 1953, and now the former committee members were trying to decide how best to use the funds the association and its fundraising committee had brought in.

The only decision made on the night saw £5 14s 7d divided equally between the YMRC Building Fund, the Old Folks Restroom Appeal, the Swimming Pool and the Dartmouth Branch of St John Ambulance. £68 raised 'for a Dartmouth project' was left unclaimed as the wrangling went on. The reason for this debacle? 'Apathy was the general consensus' said the *Chronicle*.

The reason, according to Major Forrest, long term member of the committee, was 'television' because people 'only wanted to watch that'.

Dartmouth also lost the fabled Monkey Town Regatta.

The Regatta, which had run for many decades, had last been held in 1952. The organisers had held onto the belief that it might be resurrected but all to no avail.

Dartmouth Chronicle

ESTABLISHED 1854

CIRCULATING IN DARTMOUTH, BRIXHAM, KINGSBRIDGE AND THE SOUTH HAMS

(Telephone: Dartmouth 24)   (Telegrams: " Chronicle," Dartmouth)

No. 6149   NOVEMBER 20, 1959   Price 2d.

COOKED CHICKEN from 8/6 each
JOHN WAY
St. George's Sq., Dartmouth
Telephone 83

'WATCHDOG SOCIETY' TO GUARD DARTMOUTH'S HERITAGE

PACKED INAUGURAL MEETING

NO ORGANISATION IN DART-MOUTH COULD HAVE RECEIVED SUCH A FLYING START AS THE "AMENITY SOCIETY" WHICH WAS

and Mr. P. A. Allery, among others. During the talk by Mr. Wintering-ham he showed some coloured slides, mainly of Solihull, but including other

Rowers cele victorious

Dartmouth Amateur Rowing Club certainly deserved its styling of " Celebration Event" for its annual dinner and dance last week, in recog-nition of its 1959 Regatta successes in both rowing and in organisation.

The Dartmouth & Kingswear Society is welcomed to the world by the Chronicle.

The *Chronicle* gave a clear indication what the reason for the demise was.

'Dartmouth Monkey Town Regatta provided some useful funds for a number of local organisations over a period of years, but at a meeting of organisers this week it was reluctantly recognised that the young people of today will not take their share in organising such events'.

With no one to take over the reins of office from what have been described as the 'ageing' committee, it has accordingly decided to disband this old organisation. As a significant sign of its past success – in contrast with some modern movements – the old Monkey Town Regatta was not only financially sound, but still had a considerable balance in hand. The meeting decided that these funds – amounting to slightly over £40, would be divided between existing deserving causes in the borough.

'In some parts of the town there had been hopes in recent months that perhaps one more Monkey Town Regatta might be held, as something of a 'swan song', but not sufficient active young folk volunteered to help and so the old custom is to die. There will not again be a Monkey Town Mayor, Monkey Town Mayoress (who was also a man, of course!) or a Monkey Town Clerk!'

However, on the plus side, the Old Folks Rest Room did get the Monkey Town Regatta's entire stock of cups, saucers and plates.

YOUNG BOY ON CRIMINAL RAMPAGE

Dartmouth Magistrates visited tough love on a 10 year old boy accused of stealing £10, some plasters, a pocket watch and a pocket knife.

The young boy was caught on the Embankment and admitted taking some of the items from a house, and seemed to be rather blasé about the whole thing – asked how much money he had taken he replied 'well, I didn't count it did I?' He got into a house in town when he found a key on a nail hanging in the loo outside. He let himself in, took the items and went for a day out in Paignton on the cash. He was arrested on returning as he walked up the Embankment on his way home. His pockets were full of crumpled notes and the police found this suspicious in one so young.

Coming to court the young boy was put on three years probation. His mother was told to pay the 15s costs, but was told 'to take it from his pocket money'. You get the sense this was a boy often in trouble, as he asked for two other offences, the theft of some cigarettes and some sweets, to be taken into consideration.

Tragedy hit the Britannia Royal Naval College in July with the death of Thomas McCarthy, from Wigan. Mr McCarthy, a 21 year old Naval Steward drowned in the College swimming pool on July 6 because he was ashamed of not being able to swim.

Mr McCarthy had been learning to swim for one month as previously he couldn't swim at all. After relatively quick progress he could still only do one width of the pool unaided, but was determined to learn and swim better quickly. He was described as being 'cheerfully determined' to make his swimming certificate. So determined was he that he entered the pool on his own at lunchtime on that fateful Monday, and, rather than wait for the learners class that took place there, he got in.

The Britannia Royal Naval College pool has no shallow end, if you can't swim and get into trouble, without someone there to help, it can only end one way. Despite resuscitation attempts he died in the pool and was mourned by his young wife.

The summer was scorching; ninety degree heat and no rain meant the town's firemen had to keep well abreast of the multiple fires they encountered, especially rubbish dump fires and those in farmers' fields.

Unemployment dipped dramatically from a year before – in 1958 the summer unemployed level was seventy one – an alarming figure for many during the high season but in 1959 it had dropped to thirty two. The *Chronicle* described the drop as 'particularly gratifying'.

SECOND WORLD WAR HERO WELCOMED IN THE TOWN

Field Marshal Montgomery visits the Britannia Royal Naval College.
BRNC

Also gratifying was the reception for 'Monty' – the hero of El Alamein Field Marshal Viscount Montgomery visited the College in July to take the salute in the 'Passing Out' Parade. Montgomery had famously defeated the 'Desert Fox' Rommel, and commanded all land forces in the invasion of Europe in June 1944. He was a national hero, and it shows how much he was loved as the *Chronicle* described him as the 'Most popular visitor to the Britannia Royal Naval College – vying even with HRH the Duke of Edinburgh.'

'Monty' as he was affectionately known, was 'resplendent' in full dress uniform and was watched by large crowds, who against normal practice were allowed into the College to catch a glimpse of the man who gave the first glimmer of hope in the war against the Nazis, seventeen years before, at the battle of El Alamein.

He said he and the navy personnel had 'a lot in common'. 'Whether you are cadets or midshipmen at this College,' he said, 'I suppose I seem to you to be a pretty senior sort of guy, but we have a lot in common, we both wear the Queen's uniform.

We are both pledged to our duties to the best of our ability and have definite obligations that demand the highest standard of integrity, loyalty and discipline'.

Discipline was needed by the town's rowers before they won the biggest prize in West of England rowing.

The Regatta saw the glorious win of the town's Senior Four rowers taking the Championship of the West of England with a race to spare. The *Chronicle* revelled in the win: 'Calmly, unhurried, rowing with style and delightful to watch, Dartmouth's Senior Four swept on to a six length victory to become the undisputed West of England Champions.'

The crew then went on to go one better and won the South Coast Championships, also held on the river Dart – the first such event. Dartmouth's Amateur Rowing Club did the town proud; having a placed crew in each event it entered.

But the senior fours were the main event and they won in true British sports fashion – by waiting to the last moment possible to snatch it.

'At the Floating Dock, about half way, Dartmouth was third,' wrote the *Chronicle's* rowing correspondent Racing Oar, 'and quite three lengths behind the leaders. And so the race went on. Dartmouth was seen to be slowly shortening this gap but the order of the first three boats remained unchanged. But one significant thing was seen. In spite of being behind, and the two crews ahead of them looking strong and full of good rowing, Dartmouth continued to row steadily, unhurried and maintaining the long, easy-looking stroke that is their hall-mark.

Approaching the pontoon they moved into second place: hopes were revived and all eyes turned toward the finishing line with the question, 'can they do it?', and in the minds of many a silent prayer that they would. Gradually Dartmouth moved up while the shouts of encouragement grew louder and the excitement increased to become well-nigh unbearable. And then it was over. With a well timed increase to a powerful drive Dartmouth had done it by three quarters of a length, worthy winners of a fine race in the full tradition of senior class rowing, and a great finish to a great season.'

It was a fine end to a decade which had shown the town – along with the whole nation – moving away from the horrors of war, taking advantage of the improved economic situation. Soon to come was perhaps the most socially dramatic decade in Dartmouth's or anyone's memory – the 1960s.

CHAPTER II

You've Never Had It so Good…?
1960s

THE SIXTIES: DAWN OF A NEW ERA

The 1960s dawned amidst a new enthusiasm and optimism in Dartmouth. The whole country was beginning to feel economic times becoming easier and many town businesses saw their best figures for decades. However, the continued resurgence in the world's economy and the political and social effects of the Second World War did not necessarily guarantee the town's prosperity, or its social cohesion.

Dartmouth was, more than ever before, dependent on the money brought in by tourists but the struggle to bring in visitors started a debate about how to best attract them and what kind of visitors to attract. When large amounts of tourists did visit the town they did so with so many cars that they caused congestion and so many headaches it seemed people almost wished they hadn't come.

Political power began to shift, as the Dartmouth & Kingswear Society, formed in 1959, began to try and influence the development of the town through debate and consensus building. Yet all it seemed to do was find itself entangled in long, protracted and often bitter fights with large public organisations. They fought mainly with the borough council and Devon County Council, which was in charge of planning.

The running theme of the decade, and in the *Chronicle's opinion* section, was the lack of investment by the authorities in the regular maintenance of local amenities. This meant that what could have been regular, small town work turning into vital and hugely expensive jobs by the end of the decade.

The town's sewerage system was a good example, closely followed by the roads and pavements, and the Old Market's central building, which collapsed spectacularly in 1969. Nothing seemed to move on the important capital projects needed to give the town its proper infrastructure.

The 1960s were a time of upheaval and change in the rest of the country. In Dartmouth they seemed to be categorised by arguments and long running debates which eventually left the town fundamentally unchanged.

The Higher Ferry No. 7 – *just before it was replaced by a new one made of scrap metal at the Noss Shipyard.*
DARTMOUTH MUSEUM

The Chronicle *notes the changes in the town's population in 1959 – 1960.*

DARTMOUTH BIRTH-RATE IS HIGHER THAN COUNTY AVERAGE

Population now 6,622

THIS WEEK THE 1959 HEALTH REPORT FOR THE BOROUGH OF DARTMOUTH IS PUBLISHED BY THE MEDICAL OFFICER, DR. JOHN WILDMAN AND SHOWS A PARTICULARLY HEALTHY PERIOD.

ALSO INCLUDED IN THE REPORT IS THAT OF THE PUBLIC HEALTH INSPECTOR, MR. V. E. HUGHES.

VITAL STATISTICS

Little change is shown in the statis-

TUBERCULOSIS

Once again the Borough was fortun- ate to receive a special visit from a

1960 World Events
● The first CERN particle accelerator becomes operational in Geneva, Switzerland
● Penguin Books is found not guilty of obscenity in the case of D. H. Lawrence's novel *Lady Chatterley's Lover*
● The first episode of *Coronation Street* is telecast. It had been planned to be a thirteen-part drama
● The farthing, used since the 13th century, ceases to be legal tender in the United Kingdom

1960 Dartmouth police stopped an 18 year old youth because they rightly thought he had stolen a bottle of milk and discovered he had also stolen the car he was driving too.

STOLE A PINT OF MILK AND GOT ARRESTED FOR STEALING A CAR

Bernard Prout, of Britannia Avenue, took the car in January by stealing the key from District Nurse Georgina Shirley Duncan and driving away. He did not hold a driving license and was on probation for a number of other thefts at the time.

He stole the car from the nurse's home in Townstal and drove it around the area for a week before stealing the milk from the doorstep of a flat on the Quay in Dartmouth.

The man then drove to work in Kingswear where he was found with the bottle of milk, of which he said: 'All right I pinched it'.

He admitted he knew the car belonged to the district nurse and the judge increased his sentence, despite statements in his defence from his employers and even the local vicar. The judge commented that the nurse could have been deprived of a car in an emergency and banned him from driving for twelve months and once again placed him on probation for three years.

Had Bernard been sent to prison, he would have missed the installation of Dartmouth's new and much discussed lighting system.

The town was bathed in a new glow as its street lighting was revamped for the amazing sum of £10,000, equivalent to nearly £170,000 in 2010.

LIGHT DAWNS TOO LATE FOR COMMITTEE

The first few months of the year saw this story dominate the pages of the *Chronicle*. Most of them were based around criticism of the street lighting chosen by the borough council. Most of the criticism came from the council's own highways committee. They complained that the lights were too big and 'out of scale' with Dartmouth. The lights were 25 foot high steel columns using mercury vapour lamps. Such lamps had recently been put up in Torbay. Only after the lights had been installed, did the highways committee recommend using smaller columns with sodium lamps, instead of the big mercury ones. The town clerk told the dissenting councillors that it was 'about two years too late' to complain about them now, and he was supported by the senior council hierarchy.

Alderman HJ Adams did not take the criticism lightly: 'If these lights are suitable for Torquay I think they are suitable for Dartmouth,' he said. 'We have not gone into this willy nilly but given it great thought, and when it is installed I think we shall have lighting here that will be equal to any town in the vicinity, and an improvement on lights at Totnes.'

But the argument dragged on, with the decision to use that particular system criticised in all corners, both by experts and the less well-informed.

The most stinging critics were the Dartmouth & Kingswear Road Safety Committee which sent a letter to the council complaining that not enough research into the available systems had been undertaken and that the council, and its clerk were 'out of order' to deny the charges of cutting corners.

It seemed that the main discussion was over the fact that the mercury lights gave a 'greenish tinge' to people's faces, which was considered rather unattractive, whereas the sodium lights gave a 'friendly, warm and hearty glow' to people's complexions.

The larger debate about the investment in the town was that none of the town's organisations, mainly its Chamber of Trade and the borough council, seemed to be facing up to the need for development and managed change in the town. However, this was dismissed by the town's Mayor, Cllr Harold Lloyd, who ignored all irony by stating '90 per cent of sweeping statements are wrong' and called on the chamber to work with the council to achieve more for the town, suggesting it help build a new low water landing off the Embankment.

He said that although he had 'no official information', he 'estimated' a landing would cost somewhere between '£50,000 and £100,000' or the equivalent today of guessing it may cost somewhere between £850,000 and £1.7 million.

However, he was soon wearing an uncomfortable expression because his fellow councillors slapped a ban on a private landing being built off the Embankment so the council and Harbour Commission would have to do it.

Cllr T Tozer, a supporter of Cllr Lloyd, commented that because of the involvement of the council and Harbour Commission, the town would be waiting 'two years' before a plan was finalised. He was wrong. It took six years of planning and arguments, before the idea was thrown out never to be completed.

COLD CLIMATE BUT WARM ECONOMIC WINDS

Despite the cold and even blizzard conditions early in the year, it seemed the economic climate was particularly steady. All the local councils managed to leave their rates the same, an effective drop, and made the best of their resources without putting their services under pressure.

However, Alderman H Wheatley, Chairman of the Finance Committee for Dartmouth Borough Council, said that the increase in the standard of living was putting pressure on such decisions.

Dartmouth's New Higher Ferry
– 50 Years in the Making

(See years 1959 – 2009)

PHIL SCOBLE

IN 1959 Alec Philip, grandson of George, the original owner of Dart-based Shipbuilders Philip & Son, took a look at the old Higher Ferry which the company owned, and thought about how it was in need of replacement. It was small – carrying just twelve cars – and slow, as it was steam powered and needed help from an outboard motor during strong ebb tides.

Philip & Son's yards at Noss and Sandquay had more than 500 men working in them, making them the biggest employer in the town by some margin. For several decades a successful apprenticeship scheme had been running. Many of the town's master craftsmen had a seven year Philips apprenticeship to thank for their immense skills.

But at the end of 1959 and the beginning of 1960 there was a lull in work. The yard managed to keep things ticking along for their main group of employees, but the apprentices were kicking their heels.

Alec Philip decided they needed a project to keep them busy.

The apprentices, under the watchful glares of a few old hands were asked to build a new, larger Higher Ferry.

They used scrap metal for its base. The most used crossing of the river Dart had a keel that was a quarter of an inch thick.

In July 1960 the town moved into the modern age with its new 'diesel and electric' ferry.

Mr Philip proudly proclaimed that the ferry would be good for 'Twenty five years good service'.

However it was more than forty seven years later that the Dartmouth to Kingswear Floating Bridge Company, which ran the ferry after being separated off from the Philips Group in 1999, announced it would be having a replacement installed, which would have the capacity for double its current load of cars.

This increase in the number of cars on the ferry meant that there were concerns from inside the company about tailbacks and snarl-ups. These concerns resulted in the company employing a consultant to look at the traffic situation and suggest if there was a better way of doing it. They suggested changing the direction of traffic around Coronation Park, having traffic lights at the top end of Coombe Road, and making College Way two-way right down to the Embankment.

These plans were all announced within a couple of weeks in the paper.

They were instantly attacked.

Letters to the paper from concerned residents envisaged a behemoth of a ferry, which could stretch across most of the Dart, splurging hundreds of cars into the town, causing snarl-ups, pollution and possibly Armageddon itself.

Company director Tony Tucker found himself defending the ferry, saying it would not cause traffic congestion and would not need to use the public slipway to land.

The traffic plan was also quickly dropped though. Officers at County Hall admitted off the record the plans would clearly have worked better and improved traffic flow. But the changes were considered too problematic, because they said so many Dartmothians would complain.

Pictures appeared in the paper at the beginning of 2009 showing the new ferry as it sat at Pendennis Shipyard where it was being fitted out following its construction in Holland.

The new Higher Ferry mid-stream on one of its initial crossings. The new ferry arrived in the Dart on June 12, 2009.

People began to actually get excited about the ferry, and think it might be a good thing.

Then after forty nine years, two million crossings and 528,725 miles, Dartmouth's Higher Ferry finally called it a day on Sunday June 7, 2009.

More than 150 people gathered onboard to say goodbye to the final paddle-ferry in the country, and joined crew members and seven of those that built the vessel in toasting its success and longevity. Hundreds more watched from the bank.

On the final voyage back from Kingswear the ferry stopped halfway across for a speech from ferrymanager Kerry Southern who stood in the wheelhouse over the crowds to do so. Mr Southern paid tribute to the former members of the crew and the ferry's long and distinguished service.

Dartmouth turned out en-masse to welcome the new, multi-million pound Higher Ferry as it arrived on June 15, 2009.

Hundreds lined the Embankment as the new ferry sailed in, brought by tug on a nineteen hour journey from the Pendennis Ship Yard in Falmouth.

The ferry made an instant impression as it silently and swiftly crossed the Dart.

An open day in July saw hundreds take the opportunity to nose around the new floating bridge.

And the owners also took the opportunity to 'Bless' the ferry in a ceremony using the traditional bottle of champagne.

The ferry quickly stopped being a bone of contention and became what all car ferries are: a means of getting across an awkward expanse of water.

It achieved what many believed it never could: acceptance. People appreciated its quietness and its speed, and the fact it quickly looked so at home, and not at all the monstrosity many had promised. It looked so right people forgot the old one.

Which was quite lucky: because it sat on a mooring up river for a month or so, before being dismantled for scrap. The ferry which had been constructed out of scrap by young men learning their trade and had faithfully served the town's of Dartmouth and Kingswear for nearly twice as long as it was designed to, returned to scrap almost completely unnoticed.

Tony Tucker and Kerry Southern after announcing the existing Higher Ferry (seen in the background) *would be replaced by a larger, faster version in 2009.* Phil Scoble

'We have enjoyed a year with a comparatively stable cost of living index, but the stability of prices and local expenditure is now again being threatened by new proposals for higher wages and shorter working hours,' he said. 'The county has met heavily increased charges on account of salaries and for the needs of modern education and road improvements in particular. It is therefore a matter of congratulation for us to have got off so lightly.'

The rate figure stood at one pound and eight pence per pound, and that year's budget allowed £750 for the salary award made nationally to all government workers.

Another topic which occupied much of the paper's letters section was the conduct of visiting tourists. Their 'wandering about' and leaving gates open were blamed for the loss and death of a number of farm animals.

The animals, owned by Kingswear farmer Mr H Bowley, went over the cliffs on the Torbay side of the river Dart and were washed up between Torcross and Blackpool Sands. The authorities took some time to identify the seven cattle and five sheep that were found and it appeared that walkers with dogs had indeed inadvertently driven the animals into the sea. Mr Bowley was understandably upset: 'I am very bitter about the sheer carelessness or worse of strangers who wander about my fields and leave gates open,' he told the *Chronicle*, 'and what is worse, they often have dogs who chase the cattle. With a bunch of cattle on the edge of a cliff and a dog barking, those at the rear begin to stampede and over they all go. Just an hour or two of sunshine, and out come the visiting trespassers, leaving gates open, or parking cars in front of gates, often preventing a tractor from entering or leaving a field.'

The town moved into the modern age with its new 'diesel and electric' Higher Ferry. Built by Philip & Son, which owned and ran the crossing, the new ferry replaced an old steam-driven one which was small and so lacking in power, there was an outboard motor installed to assist it during particularly strong tides. The new ferry was built at the company's Noss Shipyard up river from Dartmouth.

The yard's apprentices earned their meagre keep by putting the ferry together out of thin scrap metal left in the yard during a quiet period when they were short of work. The ferry was brought into commission in July. Though 'teething troubles' were experienced with its wires and their tension, everyone seemed very pleased with the faster crossing times and the increased space for sixteen cars on the deck, four more than previously.

The *Chronicle's* enthusiastic coverage of the new ferry may have been less prominent had the editorial team known that the keel of the ferry was only a quarter of an inch thick!

The town was 'tickled' with an appearance from 'TV Comedian' Ken Dodd.

'Doddy' was the representative of the *National Spastics Society* and as the patrons of the George and Dragon had raised 100 guineas, a little over £1,600 in 2010 money, for the society, he agreed to give a personal appearance to present a certificate of thanks. The crowds filled the pub and spilled out onto Mayors Avenue in expectation of his arrival.

He made a big impression by arriving in a 3.8 litre Jaguar with the number plate KD 11. He gave a brief speech of thanks to the landlords of the pub, Mr and Mrs Foot, giving them a certificate along with some of his own specially prepared puns: 'Congratulations on your 'feat'. I admit that last joke is a little 'corny' but nevertheless, I can certainly see you both know your 'bunions'! Perhaps mercifully he stopped there and went to have a drink with other customers.

A member of the Royal family who visited during the summer was more refined.

Ken Dodd visited Dartmouth in 1960 to thank the regulars of the George and Dragon for the money they raised for the Spastics Society, of which he was representative.
COURTESY HARRY NORTON

ROYAL VISITOR BRINGS GLAMOUR TO TOWN

The summer sun welcomed HRH Princess Margaret to the town for the July 'Passing Out' Parade at the Britannia Royal Naval College. She watched the cadets 'Passing Out', wearing a beautiful 'cornflower blue' dress and hat, accompanied by her husband Anthony Armstrong-Jones, before heading to the naval pontoon where she named a Sea Rangers Ship, The *Golden Hinde*.

She had arrived by helicopter and this dramatic entrance ensured that the crowds who had waited to catch a glimpse of her were not disappointed once she finally swept down the Embankment from the College to the naval pontoon. She was described as being 'all smiles'.

Dartmouth's population hit 6,622 and it looked like it would only be rising further, as the town's death rate was falling and its birth rate rising above the national average.

A Dartmouth boy was recognised by the Royal Humane Society for saving his friend after he had fallen down a cliff near Stoke Fleming. 13 year old Colin Jenkins was climbing the cliffs with friends at Gull Point on July 26 when Stephen Owen, his good friend and fellow Dartmouth Secondary Modern student, slipped and fell 30 feet onto the rocks below. Stephen fractured both hips and knocked himself unconscious.

Colin received a vellum certificate from the society for his bravery in climbing down the cliffs, carefully moving his friend away from the incoming tide and then climbing back up more than 250 feet to get help. A coastguard and police officer were then lowered to the boy by rope and he was taken to hospital for treatment.

1961

Coal trading started again at Kingswear after a sixteen month break, and it was front page news on January 13.

The coaling ship *Singularity* docked on January 23 to much fanfare after travelling from Goole in Yorkshire – the coal was to be used 'in the gas industry' according to the paper.

The coal used to be unloaded at Kingswear jetty to be transferred to the Torquay depot of the South Western Gas Board.

The decision to stop the deliveries had been taken in 1959 – all coal deliveries had been changed to rail – due to cost. More than a dozen men lost their jobs at the time 'and some of the men could only find temporary employment afterwards' according to the paper.

The Dartmouth Harbour Commission had struggled to convince the gas board to change its mind – as the cancellation of the deliveries had lost it £500 a year. The paper blamed nationalisation for the reversal at the time, but welcomed the partial reintroduction.

The new deliveries would not replace the full trade – at its height more than 100,000 tons of coal was unloaded on Kingswear jetty a year, and the new trade would only bring in 40,000 – but it brought much needed funds into the villages. However the aspect of the story which seemed to attract most interest was the First Mate of the *Singularity*: Alan C Clark.

He was brother to the clerk of the Harbour Commission – and had been the Captain of the Junk used in the ' million Pound' Disney film *The Swiss Family Robinson* and had spent the whole time dressed as a pirate. Unfortunately for all concerned, it was a false dawn: coaling stopped forever at Kingswear only a few short years afterwards.

FIRE BRINGS OUT THE BEST IN RESIDENTS

A fire on a 70 foot yacht in Old Mill Creek brought out the best in nearby residents. *Olanti,* owned by Mr C Thomas of Salcombe, suffered a fuel fire on January 17. Local men rowed out to him and started a bucket chain to help put out the fire.

Four men from the nearby shipyard of Ferris and Blank did admirable work when they rowed out and began passing buckets to Mr Thomas before the arrival of the fire brigade who had to run a hose a quarter of a mile long through woodland to reach the yacht – running it over rowing boats in the river.

All the effort paid off with the yacht saved and no one hurt.

The Dartmouth fire crew had a busy winter.

On February 12 the coal ship *Anja* suffered a fire in its living quarters whilst off Start Point. The Dartmouth crew used the Lower Ferry float to get out to the boat when it was towed into Dartmouth harbour and spent seven hours dousing the flames till they were out. The ship had been lucky not to become a floating bomb – as the fire was directly below a fuel store, and was started by 'an explosion' in the living quarters, which was never explained. Thanks to the efforts of not only the Dartmouth brigade, but also the navy, lifeboat and Torbay fire crews a disaster was averted.

Dartmouth magistrates rued a huge increase in public drunkenness in the borough – from zero cases to one. The magistrate described the single case as 'a fly in the ointment'.

Dartmouth celebrated the new 'Lighting Improvement Scheme'.

It was completed fifty six years after the first electric lamps were installed in the town. Six went up in 1905 and the town Mayor, JW Lee-Palin, proudly announced in March 1961 that it now boasted 350.

SHINE A LIGHT – BUT NOT THERE

However, the £9,400 scheme had suffered huge criticism from the public – for the colour of the lights, their height, the placing of the lights and the fact that the lights shone into people's bedrooms, keeping them awake.

There was also an argument about a light placed near the entrance to St Saviours Church, which was erected when the vicar was on holiday.

The Rev G Hilton Nicholson said: 'It spoils the view of the church that is so much photographed and painted from that side. There's plenty of room elsewhere in the square where it could be placed.' The Mayor was unmoved by the massive amount of criticism he and his council were receiving: 'Twas ever thus' he intoned, gaining a laugh and an award for the most phlegmatic politician in Dartmouth's history.

Dartmouth Regatta celebrated its 125th anniversary with beautiful weather and big, record-breaking crowds – it was billed as the 'BUSIEST EVER REGATTA; AND A PARKING PROBLEM THAT WAS WELCOMED!' on the *Dartmouth Chronicle's* front page.

The Philip & Son Floating Dock is taken out of the river for scrap in 1961.
DARTMOUTH MUSEUM

START OF A NEW ERA FOR PHILIP & SON

Dart Marina opened on August 25, ending the 'hundred year old tradition' of ship construction on Philip & Son's Sandquay site. The new, extremely expensive set of buildings were listed in the paper as a 'yachting centre' with 'hotel, trading centre, club, berthing and refuelling'

The manager of the new centre, an 'ex-Battle of Britain ace' – according to the *Chronicle* – Group Captain EN Ryder, said that the scheme had been 'a tremendously costly business'.

There was much discussion about the borough council in the paper during the year, and many councillors changed thanks to resignations and elections. The paper blamed public apathy towards the political process as the problem.

The paper constantly harangued the public to vote – with one headline shouting 'YOU VOTE 'EM IN!' for no apparent reason. The Mayor at the start of the year, Cllr Lee-Palin, suffered the ignominy of coming last in the popular vote in the town's first election of the year in April. He then, obviously glutton for punishment, stood in a by-election in June, against three other candidates, including fellow ex-Mayor Norman Hewson and two others.

Both ex-Mayors failed to win, beaten by first timer Mr JH Smith, who got more votes than the other three candidates combined. Ex-Cllr Lee-Palin said he was 'pleased to do better than last time' (he got 240 votes as opposed to 177 in the April election) but said it 'wasn't quite good enough'. The fact he had nearly 400 votes less than the winner meant he was stretching the definition of 'quite' to breaking point.

At the next by-election in September – for two seats caused by a death and a resignation – only one person stood.

Admiral of the Fleet Lord Louis Mountbatten, who as a Cadet, attended the Royal Naval College during the First World War between January 1915 and April 1916.
HISTORY.CO.UK

Lord Mountbatten presents the Queen's Sword to the best Midshipman.
SOUTH HAMS NEWSPAPERS

The paper was clearly not impressed, and had its front page headline as 'Council Seat Nobody Wants'.

The story began with the following sentence: 'After a brief spell of enthusiasm during the summer, when there were four applicants for one seat at a by-election, apathy has again descended upon Dartmouth so far as Borough Council Work is Concerned.'

A retired naval officer drowned due to his dinghy 'leaking like a sieve' in October.

Lt Cdr Dermod William Moriarty drowned after the canvas dinghy in which he was going to his moored yacht near Kingswear Creek sprung a leak. Lt Cdr Moriarty was found floating in the Dart not long after going missing one evening.

On his boat, *Anne*, moored on the river, a letter was found in which he had told his mother that the dinghy he was using was 'as unstable as a hip bath' and 'leaking like a sieve' after a collision with another boat.

The town was shocked in the run up to Christmas by the theft of books and vandalism at St Saviours Church on December 22. The vandals smashed the Christmas tree in the church and stole a censer, some incense and books left to loan to the poor. The vandals also broke into the town's Catholic church on the same night, but did not steal from there.

It was an inglorious end to what had been a rather less than happy year for the town – in which little was done, much was argued about, and that which was done seemed to have caused lots of disagreements. The town must have been desperate to get to 1962.

1962 Dartmouth revelled in its 'best Easter for years' when more than 20,000 people crossed the river during the long Easter weekend.

Festive spirits abounded, so much so that all three ferries gave their ticket sales figures to the *Chronicle*. They had taken record receipts.

A representative of the Boatel told the paper: 'It's been our best ever Easter and we won the unofficial dinghy race!'

The *Chronicle* reported the reason for this influx was due to the town's representatives having a stand at the London Boat Show. The Mayor and many members of the Chamber of Trade travelled to the capital for the show in January. Scores of visitors who thronged the show, were invited to give Dartmouth a try and the belief among businesses was that they took them at their word.

The paper was sold in 1962 to the *Dartmouth Chronicle Publishing Group* under the control of John C MacTavish. The new editorial *opinion* column started to anger and upset local politicians and it was vicious in some of its outbursts against any kind of 'stupid' or 'unbelievable' decisions it detected. The column continued throughout most of the 1960s and gave the *Chronicle* a campaigning voice it had not had before.

Her Majesty the Queen visited the town in July, and the town welcomed the announcement of her visit ecstatically.

However, they were all too soon less than pleased. The borough council requested that her schedule; which allowed thirty minutes for civic purposes in the town before leaving to go to the Britannia Royal Naval College to take the salute as graduating cadets passed out, be changed to allow more time for meeting the local people.

Their request was flatly refused and more than that, the Queen's time was reduced to only twenty minutes in the town. Numerous councillors responded. Alderman William Row said: 'It seems a very empty affair and hardly worthwhile putting your best clothes on for.' Alderman Dorothy Holwill said: 'We should get half an hour. When the Duke was here before he had a word with most people and that does take a little time!'

But the Mayor, Cllr Hoare quickly poured oil on troubled waters by saying: 'We still feel greatly honoured. After all, the Queen is going on to Totnes, and Totnes, who have never had a visit from her are having the benefit of a longer visit.'

Despite the curtailed time span of her visit, when the Queen did arrive on July 27, she was greeted by enormous crowds. Hundreds who waited to see Queen Elizabeth and Prince Philip arrive by Royal barge up the river Dart in the pouring rain were left disappointed, as well as wet, when the planned arrival was cancelled at the last minute and no public announcement was made.

1962 World Events
- Telstar, the world's first commercial communications satellite, is launched into orbit
- Marilyn Monroe dies from an overdose of sleeping pills and chloral hydrate
- *Dr. No*, the first James Bond film, premieres in UK cinemas
- Cuban Missile Crisis
- There are no frost-free nights from December until March 1963

The rain spoilt the Queen and Prince Philip's visit for the photographers leaving them with few pictures worthy of print. However, many residents were delighted at the Royal couples' keen interest in the training facilities at the College. The town hoped this indicated that the young Royal Princes' Charles and Andrew would attend the Britannia Royal Naval College as part of their expected military training.

The pair inspired adoration wherever they went. When Prince Philip met the councillors, who included a schoolmaster, a cobbler, builder, butcher, jeweller, estate agent, lecturer, ladies outfitter, gas fitter, food manufacturer and boat company managing director he said: 'Haven't you got a candlestick maker?'

NO RUNNING, DIVING OR…SWIMMING?

Dartmouth Swimming Club had to stop using Castle Cove for its training because of the high cost of maintaining it after gales had damaged both the cliffs and the changing facilities. The decision marked the end of seventy years of swimming at this popular spot for tourists and locals alike and was much maligned by all. Unfortunately, nothing could be done as there were no funds to repair the cove to a useable state.

The annual 'first swim' of the season happened as usual in June, but on this occasion it took place in the Boatfloat. It quickly became apparent that this location was unsuitable for bathers. The swimming club's president, Dr 'Mac' McConaghey, expressed his 'dismay' at children diving into the Boatfloat. The water, quite apart from being caked with engine oil and mud, flowed in from the river Dart, which had eighteen separate untreated sewage outlets running into it.

The *Chronicle's opinion* piece made front page, stating: 'On Saturday Dartmouth went back seventy years, for that was the last time the swimming club's opening dip was in the Boatfloat. It is fantastic to think that you can turn back the files of the *Chronicle* to the July 1893 when Castle Cove opened as a bathing place and find that even then the civic fathers were saying the Boatfloat was not a fit place for swimming. That it was dirty and full of mud and now seventy years later apparently it is cleaner! Cleaner, with dozens of petrol and diesel driven motor boats using it? Cleaner, with more visitors to throw litter about? Cleaner, with pollution of coasts and beaches higher than ever? But then Castle Cove has been lost to the local swimming club who could not afford to maintain it and they must have somewhere to teach the youngsters of the town.'

The article went on to suggest that the borough council pay the remainder needed for the planned new swimming pool, a hefty £2,500, or that the Newcomen Society, which had started to plan the transference of one of Thomas Newcomen's first steam engines to the town of his birth, should stop their plans, leave the engine in Coventry, and pay for the pool themselves, receiving the honour of having it named the Thomas Newcomen Pool. The editorial described the engine as 'tons of obsolete iron' which would do no good for the town at all.

The first Newcomen engine erected at Dudley in 1712.

STUPID OLD IRON

The final suggestion caused a great stir from the public. Mr Percy Russell, the town's foremost historian at the time and still to this day revered, had arranged for the engine to be brought to Dartmouth. He wrote pointing out that the Newcomen Society had no interest in swimming pools. Mr Christopher Milne wrote saying how Mr Russell should be congratulated for his perseverance and vision bringing the engine to the town, and that the engine would be as important to Dartmouth as an attraction as the Butterwalk.

The *Chronicle* wasted no time in replying to the letters: 'We heard of the influence of Mr Russell long before we reached Dartmouth. We respect him for what he has done and suggest he could use his persuasiveness to switch the idea. If he did he would please hundreds of Dartmothians who want the pool and not just a handful of 'head in the clouds' folk. The description – tons of obsolete iron – we do not retract. People who have seen the engine say that Coventry is glad to be rid of it. How Mr Milne can draw a parallel with the Butterwalk is beyond our ken. We are with him in every way when it comes to preserving old buildings. But to compare the Butterwalk with an engine....' it continued: 'And tell us Mr Milne, the number of people who know, or will ever know, that Dartmouth is famous for Newcomen. The first question most visitors ask when they arrive is 'Where is the College?' or 'Where does Christopher Robin live?' Can you imagine 'Will you direct me to the Newcomen Engine?' No gentlemen, it won't do, unless you want to turn Dartmouth into a museum, instead of a town for the living and younger generation who follow.'

Dartmouth Amateur Rowing Club admires its trophies.
South Hams Newspapers

The ongoing argument became ever more personal considering the townsfolk knew how Mr Christopher Milne hated to be called Christopher Robin, the fictional alter-ego he blamed for a ruined childhood.

Mr Russell accused the paper of twisting his words and eventually said that the Newcomen Society might put some money towards the pool, but the editor made it clear again on the front page, that Mr Russell had said that the money received from the society would not be enough to cover 'the cost of printing and postage' of the covering letter.

Despite the ruckus over the funding for the new pool, the borough council did agree to put in a new bridge to the bathing platform at Castle Cove. It hoped this would allow the club to use it and encourage more swimmers on the whole, without the added onus to maintain the cove.

DID NO HARM EXCEPT BY DROWNING DOG

The river Dart was also connected to an altogether darker story.

A Kingswear man received more punishment than he was bargaining for when he drowned his dog. Walter Webb, 29, took his one year old cross-collie bitch Tina and drowned her in the Dart by putting her in a sack with some bricks in and throwing her in the river. He had also drowned her two puppies a few days before. He said he had done it 'in the heat of the moment' because of numerous complaints from neighbours that Tina had gone to the toilet in the street and in their gardens.

Mr Webb commented that he had 'done no harm to Tina except put her in the sack and throw her in the river'.

He was convicted of causing unnecessary cruelty by Brixham Court, fined £5 and banned from owning a dog for five years.

He later found another dog had been responsible for the fouling blamed on Tina.

In the six weeks following the case in August, Mr Webb found himself hounded by 'poison pen' letters abusing him and threatening his family's well being if he were to act in the same way again.

Mr Webb said the letters were seriously distressing his pregnant wife and the *Chronicle* even appealed for them to stop, saying the letter writers were 'cowardly', and 'hiding behind anonymity'.

The only picture of every single local rowing participant at the Port of Dartmouth Royal Regatta local rowing finals day in 2009.
PHIL SCOBLE

47

Manor Gardens became a hot topic for many, as the council tried to install public toilets. The Dartmouth & Kingswear Society, formed just three years before, led the complaints against the toilets, even though planning permission had been granted a full year beforehand. The gardens were a gift to the town from the former owners of the land and it was felt toilets would spoil their sanctity.

However, the council argued that it was 'only a minority' who were against the toilets, mainly residents in the immediate area of them. The council decided to go ahead, creating the best place to admire the entrance to the river in the whole of the town, from the viewing platform on top of the toilet.

TRYING TO UNRAVEL THE TRAFFIC TANGLE

The society reacted furiously, but had more pressing issues on its collective mind: namely the development of the whole town.

The Dartmouth & Kingswear Society called a public meeting to examine how it could advise planners who were then putting together strategic plans for Dartmouth. The *Chronicle*, which had already accused the society of becoming solely a 'platform for the views of certain individuals' pointed out that the majority of members of the society were retired and did not depend on the economic growth of Dartmouth to survive. They could therefore not be asked what the town needed as they would want to 'protect' and that any attempt to reconcile the beliefs of the members of the society with the needs of the rest of the town would be a painstaking task for the chairman Christopher Milne, who was described as a 'benign inquisitor in chief'.

Lt Col Richard Webb, one of the co-founders of the society, suggested a series of points to 'unravel the traffic tangle'. These included; demolishing the 'slums' of Lake Street to build a car park; the pedestrianisation of Duke and Foss Street; an Inner Relief Road from Victoria Road to Mayors Avenue; an Outer Relief Road from Townstal to Coombe Road; a road from Ferndale to lower Swannaton Road; taking the Higher Ferry out of private ownership and adding a second ferry at that point; the widening of Victoria Road and South Town; banning heavy traffic on South Town and Weeke Hill; and the use of the cinema site on Mayors Avenue, which had recently been bought by the council on a long lease as a multi-storey car park.

These proposals brought a furious reaction from some of those attending at the annual meeting of the society in October. This response illustrated the complexity of the problems facing anyone trying to sort the traffic and community issues in a way which pleased everyone in Dartmouth.

However, the meeting did settle on one thing, that a link road from Townstal to the North Embankment would be a boon to the town.

A less than subtle response to a comment by Lt Col Richard Webb of the Dartmouth & Kingswear Society about the delapidated state of half the houses in Lake Street – some of which had previously been condemned.

The Royal Yacht
Britannia *in*
Dartmouth in 1963.
BRNC

1963

The town's Carnival was forced to reduce its length from ten days to four, due to spiralling costs and diminishing returns from the event.

The decision was made after the committee found itself with just £9 5s 2d left after the 1962 event, £13 less than the year before. The concerts which were such an important part of the popular event lost £2 and the collections were £169, not nearly enough.

The Chairman Mr H Lewis started an appeal to bring in funds and support from the town: 'We must get more support from local people,' he said, 'They may support us in their own little ways but that is not quite enough. We need more enthusiasm from the town as a whole. Our main objectives are to publicise Dartmouth, to give residents enjoyment and bring trade to the town.'

The event itself that year was deemed a big success, thanks in no small part to glorious weather which descended for the whole week.

The *Chronicle* left its readers in no doubt of the reality of the situation however, using a double page spread to lay out the headline 'SUN SAVES DARTMOUTH CARNIVAL FROM BIG LOSS: More Rain and this Event Would have Been Sunk for Good.'

FERRY BIG FIGHT

A plan to widen the Lower Ferry and its slip came in for some harsh criticism from the Dartmouth & Kingswear Society, who in turn came in for some harsh criticism from the borough council.

Co-founder and chairman of the society, Christopher Milne, said that the Higher Ferry should receive the investment the council was suggesting for the Lower Ferry, as it was the more logical choice.

'By concentrating on the Higher Ferry several advantages would be gained,' he said. 'It would thin the Lower Ferry queue leaving Dartmouth from the South Embankment. The slips on both sides of the river at the Higher Ferry could be widened almost indefinitely. There is also the possibility of a relief road from Townstal Farm to the lower College gates, so the logical crossing is the upper Ferry.'

The society was 'appalled' that the borough council were proposing to demolish Sunderland Terrace and although they knew it was in bad condition, felt it should be retained for its architectural importance.

The council did not take kindly to this criticism.

In the next week's edition, under the headline 'Councillors Slap the Society' they responded with both barrels.

Cllr A Parrott said: 'I think it is nearly time that the Dartmouth & Kingswear Society were told where they belong. A big percentage of their members have not even been in this town for ten years, yet they have the nerve to turn around and tell us how to run our affairs. I am fed up with them. They have a damned cheek. But I don't think I had better say any more.'

Cllr E Rimmer said: 'Dartmouth has got to live off tourists and people who come here for pleasure. If the Higher Ferry was made the main approach we would hardly see any holiday trippers at all.'

Cllr Tozer said: 'It is time the brake was put on this lot.'

ESTABLISHED 1854

Dartmouth Chronicle

CIRCULATING IN DARTMOUTH, BRIXHAM, KINGSBRIDGE & THE SOUTH HAMS

Telephone: Dartmouth 24.   Telegrams: 'Chronicle,' Dartmouth

6317   FEBRUARY 8, 1963   PRICE 3d.

MAYOR CATCHES FIRE

She escapes with burns as nightdress blazes

PRESENCE of mind saved Dartmouth's Mayor, Ald. Mrs. Dorothy Holwill, from being badly burned on Sunday morning.

She was standing in front of a gas fire in her bedroom when her nightdress flared up.

She shouted for her husband who was downstairs but managed to tear the nightdress off.

The flames burned her wrist and elbow and singed her eyebrows and hair.

She was treated for severe blistering. But later she was suffering from shock and was sent to bed.

MRS. D. HOLWILL

FLATS FOR COUNCIL ?

This is your life they're neglecting opinion

HAVE you fallen into the Boatfloat recently? If so the chances are that you won't be reading this.

It amazes us that in a river town like Dartmouth there is a great deal of slackness about life-saving equipment. Few of our schoolchildren know how to swim—or, indeed, have the chance to learn in a pool.

One of the attractions is playing and fishing around the Boatfloat. Here for the last two weeks there has been a yawning space where the lifebelt should be.

THE EASE

We understand it has been taken away for painting. But is this town so poor that

Embankment was missing and that another at Castle Cove had not enough rope on it when it was thrown out to someone in trouble.

We should have thought that by now the Council would have learned from these lessons.

UNRAILED

Isn't a normal inspection made of all life-saving equipment? If not, why not?

Another thing which disturbs us is the ease with which it is possible to fall into the Boatfloat.

There is only a small protective rail around part of the pavement. It is the simplest of things on a dark night to misjudge distance—let alone

There are great unrailed expanses of river frontage. No one is suggesting that they should be fenced off. But the emergency regulations could be tightened up.

In other towns lifeguard associations have been formed. In Dartmouth no one seems interested.

It is all very well saying that tragedies are few and far between. That is no condolence to the relatives of the first casualty.

Last year a cadet from Britannia R.N. College was drowned with all the life-saving facilities the Navy has at its disposal.

Dartmouth has few—in fact, if you walk along the whole of

What could possibly be the best headline in the Chronicle *ever…*

The society did not let it drop, though they tried to make a show at least of not rising to the bait.

Mr Milne, at the society's annual meeting said: 'The future is more important than the past. This year the town will have to make up its mind about the town plan. This calls for patience, compromise and understanding of the other person's point of view. May I urge that we all try to keep the temperature down. No good will come if we try to start a dog fight. I admit we were sticking out our necks. But I will bet that one day our analysis will be found to be correct.'

CHRONICLE STARTS A FIGHT

A real 'dog fight' broke out about a new development, but mainly because of what the *Chronicle* put on its front page.

The town was enraged about a proposed amusement arcade on the North Embankment inside the abandoned factory there.

The plans met with a mixed response, as many traders felt the town needed an injection of investment to attract more visitors, and a modern arcade with shops and games for visitors to take part in seemed just the ticket.

But many also felt it was not 'in keeping' with Dartmouth and its projected image.

Again, the *Chronicle's* front page *opinion* piece left readers in no doubt what the editor thought.

'For ourselves, dodgems, hurdy-gurdies, slot machines and candy floss are not our favourite fruit,' it said. 'In fact, you would not catch us inside an amusement arcade. But a realistic point of view must be taken. If an arcade would make Dartmouth prosper – no matter to what degree – then for the benefit of the town the council should not withhold permission. To contain amusements in one building would not be a bad idea. At least the arcade would be at the end of the town, where less nuisance would be caused by noise. It's an idea that for a certain section would brighten up Dartmouth just as much as any Boatfloat scheme. Let us hope the council will not dismiss the application, or heed too much the wishes of the Dartmouth & Kingswear Society, who are bound to make some form of objection.'

Goodbye Dolly and welcome Coun. Rimmer

'WHAT A YEAR: WHAT A MAYOR'—MASHFORD

THEY came to make Coun. E.   ago he found that for 50 per   year, except one. And that was

The end of Mayor Holwill's eventful year.

Object they did, but the company behind the scheme got cold feet and it never materialised.

The winter was very cold, Slapton Ley froze, the ice was so thick people skated on it.

It became so cold that the town nearly lost a Mayor. Dorothy Holwill was trying to keep warm in her bedroom one Sunday morning. She stood too near to her gas fire and her night dress caught fire.

Quickly ripping off the garment she escaped with blistering on her back, arm and face, but was diagnosed with shock and was sent to bed. Her husband Mr F Holwill, spoke to the *Chronicle*.

'She was very lucky to escape so lightly. I believe if she had panicked and started running about things would have been more serious. I dashed upstairs to find the nightdress alight and in fragments. It was still smouldering when I threw it in the garden. My wife did not seem very concerned. But later shock seemed to set in, so she went to bed.'

CHRONICLE CAUSES AN ARGUMENT – BY ACCIDENT THIS TIME

The *Chronicle* found itself in hot water with Totnes Rural District Council, for 'stirring up' an eviction notice.

The *Chronicle* reported that a new dental officer for Totnes and Brixham would be living in Kingswear, much to the advantage of the village, it pointed out, and that they would be living in 'temporary council housing'.

This caused a stink because the only council property that was becoming available in the right time-frame was one occupied by local family the Bryants, who were served with an eviction notice after the story went into the paper.

Residents put two and two together, and decided a less-than-perfect but still highly regarded family who had landed on hard times were being targeted to allow the new dental officer to be housed. The residents were not happy.

When the paper reported their unhappiness, Totnes Rural District Council got hot under the collar, denied that the new officer was the reason for the eviction, and publicly reprimanded the paper for printing items off the minutes of a council meeting before they had been ratified. Despite the fact that the paper could have printed them whenever it liked if it had been at the meeting.

The *Chronicle*, again through its *opinion* column, strenuously defended itself and rebutted all accusations. Totnes Rural District Council, meanwhile, mysteriously changed their mind on the eviction of the Bryant family from their Contour Heights home.

Cllr E Melville suggested that the family be allowed to stay with the rent deducted from the father of the family's wages each week direct.

'It is a heaven sent solution to our problem,' she said. 'No one wanted the family to go out, whatever we felt about the lack of payment. No one wanted to prosecute them.'

The council in Dartmouth had rather more pressing issues at the time: its election. The borough council elections actually produced good competition and exciting results.

Ten candidates contested seven seats in May and Mrs Margaret Keane, wife of Dr Giles Keane, won, beating local Fred Tremlett and a number of other people from the area to top the poll.

The poll itself saw more votes than any other in the eighteen years since the war, and Mrs Keane took more votes than any woman had ever taken in Dartmouth.

The paper was effusive in its praise.

'It was no surprise that Mrs Margaret Keane topped the poll. In fact the most surprised was...Mrs Keane. For days most people had been forecasting that she would win. But neither she nor her supporters realised she would attract 1,756 voters – 742 more than her nearest challenger. This shattering of male prestige was cheered by the large soaked crowd who waited outside the Guildhall in a rainstorm.'

Cllr Keane said: 'Thank you for the welcome you have just given me and for your votes. It was a jolly interesting election. There is no lethargy in Dartmouth with ten candidates and a jolly good poll. I promised to do my best for Dartmouth and its people and that is what I will do from now on.'

The Mayor-elect, Cllr Rimmer came last of the elected places with 794 votes; he thanked the people for their 'loyal support' and congratulated Cllr Keane on her 'glorious effort'.

HARD TIMES AT PHILIP & SON MEAN REDUNDANCIES

Less glorious was the seemingly sudden change in fortune of the town's biggest employer.

Ninety men were made redundant from Philip & Son shipbuilders in June. The turnaround in the fortunes of the yard was spectacular, as it had two sites at Sandquay and Noss and had been the powerhouse employer of the town for years, sometimes having hundreds of men in full-time employment.

The site announced that it would look to change production from metal to wooden boats, to bring in more money, while looking for more investment. It seemed suddenly as if the whole shipbuilding industry in Britain was in crisis, and Noss, a specialist and high-quality shipyard, suffered badly.

It had produced Sun Tugs for the London Shipping Company, and built more than thirty lightships for Trinity House. However, this high-end work could quickly disappear and the company spent most of the year in chaos. It had celebrated its centenary just five years before, and had seemed to be in rosy health. But it failed to adapt to the new economic times and found orders hard to come by. The only consolation for this was that it was in the same 'boat' as the rest of the British shipbuilding industry.

HOPE THAT HOUSES WILL BRING GROWTH

The building of houses made a huge difference to a number of families in the town's estate at the 'top of the hill'.

Dartmouth Borough Council spent large funds providing new homes for Townstal. In September the keys were handed over to a new development which included twenty flats, seven houses and two shops. The building cost the council

The last coaling ship, Similarity *bringing coal to Kingswear for the Torquay gas works in 1963.*
DAVID KELLAND

£50,000, and was designed by a private architect, Mr J Boyd Anderson. He claimed the development was very successful because there were double the amount of homes normally put onto developments like it, but they had 'achieved it without overcrowding'.

The development was a vital one in the minds of many in the town who saw an increasing population in Dartmouth, and wanted to keep it that way to allow the sustainability of the town's economy.

This was not helped when a guide book for tourists faced heavy criticism. The town was even 'lampooned' on television in November, over the way its guide portrayed the town.

Westward Television got interested after residents complained the guide did not give an accurate or up-to-date view of the town. A whole ten minute section on its regional news programme was dedicated to the issue, and sections of the guide were read-out and portrayed during it.

Linda Goss became one of Dartmouth's most famous schoolgirls when she headed off to Russia after being taught at the Strakhova Dance School. She was the first British person to receive training at the Bolshoi Ballet School, and is still the only Brit to receive its lauded teacher training.
SOUTH HAMS
NEWSPAPERS

The section which upset most residents, the paper and the borough council referred to a quote from the guide: 'As the ferry nudges the pontoon brown hands reach out to help you ashore.'

It referred to the hands of the ferry-men which would have been heavily tanned.

It says something of the times that the TV chose to show someone dressed, as the *Chronicle* put it: 'like a cannibal', meaning a white man 'blacked-up' and wearing a loin cloth, on the Dartmouth pontoon grabbing visitors and hauling them away to do goodness knows what to them, and that no one thought it was inappropriate.

GUIDE FOR TOURISTS 'FEEBLE'

The thing which upset the people of the town was not the inherent racism in the image portrayed, but the fact that Westward Television seemed to be openly 'mocking' them.

The borough council produced the guide, and had been defending it for a number of months after traders pointed out it gave lots of information about the town's long and proud history, but virtually none about where to park a car, have a meal or find hotel accommodation.

Town Clerk, Hugh Wright, who had played a big part in producing the guide, dismissed the television appearance as 'A Westward gimmick'. However, he had a hard time deflecting criticism when the television company showed a number of people condemning the guide, at length, on primetime television.

One such critic was Mr John Way, who said: 'The guide romances about the history and the past. It does not say enough about the facilities of the harbour and the fact that you can put big ships in it and sail in and out on any tide which you can't do in many ports.'

Mrs C Milne said: 'It does not do justice to Dartmouth, a marvellous town which we are immensely proud of. This gives a feeble impression of something that is really good. We are an old fashioned town but we are entitled to use modern advertising techniques. The guide is muck and we would like it re-written.'

Philip & Son: A Proud Tradition of High Quality Ship Building on the River Dart

(See year 1999)

The Sandquay shipyard and new floating dock in 1924. DARTMOUTH MUSEUM

Philip & Son, a company with a proud heritage, had a rollercoaster journey through the second half of the 20th century.

Running from spectacular success to abject failure, the company embodied the struggle faced by every British shipbuilding firm during that time.

The company, started in 1858 by George Philip, an Aberdonian shipwright and foreman, had an eventful Second World War. It built 230 ships and repaired battle-damaged ones, including those nearly destroyed in the debacle that was Exercise Tiger. The yard was also bombed by the Germans, in a raid which killed twenty two men, the worst loss from a single raid in Dartmouth during the war.

Thanks to this, the yard had a special place in the hearts of the town's people who had now left the war behind them. Its good employment prospects meant it single-handedly made Dartmouth a viable community, keeping men, and their families, in the area through regular employment.

1955 dawned on the business' best ever period outside the war years. It was working on some of its most famous ships, including the Trinity lightships, of which the company made more than thirty over a period of twenty years.

The company employed, at its Noss and Sandquay yards, more than 500 men at times, and was the pride and joy of the town.

The yard had the 'floating dock', an amazing contraption which allowed ships to be worked on without a slipway, which had been a shrewd investment when it was purchased in 1924. It allowed the yard to take on much bigger work than would otherwise have been the case, often keeping the wolf from the door in times of strife.

As the yard celebrated its Centenary, the *Chronicle* marked the day with pages of coverage – the firm was the town's biggest employer, and was considered very important. But behind the celebrations the company was not in good shape. By 1960 orders were hard to come by – just four years after the company's books were full.

In 1961 the floating dock, by now decrepit and beyond repair after thirty seven years, was broken up for scrap.

By 1964 the company was in dire straits: it made many men who had thought they had a job for life redundant – and was bought out by the Reeves Timber Company of Totnes.

The company took on any engineering work it could to make ends meet; it made bridges, containers, machinery. All the members of its staff remaining continued to maintain the same high standards they had been brought up with since becoming apprentices at the age of sixteen. These standards seemed at times to be the only thing that was maintained during some desperate times.

Philip Pensabene bought out Reeves shares in the company in 1969, but it seemed he had more interest in the Dart Marina Hotel, which had been built on the site of the Sandquay yard after the down-turn in the early 1960s.

But then, in 1970, the company pulled off a coup which it was felt would catapult it back into the big time: Chay Blyth and the yacht *British Steel.* Chay Blyth, the former Marine and rower of the Atlantic, decided he wanted to sail Round-the-World single-handed, against the prevailing winds. He was the first person to attempt the feat, and many felt it would be impossible. Chay decided he needed a yacht which was strong and that it should be made of steel.

He chose Philip & Son because its fame for working with steel had spread far and wide, even though the yard was past its best.

The yacht's construction was a strange and beautiful combination of the old and the new.

The men who made her – in a remarkable time of just four months – debated whether to weld a box containing trinkets for their children to the hull, so that they could then have possessions which had been Round-the-World. They decided against it because they felt that the Scot 'wouldn't make it'.

He returned to Britain triumphant after 292 days at sea. He told anyone who would listen that the hull did not have a mark on it – thanks to the twelve layers of paint with which the patient and perfection-seeking Philip & Son workers had lovingly covered her.

But it did not herald a triumphant return to fortune for Philip & Son.

Just after Chay's return, the company stopped production on steel boats

The woodwork team in the mid 1960s at Noss.

altogether and the yard made more than 100 men redundant over the next few years, culminating in the ceasing of all construction of boats on the Noss site in 1974.

Men kept working there, repairing ships and yachts, but the next twenty five years saw the Marina at Noss slowly grow and the engineering work and repairs slowly decline.

In 1999 an end was finally called.

Philip & Son called time on their engineering site 141 years after George Philip had set up in the Coombe Mud. Thirty men were made redundant.

Many felt it was the end of an era, others felt it was the inevitable culmination of the collapse of the British shipbuilding industry. But whatever was the reason for the once-great company's fall, men all over the area could still feel proud that they worked at a company which produced some of the greatest vessels ever to be launched on the Dart.

The Noss shipyard in its heyday with the Trinity House Tongue *Lightship alongside.*

Our castles in the air!
opinion

HAVE you wondered if the face of Dartmouth will change in the next year? Will 1964 alter the sleeping countenance of this 20th century anachronism?

The last year has been brimful with schemes – old and new – which may never be seen again, except in the pipe dreams of their inventors.

So come with us on a fictional tour, assuming all ideas are harnessed for a brave new Dartmouth.

We drive in from the Higher Ferry carefully avoiding the many dinghy-towing cars which are dumping their loads on the new £14,000 slipway.

Along the Embankment is a queue of youngsters for the newly erected swimming pool.

Bat to ball

Over on Coronation Park there is the sound of bat on ball – the cricket club have permission to play there.

Ten yards further on a hurdy-gurdy roars out from Greenecos. The amusement arcade has arrived, complete with the echoing timbre of skittles being scythed down by mahogany-like Dutch cheeses.

The flats at Mayflower Court are empty. Residents can't stand the noise.

Approaching the Railway Pontoon the river is choked with pleasure boats. They are all trying to land their money-laden passengers for the benefit of Dartmouth's traders – thanks to the kind thoughts of Dr. Beeching and British Railways.

A prescient article in the Chronicle *heralds 1964.*

The pontoon has been transformed since the railway retreat. Trippers sip ice-cool drinks from the glass-panelled observation section which gives a 90-degree view of the Dart. Anchored in the river is an old paddle steamer now a sailing school.

The Boatfloat is orderly and tidy. No stench, no mud, no hulks – but still swimming children, who prefer it to the pool!

Moving on to South Embankment, we pass a group of boatmen exhibiting uniform prices and handing out trading stamps.

The extension of the hospital is complete, while Sunderland Terrace is demolished and the hoardings are no more.

A new ferry slipway despatches cars less precariously while a new ferry tug speeds up the service.

Lifted face

No. 27 Lower Street is no longer delapidated and on its lifted face is an ancient building plaque.

We have to park here, because traffic is not allowed on Bayards Cove and the hill is closed.

So it's shank's all the way now – stopping to spend a penny at Manor Gardens. This part of the town has changed little – apart from a four-storey building at Ravensbury.

But moving on to Warfleet the peace is shattered somewhat by the town's second swimming pool at the end of the creek.

We plod on up to the Castle, where the gardens are neat and tidy; Sugary Green restored to its former verdant virginity and Compass Cove steps repointed and repaired.

No car

Going back to Swannaton we are glad we did not bring the car because it's one-way here now.

We pick it up again at Lower Street, just in time to get to Dartmouth Market, which has been switched to a Sunday.

This is just as well because we can't hear the buzz of the engineering factory which is in the other market buildings.

The old folk's rest room has been extended, while from the Old Gospel Hall comes a hot gospel from the record of the youth centre.

There's a new car showroom next to the Guildhall, but no longer do the bowling club perform at their green. They have moved to Coronation Park. Only cars bowl in now, while old folks live on the old tennis courts.

No fear

There is no fear of flooding in this area. The council have revived their old sewerage scheme, and we look up to a made-up elegant Ford Valley.

Higher up the road, a group of scouts return from their new H.Q. in the quarry close to the completed bungalow estate.

At Townstal a new Clochemerle has been de-cloched by the bus stop; and the residents queuing there seem more contented now that they have a community centre, a speed limit, a zebra crossing, a factory, a pub – and, of course, the lavatory.

And so on to Stoke Fleming . . . where caravans no longer rest and Blackpool Sands are saved for the residents

1964 It was promised that a new boat would grace the river Dart at the beginning of the year. The town was to experience a taste of modern engineering when Mr John Richardson ordered a 'jet powered ferry' in January, to arrive that May. Dartmouth's residents were very excited, talking about the new boat which appeared as exciting as an item from the classic, *Boys Own*. It caught the attention of one particular town councillor. Cllr H Osborne suggested using the same sort of projection system on the Lower Ferry; in fact he suggested a completely new ferry. During the council's discussions regarding the purchase of the new engine, a standard and very useable 120bhp Glenifer DH6, for the Lower Ferry tug, he said: 'I suggest an entirely different sort of propulsion. I consider that we are going back thirty years if we accept this engine. We should investigate every new method there is. A water-jet propelled boat will be coming to the river in a few months. The unit is self contained and a separate tug is not needed.'

Unfortunately for the Lower Ferry it never became jet powered, but it did continue to service the town as faithfully as it always had, using conventional propulsion methods.

Snow in Dartmouth! The winter of 1963–1964 was harsh.
REG LITTLE

The *opinion* section on the front of the *Chronicle* attracted controversy once again, this time for referring to the town's primary schools as 'hawkers' for charitable groups.

January 17 edition's front page piece was entitled 'charity at home' and featured the editor criticising schools for sending children home with envelopes for money to go towards charitable causes.

CHRONICLE SAYS CHILDREN COLLECTING FOR CHARITY 'HAWKERS'

'Charity begins at home, but some of the schools are taking this too literally in their efforts to raise money for various causes. It does not seem right – especially in the infant age groups – to send youngsters home with envelopes inviting parents to contribute to numerous charities. It is almost a veiled form of blackmail, because the child has it impressed upon its mind that either mummy or daddy should oblige. They generally do, and the child carries the envelope back full of pride that its family has come up to scratch. But is it right? What of the child whose parents won't – or can't – afford to put their hands into their pockets? Whether schoolmasters or mistresses like it or not, the infant whose envelope is empty or not returned definitely feels out of it – just as much as the child who, so the school authorities would have us believe in their efforts to get uniformity in dress, feels out of it if another youngster is better turned out in ordinary clothes. It can also lead to tantrums and heart rending at home. We are not versed in the psychological side of education but it appears that this kind of charity collecting can only lead to childhood snobbery. After all, should 5 to 8 year olds be involved in the worries of money so early in their lives? If the answer from education authorities is 'yes' then surely an appeal should be made to the children to support the causes from their own pocket money. So please Headmaster, don't let charity begin at home. There's so much of it at the front door already for the parent. Don't add another hawker who can always get a foot inside the door.'

The piece inspired a reaction from the Headmistress of Dartmouth Primary, Miss LM Gregory, which pointed out her school had only supported two charities over the previous ten years and that often the children did contribute to the fundraising out of their own pocket money. In fact the only ones who didn't were normally the 'spoilt' ones with the most to give. To educate includes teaching the desirability of helping others less fortunate than themselves. Apparently we have to try to teach at least one parent this same lesson, but the very success of the appeal indicates how few parents think along the lines of the writer of the article. Certainly he need not trouble to state he is 'not versed in the psychological side of education…' she continued 'this much is evident from the whole tenor of this most deplorable article.'

The editor, who had written the piece did not allow the issue to rest and replied by saying: 'It seems to us some of the teachers need education about the average wage in Dartmouth and also in elementary reading. There was no suggestion in *opinion* that the primary school in particular had invited parents to contribute to numerous charities. But it was suggested that donations should come from children's pocket money be it excessive or not.'

*Gross vandalism
on a massive scale
was avoided when
Kinsgwear Parish
council didn't
fill in Waterhead
Creek.*

CHRONICLE BREAKS THE LAW
THANKS TO DODGY ADVICE

The paper landed itself in hot water, and put the new youth centre in the town at risk. The paper put a lottery competition on the front of the paper in May in which readers could 'predict' the outcome of that week's election.

The proceeds would be split down the middle, with 50 per cent going to the winners and the rest to the youth centre, which needed £750 to qualify for grants to convert the old gospel hall into a much-needed youth centre.

This all seemed very straightforward, until the paper was visited by CID from Torbay and told all staff involved, including the youth centre committee, would be interviewed as part of a legal investigation.

The same day the town clerk, who had advised both the *Chronicle* newspaper and the committee that there were 'no legal problems' handed a letter to the *Chronicle* pointing out it was, in fact, in breach of Section 47 of the Betting, Gaming and Lotteries Act 1963, which stated no competition such as a lottery could be run based on a prediction of the future. The clerk refused to comment when asked, pointedly by the editor of the *Chronicle*, why this hadn't been explained.

Seemingly a very serious matter had been turned into a campaigning issue by the editor, in the midst of him facing criminal charges.

A proposal for a service unloading and cleaning sand and grit caused the Mayor to put his foot down.

Cllr E Rimmer returned from holiday to discover the town's planning committee had sent its recommendation, approving the plans by a Plymouth firm to bring its large processing and cleaning equipment to Kingswear, direct to the Totnes Rural District Council, without putting it before the full council.

He told the *Chronicle* as soon as he realised what had happened he had sent a 'hold your horses' order to Totnes, otherwise known as sending a letter asking the Totnes Rural District Council to discount the previous communication on the subject.

The mistake was not a surprise, the planning committee had been in turmoil most of the year, taking four attempts to refuse the building of a terrace in Ravensbury Drive, including two site visits when only one councillor attended, followed by the indignation of seeing it approved by the county council. This sort of farce had been repeated time and time again by the group and to be so publicly reprimanded by the Mayor must have been difficult to swallow.

The Mayor argued that the developers' deliveries and equipment would reduce yacht traffic, get in the way of the passenger and Lower Ferries and would hurt the tourist industry. To prove his point, Cllr Rimmer then played the council a recording made by a Kingswear resident of similar machinery in full swing. It was loud!

As a result, the councillors decided it was not a suitable development for Dartmouth or Kingswear and voted against it.

One councillor disagreed. Cllr G Perring said: 'The whole thing is ridiculous. People's memories are short. Just after the war there was a great conveyor belt on the site where the Boatel now stands unloading coal from the hulks. No-one mentioned a thing then about noise or vibration. I maintain that the noise of a sand washing plant will be lost in the general sound of jetty and railway noises that come from Kingswear.'

NOT JUST ANY OLD IRON RETURNS IN TRIUMPH TO TOWN

Connected to industry but much more welcome, was the acquisition of a large piece of iron which changed the world, for its inventor's home town.

Dartmouth celebrated its links with the man who fathered the industrial revolution. Percy Russell finally won his long struggle to bring one of the surviving Newcomen Engines, designed by Thomas Newcomen, born and brought up in the town, to Dartmouth.

Under the headline 'Percy Russell's Day' the paper reported the celebrations in July, which marked the end of eight years of effort on his part to bring the engine to the South Hams.

It also marked the paper dropping its long-running fight with Mr Russell over the moving of the engine to Dartmouth. The editor, through his now infamous *opinion* front page section, had lambasted Mr Russell's efforts to bring it to the town, entreating him to avoid bringing a 'lump of obsolete iron' and put the money it was costing towards a new swimming pool. The paper lauded him on the engine's arrival.

The town became the subject of national press scrutiny when it acquired the oldest newly-weds in the country.

95 year old Joseph Hall and 82 year old Ethel Miller were interviewed on the television and spoke to the *Daily Mail* when they announced their engagement and were subsequently married in September.

Ms Miller told the *Chronicle*: 'We want the companionship of each other and our families agree we should marry. There won't be a big party, just a small reception at the Regency Restaurant.'

The couple moved to a flat in Victoria Road, as neither could manage the steps in their respective houses anymore.

Thomas Newcomen of Dartmouth, the inventor of the 'engine that changed the world'.
© 2012 RICHARD WEBB

THE RESIDENTS OF KINGSWEAR CAN'T MAKE A PHONE CALL?

The people of Kingswear were written off by many after the chairman of the residents association in the village claimed '90 per cent' of residents 'didn't know' how to make a 999 call.

Mr F Small made the claim after asking the local police officer Sergeant W Cheek to 'lecture' the association members on the proper procedure of making a call to the emergency services. He felt that the lesson was needed because it was no longer a case of simply going round to the local bobby's house to find the authorities, and as there was only one telephone in the village that was available to all, many of the elderly residents 'could get flustered'. He also pointed out this was especially necessary because there would soon be an 'M1 style pile-up' on the Kingswear's roads because of the high-speed at which many cars drove along the village.

1965

Housing in the town came under the spotlight for much of the year. The main problems were the quality of the existing housing stock and the lack of new housing opportunities.

The story which brought the issues into the public consciousness was a shocking case of a family of eight living in a small two bedroomed house. The family, which included a young baby, had been in the house which was riddled with draughts and damp for more than six months.

The story broke in January, in the middle of a bitterly cold winter and in the same week as a small-pox epidemic scare ran through the town.

The borough council contacted the landlord and demanded immediate action. The instruction was not taken up with enthusiasm.

Councillors were surprised to receive a letter from him, informing them contractors were already carrying out work, when he had not discussed what needed doing with the council.

The landlord pointed out he could not start work on the property until the large number of occupants left and in such a case it was the council's responsibility to re-house them.

'A local firm was instructed to advise,' said the landlord in his letter. 'The outcome appeared to be blocked by the condition of the overcrowding which your housing committee appeared to have agreed to deal with by re-housing the tenants and the tenants to co-operate with the contractors who intended to install facilities for the utilisation of a room for a bathroom and a toilet. The contractors advised your officials of this but your officials appeared to think that the tenant should first be evicted by me. I am advised that the natural increase of the occupants of the house precludes this process.'

The landlord expressed annoyance that the amount of tenants had 'increased' through the birth of the child, and seemed to be suggesting taking one room from the eight occupants because the house lacked a bathroom and a toilet. The majority of the house was below street level and only 12 feet wide. The council expressed the opinion that the only way to solve the property's problems was to demolish it but decided against this course of action when it was pointed out the houses on either side and behind could collapse if this was done.

This was the state of much of the housing in Dartmouth at the time.

The family remained in situ for many months as the landlord and the council tried to resolve the issue. A young family suffered through a bitter winter without a toilet or bathroom inside their house, living with four to a bedroom.

Many wanted to increase the amount of houses, pointing at the successful recent completion of the Churchfields Estate as an example of how new housing should be constructed. This view seemed prevalent despite the Dartmouth & Kingswear Society describing the estate as like 'a concentration camp' and asking all residents to plant trees and flowers to brighten up the area.

HOUSING CRUSH CAUSED BY POPULATION INCREASE

The population of Dartmouth at the time was increasing faster proportionately than any other town in the south of Devon.

The town increased from 6,420 to 6,720 between 1963 and 1964. The problem was there was a blanket ban on building outside the town from the Southern Divisional Planning Committee of the county authority. This group was the final arbiter on many planning issues, and had been a thorn in the side of the borough council for many years. The paper ran stories listing the amount of decisions locally which had been overturned by the committee, including demolitions, licences for public houses and off-licences (a road which had two off-licences in it was dubbed 'off-licence alley' by the editor). Despite years of planning by the borough council, they turned down the plan for a new road linking the Market Square with Mayors Avenue to allow a bus route which didn't go past the historic Butterwalk and ease congestion.

The committee fought for and won protection for the Green Belt land around Dartmouth, meaning all expansion of the town was stopped. It was described as a belt around the town, strangling the community as the lack of people discouraged employers to invest and therefore discouraging more people from moving to the area.

ESTABLISHED 1854

Dartmouth Chronicle

CIRCULATING IN DARTMOUTH, BRIXHAM, KINGSBRIDGE & THE SOUTH HAMS

Telephone: Dartmouth 24 Telegrams: "Chronicle," Dartmouth

6419 JANUARY 22, 1965 PRICE 3d.

DARTMOUTH HIGH TIDES

	a.m.	p.m.
Jan. 22 ..	9.50	22.13
Jan 23 ..	10.22	22.44
Jan: 24 ..	10.54	23.24
Jan. 25 ..	11.38	—
Jan. 26 ..	0.17	12.39
Jan. 27 ..	1.27	13.86
Jan. 28 ..	2.46	15.19

CHEMISTS' ROTA

Sunday to Saturday (6 to 7 p.m.)

BOOTS

(except Wednesday—CO-OPERATIVE)

FAMILY OF 8 IN 2 BEDROOMS

THE perplexing problem of a family in which two teenage boys, two teenage girls and a baby share a bedroom is still bothering Dartmouth Council.

Last July the overcrowding in a house at Above Town was brought to the notice of the public health inspector. The house is also damp and below standard.

On Monday, nearly six months later, the Public Health Committee have asked the Housing Committee to give the family, which now has another infant, priority for a council house.

At the same time they agreed to give the landlord, Mr. R. Southwick, a list of defects which the committee consider need repairing.

Originally Mr. Southwick was asked in September for his proposals to bring the house up to standard. He was given three months to formulate them because the committee were considering placing a closing order on the house.

But in a letter which was read on Monday, Mr. Southwick stated: "I gave instructions to my agents to investigate the position with a view to dealing with the provision of facilities.

"A local firm was instructed to

Council to give re-housing priority

"I am advised that the natural increase of the occupants precludes this process."

Mr. A. Hugh Wright, the town clerk, said there were complications in the case. It was also a surprise to him that Mr. Southwick had instructed contractors to start work because the council had received no proposals from him. Neither was it known whether the repairs which Mr. Southwick intended to carry out would satisfy the council and avoid a closing order being made.

Not sure

"I am not at all sure that he is aware of all the work that is needed to bring the house to a reasonable state," added Mr. Hugh Wright.

"Mr. Southwick has assured me, however, that if we give him a written statement of what we think is required, he will give a written statement in return and an estimate of what he will do, together with plans in time for our next meeting."

Another snag

He also pointed out another snag. Assuming it had been possible to carry out the toilet and bathroom conversion it meant that in a house already overcrowded another room was being taken away.

Ald. A. Parrott was astonished that a full list had not gone to Mr. Southwick: But Dr. J. Wildman, Medical Officer of Health, said that although nothing had been given in writing he was sure that Mr. Southwick knew what was needed.

It was also not the committee's duty. The landlord should come with his proposals to the council who would see whether they measured up to what they wanted.

What he found in his pud

THERE have been two cases of bad food in Dartmouth already this year. One was a splinter of metal in a tin of fruit sponge pudding, the other was a mouldy meat pie.

Dr. J. Wildman, medical officer of health, told the Public Health Committee of the complaints on Monday.

The pudding was bought by a Dartmouth housewife and given to her husband. As he was eating it a splinter of metal stuck in his palate.

He pulled it out and found that it was half an inch long and appeared to be a tin-tack without a head.

The manufacturers have been told and are sending a representative to Dartmouth to investigate.

Dr. Wildman said that it would not be advisable to make a prosecution, however, because it could not be proved in court that the tack definitely came from the pudding.

It might have been in packets of

Small-pox scare

THERE was a smallpox scare in Dartmouth last month. This was revealed by Dr. J. Wildman, medical officer of health this week.

He was called in to give his

opinion

THE WEAK LINK

THERE is one glaring weakness in Dartmouth's plan for local government reorganisation which was sent to the county last week.

And that chink in the council's armour has already been spotted by Kingsbridge. It is the admission that even if the town took in Stoke Fleming and Kingswear the rateable value and population would still be below the figures the county normally seek in review proposals.

The counter that Dartmouth claims special consideration as a charter borough established in 1341 gives an indication of the looking back in envy attitude of the council, rather than looking forward in earnest.

To us the plan seems almost one of appeasement. Although the council seem vehemently against going in with Kingsbridge, they have timidly suggested taking only one parish of the

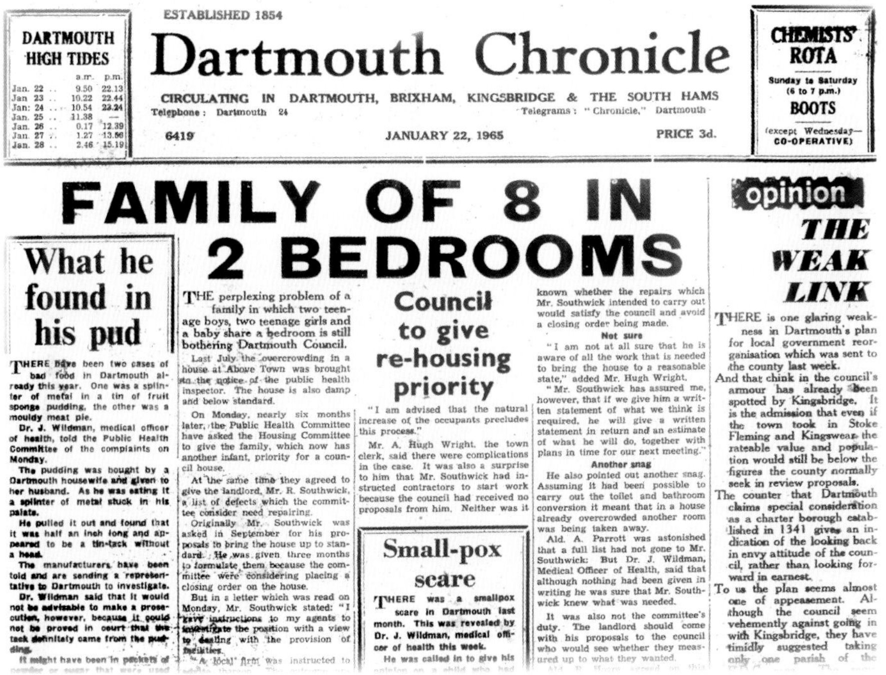

Overcrowding and slums figured heavily in the Chronicle *throughout the 1960s.*

A borough council decision to increase the size of Townstal with an extra 150 houses and flats was overturned. The council were frustrated and angry and voiced these concerns at every opportunity in the *Chronicle*. In the end the borough council resolved to do all it could to combat these problems and try to get the houses, part of a 'four year plan', built regardless and pushed on with planning, it announced in September.

These problems highlighted the gulf between the councils, and a proposed re-organisation of local government, in which large 'districts' would be created, took on great significance. Dartmouth wanted to become one on its own, but its proposals did not meet with happiness in Kingswear, Stoke Fleming or Strete, which it wanted to 'take over'.

SWIMMING POOL DREAMS AGAIN COME TO THE FORE

A proposal for a swimming pool in Dartmouth caused argument, confusion and a surprising lack of interest.

The pool committee, which had been formulated first at the end of the forties, went to the borough council to ask for £5,000 funding towards a pool.

The council, in an adroit and impressive dodge, decided to pledge general support and then ask for a public referendum to decide whether or not the pool was supported by the council with funds.

Many condemned the council for failing to have the backbone to support the pool because it was miserly and penny-pinching.

However when the big day came it turned out that the council was wiser and better connected to the prevailing views of the town than those complaining about it might have expected.

Less than 21 per cent of the electorate bothered to vote, and virtually no one from Townstal came forward. Out of those who voted, the majority turned out to be against paying for a new pool through the rates and those in favour also came out against the selected site by the town greenhouse.

Cllr Fred Tremlett who had fought hard for the pool vote said: 'Townstal has had it as far as I am concerned. It seems they want to be left out of town affairs on their own hill.'

Alderman Mashford said: 'I thought I had my finger on the pulse of public opinion but after this I reckon it is impossible to gauge in the town.'

The 'silent majority' had truly spoken, but the chairman of the pool committee, Cllr George Perring said: 'The question the public were asked to vote on was

*Dartmouth's
Embankment in
the mid 1960s
with few moorings
on the river.*
ROBIN DADSON

whether the council should make a grant. No mention was made of the council taking over the whole project and applying for a loan. It could be held that those who did not vote would prefer the council to do this. I am convinced the town will get a swimming pool and I don't think the pool committee will take a defeatist attitude and decide to pack up.'

But pool campaigner, and former Mayor, Mr N Hewson said: 'I visualised a poll of about 25 per cent, but not as low as this. I don't think there should have been any form of referendum. The council should be strong enough to make their own decisions and not so weak as to put the onus on the ratepayers who have been misled by various figures that have been bandied about.'

Later in the year discussions began about a smaller pool on Coronation Park, but this rarely got beyond the discussion phase. It seemed a pool for the people of Dartmouth would never be achieved.

A NEW WAY TO CALL

An end of an era came with the introduction of the new automatic telephone exchange, meaning the girls in Kingswear who had manned Dartmouth's manual exchange were out of a job.

They looked rather happy about it on the front cover of the February 26 edition though, and the *Chronicle* confidently predicted the end of 'the busy line' when the new fangled STD exchange opened. It had 'a capacity for 800 lines' according to its bold advert inside the paper.

The changeover was remarkably smooth, it seems, although the doctor's surgery was incorrectly listed in the new numbers directory, possibly meaning the famous Doctor McConaghey and his colleagues went untroubled over a few nights.

In August, Regatta was spoiled by gangs of youths fighting around the town. The call went out from the council to the police for reinforcements on Bank Holiday Monday, into which the Regatta then strayed, to stop disturbances.

The trouble first started the Saturday before Regatta when a coach load of young people from Plymouth got to the Guildhall for a scheduled dance and discovered that, due to disturbances at the previous dance there, the council had decided to curtail proceedings at 10.45pm, an hour earlier than advertised. Unhappy at the fact they had travelled so far for a dance which turned out to be such a disappointment, the young people got upset and started to 'clash' with Dartmothians.

The *Chronicle* reported how things then spilled over into other areas of the town, resulting in 'a whopping band of town youngsters' rushing from Foss Street to the Boatfloat and starting 'another brawl'. One of the fighters was thrown through a shop window.

The police were very clear with who they considered to be to blame for the disturbances. A spokesman told the paper: 'It is up to the Council to decide whether it is worth collecting £9 in revenue from Guildhall dances and bring all this trouble into town.'

The council demanded that more police presence was provided over the Regatta weekend because the youths might return to exact 'revenge'.

In the end very little trouble materialised, but it was the last year that Regatta ran on a Monday after the weekend, as it was decided it wasn't worth the cost or the work.

TO BE COMMERCIAL PORT OR A TOURIST HAVEN?

1966
The year started with a particularly controversial question, and one which was to be re-visited over the years.

The question was whether the harbour ports of Dartmouth and Kingswear should welcome industrial ships?

The coal ships which were unloading at Kingswear were accused of being too noisy and keeping residents awake all night, and one resident in particular made a lot of *noise* about the noise.

Mr J Holliwell of Carlton Lodge in Kingswear caused such an argument he was featured on the local television news, a rare and distinct privilege at the time. He continued to fight his corner against the ships, which he claimed were making people's lives a misery, working throughout the night.

'There seems to be a complete lack of consideration for people who live in the area by the crews of the vessels,' he said. 'The ships run all day and far into the night, which is very distressing to people living within sound range of them.'

He took his complaint to the commissioners of the Harbour Commission, who, in the main, were not sympathetic.

'This is a commercial port and if industry is to be operated then a certain amount of noise has to be put up with,' said Cllr H Adams, the commission's chairman. 'Recently one of the ships had its generator break down and the crew were unable to get light and heating. They had to work overtime to get it working. No doubt a lot of the noise could be attributed to this.'

The only member of the commission who was sympathetic to Mr Holliwell's cause was a fellow Kingswear resident, Mr S Hearn, who said that the one ship had an extremely loud generator. He claimed, without providing any evidence, that it was '90 per cent' louder than any other, and he urged that the commission used its powers to act against boats without silencers on their engines.

Nothing happened, so the determined residents association, led by its Chairman Mr W Small contacted the Minister of Transport, Barbara Castle, to try to get coal ships stopped from coming into Kingswear. Their point was that the ships, plus the lorries used to take away the coal, were creating a terrible problem for the people of the village, as they were being disturbed all hours of the day or night. Both Mr Small and Mr Holliwell said that should the coal be taken away by rail they would be happy.

SMASH AND GRAB SHOCK

The town's first 'smash-and-grab raid' took place at the end of January.

However the robbers were not hardened professionals and seemed relatively relieved to be caught within an hour of the raid at the Spinning Wheel Café and antiques shop in Hauley Road.

Very familiar, yet distinctly different; Fairfax Place in the mid 1960s.
ROBIN DADSON

Dartmouth as a Film and TV Location

The streets of Dartmouth are steeped in history – from the wooden beams of the Butterwalk to the cobbles of Bayards Cove, visitors to the town feel that they are somehow connected with the past.

So have filmmakers.

When looking to create an 'Old Fashioned' feel to their film or television series, especially when the story being told has a link to the sea, Dartmouth has been the go-to destination for many years.

There have been many visits from film crews over the years, often from London, or overseas, who are bowled over by the town's beauty and the warm welcome they receive.

Several high-profile films and series have caused a stir in the town and below follows a brief history of the most famous – and in one case infamous – productions to visit the town.

The Sailor Who Fell from Grace with the Sea 1976

This was perhaps the town's most infamous film connection. Kris Kristofferson along with his co-star Sarah Miles arrived in town in 1975 to film this adaptation of a Japanese novel, which, it was rumoured, was a bit 'racy'. Even 'raunchy' perhaps.

The *Chronicle* had great fun upping the titillation stakes for all and thanked the cast and crew for choosing Dartmouth as a location. And then they saw it.

The film featured some VERY explicit sexual material and a scene in which a cat is tortured and then killed. It is still a very well regarded film and received good reviews around the world – but will never be thought so in Dartmouth.

The paper recommended people avoid the film and criticised the cinema in Zion Place for even showing it. 'The Onedin Line' was a source of pride for Dartmouth, 'The Sailor Who Fell from Grace with the Sea' is the film everyone wished had never happened.

The French Lieutenant's Woman 1981

The adaptation of a 1969 novel by John Fowles saw Meryl Streep and Jeremy Irons star in a complicated but well-made film.

It was certainly complicated for Kingswear – which had its main street 'paved' with rubber cobbles.

It was nominated for five Oscars the next year, and won a number of awards elsewhere, including a BAFTA for Meryl Streep as Best Actress. It remains a well-liked and highly-respected piece of intelligent and ambitious film making, and Kingswear and Dartmouth were proud to be part of it.

Down To Earth 2000 – 2005

A BBC TV series about people from the city moving to Devon for a 'better life' unsurprisingly hit a chord with many in Dartmouth. The series filmed from 2000 to 2005 with three different families living on the seemingly cursed farm near a town very much like Dartmouth.

With Pauline Quirke and Warren Clarke in the first series, Ian Kelsey and Angela Griffin in the third and then finally Denise Welch and Ricky Tomlinson in the final years, it was, like 'The Onedin Line', a popular Sunday night drama, which gave many in the town their first taste of work as extras.

Ordeal By Innocence 1985

Also known as 'Ordeal to Watch' this Agatha Christie adaptation was filmed in late 1984 and featured some big names, such as Donald Sutherland, Faye Dunaway, Christopher Plummer and Sarah Miles – who obviously couldn't get enough of the town. But it was panned by the critics and disappeared without trace. Dartmouth looked lovely in the film though.

Churchill: The Hollywood Years 2004

Blackawton-based comedy veteran Peter Richardson, famous for his work with the 'Comic Strip' on Channel 4 in the 1980s, decided to use Dartmouth as the base for his spoof biography of Churchill. The premise was that American producers would replace Winston with an American GI – played by Hollywood heart-throb Christian Slater – because the American public wouldn't accept him being British and a bit fat.

The film was not successful at the box office, but the people of Dartmouth took the production to their hearts. Many worked as extras in it and the town is littered with pictures of people meeting Slater and Neve Campbell, as well as the many British comedy alumni that appeared in the film.

The Onedin Line 1971 – 1980

The TV series, written by Cyril Abraham and Alun Richards, about a down-on-his-luck sea Captain mercilessly determined to become a success at any price was screened on BBC TV between 1971 and 1980 (91 episodes). It created a sensation. The theme tune, an excerpt from the *Adagio of Spartacus and Phrygia* from the ballet *Spartacus* by Aram Khachaturian, became something people would hum through their Monday, having watched the programme on a Sunday night.

The programme made huge stars of its two leads, Peter Gilmore and Anne Stallybrass, who then went and fell in love, cementing the nation's affection for them.

The Onedin Line *transforms a building in Dartmouth.*

Peter Gilmore and Anne Stallybrass made Dartmouth their home after filming The Onedin Line *in the town.*

Dartmouth was chosen to represent the streets of Liverpool in the Victorian era, and was transformed for months at a time for various scenes. Bayards Cove featured heavily, as did the Warfleet pottery and the town's old market. Many still cherish the pictures of them in period dress, standing next to the TV series' stars.

The low budgets created some fun moments, such as the Long Wood in Kingswear becoming the Amazon by the application of filters and two palm leaves to the camera lens.

After a while the high cost of cast, crew and some large and authentic sailing ships (including the famous *Charlotte Rhodes*) began to tell and production was shifted to Exeter, but the programme will always be associated with Dartmouth.

Some other notable moments in Dartmouth's film and TV history include *The Apple Tree* in 1988, which starred Imogen Stubbs and used Bayards Cove and a well-disguised Higher Street Job Centre; the town survived a visit from hell-raiser Oliver Reed in 1964 when he made the dramatically titled *The System; Nothing But the Night* in 1972 featured Diana Dors with horror greats Peter Cushing and Christopher Lee; *Bequest to the Nation* in 1973 used shots of Bayards Cove and the river mouth in its opening sequence, the film featured Peter Finch

and Anthony Quayle; *A Man for all Seasons* in 1966 used shots of Dartmouth Castle taken from the Kingswear side; comedy *We Joined the Navy* in 1962 showed the Britannia Royal Naval College parade ground and starred Kenneth Moore and John le Mesurier.

TV highlights include *Kidnapped*, *The Master of Ballantrae*, *The Bell Run*, *Smuggler* and *Adventurer* the latter with Oliver Tobias, an advert for Honda featuring Twiggy and a motorcycle, and NatWest used the Lower Ferry for an advert in 2010.

Just forty five minutes later 27 year old Richard White and 21 year old George Thomas England were arrested in a stolen van at California Cross, with the jewellery they had taken. The jewellery items still had the price tags on. The only things in the van which they had bought for themselves were bottles of cider.

It was revealed the pair, both of whom were 'of no fixed address', had travelled down to Devon from Peckham in stolen cars before they tried to take the jewellery. Both were drunk and White admitted to officers he was 'blocked up on dope' as well. England told them White was a drug addict who was always 'taking pills'. When they were arrested it seemed to have been more akin to a scene from a *Carry On* movie than actual criminals being caught.

White told officers he 'couldn't tell them any more about the tomfoolery' (jewellery)'. After England had said that he wanted to make a 'clean breast of it', White declared 'the man is mad. He deserves an Oscar. He ought to be a scriptwriter'.

England was put on probation for three years, whereas White was sent to jail for eighteen months, mainly due to the long list of previous offences he had committed for which he not yet been sentenced.

WHO WANTS TO BE MAYOR?

Not in as much trouble, though much more embarrassed was Dartmouth Council as it tied itself up in knots trying to choose a new Mayor.

Cllr Charles Fitch-Northern was poised to become Mayor after a stormy election at the council's March meeting.

The Mayor-making process was supposed to be a secret, without anyone outside the chamber knowing the process or problems associated with choosing a Mayor. However, a number of councillors spoke to the *Chronicle* 'off the record' and the story broke.

'Fitch' as he was known, had done enough during the previous months to earn the support of six of the council members, and won the vote from Harold White, six votes to four. However, the remaining councillors were unhappy to hear from the outgoing Mayor, Mrs Vida Keane that Fitch had been 'bragging' the week before that he was going to get the job.

This led to murmurings about his suitability.

Fitch, feeling insecure and insulted, after accepting his nomination to the role, asked for a vote of confidence. This might be seen as perhaps inviting trouble, which he got.

The unhappy councillors demanded a 'run off' between Cllr Fitch-Northern and Cllr White. This was won by Cllr White as all those who had voted for others changed to support him, leaving Cllr Fitch-Northern with his original six votes.

There was then another meeting and a vote of confidence in Cllr White after complaints from the councillors who voted for Fitch. Cllr White won, but was not then confirmed as the 'official' Mayor-elect because three councillors could not be found to 'wait' on him. By this they meant go to him and officially ask him to stand. So for two weeks no final choice was made until three councillors were persuaded to go to Cllr White and ask him to be Mayor. It was a three-week embarrassment and the *Chronicle* didn't wish to let the councillors forget it.

The editor, in his front page *opinion* section, hit back at councillors who commented the paper made a great deal of the in-fighting: 'If Dartmouth can't get a Mayor without this seamy business then it would be better to pick a chairman and save the ratepayers £200 a year in Mayor's expenses. We have come under fire in this controversy, too, and have even heard that one alderman suggested we should be brought to the 'council bar' and made to divulge the name of the councillor who gave us the information. Sounds like Star Chamber Justice in a chamber with few stars.'

The pettiness continued with a number of councillors, mainly those who had voted for Fitch, refusing to actually vote for him at the Mayor-making Ceremony or go to the 'Mayoral Banquet' celebrating the election of the new Mayor. The council actually considered 'unseating' the rebel councillors, it was then decided to fine them £100, then, when it became clear they didn't have the power to do this, the council announced publicly that their actions were 'unbecoming'.

COUNCILLORS ACTING BADLY SHOCKER

The Higher Ferry in the 1960s.
ROB LITTLE
PHOTOGRAPHY

The council had bigger issues to deal with than its ceremonial leader.

There was the continuing housing crisis, with no land available for development with a great need for new houses for young families to use, along with the constant whispers about local government reorganisation, which had been handled so badly the year before.

In the previous year the council had suggested it could become its own district, despite not meeting any of the relevant criteria, especially in its population figures, to become one. It also made statements about the state of the surrounding boroughs of Kingsbridge and Totnes, alienating the very people it would have to work with and win over to become a district.

Then one of the 'rebel' councillors from the Mayoral debacle, Cllr George Perring, decided to reveal at a public meeting that there had been 'secret meetings' with the Ray Mawby MP about the direction the new arrangements for local Government would take.

Cllr Perring made it perfectly clear what he felt about proposals for a larger 'district'.

'I am not going to be hushed by the council or anyone else. If I think anything will be for the benefit of the town I will say so. Are we going to sit down and let ourselves be swallowed up without a fight or are we going to make a stand to still hold the status of our borough? This is a most serious thing for this old borough. If we are to be swallowed up we shall just become a rural borough. We should be limited in what we can spend and in so many ways.'

Despite the many arguments it was clear that a three-tier government system was coming, it was just a question of when.

COUNCILS WORK TOGETHER FOR ONCE – AND FAIL

Something amazing happened in 1966: the borough council and county council planners decided to work together after years of bickering and infighting.

And they still failed. Throughout the 1960s the *Chronicle* was filled with the on-going saga around a new low-water landing to improve loading times for the Lower Ferry and whether three houses next to the ferry slip should be demolished to make way for it. This had been argued for over five years, yet the houses on Sunderland Terrace remained standing and the low water slip remained un-built.

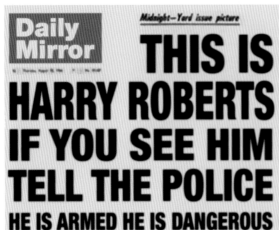

Tragedy overtook former Dartmouth man Detective Constable Christopher Head when he was shot by the now notorious Harry Roberts in London.

The plan to purchase the houses, demolish them and improve the access to the ferry slip was brought forward in 1965, but the problems dragged on into the middle of 1966.

The plan even got so far as sending the compulsory purchase order for the buildings to the Minister of Transport for ratification after the owner refused the money offered for her building.

But the planners had reckoned without the Dartmouth & Kingswear Society, which joined with a number of other groups in supporting the retention of Sunderland Terrace and its 'historic buildings'.

The plan was hit when the housing minister came to the town to look at various planning issues. The minister declared that Sunderland Terrace was wonderful and needed protecting.

He also managed to agree with the divisional planning committee on every disputed building and planning decision, much to the county council's delight and the borough council's disgust.

The compulsory purchase order was cancelled by the new Minister for Transport Barbara Castle because the scheme was flawed in its belief it would improve both access and Lower Ferry boarding times.

But within months the problem was revisited when the owner then tried to get the council to re-open negotiations in the belief a better price could be obtained. They couldn't and the buildings remained un-demolished.

The previous events made town's people wonder whether finding a low water landing slip on the Dartmouth side of the river would be a possibility. It was suggested that the Embankment be extended to achieve the same end, but this was dismissed due to its 'fantastic' cost.

DEATH OF A DARTMOUTH MAN BY INFAMOUS 'COP KILLER'

A Dartmouth man, who had left the town to join the Metropolitan Police, was gunned down in one of the most infamous police killings in British history.

Detective Constable Chris Head, who grew up in Townstal and went to Dartmouth Grammar school and whose parents had an ironmongers shop in Smith Street, had left the town in the 1950s to join the Metropolitan Police. He was a member of the Metropolitan Police F Divisional Criminal Investigation Department and was asked to check out a suspicious car parked in Braybrook Street near Wormwood Scrubs prison. Harry Roberts, a small-time criminal, aware he had three illegal pistols in the car decided that rather than risk being found with them, pulled out a Luger pistol and shot two of the officers, one of them DC Head, dead in the street. He was 30 years old.

Roberts escaped and hid out in Epping Forest for three months, using skills he had picked up while in the army in Malaya. When he was sentenced later that year, the judge recommended that he should not be considered for parole for at least thirty years. He was again refused a release at a parole hearing in 2009.

1967

The diners sitting in the Royal Castle to celebrate the new Mayor in May were not actually celebrating the new Mayor chosen by the council. Cllr Harold White had again been voted in as Mayor.

MAYORAL WRANGLINGS YET AGAIN

But he was not the most popular man outside the council chamber. There was an election between his being re-selected as Mayor and Mayor-making and he lost his seat.

This posed a problem for the council: could a man who was not a councillor be Mayor? Strictly he could, but many felt uncomfortable at the prospect of a man with no public mandate essentially leading the town.

Alderman's Parrott and Hoare were sent to talk to the Mayor-elect immediately after he lost his seat.

Poor Mr White was clearly in two minds over whether he wanted to return, but reluctantly allowed his name to go forward to the formal selection. On the night of the Mayor-making it became clear the mood had turned against him.

Cllr Mashford told the *Chronicle*: 'Previous to the election I voted that Mr White should be Mayor again. But now it is a different matter. The ratepayers have voted him out and I am afraid that I must be swayed by public opinion and vote against him as Mayor.'

Cllr Fitch-Northern, the county councillor who had been voted back onto the town council despite his unpopularity with his fellow elected colleagues, and had been beaten into second place in the original Mayoral vote, said: 'A few weeks before the election Mr White invited me into the Mayor's parlour and promised me that if he was not elected then he would stand down from the Mayoralty. This was a gentleman's agreement and I am surprised that he changed his mind so readily.'

Cllr Perring said: 'The Mayoralty is being dragged through the mud. I hate saying this, but the quicker we are taken over by someone the better even if it is only to stop this type of controversy. I am fed up with all this niggling behind the scenes.'

After an hour of heated discussion on the night of Mayor-making, those backing Mr White were defeated, by just one vote. The call was made for those who wanted to stand for Mayor, and only Cllr Middleton put his name forward.

The *Chronicle* expressed the view that Cllr Fitch-Northern was wronged, but he brushed it off, saying that the council should unite behind its new leader.

Much more serious than political wrangling was the death of one of the town's faithful servants.

TRAGEDY ON THE EMBANKMENT

It occurred in tragic circumstances, which contained within it a never-explained mystery.

Vera Eden, the matron of Dartmouth & Kingswear Cottage Hospital, died in her car in the river Dart after she drove off the Embankment, seemingly without reason, on a cold morning in March.

The heartbreaking story of the attempts to save Miss Eden as the car slipped into the river made harrowing reading.

Young student Frederick Hemingsway who watched the whole episode, said: 'I thought she was going to park on the river side of the road, but the car mounted the kerb near a seat. It came across the pavement at a slight angle. It did not seem that it was being revved but made a steady sound. I heard a bang before it went over the edge, probably from an iron ladder which it hit.

'Miss Eden was sitting bolt upright with both hands on the steering wheel. She seemed to be very frightened before the car hit the water. It went in nose-first and part of the bonnet was submerged.

She mumbled something through the open window. Then she tried to open the door, but could not.'

Richard Carnell, who also witnessed the accident said: 'Miss Eden got her right hand through the window and grabbed the ladder. I asked her if she could open the door or swim, but she said she couldn't do either. I got hold of her hand and as I was

69

doing this the railway ferry came across. It pushed the car against the wall and tried to hold it there. Mr Wakelin jumped in on the other side of the car and all the time it was bobbing up and down but as the water began to get in through the open window it sank more quickly. Matron was fairly calm and did not seem to be excited.'

Mr Raymond Wakelin, who was on the railway passenger ferry, was commended by the coroner for his bravery. For ten minutes he swam next to the car, trying to smash the windows or secure a rope to it, before it slowly slipped below the surface.

The doors of the car were locked and Mr Wakelin was forced to tie the rope around the bumper of the car as it sank below the surface. He swam down again to try and open one of the Cortina's doors, but to no avail.

A diver from the Britannia Royal Naval College was called, but his only job was to retrieve her body after she had been under the water for twenty minutes. Friends and colleagues fought to save her life at the hospital where she had been about to report for duty, but to no avail. The examination of the car showed there was nothing wrong with the brakes, but she had a swollen ankle, and experts thought if her foot had slipped onto the accelerator, in a brand new car with an automatic transmission she wasn't used to, she would not have been able to press the brake hard enough to stop.

Friends testified she wasn't a confident driver, and tended to be heavy on the accelerator. She also tended, rather than eating breakfast, to drink a cup of tea with a large brandy in it, though it was not considered to be contributory factor.

NOT SAFETY FIRST

The front page story of the *Chronicle* on June 16 gives a window on the attitude of the times: 80 per cent of Dartmouth drivers left their cars unlocked.

Police warned that they had discovered the frightening statistic after a series of thefts where the car had simply been driven away because the owner had left the doors open and keys in the ignition.

'Make sure your car is locked, especially at night,' said the police in the most seemingly straightforward advice ever given. 'There has been an epidemic in taking unlocked vehicles. While householders lock up their garden sheds they seem content to make no safety precautions for £600 worth of motor car.'

In other crime news, Dartmouth went down in 'the annals of smuggling history' after the biggest haul of illegal cigarettes ever seized was picked up off the coast.

The haul was of more than four million cigarettes, worth the then extraordinary sum of £46,000.

The man who had arranged the smuggling run was one Hendrik Smit, a Dutchman who owned a business in London. He was in a lot of debt and had turned to smuggling in desperation. His rash decision to turn to crime saw him imprisoned for a year and a fine of £25,000.

The smuggling operation was discovered when the Spanish crew of the yacht *Marie Gabrielle* turned up in Torcross asking for the number of Mr Smit in London. Customs officers were informed that there were men who had landed in the country illegally, and they found the men eating breakfast at a café. The two were being interviewed by officers in a hotel when Mr Smit walked in.

They all agreed to be interviewed in Dartmouth, but the Spanish Captain tried to sail to Brest even when there was a police officer on board his yacht, but saw sense rather quickly.

It turned out that the Captain of the yacht, Melchor Sanchez, and Mr Smit had a business relationship going back more than twelve months and had both set out to smuggle, though they had tried to do so to a number of countries before Britain, but could find no buyer for the cigarettes. The two left a huge trail of evidence behind them making detection a rather easy task for customs officers and police. These included cheques paid by Smit's company to Mr Sanchez and even a picture of the two at Torcross earlier in the year with the place for the drop-off marked in red ink.

Smit was imprisoned for a year, Sanchez for nine months; his crew were freed with conditional discharges. The men, probably only involved because of the chance of a quick buck, wept at the news and returned to their families. Sanchez could not return to his six children in Spain.

HMS Owen *dressed overall for the Regatta and graces the river with its presence in the mid 1960s.*
ROBIN DADSON

OBSESSION LEADS TO ATTEMPTED MURDER

In 1967 Dartmouth played host to a crime which was driven by obsession – and only avoided murder thanks to a million-to-one chance.

36 year old Antique dealer George Leedham tried to kill his brother-in-law, Roy Belben by shooting him four times because Mr Belben would not tell him where his estranged wife was. Described as 'tall, sandy-haired and gaunt' his story was to show what obsession could drive a man to do.

Mr Leedham, whose wife had left their Streatham home to live in Devon some time earlier, contacted Mr Belben in July of 1967 to 'be friends'.

He stayed in Dartmouth and built up the trust of Mr Belben, but all the while plotted to find his wife. He even popped into the *Dartmouth Chronicle* offices in Fairfax Place to ask if anyone knew of her whereabouts. However, his patience ran out after he had visited a number of public houses with Mr Belben. The pair seemed in fine spirits and even drank champagne before walking out onto the North Embankment. The evening took a turn for the worse.

MILLION TO ONE ESCAPE

Mr Leedham started to talk about his estranged wife and became angry. He drew two automatic pistols, shot into the river and shot Mr Belben in the thigh and calf. He then bundled Mr Belben into his car and drove him to a lay-by near Halwell, where he turned to Mr Belben and told him that his wife had known if she left him he would kill her nearest relative.

He proceeded to shoot his own hand by mistake before dragging Mr Belben out of the car and telling him 'this is your lot'.

Mr Belben tried to get away but Mr Leedham shot him in the back of the head. The bullet entered his head behind his left ear and lodged in his tongue. He staggered into the road and was saved by a passing motorist, but not before Leedham had shot him again in the abdomen.

Leedham drove into the night and crashed his car. He staggered to a nearby house occupied by a widow and her daughter. He sat down and poured out his heart to the terrified woman, after he had placed the two loaded pistols on the table. He asked her repeatedly if she would write to him in prison. When she said she would, he gave her his watch and a roll of banknotes. The ambulance and police arrived and he was arrested before being driven to hospital. The police were aware of the night's earlier events and when Leedham asked if his brother-in-law was alive and upon being told he was, said: 'Oh good. It's a good thing my mother-in-law wasn't there or I would have shot her to pieces.'

He said he was a gentle man who 'loved animals' and had had a good life with 'fast living, adultery and all that' and said his mother-in-law had 'driven' him to it by 'being on' at him 'all the time.'

He was examined by a psychiatrist and declared not mentally ill, and was subsequently sent to prison to serve a life's sentence, until 'the secretary of state decides you are no longer a menace to the public' according to the judge.

ESTABLISHED 1854

Dartmouth Chronicle

CIRCULATING IN DARTMOUTH, BRIXHAM, KINGSBRIDGE & THE SOUTH HAMS

Telephone : Dartmouth 2724   Telegrams : " Chronicle," Dartmouth

6230   MAY 10, 1968   PRICE 3d

The *China Shop* Lower Street, Dartmouth 2023
Your TABLEWARE Specialist

THE NIGHT OF WESTERN STYLE BRAWL

Crash on sentimental journey

THE retired captain who had been trained at Britannia R.N. College, Dartmouth, was making a sentimental journey with his wife and American friends, but he did not see the college.

A mile away at West Norton the...

THE night the Wilton brothers rode into Dartmouth they heard in a saloon that a local posse were out to get them. But this did not stop the Wiltons. They went into a nearby dance hall and became involved in a western-style fight which ended with a chair being broken over another man's head.

Totnes Magistrates heard of this Dartmouth Youth Centre brawl on Tuesday, but because of elements of doubt dismissed charges of assault against 23-year-old Morley John

...ley sent for the police and they came and broke it up."

Miss Lynn said that Pearn had not done anything to provoke the fight, but Morley Wilton had looked angry on the other side of the hall. In reply to Mr. J. Major, defend-

the back and saying 'Give in Charlie'." Pearn replied to a question from Mr. Major. "He did not give any indication that he wanted to stop fighting."

Mr. Major: Is it right that on a recent Saturday you had another

opinion

ONE of the requirements of making a planning application is that a block map should pinpoint the exact location. But we would go further than this in many instances by the inclusion of photographs of the surrounding area.

We say **this** because it is obvious that many of the...

DEATH OF 'CHURCHILL OF DARTMOUTH'

1968 The town mourned the loss of Bill Row, a man whose life was so full the *Chronicle* commented 'thirty four column inches is not enough to tell the life story of such a man'.

Described as 'one of the last blood and thundering debaters' on the council, who was 'the Churchill of the war years in Dartmouth'.

87 year old Mr Row had a special place in people's hearts after serving as Mayor throughout most of the Second World War, when Dartmouth and its surrounding parishes stood at the pivot of one of the world's greatest military exercises and can be said to have played an immense role in winning the war.

The *Chronicle* was unstinting in its praise for the man after he died at the end of February: 'No one served the town for so long or so great-heartedly. From 1931 until 1967 he was in council harness without stopping. Bill – as everyone endearingly called him – was the son of a Dartmouth builder and funeral director, and first had council aspirations in 1931 when he won a seat at his initial attempt.'

He was to finish top of every poll he contested for the next twenty years, including county elections.

He led the town after becoming Mayor in 1942, and was described as being as inspirational as Churchill in the way he led the town.

After the war he penned a plan for what he called 'Greater Dartmouth'. He decided to do so because he, with amazing foresight, saw that population size would be a huge influence in local government organisation and decided Dartmouth needed to expand.

He suggested a bridge across the Dart and expansion of the town all the way to Tuckenhay and Cornworthy and along to Stoke Fleming and Strete. He said that there should be a reorganisation of the town's roads, including a relief road joining Victoria Road and Mayors Avenue and a lido for Warfleet Creek.

The paper commented he was a member of 'nearly every' major organisation in the town. It said: 'In fact, it is easier to name those to which he was not connected.' He had been awarded an MBE for his wartime services. 'Bill Row was a showman for the right causes; a great front man who would be rarely caught off guard. And if he was, he would never admit it.'

HORRIFIC SCENES IN FOSS STREET

Tragedy is a terrible thing and all the more when it is witnessed by a 7 year old girl. Steven Chase, aged 5 was killed by a three tonne lorry in Foss Street in March after falling in front of it as it pulled out of Bell's Yard in the late afternoon.

Gail Hutchings, aged 7, gave evidence to the inquest into the boy's death, as the only eye-witness to the whole incident.

1968 World Events
● Martin Luther King, Jr. is shot dead at the Lorraine Motel in Memphis, Tennessee
● Manchester United wins the European Cup Final, becoming the first English team to do so
● The last steam passenger train service runs in Britain
● Former U.S. First Lady Jacqueline Kennedy marries Greek shipping tycoon Aristotle Onassis on the Greek island of Skorpios

Above: *The Chronicle editor must have liked a dramatic storyline, if this one from 1968 is anything to go by.*

Captain Robert Franks, Commodore of the Dartmouth Yacht Club by the finishing guns at Regatta (See page 272).

SOUTH HAMS NEWSPAPERS

Steven ran up to Gail and a friend in the street, asked how old they were and then turned to run back to his mother. The girls saw as he ran that he would be running in front of the lorry as it pulled out and they tried to grab him. He then lost his footing and fell underneath the wheels. The lorry then stopped on top of him, before reversing after his mother, screaming, told them to move back. The driver himself ran with the bleeding boy in his arms to the hospital, but to no avail.

The inquest revealed the driver could not tell when he got out whether he had run over a small boy or an animal.

No evidence suggested that the driver had been dangerous, it was just bad luck and bad timing, a few seconds later the boy would have run into the side of the truck, a few seconds earlier and he would have rushed back to his mothers for tea, but he died, in an almost unimaginably horrible way.

BAN THE FOREIGNERS

The call of the new secretary of the Old Dartmothians organisation was an uncompromising one in August: Ban the Foreigners.

Jack Westlake claimed at the organisation's annual reunion at the Criterion Restaurant that the rule which allowed anyone who had lived in Dartmouth ten years to join was the reason it couldn't find new members from the town: 'Many people would join but say: 'What's the use, there is a crowd of foreigners going there'. All associations in the town are gradually being taken over by these foreigners; look at the town council,' he said.

Seeking the deletion of the rule however, won him few friends.

'Anyone living in the town today is contributing to the economic welfare of Dartmouth,' said self-confessed 'outsider' M Prowse. 'Surely if a person lives here he adds to the economic growth of Dartmouth and should be entitled to join in the association.'

The association's chairman Mr A Steart said: 'Many people come here and give good service. If they have been here ten years and we can't recognise them as being good citizens, how long do you expect them to wait before they join the association.'

Schools and education occupied people's minds for most of the year.

The Chief Education Officer, Dr D Cook, told a public meeting that a combination of funding issues and a falling child population meant things in Dartmouth had to change. The meeting had been called after rumours circulated for most of the year about the stopping of secondary education in Dartmouth at the age of fourteen, where-after all children would be bussed to school in the town of Totnes.

Fighting for Castle Cove

Castle Cove is a special place for many in Dartmouth and it has been the focus of many fights and debates over its long history of use.

People probably first used the cove to swim hundreds of years ago, but it was after the opening of the Warfleet Creek Bridge in 1864 that it became a regular swimming spot.

Over the last 150 years it has been used by generations to learn to swim. The bathing platform, cut out below the castle, and its accompanying bridge increased its popularity because it could be reached at all times of the tide safely.

The Swimming Club named it its base of operations in 1893, and even had a special hut built over the rocks to allow changing and sheltering from the mercurial British weather.

But in 1958 storms damaged the cove and repairs were not forthcoming from the borough council.

Eventually the cove was repaired, but then in 1962, again the cove was closed and the swimming club had to use the Boatfloat to hold its annual 'first dip' of the season. The editor of the *Chronicle*, the feared John C MacTavish, was not impressed and described the state of the Boatfloat: it was full of 'dozens of petrol and diesel driven motor boats' and 'litter' and 'pollution'. The swimming club's

president, Dr 'Mac' McConaghey said he was dismayed by the swimming club having to move to the Boatfloat for the event for the first time in seventy years.

The Cove continued to be used for swimming by visitors and locals with joy and laughter for the following forty years – with regular grumblings from the authority responsible for it – the borough council until 1974 and the district council thereafter – whenever repairs to either the bridge to the bathing platform or the cliffs above the cove were needed. It became an everyday battle for residents to demand quicker action on 'their' cove before repairs and other maintenance were made.

Then, in the winter storms at the end of 1999, a major cliff fall destroyed much of the pathway down to the Cove.

It resulted in its instant closure on safety reasons.

It would not reopen for seven years.

In 2000, campaigners found themselves closed out of discussions with the district council. The *Chronicle* reported the comments from the council's officers, which were generally positive, vague, and ultimately meaningless.

In 2001 the Cove again reared its head as a problem as residents continued to demand it be re-opened.

Campaigners and councillors celebrate the re-opening of Castle Cove in 2006. PHIL SCOBLE

The district council found itself under serious pressure to re-open, but stalling tactics made it clear it was not at the top of its priorities list.

'It seems to us that the closed signs are staying up and that the council are not doing anything despite their claims to be working hard on the problem,' said leader of the protestors Eva Vincett. 'We want to be able to use this wonderful special place again and believe it's an amenity worth spending time and money on.'

No one appreciated quite how long they would have to fight to gain access again to their beloved bathing spot.

Four years of campaigning was to follow, in which every possible route to get their Cove opened to the public was tried.

Then someone had a very bright idea: South Hams District Council had to maintain public rights of way, by law. The County Council made the decisions on public rights of way, and it was felt it would be sympathetic to Dartmouth's cause.

A campaign was launched to document evidence that the Cove had been used, without permission for more than twenty five years – the requirement to gain a public right of way.

The cove had been used for more than 150 years so it was felt there was a good chance of success.

In 2005 Devon County Council's rights of way committee unanimously decided to recommend a £140,300 repair package. The campaign to re-open the cove had been running six years and a petition had been signed by over 7,000 people.

South Hams District Council, with, it has to be said, rather bad grace, began the work needed to the cliffs above the Cove

In June 2006 the Cove was re-opened after nearly seven years of pressure from the campaign group.

Thousands of pounds-worth of investment and safety work, including new walk ways down to the cove, the netting of cliffs to prevent rock falls and strengthening pathways had been undertaken.

There were two opening ceremonies, the 'official' one with dignitaries from the town, district and county councils, and the 'real' one with local campaigners.

The Cove, showing the incomplete bridge.
PHIL SCOBLE

The Flavel church transformed for Regatta into a haunted house in 1968!
SOUTH HAMS
NEWSPAPERS

The rumours proved to be correct. He told the meeting that the 'junior comprehensive' was planned to take students to fourteen years of age. Beyond the age of fourteen they would be educated in Totnes, and that a new county primary school would be built at Milton Lane by 1971. He delivered the crushing news that the child population of Dartmouth made any full secondary comprehensive 'uneconomic'.

Dr Cook admitted to the increasingly angry crowd that he would not be happy to have his child travel so far to go to school, but said that children would have 'more opportunities' in Totnes.

Parents angrily demanded to know what would be done, but the only answer they got was that this was the way it was and it was all 'done and dusted'.

TOWN PULLS TOGETHER
TO FIGHT FOR EDUCATION PROVISION

Mr Hugh Butterworth of Ridge Hill led the campaign against the changes with a petition and organised a poll of parents to change the mind of the education authority.

The borough council roundly rejected the plan and demanded a meeting with Dr Cook, insisting that the children of Dartmouth would be at a huge disadvantage after spending two hours on buses every school day.

The parents and teachers of the primary school called for the plan to be dropped, even though they did admit the town did not warrant a full comprehensive because of the low numbers of children.

The Mayor Eric Cook and deputation went all the way to London to put a plea straight to the education minister so that the town could secure a comprehensive for 11 to 16 year olds.

They got a reprieve, but the powers-that-be made clear it would only last a short while.

The Dartmouth & Kingswear Society made few friends, as was to be its lot for much of its history, as they aimed to create a conservation area that would cover 90 per cent of the town.

The area would put strict guidelines in place for development. The county council was proposing an area which stopped at South Town. The society, perhaps not surprisingly for an organisation which was started after the erection of a concrete wall in Warfleet, wanted to include the area going all the way out to the castle.

The borough council and the Dartmouth & Kingswear Society locked horns with regards to the project. Alderman Perring said: 'We asked for a conservation area, but our idea was something like Bayards Cove. Now the whole of the town is about to be included and I think it is all wrong. If we are going to tie ourselves to this, there is no telling where it would lead.'

The arguments continued in 1968, when the borough council rejected both the plan by the Dartmouth & Kingswear Society and the county council. Instead they decided to just conserve Bayards Cove.

Cllr A Coles said: 'Dartmouth's plans are hard enough to get through at the moment. The Southern Divisional Committee [which was the main planning authority at the time] are taking good care that we don't spoil the town, so why worry about conservation areas.'

sally brown's
of foss street dartmouth
fashions tel 2028

Dartmouth Chronicle

CIRCULATING IN DARTMOUTH, BRIXHAM, KINGSBRIDGE & THE SOUTH HAMS
Telephone: Dartmouth 2724   Telegrams: "Chronicle," Dartmouth

GIFT ITEMS
or
TABLEWARE
for your own
home
The
China Shop
Lower Street,
Dartmouth 2023

6251   OCTOBER 4, 1968   PRICE 3d

'CONVICT DREW GUN TO RESIST ARREST'

Dittisham down under

The dramatic story of escaped convict Peter Fletcher.

ESCAPED CONVICT DRAWS GUN IN ATTEMPT TO GET A CLEAN BREAK

A convict who had escaped his jailers whilst out on day release from Dartmoor Prison was re-arrested in Dartmouth, despite drawing a gun whilst trying to get away from officers.

Peter John Fletcher broke into the house of Eric Mann, of Coastguard Cottages in Dartmouth and stole a transistor radio, jewellery and a cheque book. He then broke into the Cemetery Lodge in Kingswear and stole an automatic pistol and a coat.

Ironically, it was this latter item which proved to cause his downfall.

Mr Fletcher, was spotted by the owner of the cottage, in Dartmouth. The man went to get a policeman who tried to talk to Fletcher.

When the constable asked him who the coat belonged to, Fletcher replied 'It's mine.' reported the *Chronicle*. 'Before more questions could be asked Fletcher tried to run away and drew out the automatic pistol. In a scuffle with PC Harding, he was thrown to the ground; other people went to the policeman's aid and Fletcher was taken to the police station where a loaded revolver was found in his pocket.'

Harding and a holidaymaker who helped to apprehend Fletcher were commended for their bravery.

In court where he was convicted, it was revealed Fletcher had been convicted a number of times before, the last time he was sent to prison for four years for robbery with violence.

He had been on three days release when he decided he would not return to prison. He absconded and broke into the Stoodley Knowle Girls' School to try and steal money and clothes. After being disturbed by one of the students he gagged her and tied her up before escaping down a drainpipe and ended up in Kingswear and Dartmouth.

The man whose coat and pistol had been stolen found himself in court a month later. Michael Reynolds was convicted of failing to comply with the conditions of a firearms certificate by not keeping the gun in a safe place.

Reynolds responded 'Well I've never heard of that before.' when told he should not have been keeping ammunition with the gun. He was fined £50.

AN INTERNATIONAL AIRPORT – AT CALIFORNIA CROSS?!

The front pages of the *Chronicle* were dominated for months by something that wasn't even going to happen in the town: an international airport at California Cross.

The town council, the *Chronicle* and, everyone in Dartmouth it seemed, wanted jumbo jets to be flying into the newly planned airport. However it seems they, and the developers were very much alone in that view.

The *Chronicle* was even mocked by other newspapers, including the *Devon Times Guardian* which ran cartoons about the views of the Dartmouth people, showing them as dumb yokels who didn't understand anything about the economics of the proposal and thought 'jumbo jets' were flying elephants which would fertilise their fields.

The *Chronicle* responded with vim and vigour but the airport was a dead duck from the start, and when Plymouth Airport was given planning permission the same year, the plan was quietly dropped.

Left: *A saviour for Noss Works arrives in the shape of Philip Pensabene.*

Right: *Regatta 1969 – the new format* Chronicle *resulted in some interesting editorial decisions such as the strange angle for this picture on page 3.*

1969 The *Dartmouth Chronicle* had been bought by the company Kay Sons and Daughter, an international publishing concern in June 1968. The company had been using the paper to publicise its own brand of books. It managed to pull off an amazing *coup* for the first edition of 1969. The *Dartmouth Chronicle* was to become the most modern newspaper in the west-country with the area's first computerised press.

A new production line would be based on Dartmouth's Townstal estate and a series of books, including the exciting *Dictionary of Autobiography* was planned, which would result in an export industry worth, according to the *Chronicle*, hundreds of thousands of pounds.

The main difference visible to the readers of the newspaper would be the use of an IBM Web Offset Press, which produced papers with clearer type and pictures, the paper claimed.

And by golly they were right.

The April 4 edition, under the headline 'NOW YOU ARE READING PRINTING HISTORY' showed off type so clear it really did make people sit up and take notice. The pictures especially were now crystal sharp and the *Chronicle* logo had been redesigned in the modern font type 'Arial'.

The first paragraph proclaimed: 'The words you have just read have made history. This week your *Chronicle* has been set by computer for the first time. History? No other newspaper in the southwest of England is using the IBM Type computer system which has been installed at Duke Street, Dartmouth.'

The company brought in Sir Francis Chichester to open the new Townstal factory: crowds gathered to catch a glimpse of the spindly grey man who had braved the elements and conquered the seas single-handed, sailing Round-the-World for the very first time. He did however shock those who attended by answering the question 'Why did you sail Round-the-World?' by replying 'Have you met my wife? If you had you would understand'.

ARCHWAY TO ARGUMENT

An arch at the Norton Park Holiday Centre caused an argument which ran for more than a year.

The archway at the entrance to the holiday park before the Norton bends on the outskirts of the town had obtained planning permission in 1968, with no comment from anyone.

However that had been for an 'open box' style arch made of wrought iron. But then the owners decided they wanted a wooden archway instead, in the style of a grand prix bridge. They consulted the divisional planning officer and got his permission to change this. However they didn't get his permission to move the

arch tens of feet forward to be right next to the road. This was done to 'increase safety' because cars following those behind visitors to the park would 'not be surprised' by them 'suddenly' turning in, according to the park's architect.

The borough council were horrified. Councillor's described it as 'like the entrance to a nuclear power station'. They immediately sent a notice to the park ordering them to 'take it down'.

Cllr Irene Scawn said: 'It is not a wrought iron arch as was indicated on the plans. We should tell them that it must come down. All they have done is put up something which they have decided is better. If it was a private householder who had contravened a planning application we would order them to conform.'

One of the owners of the park, Eric Waldron, was so angry he slammed the council for the 'eyesores' it had allowed to be built, which he said ruined the visits of his customers, whilst persecuting his park.

The council did not help this fiery relationship when it refused the initial planning application for 106 new chalets on the site, demanding that it reduced the number. They got their way. A new application featured only eighty chalets. However there had been a large group of people in the area fighting any increase in development on the site, so the approval of the plan was met with howls of dismay.

The chalets were counted as part of the permitted development for housing Dartmouth could have, meaning a development of eighty chalets would significantly delay new council housing. The borough council said 'yes', before the county committee in charge of development refused the plans because the sewerage drainage system was not adequate to take the new dwellings, meaning council housing again came onto the agenda.

The arch continued to inspire comment and argument, but stayed resolutely where it was until the next October when high winds brought it down, much to the relief of many but the consternation of the owners. It was not replaced.

Left: *The area above Coronation Park before the building of College Way in 1969.* South Hams Newspapers

Right: *The view from the river as College Way is constructed.* South Hams Newspapers

Below left: *Dartmouth Amateur Rowing Club's Centenary Celebrations.* South Hams Newspapers

Below right: *The Queen Mother made a big impression when she visited in 1969: here she is alongside Mayor Eric Cook.* South Hams Newspapers

Yellow lines caused a stir in the last year of the decade.

NO! Those yellow lines must stay

THOSE YELLOW LINES are staying. Despite a wave of protest from both business people and residents, Dartmouth Council decided on Tuesday night not to consider revoking the new traffic order, which has turned both side and main streets into long ribbons of double yellow lines.

The only sop for the objectors is the promise that after a trial of a year the council may review the situation.

Coun. G. Evans, chairman of the Works and Highways Committee, pressed his fellow members to remain firm.

He contended that parking was a serious problem, and that no-one liked to have yellow lines splashed around the town, but the

seeing if the no-parking and one-way order worked properly and it must be given a trial.

If the County council were asked to squash the order they would wonder "just what this council is up to."

A YEAR

He added that even if it was agreed to change their minds, it would take a long while

NO! KINGSBRIDGE MISS BIG MONEY GRANTS

KINGSBRIDGE will not benefit from special development grants and benefits.

It was decided this week by the South West Economic Planning Council that the employment exchange area of the town should remain outside Plymouth intermediate area.

"When recommending development area status for Plymouth in their draft strategy, the council recognised that because much of Kingsbridge is designated as an area of outstanding natural beauty it would be inappropriate to include it in the development area.

SEWERAGE WORK DEMANDS HUGE INVESTMENT

Dartmouth Borough Council began to realise what 'false economy' really meant in 1969.

The council had been very proud of its record since the war in keeping the rates low. The *Chronicle* watched and reported every proposal for changes in rates, almost always negatively if they went up. You can understand councillors not wanting to be seen to be raising them on a yearly basis but this contributed to a culture of leaving repairs and maintenance until the last possible moment.

The headlines in February were related to the need to spend £380,000, or equivalent to £5 million in 2010, on a new sewerage system. The council was told the work could take twenty years, but it was necessary as the days of 'burying sewage in the garden' were long gone and 'flushing toilets' were here to stay.

In the Dartmouth area alone there were eight sewage outfalls, completely untreated. They went direct into the river. One ran alongside the Boatfloat which housed swimming throughout the summer and competitions during Regatta.

If the possibility of the 7,000 residents of Dartmouth bearing this cost in their rates was not enough, a week later the *Chronicle* was reporting the need of the borough to spend more on repairing the roads and pavements around the town. Cllr G Evans, chairman of the Works and Highways Committee, told the council: 'There is a tremendous amount of work that has to be caught up with at a greater expense than if it had been done when necessary in the ordinary course of maintenance. We have a low standard of maintenance and it is my intention, if you allow me, to see it put right.'

There was bad news, yet again, for the education of the town's children.

After serious discussions the year before about the future of schooling in the town, residents were dismayed, but not shocked, when a proposed brand new primary school for the town was seriously delayed.

The new school had been in the 'new design list' of Devon County Educational Committee and was to be built between 1968 and 1970. However, with no movement on the project the announcement in May was not too much of a surprise.

The sub-committee in charge of organising the building of new schools said in a statement: 'It is an indication of the great difficulties with which the committee is likely to be faced that the Department of Education and Science has only approved two of the nine projects included in the design list.'

The new school was not built until 1974, six years late and by then much needed.

1969 saw the arrival of a menace in Dartmouth: double yellow lines.

The town, and especially its business community, reacted with horror.

The lines arrived in April, imaginatively dubbed 'Yellow Line Day' in the *Chronicle*. However, the residents were horrified at the difference it made to their town.

Henry Baguley, managing director of the Raleigh Hotel on the South Embankment said single yellow lines outside the hotel had cost him £1,000 a year. He was, perhaps unsurprisingly, unhappy at the arrival of double yellow lines.

'We have learned to live with this [single yellow lines],' he said, 'but two yellow lines will affect the business even more. The lines tell visitors 'don't stop, carry on to Torbay'.'

*Future Mayor
Richard Rendle
– then secretary
of Dartmouth
Rugby Club
– chats to one of
American Sailors
from the destroyer*
Bordelon *visiting
for the 25th
anniversary of
D-Day.*
SOUTH HAMS
NEWSPAPERS

The businesses in the centre of town were aggrieved to discover that the borough council, who had instigated the traffic order covering the town with double yellow lines, had requested that none be painted outside the Guildhall.

A challenge was raised by the businesses in the town and it was again discussed by the borough council who ultimately resisted any change.

Cllr G Evans had a stern message for his fellow councillors: 'They are necessary for the control and guidance of the small minority of motorists who have no regard for the convenience of other users of the road,' he said. 'Dartmouth is not unique in having yellow lines. Many larger and smaller towns up and down the country have more. In South Devon you can hardly pass through without seeing double yellow lines with a mass of signs.'

Along with this sobering message he also pointed out it would take more than a year of legal red tape to reverse the use of yellow lines, even if the council wanted to get rid of them, and this probably had as much of an impact as any of his other points.

The lines stayed.

Dartmouth marked twenty five years since D-Day, the Longest Day, when more than 400 ships sailed from the harbour, carrying thousands of men to the beaches of Normandy. The town will forever be indebted by the sacrifice of these young men.

The town was visited by American destroyer *Boredelon* as part of the celebrations.

It sailed in for the special day and its crew formed a guard of honour along with Royal Navy personnel from the Britannia Royal Naval College. The comrades lined up along the Embankment by the special memorial to those who risked and lost their lives fighting for the freedom and civil liberties of their countries.

The visiting American sailors and Dartmothians were also involved in some friendly rivalry. The American's brought baseball equipment ashore and challenged the town's rugby team to a game on Coronation Park. The *Chronicle* reported on the game, mockingly praising the Dartmouth team as having, 'showed plenty of willing, if no expertise.'

Perhaps kindly, they did not print the score of the match.

Not so kind was the reaction of the *Chronicle* to a serious and potentially dangerous collapse of a borough council building.

Dartmouth Council found itself in hot water with the carnival committee when one of the walls of the Old Market's central building fell in June. The top floor of the east side of the old building simply collapsed, ruining the throne which was to be the seat of the carnival queen just a few weeks later in July.

The repairs were estimated at £380, or £5,000 in today's money, and councillors were sternly told that they had, yet again, made false economies in previous years when warnings were given about the building's structural integrity.

Left: *In 1969 the building in the centre of the Market Square nearly fell down after years of borough council neglect.*
SOUTH HAMS
NEWSPAPERS

Right: *Carnival Queen 1969 Susan Lumley and attendants but not on the right throne, thanks to cuts to maintenance budgets by the borough council.*
SOUTH HAMS
NEWSPAPERS

The carnival committee were livid that their advice of many years had not been taken up by the council, that the wall was structurally unsafe and needed repairs.

The borough engineer, Mr J Vince told the *Chronicle*: 'The wall has been leaning badly for some years. After I heard from the carnival committee I went and inspected it. It was leaning inwards quite considerably. The council were aware of the situation. It was brought to their attention by the president of the Society for the Preservation of Ancient Buildings when they presented their plans for the market. Had the council spent part of their money on restoring the wall four years ago the trouble caused and the possible danger to people in the vicinity could have been averted.'

LACK OF INVESTMENT LEADS TO BAD FLOODING

Lack of investment caused more problems elsewhere when floods created a huge stink, thanks to the inadequate drains.

In July, a year after Dartmouth Borough Council had finally agreed to put huge investment into the town's sewerage system, torrential rain proved why upgrading works should have been undertaken years before.

Lake Street and Victoria Road in particular were badly hit.

John Lord, landlord of the Commercial Hotel, said: 'It started about 2.30am. Firemen woke up a front room resident who then knocked us up. We only had time to take up the carpet in the lounge bar. The whole ground floor was submerged beneath two to three inches of sewage. Normally when we get flooding it is just surface water, but this time it forced sewage up out of the drains. The back of the pub was under five–to–six inches of sewage and Lake Street was a river of it. It took two hours for us to shovel it out of the hotel.'

The flooding was all the more frightening because it had been a low tide at the time and therefore, totally unexpected.

Only a week later a 'twenty year' storm hit which caused as much chaos, and even more damage.

The storm rolled in on August 1, causing more flooding along Victoria Road again and further along into Coombe Road. The storm was an electrical one and scores of properties were hit. The *Chronicle* reported more stories about the town's television reception being absent for more than twenty four hours than the devastation caused to peoples' homes.

As the decade drew to a close the *Chronicle* looked forward to the 1970s with optimism, hoping the large investment the town needed would be forthcoming and that the town's politics would settle down, becoming less about personality and more about substance.

It was to be sorely disappointed.

CHAPTER III

Hard Times Ahead
1970s

INFLATION, INDUSTRIAL UNREST AND TURMOIL

The decade began in the twilight of the old local government system, and was beset by turmoil: political, financial and social. Dartmouth could not escape the effects of these problems, and saw some of the most profound changes in its recent history.

Along with the loss of its Royal Charter, bestowed by Edward III in 1341, in the local government re-organisation of 1974, the town acquired two brand new schools and debated the need for more housing and industry throughout the decade.

Industrial unrest, economic hardship and the quest for development were also constant concerns. The ferries became a persistent source of problems for the various councils and companies that were foolish enough to try and run them.

Kingswear tied itself up in knots over a new marina, and how it was to be realised. Small town and parish councils in the area all began their long battle for recognition, power and investment from South Hams District Council, when it came into being in 1974.

The quest for a swimming pool and parking debates dominated much of the news in the decade, as scheme after scheme came and went, with nothing actually being achieved.

The decade also saw a lot of change for the *Chronicle* itself: the paper group was bought by South Hams Newspapers, and began to be printed in Kingsbridge.

The paper lost its *'Britannicus'* report from the Britannia Royal Naval College, and gained a gardening column. The style of the paper became more 'tabloid', while the look of it became more traditional, with the reversion to a more decorative look for the paper's name. The paper grew in size, and increased in cost thanks to the financial hardships and problems which categorised the decade.

The 1970s proved a hard decade for the whole country, and Dartmouth adapted to suit the times. Events, places and people all changed – some for the better and some for the worse. Despite all the challenges, however, the town never lost is sense of community.

Raising funds for a proposed new unit at the Dartmouth Cottage Hospital with bell ringing.
TOTNES IMAGE BANK/ SOUTH HAMS NEWSPAPERS

1970 Residents of Cross Parks were dismayed to find that the road improvements they had helped pay for – with the not insubstantial contribution of £220 (or £5,000 in 2010) each – stopped them from opening their garage doors. Some even had their cars inside at the time.

The road level had been raised, after the addition of a permanent tarmac road, by more than a foot in some places.

Cllr Eric Cook claimed the problems had been caused by the garages not being built 'as they should be in the first place'.

In January the Ministry of Defence was also unpopular, after it was decided to charge local organisations £54 a year to have the use of its swimming pool at the Britannia Royal Naval College for an hour a week during term time. The person who made the decision was described, with pleasing honesty, in these terms by the *Chronicle*: 'Someone, somewhere tucked away behind a tea-cup stained desk in Whitehall has made a miserly decision that town organisations must pay for the use of the swimming pool at Britannia Royal Naval College, Dartmouth. This niggardly piece of cheese-paring means that the Dartmouth Cubs will be denied instruction at the pool'.

Local businessman Eric Waldron, who owned and ran Norton Park Holiday Camp, donated £54 to the local cub pack the following week.

The town's own swimming pool plans were still causing problems. A site was chosen in Mayors Avenue and planning permission obtained. Everything was moving forward. However the swimming club objected to the plans for an outdoor swimming pool, saying it would be pointless having one as it could only be used for three months a year and the club would lose its space at Britannia Royal Naval College. The club boycotted a public meeting about the project. The *Chronicle*, in rather strong fashion, said the meeting 'wasted' the hard work of the swimming pool committee and council over the last six months.

In the end the committee decided to follow up its plans for an open air pool in Mayors Avenue without the support of the swimming club, who kept on calling for a competition sized pool in Townstal.

PARKING PROBLEMS BEGIN TO 'STRANGLE' TOWN

Dartmouth Borough Council were warned that Dartmouth would be 'strangled' by parking problems in just a few years if something were not done.

They then proceeded to do nothing about it – throwing out the first of many well intentioned solutions from innocent councillors. George Evans earned a smart rebuke from Cllr Alan Coles when he suggested building a multi-storey car park on the New Ground. The councillor said it would be 'a terrible' waste of officials' time if they had 'no intention' of proceeding.

A removal van can't cope with the steep new College Way – and crashes at the bottom.
Totnes Image Bank/ South Hams Newspapers

Also in 1970 Devon County Council refused to build a new car park to the north of College Way due to having 'road safety' concerns about more vehicle access off the fast steep road. It was then suggested that by building 62 feet out into the river from the Higher Ferry slip to the end of Coronation Park, parking for 135 cars and seventy dinghies could be created.

The Borough Engineer John Vince estimated the project could cost as little as £30,000.

The Dartmouth & Kingswear Society along with, it seems, most of the town, resisted the idea. In a newsletter it said: 'Do the town leaders really understand why people choose to come to Dartmouth and why, with changing trends they may not want to come here in future?' The message got through and after much to-ing and fro-ing a borough council planning application was refused by the Southern Divisional Planning Committee.

Started work in local bookshop; now Publishing Company director

The Chronicle *was proud to report on the success of one of its own, Richard Webb. After working for Condé Nast magazines (*Vogue*), he had at the age of 27 had just been appointed to the board of Michael Joseph, the leading London publishing company then owned by* The Times.
SOUTH HAMS NEWSPAPERS

A report from the Port Medical Officer Dr Andre Verniquet advised councillors there were no public health reasons to stop pouring raw sewage into the river from eighteen separate outlets. '…except for aesthetic reasons, the health hazard can, for all practical purposes, be ignored.' The only suggestion for a solution was to 'extend the outflow pipes by fifty metres'. Fancy a swim?

The report was later slammed by the Medical Health Officer, Dr John Wildman, who claimed Dr Verniquet had drawn 'the wrong conclusions' and said the report Dr Verniquet had produced was 'laissez-faire'. He said that untreated sewage in the Dart was 'a potential hazard for health'. The warning seems to have worked – the council agreed, later that year, to pay towards a £500,000 new sewerage scheme – which unfortunately was then delayed indefinitely.

One letter writer to the *Chronicle* summed up the problem for the popular tourist destination in rather simple and direct language: 'Until the recent cloudburst on the upper reaches of the Dart last summer there were tennis-court-sized patches of excreta sludge floating up and down the river for weeks.'

The swimming club were so worried that a build up of pollution would be detrimental to the health of its members it moved its symbolic first dip of the season from the Boatfloat to Bayards Cove, unfortunately about three hundred yards closer to a sewage outflow pipe.

Later that summer the 125th Port of Dartmouth Royal Regatta swimming gala in the Boatfloat was hailed by the *Chronicle* as 'one of the finest in memory'.

However it did not escape controversy. Two swimmers complained of feeling ill after swallowing water during races. Gary Ash withdrew from all competitions after complaining of headaches after his first race.

He said: 'It was absolute filth to swim in. I just could not have gone on any more, on the final lap I swallowed a mouthful of water and felt my head go round.'

One wag of a sub-editor marked the picture on the front of a swimmer in the gala with the note 'they scooped the muck off the surface first'.

TAXES HIT HEADY HEIGHTS OF 12 SHILLINGS AND SIX PENCE IN POUND

In other cost-related news, the borough council put up taxes to the highest rate it ever had – one shilling in the pound.

That represented a 44 per cent increase in the local rates. Twelve shillings and six pence were now taken from every pound in Dartmouth. The rise was blamed on 'false economies' by previous councils, resulting in bad roads and a backlog of works for the borough's maintenance men.

A Christmas party with Father Christmas at St Clements Church Hall, Townstal.
Totnes Image Bank/ South Hams Newspapers

The Townstal Community Association's vote for a May Queen left the 12 year old winner crying bitterly and throwing down her sash after the decision was booed by spectators – because the girl had won for the second year running.

Susan Lumley – who had won after a vote by a brand new committee – understandably burst into tears and threw her winning sash to the runner-up after a group of bitter parents booed and shouted 'Fix!' when the winners were announced.

Parent Joyce Olver pointed out that the normal way of doing things was for the previous year's queen to crown the new one. With clear thinking she said – 'but she can't crown herself'. The poor girl's parents decided that she should not be queen following the controversy, forcing the committee to overhaul its rules.

The story had a happy ending though, as when the eventual winner, Sandra Edwards, 14, was crowned by Angela Rippon. Miss Rippon was handed the crown by young Miss Lumley.

An angry colonel died in Dartmouth in April, still without the Second World War pension he claimed he deserved.

Colonel Frederick William Wagg of Newcomen Road complained to various government officials, several prime ministers and a number of decorated war heroes, including Montgomery and Eisenhower, that he, as a colonel, was owed an £800 a year pension.

He seemed to be an extraordinary character – protesting against car tax by handing in his licence and giving away his car; giving away his television set in protest at 'poor television programmes', and sending back all the decorations he picked up from service in both World Wars to the Queen herself in protest against the Beatles' MBE.

He also sent a rude postcard every week to a firm of solicitors he claimed had lost him money. His passing must have been mourned almost as much by the *Chronicle*'s editor as his family.

The new flood defence system running down Victoria Road was nearing completion on May 5 when contractors failed to put the stops in either end of the pipe.

A particularly high tide saw water rush into Charles Street and Victoria Road. There was no damage after firemen spent most of the night pumping water away from the stricken areas. Problems persisted with the scheme as it was revealed that the outflow pipe would be visible at low tide and could prove a danger to shipping.

The *Chronicle* tempted fate by declaring 'this might be the last flood in Dartmouth's history' and it was promptly proved wrong.

Within two months of this dangerous statement another two floods had occurred – amounting to five in just twelve months.

In September more than three inches of rain fell around Dartmouth in just a few hours and the flooding went past the Guildhall in Victoria Road. Be careful what you print.

1971 World Events
● BBC Open University begins in the United Kingdom
● In Britain, Rolls-Royce goes bankrupt and is nationalised
● Decimalisation Day:
– The United Kingdom and Ireland both switch to decimal currency
● The number of British troops in Northern Ireland is raised to 12,500

1971 Decimalisation was the big worry to many in February 1971. During the changeover, apart from the need to adapt over 230,000 phone boxes, the main trouble seemed to be letting the public know how much their money would be worth.

However, shopkeepers remained relaxed about the prospect – saying that once the old coinage was out of circulation everyone would be much happier. For a few short days confusion reigned however, with old money taken for goods but only new coins given in change.

HARD TIMES AT NOSS SHIPYARD

Noss Shipyard, the subject of hope and enthusiasm just over a year before, when it was bought by businessman Phillip Pensabene, made fifty three members of staff redundant in April and another 30 in July.

This resulted in the workforce being reduced from 144 to sixty four. The site manager said the first jobs cuts would reduce the size of the organisation to 'more workable limits'. He said that the management hoped to re-build the site as a boatbuilding centre. Just months before the site had received international recognition as it built Chay Blyth's Round-the-World yacht – *British Steel*.

The second round of job-losses was blamed on a 'rationalisation taking place in the shipbuilding industry together with the depressed market for steel fabrication work'. The yard cheerfully announced it would be increasing the work it did in glass fibre and would be exhibiting at the 1972 boat show.

The department of employment told the *Chronicle* that the men who had lost their jobs had 'little hope' of finding new ones. Better news appeared the same month when the old Normand boatyard, which had closed in 1969, was bought by TTB Fabrications. The site in Townstal allowed the business to double the size of its works, with plans to increase its size even further. The move created fifty jobs.

Economics of a different kind caused problems before the summer.

Many traders had hoped to open on Sundays during the summer months, but the council kept failing to send out the promised questionnaires needed to collect proof of their support.

After a front page criticism of the council in April by the Chamber of Trade, the council sent out questionnaires on a Thursday morning in May to traders, with a request to return them by the same evening so the health, housing and estate committee could discuss the possible change of licensing.

However, the town clerk told the committee they could not make a decision that evening as that would have to be done by the finance committee a month later.

Then it would take another four weeks, or until mid July, before the licensing could allow shops to open legally. Some got so fed up they opened up illegally, risking a fine.

The Mayor's Civic Dinner.
TOTNES IMAGE BANK/ SOUTH HAMS NEWSPAPERS

The traffic lights at Dartmouth's Higher Ferry, installed in 1970 to much criticism, continued to cause chaos with many motorists being summoned before Totnes magistrates for going through red lights.

Most did this because they either hadn't realised there were two sets, or because they were sick of seeing the ferry come and go three or four times empty without them able to move.

It seems Dartmouth police were on shifts waiting for unlucky motorists to jump the lights, with sets of four or five at a time getting the standard £4 fine and an endorsed licence.

In March several drivers were still fined, but for just £1 and did not receive endorsement because a clever solicitor, Mr B.C. Reade, pointed out to the court that the lights clearly didn't work very well.

The *Chronicle's* editor obviously had a run in with them later in the year and declared himself 'sick and tired' of their problems. His angry tirade against the lights ended: 'Somebody in authority wants a kick in the pants and if it means a trip to County Hall in Exeter to inflict this well-justified punishment, we suggest a party of councillors should make that trip pretty smartish.'

PRINCE CHARLES ARRIVES AT BRNC

Rather more civilised however was the arrival, in Dartmouth, of the heir to the throne. Prince Charles attended the Britannia Royal Naval College for six weeks from August until October 1971.

His arrival in a blue Aston Martin DB6, two days after the rest of the cadets, made a big impression – possibly on his fellow cadets.

The paper said it intended to 'leave the lad alone!' and warned its readers: 'don't ruin the all too brief period of his youth by trying to crowd him out or make him feel embarrassed when he is simply seeking to mix on an informal basis'.

The *Chronicle* took pains to point out that the '£31 per week Acting Sub Lieutenant' would be 'NO DIFFERENT FROM OTHER OFFICERS UNDER TRAINING' – that is the *Chronicle's* capitals by the way.

However, the Prince would have a 'single cabin in the main College building with unrivalled views of the Dart'.

The paper was rewarded for its honourable stance on the Prince with an EXCLUSIVE visit to the Guildhall with the Prince when he left the College in October. However, the paper failed to get an interview with the heir to the throne.

Prince Charles enjoys a joke with the councillors including Eric Cook (second right) at a reception at the Guildhall to mark the end of his time at the Britannia Royal Naval College. The Chronicle *were granted exclusive access as a thank you for not reporting on his time training.*
TOTNES IMAGE BANK/
SOUTH HAMS NEWSPAPERS

TOTNES IMAGE BANK/
SOUTH HAMS NEWSPAPERS

ONEDIN LINE STARTS FILMING

Another boost for the town began in May, when the BBC began shooting a new television series – described by producer Peter Graham as 'a *Forsyte Saga* with sailing ships' – around Dartmouth and Kingswear.

The *Onedin Line*, the *Chronicle* reported, would star 'young actors' Peter Gilmore and Anne Stallybrass.

Bayards Cove and the Market Square would be the main locations, being transformed into Liverpool of the 1860s. Producers hoped that the show would run for 'five years' if successful.

The series ran in total for nine years (91 episodes) and would be the beginning of many great careers, including that of Jane Seymour, who was informed of her casting in the Bond film *Live and Let Die* while staying at the Dart Marina Hotel.

It seemed that most of the Dartmouth community took part as extras in the filming and every Sunday it was a good game to watch the programme – led off by *that* music – to try to spot which locals appeared and which parts of Dartmouth had been used that week.

During the series' long life, the producers employed many tricks of the trade to maximise the budget, using Bayards Cove and Kingswear to replicate several different locations, including New Orleans and the Caribbean. The Longwood near Maypool even doubled as the Amazon rain forest.

In more prosaic news, the change to a three tier local government system caused much debate.

Alderman Jack Mashford said Dartmouth should join Torbay 'forcing Kingswear to do the same', as 'we have the river which is what they want'.

This caused much ire in Kingswear, as they felt it was presumptive to describe Dartmouth as 'having' the river. The village was also not happy at the suggestion that they 'had' to do anything Dartmouth told them.

The large meetings arranged by the county council to discuss the re-organisation saw a vote on 'area 6' – basically what became the South Hams district. Ald Mashford claimed that Dartmouth 'as the largest town' would have the most influence.

The details of the new local government structure were announced in November, showing Dartmouth would be included in the new South Hams area, and so April 1, 1974 was set as the new beginning of three tier government, and the end of the historic and ancient Borough of Dartmouth Clifton Hardnesse.

Kingswear had more pressing problems when British Rail announced it was to close the Kingswear Branch line.

The Dart Valley Light Railway, which had two years previously opened the Buckfastleigh to Totnes branch line, announced it was negotiating to buy the seven mile stretch of line in August. In November it agreed in principle to buy the railway line from Kingswear to Paignton, but only with plans to run the train as a tourist attraction, not as a public transport service.

Nicolette Milnes-Walker MBE

Best known locally as Nicolette Coward, wife of Bruce Coward, the joint owners of the Harbour Bookshop, Dartmouth after Christopher Milne's ownership. Nicolette was the first woman to sail non-stop single handed across the Atlantic. She left Milford Haven in her 30 foot yacht Aziz *on June 12, 1971 and reached Newport, USA forty five days later, arriving on July 26, 1971.*

The Townstal nativity was enjoyed by all the parents – though perhaps not all the children.
TOTNES IMAGE BANK/ SOUTH HAMS NEWSPAPERS

The passenger ferry was also the subject of much debate during the year – mainly because British Rail (BR) wanted to sell it off to the borough council.

BR offered the passenger ferry to the borough council for £20,000. In return the council offered £9,000, and BR accepted. Who said that publicly owned companies don't know how to run a hard bargain?

SCHOOL 'SLIDES DOWN THE HILL' CAUSING CHAOS

The secondary school spent much of the year in flux and uncertainty. The Ford Bank annexe of buildings were declared unfit for human habitation after the foundations gave way, leading to the widely held belief that the buildings slipped down the hillside.

The buildings were closed in February and 300 pupils had to cram into the space previously occupied by 150 at the Victoria Road site. The county council provided temporary classrooms, but at the expense of space in the playground.

The town worked itself into a frenzy after the 580 foot long, 22,000 ton Greek ship *Queen Frederica* came into the harbour.

Booked to stay for six months, the massive ship managed to obscure much of Kingswear from view in Dartmouth and vice versa. She was the largest vessel to visit the harbour in twelve years.

John Lewthwaite, owner of the Gunfield Hotel in Warfleet said: 'We are absolutely furious. There are many people surrounding my property who feel the same way as I do. [I] intend making an application for reduction of our rates because of the loss of amenity to our properties.'

Cllr Eric Cook, chairman of the Dartmouth Harbour Commission said: 'We are here to run the harbour as a port. Other beauty spots like Nice and Naples contain large commercial vessels and I see no reason why Dartmouth is in any different position.'

The ship inspired weeks of correspondence in the pages of the paper, with opinions divided straight down the middle.

Cllr Cook revealed he would recommend that the proposed harbour dues increase be delayed, thanks mainly to the extra funds brought in by the *Queen Frederica*.

Queen Frederica laid up in the harbour.
REUBEN GOOSENS

1972

Dartmouth Town Council purchased a plot of land in Townstal in the early part of the year to allow it to extend the area's industrial estate. The £34,000 purchase would help promote more business in the town. Enquiries from potential purchasers didn't get far until the council installed link roads, sewerage and electricity supplies to the site. Cllr Brian Goss said the council had to move faster as local people were suffering through high unemployment.

'I am not pessimistic, but I am a realist and have not got my head in the clouds either. I have seen this town dwindling and I have got people in my family who are unemployed.'

The council offered sites on the estate at cost price – between £2,800 and £5,200 – to try and encourage as many businesses to come in to help the town's ailing economy. However, by the end of the year none had been sold and only interest from a suspicious 'video tape' producing facility had been shown.

NOT BLOOMIN GOOD ENOUGH

Dartmouth decided not to enter Britain in Bloom this year due to a 'lack of response' from local organisations.

The town's borough council, who had been heading up the appeal to get an entry going, received just two letters of interest about it and therefore let it drop. Cllr Vida Keane said she was 'very angry' about it, and said 'if we do not have the support of the town, there is no point going on.'

Parking reared its head again – with the Dartmouth & Kingswear Society arguing for large car parks in Townstal and a 'free bus ride' to and from the town. However, many felt that shoppers would not want this – especially if they had heavy bags.

Traders complained in early May at a new 'rash' of yellow lines around the town saying they would 'strangle' it.

Chamber of Trade Chairman Fred Tremlett said: 'The whole thing is ridiculous. The council have put the cart before the horse and before imposing additional restrictions should have provided more car parks.'

Borough Cllr Leslie Briers said that the new parking restrictions would mean a loss of 125 car parking spaces around the town.

He said: 'Unless more car parks are provided we will strangle ourselves. Double yellow lines have made Vicarage Hill a most hideous sight. Ours is the only country which disfigures roads in this manner with broad, bright painted lines. Other countries manage to do it in a more harmonious manner.'

In the quiet days of September, Borough Cllr Brian Goss decided the council needed to 'think big' about the town's parking problems.

'He felt they were all guilty of not thinking big enough,' the *Chronicle* reported. 'Dartmouth was being overburdened with retired people and they were losing out on the family man. If they did not think progressively he guaranteed in twenty years that it would be a dead town. They did not have a progressive plan and this was where they were falling down.'

Cllr Goss proposed a tunnel under the river rather than a bridge, a car park on Jawbones and a way to the town via a 'scenic railway' from this car park.

Instead the council decided to send a letter to a number of developers, inviting them to give ideas about how to generate more car parking spaces in the town.

1972 World Events

- Bloody Sunday: The British Army kills fourteen unarmed nationalist civil rights marchers in Londonderry, Northern Ireland
- Watergate scandal: Five White House operatives are arrested for burgling the offices of the Democratic National Committee
- Rioting Maze Prison (Northern Ireland) inmates cause a fire that destroys most of the camp
- The last major epidemic of smallpox in Europe breaks out in Yugoslavia

Top left: *Being a successful actor in TV's most exciting new show does not protect you from the Devon weather.*
Totnes Image Bank/South Hams Newspapers

Top right: *The* Onedin Line *continued to cause a stir around the town.*
Totnes Image Bank/South Hams Newspapers

Dartmouth Celebrity Chefs – A Brief History

(See years 1974 to 2010)

Dartmouth seems to have an embarrassment of riches when it comes to notable and well-renowned chefs, some of the most eminent are listed below.

Joyce Molyneux

In the 1970s, the Hole in the Wall in Bath – owned by George Perry Smith – was THE place to eat. The Lancastrian restaurateur used influences from across Europe to infuse his menus with beautiful dishes people flocked to try.

Into his kitchen one day walked a 'domestic science' student called Joyce Molyneux, who wanted to be his cook.

She showed herself to have consummate skill, and yet was still immensely humble, and when Perry Smith came to Dartmouth with her in 1973 to look at a building on the South Embankment, he knew she was ready to run a fantastic and highly-regarded restaurant on her own.

The Carved Angel opened in 1974, and quickly became regarded as the finest restaurant anywhere in the country. Chefs from London and beyond came to taste the food created by a woman who claimed she was a 'magpie', taking the best bits of other people's ideas. She demanded a friendly and happy kitchen, with staff all working in the kitchen and serving food as well.

Joyce Molyneux in the early days of The Carved Angel TOTNES IMAGE BANK

Keith Floyd

Keith Floyd was a unique, fascinating and ultimately flawed man who ignited television with his wine-fuelled cooking sessions on his many TV series, starting with *Floyd on Food*.

Floyd started his gastronomic career at his bistro in Bristol. He came to the attention of TV bosses and several series later the former Tank Regiment dropout had basically invented what we now call a 'celebrity chef'. He was rude, irreverent and often drunk – but he was always watchable, interesting and actually very likeable. Floyd was always himself, no matter how bad that looked, and the TV audiences found that extremely attractive.

He clearly LOVED the food he cooked and respected great cooks and chefs in a way he couldn't respect anyone else. He craved good company, good food and good wine, and often found all three.

He came to the Maltsters Arms in Tuckenhay in the 1990s, pouring £1 million into a business off the beaten track and to which he rarely gave his full attention. He married a beautiful Dartmouth girl, and their relationship was played out in front of the media until their eventual split and divorce in 1994.

Then Floyd, perhaps not before time, went bankrupt, reportedly after accepting a cheque for a £36,000 bar bill at the Maltsters – which then bounced.

He left South Devon at that point, and ended up in the South of France, in his final years striking out angrily at the celebrity chefs he himself had helped to create. He died in 2009.

John Burton-Race

John Burton-Race celebrates getting a Michelin star. PHIL SCOBLE

John Burton-Race, Michelin-starred chef, appeared in Dartmouth in the summer of 2004 following the purchase of the Carved Angel – which was renamed the New Angel – with a reputation.

In 2004, he went to France with his wife Kim and their many children. The year away was documented in the TV series *French Leave*, and highlighted his fiery temperament and tendency to make snap, and sometimes unwise, decisions.

His return from this self-imposed exile was to take on the previously renowned Carved Angel and reshape it in his own image, incorporating new ideas brought about by his time away. This again was documented in a television programme, called *Return of the Chef*. It again showed his difficult and mercurial nature and his great cooking.

The business gained a Michelin star in 2005.

The town seemed to benefit from his presence and the continual TV exposure he brought, with 2005 and 2006 being particularly good summers for the tourism industry thanks, said some, to the 'Burton-Race effect'.

But trouble was just around the corner: he was revealed to have had a child with another woman and split from his wife. He then seemed to get a lifeline thanks to a spot on *I'm A Celebrity....Get Me Out of Here!* at the end of 2007. But while he was in the jungle his estranged wife was closing the New Angel restaurant they jointly owned.

On his return, Burton-Race was instructed to liquidate all his assets for the divorce and it seemed his short tenure in Dartmouth was over. He did return briefly to work for the restaurant's new owners, but left soon after to 'concentrate on TV consultancy'.

Mitch Tonks

One of the most interesting chefs to be linked to Dartmouth in the recent past – Mitchell Tonks turned his back on accountancy to become a fishmonger in 1995. His Bath fish shop soon had a cookery school and restaurant added to it, and became Fishworks, a new way of selling and promoting seafood.

Mitch Tonks with his sometime TV presenting partner Matt Dawson. PHIL SCOBLE

Fishworks quickly expanded and was even floated on the stock exchange. Mitch then started appearing on TV programmes, and his wide smile and friendly personality proved a hit with viewers.

He was voted Restaurateur of the Year by *Tatler* magazine in 2006, the latest in a string of accolades.

He stepped down from his hands-on role with Fishworks not long after that award, and was then searching for a new project.

Mitch came to Dartmouth in 2008 to see what there was available. He saw, just a few doors down from the now famous New Angel, a perfect opportunity for his new venture. The Seahorse, which opened summer 2008, instantly earned a stellar reputation, for both its food and ambience.

In 2010, Mitch and friends bought another premises just five doors down the Embankment, and opened the Rockfish, the second in a new high-end fish and chip restaurant chain. It was an intriguing and an original concept for Dartmouth, but a successful one.

Top left: *Cubs line up.*
TOTNES IMAGE BANK/SOUTH
HAMS NEWSPAPERS

Top right and
above: *The first
dip of the year
for Dartmouth
Swimming Club
in the Boatfloat
seems to be a
chilly one.*
TOTNES IMAGE
BANK/SOUTH HAMS
NEWSPAPERS

BEWARE THE 'MIDLANDERS'

With 'the coming of the M5' many feared a huge influx of 'Midlanders' swamping the town in their cars.

One borough council meeting was told that two proposed schemes on Ridge Hill and the North Embankment (which was to include a boat park) would be dependent on funding from central government. The borough council had looked at buying land along Mayors Avenue for a multi storey car park but found land owners did not want to sell.

Dartmouth discovered it would now have a new purpose built school campus on Milton Lane featuring both secondary and primary schools. The borough council expressed concern about the traffic on the road and the lack of parking allocated to the schools, but then gave their consent in March.

Building on the new primary school, next to the existing St John the Baptist Roman Catholic School, began in early summer with plans to complete by the beginning of 1974. The new primary school would replace the old school in Higher Street which had opened in 1873. It would be open plan 'with no interior doors at all' and would be able to accommodate 480 pupils 'in comfort' rather than the current 'cramped' conditions for 410, according to Miss M Gregory, the Headmistress.

The new secondary school was also looking for a 1974 completion for its £204,000 'first phase'. The new buildings, very near to the new primary school, would be 'as fine as any in the country'.

The Greek liner *Queen Frederica* continued to cause controversy. The mooring of the 580 foot long 22,000 ton ship had caused outrage in some parts of the community the previous year.

Accusations had been made that the placing of the liner opposite Warfleet Creek was a danger to shipping, that the liner was leaking oil and fuel and that she was an eyesore.

All this was refuted by the Harbour Commission and the liner stayed. The ship got into trouble at the beginning of February when violent storms followed hot on the heels of snow showers. Heavy winds and a high tide resulted in the loosening of the ship's mooring and it drifted more than 130 foot onto a mud bank.

The same storms knocked a 15 foot hole in the sea wall below Kittery Court.

The huge liner left port on June 2 with many sad to see her go but also with many glad to be rid of her.

It was revealed after her departure that the ship had contributed more than £1,700 to the Harbour Commission during her months in the harbour. The harbour's honorary Commissioner P. Gilbert, said that the *Queen Frederica's* visit was the only reason the harbour was not in the red and the harbour 'would be wise to review the various charges levied on the river.'

Dartmouth's biggest day in years took place on Monday July 31, when Her Majesty the Queen, Prince Philip, Princess Anne and Prince Andrew came to the town onboard the Royal Yacht *Britannia*. Huge crowds met Her Majesty who had specified she would like to walk through the town before taking the Royal Salute at Divisions at the Britannia Royal Naval College.

The headline on the *Chronicle's* front page, read: 'Our Regal Queen, Wise-Cracking Duke and Gay Princess'. The respect shown to all three in the report is something to behold in these days of paparazzi-hounded royals.

Greeted by the Lord Lieutenant of Devon, Lord Roborough, and the Mayor Frank Mullett, the Queen spent a long time walking around the rain-soaked town and the *Chronicle* complimented her on having 'the right word in the right place every time.'

Prince Philip was a huge success during the visit – having the 'crowd roaring most of the time'. 'Nothing about him was stiff or starchy, in spite of the yards of gold braid'. The *Chronicle* said the people of the town were 'privileged to see him at such close quarters'. It did reveal he was 'baffled' by a demonstration of judo. 'What is this jargon they keep on mumbling?' he asked of an aide before roaring with laughter himself.

From left to right:
The Queen is not deterred by the weather during her walkabout in Dartmouth.

… and spent a long time chatting to the crowds, to the delight of all.
Totnes Image Bank/
South Hams Newspapers

QUEEN'S DEPARTURE FROM DARTMOUTH

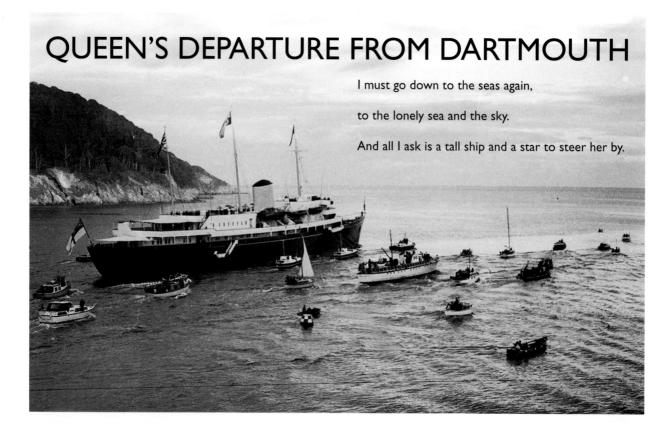

I must go down to the seas again,

to the lonely sea and the sky.

And all I ask is a tall ship and a star to steer her by.

Top: *The Royal Yacht* Britannia *departs Dartmouth Harbour and the* Chronicle *leaves no doubt about the feelings the people of the town have about her visit.*

Below left: *The Queen inspects the cadets during her July visit.*

Below right: *The Queen is clearly delighted to see the Dartmouth Cubs lined up.*

ALL IMAGES TOTNES IMAGE BANK/ SOUTH HAMS NEWSPAPERS

END OF ERA AS BRITISH RAIL LEAVES KINGSWEAR

On more prosaic ground, the Dart Valley Light Railway claimed it would provide services for school children after it took on the seven mile track from Paignton to Kingswear at the end of the year.

The enthusiast-run company had stated it would run the service as a tourist attraction in summer but was forced to agree to run a school service during the nine months of the school year.

Dart Valley Light Railway Manager Barry Cogar said that 'although the company charged tourists double the standard BR rate for trips, locals would not be asked to pay that price'.

When the day finally came, October 28, the company asked for a few weeks grace, with a skeleton service of only four trains a day, back and forth. The county council stated that a reduced service such as that 'had to be expected'.

The sale had been opposed and Kingswear Parish Council wrote to the minister for the environment asking them to check the legality of the sale as it should have been offered to the local authority for sale first. The parish council and residents association joined together in a call to the county council to bring better bus links to the village.

'Councillors claimed, the lack of trains put those employed in Torbay at risk of losing their jobs. The parish council wrote to the Dartmouth Borough asking for support. The borough responded with a strongly worded call of support and even the Torbay Trades Council came out with a call for a better service.

Blackouts in this year caused annoyance and discomfort to many in Dartmouth, as it did across the country.

A new housing complex for the elderly in Townstal was opened in August to much acclaim. The complex, which included a mini-market in Townstal Crescent, was opened by the Mayor.

The first two occupants, rather than celebrating, had to deal with the jealousy of other Townstal residents. One of the visitors to the new complex was quoted as saying 'just look at all those cupboards. I didn't even have one.'

The 'Historical Pageant' held in St Saviours Church to mark its 600th anniversary. The performance featured every famous historical figure to be connected with Dartmouth in that time.
TOTNES IMAGE BANK/SOUTH HAMS NEWSPAPERS

… including, in one bizarre scene, Sir Francis Drake, Queen Victoria and the then town Mayor Cllr Frank Mullett as George V.
TOTNES IMAGE BANK/ SOUTH HAMS NEWSPAPERS

600 YEARS OF ST SAVIOURS CHURCH

In October the 600th anniversary of the founding of St Saviours Church was marked by many events.

The Bishop of Exeter, arriving by boat, led prayers and thanks for the presence of the church, first built in 1373. The Chancel extension was funded by John Hawley, a 14th century merchant and privateer and probably the inspiration for Chaucer's 'Shipman' in the *Canterbury Tales*.

A specially arranged pageant was performed in the church – taking more than 100 audience members through the principal events concerning the church in the past 600 years starting with a visit from Edward I in 1286 who had asked for the building of a riverside church leading directly to the building of St Saviours.

The pageant took place over three nights and featured Chaucer's alleged meeting with John Hawley, and a scene oddly involving King George V, Francis Drake and Queen Victoria.

On a lighter note, Mr E.C. Marshall took the council's feedback about his proposed sign for a restaurant too much to heart. He had asked to have an illuminated sign with 'Ernie's Eatery' at 15 Victoria Road, but this was thrown out because councillors did not like the name.

He then suggested 'Epicurean Restaurant' instead, which was again thrown out. Cllr Richard Hoare said it was going 'from one extreme to another.' It was too long anyway, meaning the sign would be too big and intrusive.

The Mayor and staff are amazed by Dartmouth's new, electronic telephone exchange.
SOUTH HAMS NEWSPAPERS

1973 World Events
● The United Kingdom, the Republic of Ireland and Denmark enter the European Economic Community (EEC)
● The World Trade Centre officially opens in New York City
● Princess Anne marries a commoner, Captain Mark Phillips, in Westminster Abbey
● Due to coal shortages caused by industrial action, the 'Three-Day Week' electricity consumption reduction measure comes into force

Irene Scawn, the last Mayor of the ancient Borough of Clifton Dartmouth Hardness
DARTMOUTH TOWN COUNCIL

1973 The plans for the new 'video studio' at Townstal were unveiled in the January 19 edition. The company behind the plans to build a studio and reproduction complex, Learning for Pleasure (LFP), was owned by Ronald Dilworth. He claimed that the company would have its headquarters in Dartmouth, but have offices 'all over Europe'.

However, the plans appear to have been nothing more than pie in the sky. The borough council tried to contact the company in October with a twenty eight day notice telling it to complete the purchase or lose the deposit it had paid.

Solicitors for the firm asked for an extra seven days because 'all the directors were either on holiday or ill'.

The sale did not go through despite the 'not inconsiderable' deposit already paid by the company. The council began to look elsewhere to fill the large amount of plots LFP had reserved with little or no success.

END OF THE BOROUGH ERA

The Borough of Clifton Dartmouth Hardnesse elected only its third female Mayor since Edward III had created the borough by Royal Charter.

Irene Scawn said she was sad that the borough days were coming to an end and said: 'I love history and ceremony and to think that this is to be practically the end is very sad and it seems depressing that we are caught up in this whirlwind of progress that makes it difficult to see where we are going.'

The Mayor-making Ceremony was very popular, as many felt it was the end of an era – after this the Mayor's role would be purely symbolic and hold virtually no power.

Cllr Scawn was not ambiguous on her feelings towards the changes at her inauguration as Mayor: 'It seems incomprehensible to me how a charter granted 632 years ago by a reigning monarch giving Dartmouth the status of a borough 'for our heirs and successors forever' can in this modern age be wiped away by the stroke of a pen.'

The St John Ambulance Association upset the borough council. They held a lease until 1997 for rooms on an old factory site on the North Embankment, which the borough council was trying to sell for development. They refused to budge until 'an adequate replacement premises is offered'.

In January St John Ambulance refused a proposal for a new base attached to a sports pavilion on Coronation Park because it would 'lack sunshine' and have no special parking area for the ambulance staff to use.

Ald Jack Mashford said: 'Surely no one can stifle progress like this. The council have bent over backwards to find a solution.'

Lt Col Richard Webb, President of the Dartmouth St John Ambulance Association, said: 'We have stressed the fact that many of Dartmouth's citizens subscribed money for the erection of this headquarters and that we are morally obliged to bear this in mind in any action we take. So far nothing satisfactory has been offered to us.'

Top left: *The Mayor Irene Scawn pins the Silver Oar to Regatta chairman Fred Tremlett at the start of the 1973 Regatta.* TOTNES IMAGE BANK/SOUTH HAMS NEWSPAPERS

Top right: *Six former senior officers from Dartmouth Fire Station meet for a chat about the old times – including Albert French, who would later win the MBE and see his son Barrie go on to also become the Station Officer at Dartmouth Fire Station.* TOTNES IMAGE BANK/SOUTH HAMS NEWSPAPERS

Bottom left: *From left to right: Irene Darby, Don Darby, David Kelland, Joyce Darby dress up for a special Edwardian Day during Carnival week.* TOTNES IMAGE BANK/SOUTH HAMS NEWSPAPERS

So desperate were the developers to move forward that they offered St John Ambulance a place in the new development and even invited them to come up with their own suggestions for an acceptable rent. However, the council were less happy as the developers wanted to reduce the amount they paid for the site because they were, of course, now going to get less for their investment. Ald Jack Mashford summed it up, after the council had also been asked to make a financial contribution to the new scheme: 'They have us over a barrel'.

They certainly did – and sat tight for the next five years too – when the developers, tired of waiting, began to build elsewhere on the site.

More unhappy building news was mentioned when the planned extension to Dartmouth hospital was delayed in February by 'at least six months'. The delay came after the regional health authority decided that it wished to make a decision on the new physiotherapy wing at Dartmouth, after it had decided on any expansion to the beds offered across the region.

The friends committee continued their sterling efforts to raise £10,000 to pay for the extension, and had reached £3,300 by mid March.

The fundraising paid off when, in October, it was announced that the new extension's foundation stone would be laid in January by Mayor Irene Scawn, who had started the very first fundraising push for the new extension herself.

FERRY 'CROSS THE DART – PROFITS AND PROBLEMS

Dartmouth Borough Council took over the running of the passenger ferry – and immediately raised the ticket prices. The price of a crossing went from 2½p to 3p. The Lower Ferry, also run by the borough, had its ticket price increased by 200 per cent – to 3p – so that one borough service was not undercutting another. Despite these rises, Borough Treasurer Jack Bates indicated he expected to make a loss over the year for the service.

Left: *Some young
models showing
off the clothes
they wore at a
fashion show to
raise funds for
a new Hospital
Extension
– Allison (10)
and Deborah (8)
Emery, Tanya
(7) and Anton
(4) Rundle,
Julian Hollis (4)
and Gary (6)
and Emma (3)
Nightingale*
TOTNES IMAGE
BANK/SOUTH HAMS
NEWSPAPERS

Right: *Alfred
'Jack' Mashford is
made Alderman
of the Borough
of Dartmouth by
Dartmouth Mayor
Irene Scawn.*
TOTNES IMAGE
BANK/SOUTH HAMS
NEWSPAPERS

The ferry proved an extraordinary success early on, carrying 75,000 passengers in its first two months as a borough operation. The summer influx of passengers from the train was helping to swell the numbers and some days the ferry was carrying 4,000 people across the river in both directions.

The borough council decided that automatic machines were just the thing to increase efficiency and profitability on the ferry. The ticket machines required a bulk order of tickets – so the council ordered one million.

However, the high volume of passengers, with more than 345,000 in June, July and August, and the less than satisfactory operation of the machines showed they were a false economy as the staff had to stop using them at busy times because they just didn't function very well.

The third week in February saw work begin on phase one of the new secondary school in Milton Lane, before the work began on the long planned new primary school. The terrible state of the existing secondary school had spurred the county council into action, but the primary school new build had been held up by problems in the tendering process.

The new secondary school Headteacher was announced as Mr Trevor Pankhurst, who promised a truly democratic school with decisions made by a committee of staff members rather than him alone.

The builders hoped to have everything finished by Easter 1974 a few weeks ahead of their deadline. The 284 students would then work in the new buildings while plans moved forward for phase two.

Building was also on the minds of Kingswear residents. The new marina, proposed on old railway land next to the station, became a huge talking point.

Rumours from those involved with the development said there were no actual plans and the developers it seemed, only proposed to come up with them once permission had been given.

The developers agreed to hold a public consultation event to publicise their plans.

The consultation event, on May 15, was a stormy affair and achieved little.

In the end the planners came to the campaigners' rescue and the marina plan, with a multi storey car park included – was thrown out by the Totnes Planning Committee in February 1974. Was this a happy end to a divisive and strongly fought battle? Unfortunately not; the saga of the Kingswear Marina would not be sorted out until the 1980s.

CLOSED AFTER 142 YEARS –
THE CHURCH IN THE WRONG PLACE

St Barnabas Church was closed after 142 years because of changing patterns in worshipping in the parish. The church had originally been built to avoid the winter crossing at the head of Warfleet Creek, to get to St Petrox. This had resulted in St Petrox falling into disrepair. Now the boot was on the other foot and a shift in population and better roads had resulted in St Barnabas being unpopular as well as being expensive to maintain.

Reverend Harvey Phillips said: 'We've all known for a long time that for our population and resources we cannot go on affording four churches. I cannot say more

Left: *Making the most of a hot summer, Dartmouth's cricket team, featuring future town Cllr Francis Hawke in the centre, line up before a match.* SOUTH HAMS NEWSPAPERS

Right: *Townstal Brownies celebrate their 21st Anniversary.* SOUTH HAMS NEWSPAPERS

of the future use of St Barnabas than has already been said, that we all hope for a most worthy service to the community in whatever role it may be.' The church would remain empty until 1979 when Bob Trevatt opened it as a furniture workshop.

The swimming pool committee shelved plans for an open, unheated swimming pool in Mayors Avenue, due to the high cost and the fact that it could only be used for a few months a year. The committee announced in November that it was now pushing for a 'covered, heated swimming pool' on the new school complex. The group said that such a project could cost a quarter of a million pounds.

The assistant county education officer said the education committee would love to support such an idea, but that it would face major challenges which would not be easily overcome, which they certainly were not.

Dartmouth was shocked by the deaths of four naval officers in a helicopter crash in a field at Milton Farm, Townstal.

Their Wasp helicopter came down during a training flight on the afternoon of December 12. Two were killed instantly and the other two died on their way to hospital. The cause of the crash was found to be the detachment of the rear rotor blade. The pilot was dragged out of the burning wreckage by a ground mechanic at the Norton base but to no avail.

Firemen from Dartmouth and Torquay fought the blaze that erupted from the helicopter to bring it under control.

The dead men were named as Midshipman J. Barlow of Northumberland, Midshipman M. E. Bond of Plymouth and Midshipman O. C. M. Gudgeon Barnes of London; all three were single and officers under training at Britannia Royal Naval College. The pilot was Lieutenant K. J. W. Taylor RN of Wyke Regis. He was married and attached to the Royal Naval Air Station, Portland, HMS *Osprey*.

Gordon Harris of Britannia Avenue saw the crash: 'It went up on its tail and a little pale red light was showing. The big rotor was working. He levelled out and then went for a little while on a level angle then he started to make a normal spin round on its axis. Then he seemed to drop and I saw two of the crew bale out but I did not see any parachutes open.'

Left to right, *Willis Hart, Paul Williams, Tessa Mashford – Town Mayoress, Rita Bowden, Bill Bowden, Wayne Barrow, Chris Pillar. The boat, to be used by Dartmouth Amateur Rowing Club, was being named in Mr Bowden's honour.* SOUTH HAMS NEWSPAPERS

The Best Laid Plans

(See year 1983)

Dartmouth changed a lot in fifty five years, but the town could have been so very different if the plans made by many of its erstwhile leaders had come to fruition.

The front page of the *Chronicle* has often been filled with Mayors, councillors or perhaps even chairmen of the Chamber of Trade, stating what 'could' happen in the town in the future.

Here is a non-exhaustive list of some of the more exciting promises or terrible events predicted: a car park on Coronation Park, a car park under Coronation Park, a car park built out into the river on top of a sewerage plant in front of Coronation Park, the inner relief road, a swimming pool on Mayors Avenue, a multi-storey car park on Mayors Avenue, the deep water quay at Noss, Dartmouth the channel ferry port and the closure of the Naval College.

A few of these I have looked at elsewhere in this book, still others were simply the mad ideas of individuals, but some were actually quite close to being achieved, and deserve some further examination here:

THE CROSS-CHANNEL PORT

The idea of making Dartmouth a cross-channel port is not as crazy as it might first appear.

The town is one of the deepest, and most beautiful, natural harbours in Britain and is near many large population centres, such as Plymouth, Torbay and Exeter. It has mooring points for large vessels, and a harbour authority used to bringing in large ships on a regular basis.

This had given both Kingswear and Dartmouth residents the belief that all that was needed was some interest from ship owners, and the ferries could start steaming in.

These positive points helped two firms in the 1980s start to believe Dartmouth could conceivably be the centre of a new economic boom.

The two companies announced their plans within months of each other, and Harbourmaster Colin Moore was truly excited by the opportunity.

The feeling was that smaller ferries, including car ferries, could come to Dartmouth offering holiday makers a superior way across the channel. Dartmouth and Kingswear's beautiful harbour and even more beautiful views could have been a draw for those wanting to cross the channel by boat, but not use the impersonal and ugly larger ports at Southampton, Portsmouth or Plymouth.

However, there were negative points to the plans – namely the geography surrounding Dartmouth. The hills around the two towns made the need for investment extremely high. Winding narrow lanes, steep hills and a lack of infrastructure in the towns themselves meant that the figures never added up.

Despite the complaints of the Harbourmaster, the two companies turned their back on the harbour, and the chance of the town being an international ferry port for holiday makers was gone.

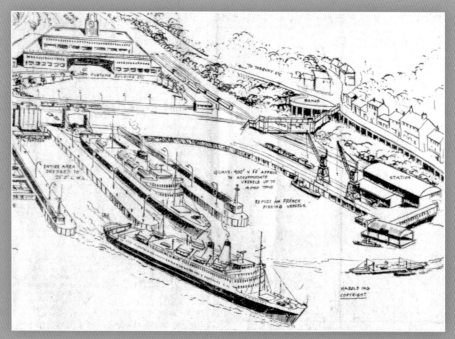

An artist's impression of Kingswear as a cross-channel ferry terminal.
HAROLD ING

THE DEEP WATER QUAY

In 1983 a suggestion for a new deep water quay at Noss Marina caused uproar at committee meetings around the county – with the owners of Noss Shipyard opposing the plans and Devon County Council refusing to support it.

The idea was proposed by the Harbour Commission, and it felt it would change the face of the Dart forever, securing large shipping and prosperous contracts for Dartmouth, Kingswear and Torbay businesses to service them.

But there were some fearsome objections to it.

Possibly the most important objector was the man who owned the Marina which would be the home of the quay.

Philip & Son owner Philip Pensabene was angered the plan would require major vehicular access through his Noss site, actually reducing its profitability.

His objection was a bit of a problem for the Harbour Commission. He made it very clear he would 'never discuss it'.

He had a lot of bargaining power as he was chairman of the Harbour Commission planning committee, which would have to approve the plan before anything got built.

The plan was put in serious peril when Devon County Council recommended that no money should be given towards a £20,000 feasibility study on the plans – which it was thought would cost £2 million.

This effectively stopped the plan: Philip & Son refused it to be sited at the south side of the Noss shipyard, and the National Trust, which owned land to the north which could be used for access and the quay area, said it would not release the land until a feasibility study could be carried out. The county council would not support the feasibility study until the land had been agreed, and so the quay which it was said could have brought huge amounts of large-scale shipping business to the town could not be built.

However the arguments went on well into 1984.

At one point the town council pledged to give the feasibility study its support and then had the loan to fund it refused.

The district council did finally agree to support the study but unfortunately this decision was made around the time Mr Pensabene refused to allow the scheme to use Noss Land and the National Trust denied any use of its land to the north as well.

The plan never gained the support of Devon County Council's officers, all of whom were required to put in large amounts of work in the planning stages to get the scheme off the ground. Without their support, and in fact with some of them actively promoting and supporting a rival development in Plymouth, it never got beyond detailed planning.

1974

The year began on a downturn. The 'Three-Day Week' and massive fuel shortages put pressure on many businesses and created worry and uncertainty. TTB Fabrications had been stockpiling fuel which in conjunction with a large generator allowed them to 'more or less' work a five day week, but other businesses were less lucky.

The *Chronicle* said that the town was 'coping well' with the situation thanks to 'friendly co-operation and sympathetic understanding between work people and management'. The paper said thanks to the 'family-like' relationships between companies in the town with many able to get by without laying off staff.

The set 'power days' meant that many companies had to bring in staff at difficult or inconvenient times. New Year's Day was a power day so many companies brought in a near to full staff and most were happy to come. As a result the celebrations for the New Year were muted in town as many people had to be at work bright and early the next day. The outlook, according to most, was 'bleak' for the year, but the town seems to have tried to put on the bravest face possible and ride out the bad times.

Adverts throughout the paper confirmed the crisis was serious enough to become an advertising theme, including: 'I'm buying a Saab because I'm rationing petrol'. Street lights were switched off around the borough with the only exceptions being where there was danger of an accident.

The start of the new season at Easter, as always, helped optimism rise. Many hotels reported being 'chock-a-block' over Easter and hopes were high for a good summer to push away the high-inflation blues.

A landslide on Swannaton Road nearly took the life of two people.

On January 13 Peter and Joan King had been happily chatting to a man below the 15 foot retaining wall which they noticed was developing large cracks as they leisurely made their way up to the house of a friend. Mr King said: 'To my great interest, rather than alarm, and like a slow motion film, the wall began to slide down with a sound like falling snow.' Except falling snow doesn't weigh 400 tons. The couple then got their friend out of the house as a second landslide began. This left the house just 10 feet from a new cliff edge.

The owner of the house, Mrs Rachel McCoy was left with perhaps an even bigger shock than that of seeing most of her house's foundations slip down the hill – she would have to pay £15,000 to get the wall replaced.

Top left: *Borough Gardener Mr J Bowhay votes in that year's October elections.*
TOTNES IMAGE BANK/ SOUTH HAMS NEWSPAPERS

Top right: *Car dumping seemed to still be a problem in Dartmouth in 1974 – unless this was the only way they could fit in the spot….*
TOTNES IMAGE BANK/ SOUTH HAMS NEWSPAPERS

Left: *Dartmouth United allow their club secretary Stan Prowse – who had waited his whole life for a cup win – to hold the Herald Cup after the team finally won it.*
TOTNES IMAGE BANK/ SOUTH HAMS NEWSPAPERS

1 April 1974

This was the actual date when the ancient Borough of Clifton Dartmouth Hardness ceased to exist. King Edward III had established Royal Borough status in 1327, followed by a Royal Charter granted in 1341.
After over six hundred years, the history, trappings and most of the powers of the Mayor and Corporation, Aldermen and councillors, were swept away overnight. In its place came the new district council that was formed under the Local Government Act 1972. The borough or district councils of Dartmouth, Kingsbridge, Plympton St. Mary, Salcombe and Totnes all merged into the new South Hams District Council on April Fools' Day 1974.

South Hams
District Council

Her insurance company agreed to pay half the £30,000 costs but this still left her with more than the value of the house to find herself. Mrs McCoy was left with few options, the most attractive of which was a 'loan' from Devon County Council that would involve her handing over the house as payment. After a number of years of struggle, Mrs McCoy, a widow, would be forced to sell her beloved house to pay to repair part of the wall.

YET MORE STINK FROM THE SEWAGE

The borough council discovered the proposed sewerage scheme, which had been discussed many times since 1971, was to cost more than £2 million. The original plan was costed at £500,000.

Cllr Dennis Hopker nailed it when he said that 'this is one of those things where time lost has cost a hell of a lot of money.'

The lowest tender was for £2.3 million and the most expensive for more than £2.5 million. At today's prices this would equate to more than £10 million. Councillors reportedly gasped with amazement when the figures were read out in council.

Inadequate sewerage was becoming a popular reason for refusing new planning applications with the river Dart having more than eighteen raw sewerage outlets running into it. The new system would see all of them removed with new pumping stations leading up to Old Mill Creek where a treatment works would be installed. The regional water authority would have to approve the plan before it could then go to the Department for the Environment. The town council could then apply for grants to pay for the massive scheme. However, the plans were mired in problems until the end of the decade when the water authority announced no new scheme would be installed until 1990.

Three men were lucky to escape unhurt after a lesson in underwater explosives went wrong and blew up the instructor's boat. Glenn Chadwick, of the British Underwater Centre, was in the process of showing a small explosive charge, known as a 'pill, to two students' when a combination of wind and tide resulted in the charge getting caught up in the propeller of the small dory the three were in, blowing the engine off the back of the boat. The three rowed back to shore in their slowly sinking boat with only the pride of the instructor hurt.

The Canadian Kitsilano Boys during one of their many visits to Regatta.
Totnes Image Bank/ South Hams Newspapers

BUSINESSES NOT WANTING TO PAY TO BE RID OF RUBBISH

Anger and wrath was directed at district councillors by traders after the decision was made to charge for the collection of trade waste. Their mood was not improved when they were told that they should have been paying for the collection of their waste since 1936. It was made worse when they found out that caravan parks and hotels would not be treated as 'trade' and boiled over when they were told that the charges levied were 'nominal' and would not 'cover the cost' of collection.

The traders organised a petition voicing a 'vehement protest at this iniquitous surcharge when traders are already paying high rates'. The anger of traders in the town had first been raised by a letter from Mr J Yeo, Technical Services Officer for the district, informing them that payment for collection would be needed. The letter was described by Chamber of Trade members as 'a disaster in the art of diplomacy'.

The borough council had never charged for collection, even though they should have, because 'it would cost too much to collect the money'. That state of affairs had existed since legislation in 1936 – and the district council were in no mood to allow it to continue.

District and Borough Cllr Brenda Breakwell was obviously aware who her electorate were when she told the Chamber of Trade, 'you need to get militant. We have seen what can happen when people get angry enough'. It was not recorded whether she handed out pitchforks and burning torches to an angry mob.

A letter to the *Chronicle* made a rational point when it said the area was being penalised because 'there was no tip in the neighbourhood where they could take the rubbish to burn.'

The district council decided that Dartmouth had to pay the fees, just like everyone else, but probably decided that Mr Yeo would not be sending the letter informing the Chamber of Trade of this, as this time it would, apparently, be 'a clear but gently worded letter of explanation'.

The town geared up for the second general election in eight months in October after the chaotic financial situation brought down the government.

Again Conservative Ray Mawby MP did battle with Liberal Tony Rogers, who had cut the standing MPs majority to 9,643 at the last poll in March. Also standing was Saxon May Spence for the Labour party, the first female candidate for Totnes in nearly fifty years.

The paper worked incredibly hard to be fair, claiming until the very last minute 'the result is still open and could go any way'. Labour won the national competition, though without being able to form a majority government, but once again Ray Mawby was returned as MP for Totnes. His majority was 6,400, although reduced by Mr Rogers, who vowed to fight again. The Labour vote dropped by 883.

Veterans of the British Armed Forces march along the Embankment to mark Armistice Day.
Totnes Image Bank/South Hams Newspapers

1975

The Lower Ferry became the centre of rumours as its loss making resulted in fears it would close. The ferry was reported to be making a loss of between £15-20,000 a year and the district council was not prepared to support this position.

FERRY FIGHT

A spokesman for the council said: 'The council has never considered any curtailment of the service in the past but at the same time, if the ferry continues to show a heavy loss, the council may consider any curtailment it deems necessary.'

Devon County Council decided to support the ferry, but the operation was still losing thousands of pounds each year.

The district council took a most controversial decision by increasing charges on the ferry by more than 75 per cent for cars and double passenger costs. Cars cost 35p from March 1, up from 20p. Passenger fares increased from 5p to 10p. Charges were also introduced for old age pensioners for the first time.

It was pointed out by a correspondent to the paper called 'Doomwatcher', that the charges were more expensive (per mile) than taking a jumbo jet to America.

The district council then decided it needed to 'discourage' passengers from using the Lower Ferry and to encourage them to use the district council owned passenger ferry instead. The foot passenger fare was increased to 20p in the summer.

The rise in prices caused anger and resentment throughout the year with countless letters to the paper. A petition was raised from traders in Lower Street concerned the price hike would affect their already meagre profits.

The passenger and Lower Ferry saw a reduction in trade by more than a quarter after the rates were increased.

Problems abounded for both services with the introduction of new ways of working resulting in one memorable instance of a full passenger ferry crossing the Dart with no one being charged. Those supposedly collecting fares on the pontoon on the Dartmouth side 'left their posts'!

The Higher Ferry had been stopped from putting up prices before September, because as part of the road network, it had to go through a lengthy process to request increases from the Department for the Environment. When it did increase its fares, the proposed charges caught in people's throats: 50p a crossing and 10p for passengers. Many thought this would make it worth their while to go round by road to Torbay.

Rises were delayed in 1976 by a public enquiry but many knew the writing was on the wall.

1975 World Events
- Margaret Thatcher defeats Edward Heath for the leadership of the UK Conservative Party
- Bill Gates founds Microsoft in Albuquerque, New Mexico
- The United Kingdom votes 'Yes' in a referendum to stay in the European Community (EC)

Left: *Trying to jump the Dart!*
SOUTH HAMS NEWSPAPERS

Right: *The Middleton family of blacksmiths proudly display a piece of their handiwork.*
TOTNES IMAGE BANK/SOUTH HAMS NEWSPAPERS

Storms in March brought down many trees, including this one in Kingswear.
TOTNES IMAGE BANK/SOUTH HAMS NEWSPAPERS

TWINNING WINNING

To try and detract from the economic doom and gloom the idea of twinning with a French town was put forward. The town council decided that although twinning was a good idea it was not something for which ratepayers should foot the bill.

The secondary school had already made a strong contact with Courseulles-sur-Mer, a town of 3,000 which swelled to a population of 25,000 in summer. The similarities between the two towns were quite striking.

However, councillors did raise fears that Dartmouth would come off badly in comparison with their Gallic cousins in the event of a twin. What if the French municipality decided to support the French twinning association with large financial backing? Cllr Breakwell said if the French showed great and expensive hospitality to the English 'our civic pride would be very sorely damaged if we could not return it.'

She then made a good impression when the Mayor of Courseulles-sur-Mer visited the town in May – as she had, by then, become Mayor of Dartmouth. Monsieur Jean Pierre Baudard was very impressed with the town and the two groups must have really hit it off because in September the decision was made to take the plunge to twin with the French town in October.

However, the Chamber of Trade were unhappy at the decision and demanded the town have more say in the choice of a twin town, calling the speed at which the choice of Courseulles-sur-Mer was made as 'unseemly'. It wrote to the twinning committee saying it was behind the idea of twinning, just not with Courseulles-sur-Mer.

However, the twinning did not go ahead as planned. It transpired that the Mayor of Courseulles-sur-Mer, the happy Monsieur Baudard, had been convicted of corruption and would be spending some time in prison. He appealed against the decision but was found guilty of accepting more than 800,000 Francs in bribes to approve certain building contracts around his town and its district.

The town council said it did not want such a man to be signing a charter with the town and despite pressure from the twinning association, Devon County Council and the British Council, Mayor Brenda Breakwell refused to sign. The Devon County Council Chairman Charles Ansell, told her if she did not, he would sign it for the town. The Twinning Association Chairman Trevor Pankhurst expressed his 'disgust' that the Mayor would not sign.

The twinning association disbanded, but within a month a rather similar Anglo-French association had been formed, with an agreement written and signed between the two towns remarkably similar to the original twinning charter. As the *Chronicle* stated: 'Entente cordiale flows once more between Dartmouth and Courseulles-sur-Mer.'

The people of the French town sent an open letter in November to the Mayor stating their support for the council's decision and saying the two towns should not twin until Monsieur Baudard was removed from office. A petition signed by 577 residents to the disgraced Mayor read: 'The king is exposed. Your English friends have given you a lesson in democracy. The twinning charter cannot be signed by your hand.' It stated that in the autumn of 1976 he could be removed and then twinning should continue, 'with a Mayor on our side worthy to represent us and to welcome you.'

CARNIVAL BRINGS TOWN INTO DISREPUTE

Dartmouth Carnival, while trying to arrange the large event, was marred with internal arguments which were made very public on the front page of the *Chronicle*.

Cllr Brenda Breakwell visited the committee in early June in her capacity as Mayor, stating 'I am not prepared to stand by and let you bring this town into disrepute.' She informed them that if they could not settle their differences she would 'suspend their constitution' and have the Rotary Club run the carnival.

The chairman stepped down and the Mayor installed the Deputy Mayor Mr Brian Goss as new chairman and told them in no uncertain terms to sort it out, saying 'you do not appear to be able to run your own affairs.'

When carnival time arrived it was considered a 'great success' despite near tragedy when a car carrying a family on holiday ran towards the Boatfloat out of control, only to be stopped by two thin railings from a ladder. The carnival procession, a big annual event, really benefited from beautiful weather and several imaginative entries. The Carnival Queen, Patricia Rowsell, travelled on a huge float in the shape of a peacock that barely fitted down some of the streets, followed by the procession.

There was also a wonderful bit of fun with the 'TTB Fly the Dart Challenge'. TTB Fabrications offered a reward of £10,000 to anyone who could launch from one side of the river Dart and make it to the other in a homemade, un-powered craft. The early Flugtag brought out the crazy people that always take part in events like this with Batman, a man with just an umbrella and one man even took off on a rocket powered bike!

On a more sombre note, Dartmouth lost one of its most beloved servants in August, with the death of Dr Richard McConaghey.

The town was lucky to have such an esteemed doctor – known as 'Doctor Mac' – caring for its populace. Dr McConaghey co-founded the Royal College of General Practitioners and for fourteen years was the editor of its journal, and was co-editor of the *Encyclopaedia of General Practice*. In his spare moments he also cared for patients. His bedside manner and dedication to his role within the community were legendary. The paper's headline showed how he was regarded: 'Dartmouth loses doctor, friend and counsellor'. 'Apart from being an outstanding general medical practitioner,' the *Chronicle* said, 'he was a sympathetic, understanding friend and counsellor and was truly loved by all those who had the good fortune to meet him. He will be greatly missed, for his interest in local organisations was considerable.'

Mayor Brenda Breakwell inspects Naval cadets outside the town's Guildhall.

DON'T SWAP WITH MR DEPLEDGE

On a more prosaic, and some would say lighter note Mr Les and Mrs Barbara Green got more than they bargained for when they did a house swap with Dartmouth man 'Mr Depledge' from Yorkshire.

In swapping the council house in Britannia Avenue, they asked Mr Depledge to fill in a pond in the back garden as they had four children and wanted more play space for them. When they moved in they were satisfied with the nice job he had done. However, some time later when one of their children put a foot through the topsoil and a foul stench emerged they began to smell a rat, so to speak. On digging down they found a huge amount of rubbish including old clothing, tin tubs, bricks, mirrors and a plastic bike. However, after a year of demands to the district council it emerged that they would have to clear up the mess themselves, despite a council worker 'mistakenly' telling them the council would 'sort it out'. They didn't and the Greens were left rueing the day they ever swapped with Mr Depledge, who was nowhere to be seen.

The visit of The World, *the biggest cruise ship ever to dock in Dartmouth in July 2010.* *(See year 2010)* KEVIN PYNE

*The drought in
1976 meant that
the town's main
reservoir dried up
almost completely
by September.*
SOUTH HAMS
NEWSPAPERS

1976 World Events

● The first commercial Concorde flight takes off

● Apple Computer Company is formed by Steve Jobs and Steve Wozniak

● The Great Clock of Westminster (or Big Ben) suffers internal damage and stops running for more than nine months

● The brand new Intercity 125 High Speed Train is introduced in the United Kingdom

● The Sex Pistols achieve public notoriety as they unleash several 4-letter words live on Bill Grundy's early evening TV show

1976 Hopes again were raised for a new swimming pool, on the site of the new comprehensive school.

Suddenly people felt that here was a proposal that could be successful and they quickly supported it in January even asking Torbay education authority to look at the figures and perhaps allocate funds.

However these hopes were dashed almost immediately as the authority informed the committee that there would be few funds available and put conditions on its use. The committee decided to 'shelve' the idea, putting £7,000 aside to wait for the right time to dust the project down again, possibly when the financial situation improved across the country.

The committee continued to raise funds but it all collapsed again when proposals were made to shelve any ambitious plans and stop fundraising 'indefinitely' later in the year.

REGATTA PAYS FOR ROGUE 'CHIT'

Also suffering frustrating times were the members of Dartmouth Regatta committee, which was forced into a loss by a bill that it had never expected to receive from the district council.

If paid it would take the large event from a £100 profit to a £260 loss. A letter to the district council accompanying the bill sent back to Follaton House, included a detailed account of which parts – i.e. all of it – the committee considered 'excessive'.

The district council offered to reduce the bill but this offer was rejected out of hand.

However, when the committee secretary looked again, he realised he had signed a 'chit' agreeing to pay extra costs during the event.

Both sides admitted a 'misunderstanding' and the district council agreed to waive a number of costs for the 1976 Regatta to offset the cost incurred in 1975, which the committee then agreed to pay.

A man was forced to 'help' the RSPCA with its investigation after a gruesome find in the river Dart. A dog was found wrapped in a plastic bag floating in the river with no coat left after serious neglect and mistreatment. The discovery, made by staff of the Lower Ferry in the early days of January caused a public outcry and soon a man was singled out and brought forward for questioning. A young man with mental health problems had tried to sell the dog, which he had been given, when he realised he could not cope with looking after it. After finding no one to take the poor animal into their care, he tied it up in a bag and threw it over a cliff past the castle. He said he 'did not think it would suffer'. He was fined £5.

The Dart Harbour and Navigation Authority (DHNA) was formed in March with the election of its commissioners. For the first time private owners were represented (by Captain Robert Franks of Dartmouth) along with local representatives, district councillors, the MoD, South West Water Authority, and the owners of the river 'fundus' The Duchy of Cornwall.

The Duchy brought a shock within two months, demanding £5,000 'rent' for the use of the river. The Duchy had demanded no such rental in the past and many were taken aback by the demand. The Duchy said it was the same figure as negotiated for rivers in Cornwall and it had to 'do nothing' for the money. The rest of the commissioners decided to fight the request as it would mean that prices for their moorings would have to go up. The figure requested represented more than 10 per cent of their annual income. However, the authority soon realised it had to capitulate on these charges and agreed to pay them.

Left: Cars being scrapped after their dumping in the New Ground Car Park.
TOTNES IMAGE BANK/ SOUTH HAMS NEWSPAPERS

DISTRICT COUNCIL PR MISTAKE SHOCKER

South Hams District Council proved it had learned nothing from the furore about Lower Ferry charges in 1975 by suggesting each additional passenger in cars pay an extra 10p on top of the 40p fare for the car.

The ferry was a loss making enterprise for the council and the suggestion was made in March after a series of disappointing figures. The economic outlook at the time was not good, and rates were rising across Devon, so the decision was very unpopular. Letters again poured into the paper; with just about everyone pointing the finger at the district council, saying incompetence was the reason for the losses, and forgetting of course it had made losses just as large when it was run by the borough council before 1974.

The district council did decide to keep hold of it in the long term – providing a £5,000 subsidy from the county council remained.

The passenger ferry was also in the news in July when the district council decided to sell it. Again showing perfect timing, it had decided the best time to offload the operation would be when it would stop being profitable in September – thus making it an amazingly unattractive prospect for anyone to purchase.

Dart Pleasure Craft, who had expressed an interest the year before into buying both the passenger ferry and the Lower Ferry demanded that they sell it 'immediately' to allow them to make some money out of it in the first year.

The district council then launched a bid to be the first council with all of its appendages lodged firmly in its mouth – by making a firm decision NOT to carry out a consultation into the sale of the ferry with local councils and residents.

The district council continued its streak of PR blunders when it decided not to accept an offer of £10,000 for the two pontoons on either side of the river from a private business but accepted a bid of £1,000 from DHNA. The council said it wanted to keep the pontoons in public ownership.

It later turned out that the DHNA had offered the passenger ferry service as a tender, which had been taken up by Dart Pleasure Craft.

The Higher Ferry's owners, Philip & Son, were also forced to justify its call for an increase in ferry fares at a public enquiry. 'The ferry had lost more than £15,000 in two years', said the company and the increase would not only cover these losses but allow it to start putting money aside to pay for a new ferry in the next few years, which it said was badly needed.

Right: Carnival parade.
TOTNES IMAGE BANK/ SOUTH HAMS NEWSPAPERS

It was finally agreed in April to increase the charges to 50p for a car for a one way crossing and to 10p for a passenger making it more expensive than the Lower Ferry.

Dartmouth Primary School came under fire in June when parents of a number of children warned they would 'remove' their children due to 'falling standards and lack of discipline'.

The fears were raised in a special meeting arranged after parents met Irene Scawn to express their opinions.

A subsequent meeting, attended by more than 180 parents, became, according to the *Chronicle*, a bad tempered and angry affair. The basic fears of parents were expressed by Marigold Richardson who was invited by the Headteacher Jack Baker because of her 'educational qualifications'. She said: 'Punctuation, paragraphing and spelling [have] begun to fall away.' She claimed she 'spoke for 90 per cent of parents' when saying people were worried about their children at the age of nine having not mastered these skills. She said: 'Creativity is not always controlled and soon we will not be able to understand what children are trying to say.'

Mr Baker took exception to Mrs Richardson's comments: 'Speak for yourself and no one else. I don't like your attitude.'

Parents criticised the 'open plan' of the school, saying that children just 'ran around' with no control and that they 'do nothing'. Mr Baker said he had total confidence in his staff and said that more could be done by parents – he said that many were 'not concerned' and many children appeared at school 'hardly able to speak at all'.

The *Chronicle* incurred the wrath of Mr Baker, through a letter the week after the story appeared on the paper's front page. The meeting was attended by many who were positive, wrote Mr Baker, and if six children were taken out of school and went to Stoke Fleming, that was not such a bad figure 'out of 370'. He also commented that maybe the people of Dartmouth did not need a choice between schools, but 'a choice between local papers'. Unfortunately for a man defending 'progressive' schooling against traditionalists, Mr Baker started his letter 'The teaching staff and myself were...' whoops. This did not go unnoticed, and one correspondent wrote in to tell readers he was 'astonished' at the grammatical mistake – which the *Chronicle* printed again in case anyone hadn't seen it.

DROUGHT DRAGS ON – CAUSES HEADACHES AND DANGER FOR FIREMEN

The summer of 1976 was one of the hottest and driest recorded, the conditions got so bad that Dartmouth fire fighters were called out on countless occasions to deal with fires caused by tinder dry conditions.

A number were caused by sparks from the Dart Valley Light Railway trains in Kingswear, and many farms saw fields burn over the summer and in one day a total of five fires ignited around Strete, all beginning at the same time.

A number of cattle died or had to be put down after eating bracken when the grass died across pasture in the area.

Firemen were described as being 'out on their feet' with exhaustion. Drastic controls were brought in to ensure the scant water resources were not wasted. Orders were sent out to residents to cut their water consumption by '50 per cent' to protect reserves of water.

The weather was so hot and dry that Slapton Ley almost dried up and the Old Mill Reservoir did just that, meaning Dartmouth had to be connected to the Avon Reservoir, which itself was getting very low by the end of the summer.

In fact the first rain came during Regatta, which was typical, but the runners in the road race were certainly pleased for it.

The heavens opened very seriously just after Regatta at the same time as the Stoke Fleming Horticultural Show was held. In the words of the *Chronicle* it 'tipped down' and 'rained stair rods'. The show, which gardeners prepared for throughout the year by furiously saving water, turned into a quagmire. They certainly didn't let it spoil their fun, even if it did spoil their shoes.

1977 The problems and anger relating to the sale of the passenger ferry by the district council continued in the new year.

A statement calling for such 'chaos' never to be repeated, signed by six district councillors was sent to the Chief Executive Simon Bradley.

One of those councillors was Charles Fitch-Northern of Kingswear, who found himself in hot water for another letter written to the district council. In it he made a number of accusations of maladministration and corruption. It was described by one of his fellow councillors, Mr Robertson Cooper as 'the most scurrilous piece of paper I have ever seen'. Simon Bradley sent the letter to the police, claiming he 'could do nothing else'.

Cllr Fitch-Northern claimed at a council meeting that he had not meant to 'attack any personality', which was met with loud cries of disbelief from his fellow councillors.

The councillor only lasted a few more weeks in the job however as a serious car accident which did not injure him but wrote off his car ended his political career. Mr Fitch-Northern had tried to stand down from the district council role once already but had been dissuaded from doing so by the Kingswear Parish Council in early March. He said the recent problems he had faced at district council, plus ill health, made him want to stand down. The very next day he crashed his car and being unable to attend any meetings without it, and also being unable to afford a new car on a pension, tendered his resignation. So many years of hard fighting and political manoeuvring came to an end and the indomitable 'Fitch' hung up his political boots.

The Lower Ferry again became an issue of some discomfort for the district council.

After another year in which losses ran into thousands of pounds, despite the increase in charges the year before, the council decided to put prices up again – from 50p to 65p for cars and from 10p to 15p for passengers. The letters pages were yet again full for weeks, with angry responses from residents who would now find it even more of a challenge to pay the fees.

Left: *The march to the Royal Avenue Gardens to celebrate the twinning ceremony.*
Totnes Image Bank/South Hams Newspapers

Bottom left: *The signing of the official Twinning document, linking Dartmouth to Courseulles-sur-Mer 1977.*
Totnes Image Bank/South Hams Newspapers

Bottom right: *The winning Dartmouth badminton team accept their trophy after beating the visiting French team.*
Totnes Image Bank/South Hams Newspapers

115

Left: *The twinning tennis tournament was also won by Dartmouth.*
TOTNES IMAGE BANK/SOUTH HAMS NEWSPAPERS

Right: *The football team Captains for Dartmouth and Courseulles-sur-Mer exchange pendants before their match during the twinning celebrations.*
TOTNES IMAGE BANK/SOUTH HAMS NEWSPAPERS

DUCK CAUSES SENSATION

A female duck became something of a news sensation in Dartmouth over the end of 1976 and the beginning of 1977. 'Snowflake' the mallard was convinced she was a swan, and spent most of the winter following a pair of swans up and down the river. The young duck, probably the very opposite of the 'Ugly Duckling', was bemused when the two swans flew off in January. She was very pleased to receive the gift of a husband from RSPCA Inspector Tony Eden, who brought down a drake he had recently nursed back to health after it was shot by some cruel individual with an air rifle. He released the now well 'Snowdrake' near to 'Snowflake' and it seems the species confusion she had been suffering soon abated.

'Snowflake's' story did not seem to be destined to end happily however, despite hopes for ducklings (perhaps inevitably known as 'the Snowballs') just five weeks after meeting, 'Snowdrake' was dead, poisoned by eating some industrial pollution on the river. As the *Chronicle* poignantly put it: 'Snowflake' has been left, once again, without a mate to call her own.'

'Snowflake' was obviously badly affected by this loss, and was later found wandering down the Embankment, underfed and covered in oil. She was taken in by farmer Bob Langford and made friends with a number of birds on his farm. She spent her days wandering around the idyllic area near Blackawton, well fed and, seemingly, content. The paper reported six months after her tragedy that she now had eleven 'Flakelets' fathered by Maurice the Mallard, who was feeling rather proud of himself.

The town's twinning with Courseulles-sur-Mer went ahead after a two year delay on May 21.

The event was hailed as 'C'est Magnifique' by the *Chronicle*, who also took great pleasure in pointing out that Dartmouth had won all but one of the sporting competitions, including a 4-1 drubbing of the French during a football match on Coronation Park, and nearly made it a clean sweep apart from a loss in table tennis.

The Mayor of Courseulles-sur-Mer, never named in any of the coverage, was not present, so it was not clear whether he was the same Mayor who had caused the previous twinning to stall after he was convicted of corruption. No matter, Courseulles-sur-Mer Deputy Mayor M de Mercastel signed the Twinning Treaty with Cllr Richard Hoare after a march to the Bandstand in the Royal Avenue Gardens. The events of the weekend were well planned and executed without a hitch according to the paper – with a Mayor's reception, sporting events, children's party, a Twinning Ball and many more exciting happenings.

The favour was returned in the French town in October, with a huge variety of events, parties and fun for all who went over.

The French even donated a street name plate, with the hope the North Embankment would be renamed the Rue de Courseulles-sur-Mer. The Dartmothians won all the sports events again.

FALSE DAWN FOR JOBS

1977 seemed to be a better year for commerce in its early months, with seven new industrial units announced in Townstal, creating fifty five jobs. Philip & Son continued to be booked up to the rafters, as did TTB Fabrications, and even the Kingswear Marina, the bane of residents' lives for five years, got a new lease of life. Ernest Ireland, the owners of the site who had caused so much anger in the village, went into receivership in January. The new owners of the company, Darthaven, formed from the remainder of Ernest Ireland and Upham Ltd. who bought it, confirmed the build would go ahead during 1977 and phase one would be completed by February 1978. The new company pledged to communicate better with residents and 'improve the general appearance of the site.'

This trend took a considerable dent with the news in April that Paul Pinch Ltd., a television and electrical retailers, were bought out and decided instantly to close their Dartmouth branch.

Then, on April 20, workers at TTB took strike action in a dispute over a productivity bonus.

The factory had recently been awarded the Queen's Award for Industry. The dispute left a trail of harsh words and distrust, sparked by an accusation from the Amalgamated Union of Engineering Workers that the TTB Management had 'gone back on its word' over promises to discuss bonus payments. This was strongly denied by the management, who said: 'We can't give more money without more effort.'

Good news again found its way into the paper in June with the announcement that a fish processing factory was planned for Townstal, run by Town and District Cllr Brenda Breakwell.

A petition was handed in with 413 signatures against the plan. This was treated with less respect when it was noticed that a number of names appeared more than once and in the words of one officer 'some houses in Dartmouth appear to have a lot of people living in them.' The factory's plans were approved.

The seven units supposedly 'filled' in February turned out all to have fallen through, bar one, and the fish factory, which would create fifty jobs, was hoped to be a saviour for the industrial estate which was stalling badly.

However, the factory began to find it difficult to gain funding and by the end of the year no firm plan was in place for its development.

The bad economic situation also forced Darthaven to scale back its building plans in July. The new plans met with yet more opposition and the residents appealed against a decision to approve the plans on the grounds there should be car parking allocated for local people, not just berth holders.

Then in August businessman Reg Bonsey retired, shutting his four businesses as he did so.

The news was another blow to the town, which had official unemployment running at 12 per cent, much higher than the regional average of 8.5 per cent. The town had a total of 256 out of work, with prospects bleak. The figure went up again in October to 14.4 per cent, and many worried that Dartmouth was in financial meltdown.

Left: *The dismantling of Dartmouth's gas holder.*
Totnes Image Bank/South Hams Newspapers

Right: *Celebrating the Queen's Jubilee on Crowthers Hill.*
Totnes Image Bank/South Hams Newspapers

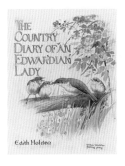

Richard Webb from Dartmouth (as Webb & Bower, his jointly owned publishing company based in Exeter) published The Country Diary of an Edwardian Lady *by Edith Holden in June 1977 and received a Gold Plaque for the first million copies sold. The book went on to sell over three million copies in 13 languages. It achieved a place in* The Guinness Book of Records *for the longest-running No.1 Bestseller. It also became an international brand name with a wide range of merchandise.*

Left: *Julie Tremlett becoming the only girl, and only one of four who crossed the Boatfloat on a rope during Town Week 1997.*

Totnes Image Bank/South Hams Newspapers

Right: *David Dimbleby gets involved in the fun and games at Dittisham Regatta 1977.*

Totnes Image Bank/South Hams Newspapers

END OF AN ERA FOR *ONEDIN*

Dartmouth mourned the passing of one of its most lucrative claims to fame – the *Onedin Line* stopped filming in the town in May. The BBC confirmed that the new series would be filmed at Milford Haven. The expense of taking down the *Charlotte Rhodes'* masts to get under a bridge at Exeter was cited as a reason to relocate production. The corporation said it was 'very sad' about the decision, but the economics could not be ignored.

The Queen's Silver Jubilee was celebrated across the country with gusto, and no less so in Dartmouth.

Street parties took place across the town, from Townstal through the lower town and along to Warfleet. All the villages got into the act with a Brownies' Jubilee Show at Kingswear Hall and a sports day at Dittisham.

No-one, it seemed, missed out on the opportunity to celebrate and a huge bonfire created by the Scouts went up in flames to mark the day.

The police were the targets of much anger as they put out cones to enforce parking restrictions on College Way, where more than seventy cars had been parking daily. The cones mysteriously disappeared overnight but it only put a temporary stop to the restrictions.

A police spokesman vainly tried to explain that it had always been illegal to park on the hill, while admitting a 'blind eye' had been turned towards it in the past. However, when large continental coaches started to park on the road, action had to be taken.

TTB Fabrications set up its own park and ride service, running from a field next to the heliport, with Western National buses running thirty one seaters between the park and town throughout the summer. Despite a recent decision by Devon County Council that such a scheme was 'not viable' the plan seemed to work rather well.

At the end of the summer, the Rotary Club, headed by Basil Williams put together a plan to reverse the roles of the Mayors Avenue car park and Coronation Park, thereby creating some more spaces and losing 'little' amenity spaces. The tennis courts and putting green would also be moved to the New Ground under the plan.

However, this threatened another local project as Coronation Park was now the preferred site for the twenty five metre swimming pool. The plans proved immensely unpopular in the letters pages of the *Chronicle*, and never got anywhere near becoming a reality.

1978 Townstal Post office managers Ronald and Christine Foot suffered a huge blow in early January.

Their home was completely destroyed by fire as they were driving to Southampton on January 8 to take Mr Foot's mother home after a Christmas visit.

The fire started in the basement of the property in Church Road, Townstal, and 'all but destroyed' the house. Mr Foot showed the spirit that got Britain through the Blitz and the Black Death, stating: 'Well, that's the last six years gone up in smoke. Now we shall have to start again.'

SOMETHING FISHY IN TOWNSTAL

Also in January the planned fish factory for Townstal estate, planned by Town and District Cllr Brenda Breakwell, appeared to be 'floundering'.

The problem was that no start up funding could be found as Dartmouth was not in an area designated to gain vital European Economic Community (EEC) cash for businesses. Miss Breakwell said it was frustrating to be working on the project, which it was hoped would have brought fifty jobs in a viable canning facility, if only they could get funds.

'Yet none are willing to put in capital, or at least the amount we need.'

Miss Breakwell had a stern answer for those accusing her of simply looking for personal gain.

'One Government department suggested we took the factory to Lee Mill, an assisted area [where funding was available from the EEC]. We would have received the money we needed, drawn labour from Ivybridge and cut down costs. We refused because we wanted to do something for Dartmouth.'

The news was particularly disturbing as unemployment was skyrocketing in the town – it was at 16 per cent in January – a 4 per cent rise in three months. Although the figures would certainly drop in season, many hoped for more permanent jobs in the town but were sorely disappointed.

1978 World Events
● Cricketer Ian Botham becomes the first man in the history of the game to score a century and take eight wickets in one innings of a Test match
● Phil Scoble born in Hastings, East Sussex
● Pope John Paul I succeeds Pope Paul VI as the 263rd Pope

Left: *The age-old ceremony of blessing the river on Rogation Sunday.*
TOTNES IMAGE BANK/SOUTH HAMS NEWSPAPERS

Right: *The demolition of the old Parade House.*
TOTNES IMAGE BANK/SOUTH HAMS NEWSPAPERS

The incomplete sports hall at Dartmouth Community College – the builders went out of business before they could finish it.
TOTNES IMAGE BANK/SOUTH HAMS NEWSPAPERS

It's a Knockout TV Game Show comes to Dartmouth

(See year 1981)

The Dartmouth It's a Knockout *team.* TOTNES IMAGE BANK/ SOUTH HAMS NEWSPAPERS

Dartmouth's councillors and residents thought winning the right to host *It's a Knockout* would be great publicity for the town in 1981: it turned into the most amazing story of triumph over adversity.

It's a Knockout was a massive, massive deal featuring teams taking part in some of the most ridiculous games ever conceived, wearing outlandish and sometimes dangerous costumes often throwing themselves into big tanks of water in the process. Everyone did so for nothing more than pride as there were no cash prizes available for the winners.

Towns entered in the hope that they would be chosen to host an edition of the programme which commanded viewing figures up to 20 million at times. It was considered a huge honour to host the programme and the news that Dartmouth had done so, beating the city of Plymouth and fellow seaside town Exmouth was a huge boost for the area.

However, the town could not have known or ever anticipated the huge journey the team's members would undertake, the heartache they would have to endure and the ultimate triumph they would taste against all the odds.

Hosting was an expensive process and the town needed a loan of £5,000 from South Hams District Council to pay for the infrastructure of the show which it was hoped would attract 5,000 visitors.

On the day there were torrential downpours and chilly conditions. It meant that the excitable and Shakespeare-quoting host Stuart Hall described the day as 'the coldest in *It's a Knockout* history' which

wasn't the type of publicity the town needed, and three thousand unsold tickets was not the financial return the town was hoping for to allow it to repay the 'loan' from the district council.

Dartmouth were triumphant in a nail-biting competition, winning when Sid Davies, Physical Training Instructor at the Britannia Royal Naval College won the 'Castle Capers' game and won the overall competition for the team.

The win set up a visit to Charnock Richard in Lancashire on June 14, for the next round of the British competition and also the chance to go to Portugal for the European competition heat. The win prompted delirious, though very damp celebrations on Coronation Park which had turned into a mud bath.

But it seemed the event and the team's win would be forever tarnished by its financial failure, and the problems deepened when it was revealed the BBC's own employees had been selling tickets on the cheap to make a quick buck.

But the accusations and finger pointing which had begun almost as soon as the broadcast finished, quickly paled into insignificance as tragedy struck.

Team member Barry Wilson, 34, had a heart attack during a training session in May on Coronation Park. Valiant efforts by the team to save him were to no avail, and his death on the park left many of them traumatised and distraught.

Team manager Tim Price told the *Chronicle* Barry had been the team's resident joker who could always lighten the mood: 'Every team needs a member like Barry,' he said.

It looked like the end of the dream.

But then his widow Yvonne visited the team to personally ask them to carry on competing in his memory. Her strength and fortitude in the face of his loss seems to have given them more determination to take part again and do well. They resumed their training with vigour.

The visit to Charnock went well; they were joint winners with Dunfermline, and the town began to look forward to the European Heat in Lisbon. Then it was revealed that the BBC would only pay for the twelve participating team members to go. The group of more than twenty had bonded so much, and supported each other so well over the tragedy many felt it would be a huge disadvantage to only have a few travel.

The town did what it always seems to in times of difficulty: pulled together to overcome a challenge.

The town rallied around to raise the funds needed to get the whole team to Portugal. More than £2,000 flooded in to pay for them in just a couple of weeks, allowing Barry's children and widow Yvonne to go along too.

The team gave an inspired display in the heat of Portugal to come second, and found themselves, thanks to their combined total, the British representatives at the *Jeux sans Frontieres* final in Yugoslavia.

They were the smallest town ever to reach the TV programme's prestigious final, and Dartmouth revelled in their tag as 'underdogs', in true British fashion.

In totally un-British fashion however, they actually won the competition.

The team, high on the unexpected and fantastic nature of their win, flew home to Britain and received universal acclaim – they were and remain the smallest town ever to be crowned winners of the competition. They were received like Royalty in the appropriately named Royal Avenue Gardens and toasted their success with the crowds, no-one quite believing that this small group of dedicated individuals, forged into a team by circumstance and tragedy, had punched above their weight consistently. It was the most positive story of the year and is still a source or pride in the town. A reformed version of the team competed in a special competition at Dartmouth Community College in 2006.

Everyone was delighted to see the magic had not deserted them: they won the competition.

The qualification for the European final was incredible for Dartmouth but not so incredible as actually winning it!

Left: *The summer was not blessed with the best weather, as these holiday makers found out to their cost.*
TOTNES IMAGE BANK/SOUTH HAMS NEWSPAPERS

Right: *The first ever performance by the Red Arrows at Dartmouth Regatta was a major success.*
TOTNES IMAGE BANK/SOUTH HAMS NEWSPAPERS

In February good news appeared with a company called Tidal Marine planning to set up in the old laundry building in Victoria Road. It would employ twenty men using fibreglass to make boats sold through its offices in Chichester and Southampton.

The district council decided to meddle in Regatta and, simply, got everyone's backs up. They decided, perhaps reasonably, that as the fair was on the New Ground car park, which it owns, it should negotiate directly with the managing company Whiteleggs, and take the money. These funds were the main income received by the Regatta, and many felt it would 'kill' the event.

Added to this, the district council decided that after heavy rain had resulted in a heavily cut up surface on Coronation Park, no parking would be allowed on it. Visitors could use the park and ride if they needed somewhere to park.

Chamber of Trade Chairman Frank Rochford said: 'If this goes ahead it will kill off not only Regatta, but the best two weeks trade in the year.'

Brenda Breakwell, town councillor and chairman of the district council told South Hams councillors: 'I have never known anything create as much distress as these recommendations.'

The council, after seeing the huge reaction in the letters pages and in the personal response of everyone involved with the Regatta, quietly overturned the plan in late February.

TOWN 'MOST DRUNKEN'

The town of Dartmouth is never satisfied until it has achieved the very height of perfection in all things – views, Regattas, shipbuilding and… drunkenness?

Yes, after achieving the notable feat of having fourteen out of nineteen drunk and disorderly convictions against it in 1976, ALL those convicted of being drunk and disorderly at Totnes magistrates in 1977 were from Dartmouth. George Lawson, 78, a war veteran left the Red Lion in Dittisham at closing time when his 'foot gave out' in the graveyard, he fell down, smacked his head, and passed out. Despite freezing temperatures he was woken by a passer-by at 6am. He was taken to hospital but just found to be 'a bit cold'.

He wrote a letter to Guinness saying the drink had saved his life – and they fittingly gave him some more.

The Kingswear Quay became the focus of another dispute after owners Darthaven tried to increase the rent for fisherman from £120 to £5,500 pa.

The rent came under fire when the old deal of £120 a year ran out in March. The seventy or so men employed on crabbers that used the quay were desperate

to find a cheaper solution. It was the only area they could use to unload as the Dartmouth side of the river often became inaccessible at low tide. A group of them considered buying it themselves and developing it further as a commercial fish quay. This prompted South Hams District Council to become involved as they felt it should be kept in public ownership.

The arguments over the use of the river and its amenities continued after the DHNA put up its fees to offset rising costs. This incurred the wrath of the Torbay based passenger ferry company Torbay Boat Construction which stated new fees for entering the harbour were 'so great the company has strong doubts as to whether a service to Dartmouth is economically viable, if a satisfactory conclusion cannot be reached they will have to consider terminating landings in Dartmouth.' The group told the *Chronicle* that it was 'not entering the harbour' until the DHNA lowered the charges.

FERRY BAD ARGUMENT

However Tony Freeborn, clerk to the DHNA, said that the company had been 'told' not to enter the harbour by them until they paid up and had actually been entering against those instructions. He said: 'In the past these boats have been paying a ludicrously low fee without contributing to the upkeep of the river.'

He said that the boats would be confiscated and sold if they continued to enter the harbour.

The DHNA were also arguing with Dart Pleasure Craft (DPC), who ran the passenger ferry. For the first year since the company had taken over the service, the DHNA had charged it 10 per cent of its turnover for using the pontoons. The authority wished that to remain the same, but in September, DPC asked for a reduction prompting DHNA to call in a mediator.

Mr Freeborn said that the pontoons were too expensive to run and that DPC owed the DHNA '£3,000, possibly more' for landing on the pontoons.

The mediator took until 1979 to make his decision, leaving an uneasy standoff between the two organisations.

Dartmouth police confirmed the old saying that 'a few troublemakers that give the rest a bad name' – when nineteen burglaries were attributed to just four teenagers.

The boys broke into varied premises including a supermarket, a Townstal store, Norton Park holiday camp, the Britannia Royal Naval College and St Clement's Church hall.

The prosecutor said that the raids were 'carefully planned' by the group. They had to pay £500 compensation and court costs.

Round-the-World yachtswoman Naomi James triumphantly returns to Dartmouth in June.
SOUTH HAMS NEWSPAPERS

NAOMI HOME

Naomi James with her husband Rob about to tour the town on her return.
TOTNES IMAGE BANK/
SOUTH HAMS NEWSPAPERS

Dame Naomi James. See Feature on page 147

Not in the least bit tempted to cause trouble, Kingswear yachtswoman Naomi James sailed into harbour, not quite the first woman to sail single-handed Round-the-World, but certainly the fastest.

Mrs James, 29, had undertaken the 15,000 mile round trip in 272 days, beating the record of Sir Francis Chichester by two days.

She was the first woman to complete the circumnavigation via Cape Horn, a place she admitted 'scared me a lot'. Her boat, *Express Crusader*, owned by Kingswear's other famous sailor Chay Blyth, underwent a serious beating but looked fantastic as she sailed into the harbour at 9.30am on June 8 to a heroine's welcome.

Hoards of people greeted her as she sailed into Dartmouth with a flotilla of boats milling around her as she made her way in. The park and ride was brought back for the day to cope with the visitors who came down to see her arrive.

Her Majesty's Band of the Royal Marines played as she stepped ashore and she was driven around the town in an open top car to wave and smile at the assembled throng. The church bells of the town rang out as she arrived and the carnival atmosphere infected all, the *Chronicle* said she was 'radiant' and she 'captured everyone's heart with her big friendly smile and cheerful wave at a time when she must have been ready for some peace and quiet.'

The amazing year for Mrs James was rounded off with the announcement she would be made a Dame Commander of the British Empire in the Queen's New Year's Honours list.

Perhaps not willing to be outdone, her husband Rob announced the week after her triumphant return that he would be undertaking the Round Britain race with Kingswear super-sailor Chay Blyth.

This brought another big day to the town when the Duchess of Kent arrived to name the pair's new trimaran *Great Britain IV*.

The Duchess presided with regal calm over proceedings when hoards of people again lined the streets of the town, hoping she would stop and talk. Her magic touch seemed to work as Chay and Rob won the race.

Chay Blyth.
See Feature on
page 129

NEW WING FOR HOSPITAL

In June the Dartmouth and Kingswear Hospital League of Friends got good news that the new geriatric wing would be built in 1979.

The cost of the scheme was suggested to be around £135,000 with Torbay Health District bearing the brunt of the costs and the League of Friends agreeing to help with the purchasing of equipment. However, by late July, the estimated cost had grown to £250,000 and the health authority said it would not pay more than £165,000. Fears were understandably raised that the wing would never be built.

The Friends agreed in November to guarantee half the extra costs of the build, on condition 'work begins by July 1979'. This represented a huge gamble on behalf of the committee, as they had just over £19,000 in their coffers and needed to raise £10,000 in six months. The fundraising again got underway and by December the Friends had now got a balance of £27,000. The hard work paid off and in the last weeks of 1978 the health authority agreed to build the wing. Irene Scawn called it 'the best possible Christmas present.'

The Carnival was a great success, but only just got together a committee to organise the 1979 event. The Mayor and Carnival Chairman John Tremlett made very public appeals for more people to join the committee. Seventeen people turned up to the subsequent public meeting and ten joined the committee.

The 133rd Regatta was a roaring success, attracting more people than ever before thanks to the appearance of the Red Arrows for the first time. The *Chronicle* said the display was 'astonishing'.

Their appearance did elicit one complaint about the noise but, as the *Chronicle* said, that was 'soon forgotten'.

Flooding hit the
town in February
1979.
JIM COZENS

1979 World Events

● Ayatollah Ruhollah Khomeini returns to Tehran, Iran after nearly fifteen years of exile

● Philips demonstrates Compact Disc publicly for the first time

● Margaret Thatcher becomes the country's first female prime minister

● Lord Mountbatten of Burma and three others are assassinated by the Provisional Irish Republican Army.

Above: *Crowds gather in the Royal Avenue Gardens for the St George's Day Parade.*
Totnes Image Bank/South Hams Newspapers

1979 Industrial action, a headache throughout the 1970s, reared its head in the town in January.

Forty three workers from TTB Fabrications went on strike over the long running dispute over bonuses and pay rises.

The argument was over basic wages – the 'minimum wage' was £60 per week for a skilled labourer, but the company were only paying £54.

TTB agreed to pay the £60 a week, but said £3 of this would have to come from the worker's bonus payments.

Union representative Francis Hawke said: 'The management is giving with one hand and taking with other. By the time tax has been taken off the increase there will only be enough left for a pint of beer.'

The strike went on for two weeks before an agreement was made to raise the workers' wages to £58.50 and leave the bonus untouched.

Everyone was hit when the National Union of Public Employees went on strike at the end of January. The Lower Ferry stopped and rubbish was not collected.

National strikes took their toll on the town, not least from haulage drivers, who impeded deliveries already hard hit by the inclement weather.

NO PAPER? NO PROBLEM

This caused a problem for the *Chronicle*, indeed the whole *Gazette* series, as there was no paper to print on. They decided that they just had to use seven point lettering and fit more stories on the page. You had trouble reading them though.

Blackpool Sands 'disappeared' in late January after strong southwesterly winds washed away most of its beach.

Onlookers commented that the waves which removed the beach had even broken over the café and conditions could only be described as 'treacherous'. The front walls of the café were knocked down and the café itself was flooded just a week later.

Fears for trade in the summer, which the continuing economic crisis had already put in jeopardy, grew substantially around the attraction.

However, Lady Newman, owner of the beach, said: 'a similar shift occurred in 1963, but returned in time for summer.' She was right and it was back in all its glory.

The traditional start of the 'season' proved a bumper success. Long periods of foul weather all across the country up until April meant that when the first truly warm weekend came at Easter the crowds flocked to the seaside. Dartmouth's Easter weekend 'broke all records' delighting the business community.

However, strikes and oil crisis' took their toll and the petrol dried up. The summer threatened to grind to a complete halt after holidaymakers stayed put, not confident the petrol they had would last to get them all the way to Devon, and then not sure if there would be any petrol here to get them back.

On a happier note, following on from Naomi James' amazing Round-the-World antics; Dartmouth now seemed to have an export industry in brave and reckless sailors.

Shirley Ravenscroft, 53, became the first grandmother to sail across the Atlantic single-handed. She suffered many setbacks, including concussion and severe bruising in a force ten gale and a husband who pleaded with her to turn around. The achievement is made all the more impressive when it was learned that two years before her crossing Mrs Ravenscroft was 'crippled' with arthritis.

'For the first two weeks I was terrified,' she said, 'but once I hit the trade winds the voyage was like a journey through paradise and I arrived exactly where I planned.'

She said she would not sail single-handed Round-the-World because she would 'get terribly bored'. She claimed the journey had helped her lose two stone and said she 'hadn't felt so well since I was a teenager.'

MORE FERRY WOES

The passenger ferry cut its service back after an arbitration panel forced it to pay more for the use of the Dartmouth and Kingswear pontoons than it could afford. The panel was looking at claims from both the Dart Harbour and Navigation Authority and Dart Pleasure Craft who ran the passenger ferry.

In its first year of operation the company paid 10 per cent of its turnover to use the pontoons. The DHNA wanted this to continue, but DPC wanted to reduce it to 2.5 per cent. The dispute began at the beginning of 1978 and was not resolved until February 1979 when Devon County Council decided the amount paid should be 7.5 per cent of turnover.

The decision meant that DPC had effectively lost £2,000 during 1978. The DPC Director Arthur McLoughlin said: 'We are being victimised, singled out by the authority. We are very disappointed at the outcome and have no option but to cut the service.' The company then announced prices would also be rising by 5p to 20p for a crossing, and that sailings would stop at 6pm during the winter.

The town entered the 'Britain in Bloom' competition for the first time after years of efforts to get behind such an idea.

Left: *Mark Wingett and Jack Wild on location in Dartmouth filming the children's television series* The Ravelled Thread. TOTNES IMAGE BANK/SOUTH HAMS NEWSPAPERS

Right: *Star Robert James about to film in* The Ravelled Thread *which filmed in and around Dartmouth for a number of weeks.* TOTNES IMAGE BANK/SOUTH HAMS NEWSPAPERS

Left: *Transatlantic sailor and grandmother Shirley Ravenscroft is welcomed home by her family and the Mayor Dennis Woods.*
TOTNES IMAGE BANK/SOUTH HAMS NEWSPAPERS

Right: *The Royal Avenue Gardens were full to bursting point for the Town Week Olde Worlde Fayre.*
TOTNES IMAGE BANK/SOUTH HAMS NEWSPAPERS

After a public meeting brought a very poor response town Mayor Dennis Woods, took a new tack. He invited all the town's organisations to send one representative to the Mayor's parlour for an 'informal meeting' and gained enough sponsorship to launch a bid. The town began to prepare in February for the judging in June and competition fever began to take hold, bringing more and more secret gardeners out of the woodwork.

The effort paid off with the town winning the Gordon Ford trophy for Outstanding Effort in the competition. Cllr Woods pointed out it was 'very unusual' for a town to win something at the first attempt and said he hoped it inspired the town to enter again.

An election in May was called after the prolonged economic problems faced by the Labour Government.

Mrs Thatcher was thrust into No 10 with a huge swing and Totnes went to the Tories in the party's biggest ever poll in the constituency, 35,010 votes, nearly 11,000 ahead of the Liberals. Mr Mawby called it a 'vote of confidence in Mrs Thatcher'.

DON'T LIKE THE NOISE?
DON'T OPEN YOUR WINDOWS DURING REGATTA

A single complaint from a woman in Clarence Hill at Regatta prompted the district council to attempt to curb amplified music in the Royal Avenue Gardens. The complainant guaranteed herself hate mail and abuse in the street after the *Chronicle* printed her name in connection with the complaint about the Regatta Rock party during the 1978 event. Council officers attended, took readings and agreed that the noise levels were unreasonable. They decided to ban public announcement systems in the Gardens from 7pm throughout the year.

The decision was relayed to the town council in June 1979 which was quick in its condemnation of the move. Mayor Dennis Woods, recently returned as Mayor for a second term, said: 'To close down at 7pm is ridiculous. These events are designed for the greatest happiness of the greatest number of people.'

Brenda Breakwell said: 'This is just one person whipping up a storm in a teacup and the attitude is thoroughly out of proportion.'

Miss Breakwell said that anyone who didn't like the noise should either 'put up with it or arrange to go away during the time they are taking place.'

Below: *Blackpool Sands after a storm washed away most of the beach.*
TOTNES IMAGE BANK/SOUTH HAMS NEWSPAPERS

CHAY BLYTH *Sailor*

(See year 1978)

The first sailor to be truly associated with Dartmouth, in the era when sailing Round-the-World was a challenge in itself, rather than a requirement of a job, was Chay Blyth.

The former Royal Marine had won the British Empire Medal after being part of the first pair to row across the Atlantic Ocean. He then decided, after very little experience of sailing in crews, that he would sail single-handed Round-the-World, against the prevailing winds. The feat, in 1970 when he left, was considered suicide, and many predicted he would never make it home.

Blyth knew the risks and decided he wanted to use the safest, strongest boat he could, so decided that he wanted it built of steel. The fame of Philip & Son on the river Dart as a shipbuilder of steel vessels was widespread, and Blyth handed the contract to the yard in 1970, confident the yard's workmen would do him proud.

They did.

Taking George Clark's design they produced a yacht both classic in its lines and at the time revolutionary in the way it was constructed and kitted out. Blyth took the yacht on its 'impossible' journey and returned 292 days later, triumphant and in an unscathed boat. He told the world it was incredibly well constructed.

The yacht began a long association with Dartmouth, where it was used as a training yacht, eventually bought by the 'Super Yachtsman' Pete Goss.

The Duchess of Kent names Chay Blyth's Great Britain IV *in Dartmouth in 1978.*
TOTNES IMAGE BANK/SOUTH HAMS NEWSPAPERS

Chay Blyth sailing on the Dart.
TOTNES IMAGE BANK/SOUTH HAMS NEWSPAPERS

When his *Team Philips* project failed so spectacularly, *British Steel* was handed to creditors. It still sits on a mooring in Kingswear, a proud and lasting tribute to the bravery of Blyth, but also to the workmanship of the shipwrights and steel workers of the river Dart. Later honoured, is now Sir Charles Blyth CBE CBM but will always be known as Chay Blyth.

The improbably named Gay Abbott had to face accusations of loud and anti social behaviour.
TOTNES IMAGE BANK/SOUTH HAMS NEWSPAPERS

A storm nearly caused this tree to come down on the Bandstand in the Royal Avenue Gardens.
TOTNES IMAGE BANK/SOUTH HAMS NEWSPAPERS

Edward Fox caused quite a stir when he visited the Guildhall to meet the Mayor.
TOTNES IMAGE BANK/SOUTH HAMS NEWSPAPERS

The wasteland formerly occupied by the council engineering works was wanted for development.
TOTNES IMAGE BANK/SOUTH HAMS NEWSPAPERS

Blacksmith Alan Middleton with the penknife he prepared for Prince Charles when he visited the town in 1979.
TOTNES IMAGE BANK/SOUTH HAMS NEWSPAPERS

The New Zealand 'Suburbs Team' perform a Haka before their match with Dartmouth, which they won convincingly.
TOTNES IMAGE BANK/SOUTH HAMS NEWSPAPERS

The outbursts won the day and the district council decided to back down because of the 'tradition behind the events.'

The school hall, named after Chairman of the school governors Harold White, was opened in July – nearly nineteen months late.

The hall had been in the middle of construction, ten months behind schedule already in October 1978, when the company building it went into administration.

The county council spent months trying to find a contractor to finish the work, of which only four weeks was needed, but only managed to find one in May. The hall helped the school truly become 'comprehensive' with sports and meeting facilities at the Milton Lane site for the first time.

The Regatta, flush with the knowledge that the Red Arrows were returning to boost visitor numbers, had a badge of office made for the Regatta Chairman. This was worn proudly by John Bowden for the first time at the opening ceremony – 145 years after the first event. The committee obviously got behind the idea of self-promotion by printing up tee-shirts available for the first time too.

The Regatta, the last of the decade, proved a huge success, with the town packed throughout the week and the Red Arrows pulling out all the stops.

It is not often a local paper has to report real tragedy, but the death of Leonie Clare, known to all as 'Mimi', can only be called that.

Mrs Clare was killed just six days after her marriage to Lt Troy Clare RN at Britannia Royal Naval College. Mimi was killed when a motor cruiser struck the yacht they were sailing in Monaco for their honeymoon in August. Both were thrown into the water by the impact, but Mimi was thrown forwards and was struck by the cruiser's propeller. Mimi's husband retrieved her body and brought it to shore.

She was buried after a service in the Britannia Royal Naval College chapel just days after she had been married there.

Top left, top right and above left: *Eddie Kidd puts his life on the line for the crowds around Coronation Park.*
TOTNES IMAGE BANK/SOUTH HAMS NEWSPAPERS

Above right: *A car performs a stunt on Coronation Park as part of the visit from Eddie Kidd.*
TOTNES IMAGE BANK/SOUTH HAMS NEWSPAPERS

Right: *Prince Andrew surveys the view from Britannia Royal Naval College as he begins his training.*
TOTNES IMAGE BANK/SOUTH HAMS NEWSPAPERS

PRINCE ENJOYS HI-JINKS AT BRNC

Prince Andrew arrived at Dartmouth ready to begin six months of training at the Britannia Royal Naval College. He joined Hawke Division in order to become part of the Fleet Air Arm of the Royal Navy.

He made a more formal entry to the College than many cadets and certainly more formal than his brother Prince Charles who had arrived in his Aston Martin two days after the rest of the College in 1971.

However, as the other cadets arrived on the parade ground in coaches, Prince Andrew, 19, arrived with his kit in a blue Rolls Royce.

His training, the College promised, would ensure he got 'the same treatment as all the other midshipmen'.

Rather than have a 'news blackout' as it did for Prince Charles, the paper kept readers updated, in a modest way. It seemed a little news often stopped people from being too curious about the Midshipman's time at the 'cradle of the navy'.

The world's press made a meal of the Prince's taking part in the 'drills' tradition on the parade ground in October, where he was dressed in pyjamas for part of it, but bless the *Chronicle* as it refused to print the pictures.

Christmas proved an unhappy one for many Dartmothians, despite efforts by the Chamber of Trade to boost trade in the town. A burst water main in Victoria Road meant many were without water on Christmas morning.

Add to this the mysterious disappearance of Arthur and Stuart Rendell in the middle of the month whilst picking winkles along the river. They disappeared, leaving a boat and some remnants of clothing, but little else. It was thought at the time that they had been cut off by the tide and tried to swim for shore, and were then both sucked into the mud and drowned. Finally to add to all this the news that Philip & Son were increasing fares by 20p for cars for the Higher Ferry, from 60 to 80p, it was all enough to make Dartmothians weep as they sang Auld Lang Syne. Happy 1980!

CHAPTER IV
A Decade of Promises
1980s

SOME OF THEM KEPT

The Eighties began with the town still suffering the effects of the economic turmoil of the Seventies but with more hope than for a while. However, the recession in engineering did little for the town's major employers on the Townstal industrial estate.

The decade also saw a major series of proposals for the town, some saner than others, some desperately needed and some mystifying in their purpose. The only thing they had in common was the fact that each one was argued about in detail in the pages of the paper.

The main project to be undertaken was the mammoth Embankment renovation with flood defences and a sewerage scheme. The Royalty cinema was also demolished and replaced with a new health centre offering services the town had desperately needed for years.

The town also got new fire and ambulance stations on College Way, giving both services the kind of headquarters their professional workers deserved.

Of those that never came to fruition the river-based car park and sewage processing centre, a car park on Coronation Park and the ill-fated 'inner relief road' – which no one ever proved an actual use for – are notable for the enormous reaction they caused in the *Chronicle's* pages, especially through residents' letters to the editor.

The Dart Deep Water Quay at Noss set new records for prolonged, embarrassing and doomed efforts to keep a project going. The discussions and arguments lasted the best part of a decade.

The decade saw more changes with the paper as Tindle Newspapers, owned by Ray Tindle, OBE, bought South Hams Newspapers in November 1986, although the *Chronicle* claimed the purchase would result in no changes.

The 1980s were a 'can-do' decade and people dreamt and fought for what they felt would help their community. It was certainly a dynamic period but more than that, it was ten years in which everyone in Dartmouth felt the town could change for the better.

The Onedin Line *ended after ninety one episodes with the final screening on October 26, 1980.*

Dartmouth as a Film and TV Location.
See Feature on pages 64-65

RADIO TIMES

1980 World Events

● U.S. President Jimmy Carter announces that the United States will boycott the 1980 Summer Olympics in Moscow

● Iran Embassy siege in London

● Mount St. Helens erupts in Washington, killing fifty seven and causing US$3 billion in damage

● British Leyland launches its new Metro

● John Lennon is murdered in New York

1980

The decade began with the dramatic story of a fire on board the ship *Butaseis*, carrying 740 tons of butane gas, resulting in it being dubbed the 'floating bomb'.

All Dartmouth's retained firemen answered the call and went out onto the ship in Torbay to fight the fire during the last weekend of 1979. They had to endure 'indescribable heat' and saw their oxygen running out fifteen minutes early because the terrible conditions caused them to gasp so much for breath.

Two teams, one led by Leading Firefighter Terry Millman and one by Station Officer Peter Denning, helped subdue the flames even coming through a dangerous moment when diesel fuel on the water around the ship ignited.

Mr Denning said: 'I am very proud of them all, conditions on the boat had to be seen to be believed and they did a first class job.'

It was not too long before people started to seek political capital out of such a dramatic incident. Tony Rogers, who happened to be looking to become the parliamentary candidate for the Liberal party in the South Hams, came forward to say the situation was much more dangerous than had been reported and that no one should have been allowed to go on board.

Confusingly he also said that the ship, had it exploded, would have caused incalculable damage to the Torbay area, which is why, of course, men brave enough were sent to stop it doing so.

Parents of pupils at Dartmouth Primary School got angry when its opening times were changed – to fit the bus timetables.

Western National changed the timings of their bus runs so that the earliest bus which could bring the 150 school children to the Milton Lane site would arrive at 9.10am. The school day was changed accordingly to start at 9.15 am.

Parents at the school were still not satisfied.

The County Council, as the Local Education Authority responsible for the school, said it was 'not happy' about the changes either, but it had 'no choice'.

Council officers also decided that this *really* was *the* time to tell parents that the traditional subsidy for school travel was being taken away from April that year which would result in doubling the charge paid by most families.

Parent, Sally Jenkinson said she was angry no consultation had taken place.

'I am angry at the cavalier way the county has run roughshod over us,' she said. 'Many parents have to go to work and the two weeks notice given to us is simply not sufficient to allow alternative arrangements to be made.'

FRENCH ADMIRAL'S WAR

Kingswear was visited in November by French Vice Admiral d'Escardre de Cazanova from where he had operated a Motor Torpedo Boat during the war.

The Second World War was still within the experience of most people in the town, and the Admiral's visit, to the famous HMS *Cicala* – in fact the Royal Dart Hotel (which Lord Haw Haw had announced as being 'sunk' by the Nazis) – and other important buildings which had sheltered the Free French in the harbour during the war, was deemed a great success.

A life and death situation, which brought home how a connection with the sea could put people in danger, also took place that month.

Dartmouth trawler mate Will Gillespie was reunited with his wife Clare after his boat *Piete Anje* sank and he spent hours in a life raft.

Several of his crew mates died during the accident. He looked relieved in the pictures of the couple at their home.

The trawler capsized in heavy seas off Start Point in November, and was the first of a number of near misses and deaths linked to Dartmouth during the 1980s. It was a reminder of how dangerous fishing was, along with any job linked to the sea.

Stoke Fleming celebrated the 100th birthday of the woman they called the village's 'Queen Mother' – Keturah Forster. She was pictured surrounded by her great grandchildren grinning like the cat who got the cream, and who could blame her? She lived through twenty one years of Queen Victoria's reign.

Mayor and Mayoress Miss Irene Scawn and Mrs Viola Smith, along with deputy Mayor and Mayoress Mr and Mrs Fred Tremlett delivered more than 200 presents to various good causes all over the area in a special Christmas giveaway. The recipients included eighty housebound people and seventeen old people's homes, along with the traditional Christmas Day visit to Dartmouth Hospital.

The Christmas time goodwill was not in the air when Town Cllr Eric Cook was accused of trying to take money from the Council. His firm was in charge of the maintenance of the Christmas lights. The Director of Public Prosecutions decided to take no action after it was discovered that 'errors' amounting to £550 had been found in the bill submitted to the Council.

Free French Motor Torpedo Boats (MTBs) and their depot ship HMS Belfort moored alongside their Hoodown headquarters during the Second World War.
DAVE GRIFFITHS

Mr Cook agreed the sum and paid it back. This conclusion served as just an appetiser for many who felt this kind of 'mistake' should not go unpunished.

His fellow town councillor Capt Fred Hewitt demanded an apology in a stormy Council Chamber but found no support from his fellow councillors in the demand. Cllr Brenda Breakwell commented the investigation had been for both 'the council's and Mr Cook's good' and that no apology was needed. He gave none.

Of a less controversial nature, 'Dartmouth in Bloom' celebrated the news it had won its second cup in the 'Britain in Bloom' competition – in its second year of entry.

In 1979 the town won the Gordon Ford Trophy – and in 1980 it took home the Sargent Cup for outstanding effort and achievement after scoring highly with judges, although not highly enough to go forward to the national final. The town's participation was in itself a minor miracle, after years of failed attempts to mobilise the town to take part throughout the 1970s.

Dartmouth was revealed as being on the list of targets for the Russians in the event of a nuclear war – but no one was really sure why.

Although a training establishment for the Royal Navy, most thought that there was no real reason to attack the BRNC – unless the 1905 building hid a few secrets.

The MoD were remaining tight lipped – they told reporter Steve Peacock to 'ask the Russians' why the town was targeted – and rumours spread that it held some sort of Command Centre for operations after Armageddon – if there remained anyone to command of course. Everyone apart from the MoD just said 'we don't know why' or 'I can't really talk about that'.

The only person who seemed prepared to make a definite statement was 'nuclear tactics expert' Brigadier Thomas Helby who said, rather cheerfully, that if the town was hit directly 'there wouldn't be anything left. The whole countryside would be thick with radiation.'

ROYAL VISIT

The town was lucky enough to be visited by a number of Royals during the year – Princess Anne, Prince Andrew, the Queen and Prince Philip all came to the town. The Queen's visit for Lord High Admiral's Divisions in April was a big success. The motor cavalcade in which the Royal couple were travelling stopped unexpectedly when an 11 year old schoolboy ran into the road carrying a bunch of flowers. Her Majesty ordered the car to stop, rolled down her window and took the posies from the excited child.

The Long Road to a Heated Swimming Pool – and then the Long Road to a Heated, Covered Swimming Pool

(See year 1987)

Perhaps nothing sums up the never-say-die attitude of Dartmothians like the campaign to build a covered swimming pool in the town.

First suggested in 1949, the different schemes to raise funds for it were highly imaginative; from recycling paper and foil, to the sixpence a week plan, to the *Happy Families* cards (used on the endpapers in this book) which featured such notables as Killer the Chemist, Blewitt the bookie and of course Drew the artist...

Mr Drew's card from Dartmouth's Happy Families *fundraising game pack.*

MR. DREW

The Artist

Above: *Members of Dartmouth Swimming Club enjoying a dip at Castle Cove.*

The pool was first suggested in 1949 and a plan to start fundraising towards a pool was put together.

After a strong start, the support began to wane, and by the mid-Fifties the group considered disbanding and circulating the few pounds that had been collected amongst other town organisations.

But this was rejected in May 1958 and a new 'sixpence a week' scheme was suggested: every household in Dartmouth was to give sixpence every week until there was enough for a pool.

An overwhelming majority at the packed meeting voted for the scheme, which it was hoped would bring in £1,300 in two years to use to get a bid going for a pool, hopefully somewhere around the lower town – sites were suggested on Mayors Avenue, one on the site of the community greenhouse.

The plans kept being discussed, the sixpences kept being collected, and yet the town seemed no closer to a covered, heated swimming pool.

In the 1960s constant closures of Castle Cove brought a strengthening of resolve: campaigners really rolled their sleeves up and decided to do more.

More fundraising schemes, the recycling and special events among them, were organised to bring in cash, and when the 1970s dawned

there was again renewed hope. The committee started to look seriously at sites with the help of the local councils, first the borough council and later the town council in conjunction with South Hams District Council which came into being in 1974.

The Mayors Avenue site near to the Embankment seemed to be the best option and plans were drawn up.

Everything seemed to be going well – the plans were in place, the councils' were in agreement, there was enough money in the bank; nothing seemed able to stand in the way of Dartmouth's dream pool being built.

Except that there was: inflation.

The economic and social chaos that engulfed the mid to late 1970s resulted in double figure inflation from 1974 through to 1981. The budget for the pool, basic though its specifications were, was out of date before it had been approved. The cost of building the pool was moving ahead of the committee too fast – they couldn't raise money to fill the hole left by rampant cost increases.

It seems to have broken the resolve of the committee – which effectively disbanded, leaving £7,000 in an account with no campaign to spend it.

The plans seemed ruined forever. But then a new committee got together in 1985 and decided the chance was again there to build a pool on the Milton Lane school site. It was thought that with the help of the Local Education Authority and new funding streams the dream was indeed again possible.

The campaign got up and running very quickly and plans were submitted almost sooner

Taking the plunge in 1987 after thirty eight years waiting.... Sᴏᴜᴛʜ Hᴀᴍs Nᴇᴡsᴘᴀᴘᴇʀs

than anyone could have hoped. The funding was agreed and construction began in late 1986.

There was a last minute panic when campaigners realised the plans meant effectively a covered pool was an impossibility unless the foundations were strengthened. But stronger foundations cost money, and they didn't have enough. Step forward the old committee, who brought in the £7,000 left in its account to provide stronger foundations, in readiness for the addition of a roof in later years.

The pool opened in July 1987 to great fanfare and huge celebration, with many claiming the wait for a pool was over after thirty eight years. Though strangely the committee decided to 'finish' the pool without changing rooms, so the first couple of years students were forced to get changed in the College and run across the car park to the pool.

After nearly twenty years of good service, it became clear that the Milton Lane site was coming to the end of its useful life, and the campaign for a pool became a topic of discussion and argument yet again in the new Millennium.

Hopes it could be included in the planned sports centre were dashed when South Hams District Council negotiators made it clear they would not discuss one.

Then a survey in 2004, conducted by the Market and Coastal Town's Initiative group, formed to kick start community projects in the area, found that for local people a swimming pool was the number one priority – the people demanded a pool.

This was the spur that got the new campaign going, and although there have been many set backs, it started to gain momentum.

The group gained £1.5 million from Devon County Council in December 2008 and a pledge for £400,000 from South Hams District Council few months later. The pool committee used these pledges of support to go for funding from Sport England for the remainder of the funds.

The fundraising continued throughout 2010. Popular events and a strong community support seemed to be giving it again a fighting chance of coming to fruition.

But there was to be no Christmas 'ground breaking' ceremony as some had hoped, and the project went into 2011 still hoping, but with no final agreement to build.

The town was shocked in late April by the death of ex-restaurant owner John Way – whose body was found in the burnt out remains of his Northford Road home. Mr Way had just that week been charged with criminal damage, and had been suffering from alcoholism. His condition had become so bad that he had been forced to sell his successful Tall Ships restaurant in the town. After the sale – three months before his death – the police had been called out on sixty eight separate occasions to deal with fracas between Mr Way and his estranged wife.

On the night he died he had managed to run his car into the river Dart, verbally abused and threatened friends and three separate policemen – one of whom had gone into his home to put out a fire caused by an electric heater put too near Mr Way's bed. Mr Way shouted at the officer until he left. Not long after the police and fire brigade were called to the Studio Flat where the fire was so ferocious it threatened to engulf nearby properties. The coroner concluded Mr Way had 186 milligrams of alcohol in every 100 millilitres of his blood which is more than double the 2010 drink-drive limit.

It seemed tragedy would be linked with alcohol in this year: Lower Ferry Captain Robert Floyd, 48, drowned after falling out of a small launch at the end of his shift.

Mr Floyd had been celebrating the birthday of his colleague and had drunk three and a half pints of beer, three whiskies and two vodkas whilst on duty.

After the end of their shift Mr Floyd dropped off colleague William Farrand in Kingswear and then headed back across the river to Dartmouth. Mr Farrand soon heard the launch going round in circles and raised the alarm. The 16 foot-long clinker-built boat was later found in rocks with its engine still running. A huge search was launched but called off due to bad weather. Mr Floyd's body was found floating in the river the next morning.

THE FRENCH LIEUTENANT'S WOMAN

The Lower Ferry stopped running for the filming of *The French Lieutenant's Woman* in Kingswear.

The high-profile film, starring Jeremy Irons and Meryl Streep filmed in the village in October and by all accounts made a major impression.

The Steam Packet Inn was transformed into Endicotts Hotel, the Royal Dart Hotel and Railway Station were repainted and the low wall on the river side of the street was faced with imitation stone. The streets were paved with imitation rubber cobbles for good measure.

The changes were intended to make the village look as if it were straight out of 1880 – and was perfectly timed out of season to give a big boost to the town's economy and also not disturb the holidaymakers with the stopping of the Lower Ferry.

The filmmakers had originally asked to film in summer, in the middle of the peak season, stopping the ferry at its busiest time.

Dartmouth as a Film and TV Location. See Feature on pages 64–65

Town councillors and local business people complained this was commercial suicide in a summer already blighted by terrible weather. All breathed a huge sigh of relief when filming in Dorset on the project overran and pushed the Kingswear date back.

Everyone was even happier when an Indian summer in September and early October allowed Bed & Breakfast premises and all the other businesses in the town to claw back some income.

Sean Tucker of Dittisham earned the respect of all, and an award for bravery, when he went under the knife for closed heart surgery. 9 year old Sean came through looking none the worse for wear – his picture in the *Chronicle* proving a bright and happy story after fears for his safety ever since his birth.

1981 The programme *It's a Knockout* was massive in the early 80s, and excitement reached fever pitch when it was announced that the programme would come to Dartmouth and take over Coronation Park.

The day was cold wet and miserable – the programme's presenter Stuart Hall was not impressed – and it made a massive loss for the town. However, against the odds the team won thanks to a valiant effort from Sid Davies, the PT Instructor at the Britannia Royal Naval College.

While training for the next heat in the competition, team member Barry Wilson collapsed and died of a heart attack. The team nearly gave up the whole thing – until his widow Yvonne asked them to continue in his memory. Team manager Tim Price and the 'Dartmouth Dozen' as they were known, decided to carry on.

And they did Barry proud.

They came through the European heats in Portugal to eventually win the 'Jeux Sans Frontiers' title in Yugoslavia – the smallest town ever to do so. To say their reception on returning to Dartmouth was rapturous is an understatement.

The new extension to the Dartmouth and Kingswear Hospital was finally begun in June paid for with £30,000 from the town's League of Friends.

The extension had taken eight years to get off the ground and the difference in costs showed how high inflation had affected the cost of living in 1973 the cost had been estimated at £62,000 in 1981 it was around £340,000.

The work was barely begun however, when cracks began appearing in the sea wall.

The contractors, while admitting the building posed some difficult challenges namely having to drive piles 40 feet down to find solid ground on the reclaimed land said the cracks were nothing to do with them.

However, after the initial hiccups the extension ran to schedule with the new bridge from one building to another provided two new six-bed wards, a day/dining room and ancillary rooms.

Nuclear fears brought the autumn's hot topic – the plans of local authorities in the event of a nuclear attack.

Dr Steven Huggett of Plymouth sent a request to sixty southwest councils asking what plans they had in the event of an attack. He got thirteen replies.

Dartmouth was one of those councils which replied. Reacting to that reply Dr Huggett said: '[The Council] have made no preparations as far as I can tell and they don't intend to.'

The article in November about the good Doctor's enquiries created a long running debate in the pages of the *Chronicle* in the form of letters, some of them from Caroline Drew who stated: All residents have the right to know the details of whatever post-holocaust activities may have been mapped out for them by councillors.

This prompted a reply from ex-councillor Charles Fitch-Northern in Kingswear, informing the town that a Nuclear plan had been in place since the 1960s, and that it was most competent. He said that he had been on the committee that put

The It's a Knockout *team in training.*
TOTNES IMAGE BANK/ SOUTH HAMS NEWSPAPERS

It's a Knockout TV Game Show comes to Dartmouth. See Feature on pages 120–121

Left: *The Queen Mother visits Dartmouth.*
TOTNES IMAGE BANK/ SOUTH HAMS NEWSPAPERS

Right: *The Queen Mother is presented with a bouquet in Dartmouth while Mayor Irene Scawn looks on.*
TOTNES IMAGE BANK/ SOUTH HAMS NEWSPAPERS

the plan together and outlined, in great detail, how the Soviets missiles were a great threat and in the event of a strike, a secret plan, known only by a few, was essential to maintaining Law and Order and avoid looting and sabotage.

He also accused Mrs Drew of being part of a plan by the Soviets, who had organised a peace movement to prevent the deployment of Cruise missiles and Pershings as a deterrent to their SS20s. Whenever this Peace orchestra plays, the fellow travellers and the CND begin to dance to the Soviet tune. He went on to say that the success of the CND or Labour would reduce our survival time after a nuclear strike from years to weeks.

Mrs Drew also replied to his points at length, making an impassioned plea for disarmament, and also making the salient point: 'I cant help thinking that after the holocaust looting and sabotage with be the least terrible of all our problems in the unlikely event, that is, of anyone surviving at all.'

QUEEN MUM DELIGHTS THE CROWDS

The Queen Mum came to Dartmouth on April 9 – and the town turned out in force to greet her. She was there for Lord High Admiral's Divisions, but took in a walk around the town and even found time to visit Major General Sir Julian and Lady Gascoigne in Stoke Fleming for a 'private visit'.

She arrived on the Royal Yacht *Britannia*, which was welcomed by a 21-gun-salute, with the crew lined up in view of the crowds and with a band playing on deck. The *Chronicle* reported that the yacht turned at the Higher Ferry and that 'as she made her way back the sun suddenly broke through the mist to add the finishing touch to the Royal occasion'.

After bringing perfect weather, the Queen Mother swept through crowds that had been gathering since early in the morning to the Guildhall to meet the 'town's dignitaries' and hundreds of excited school children.

There would have been no red carpet for the Royal lady to walk on, if it had not been for the athletic efforts of Rose and Chris Routley. The carpet shop-owning couple were called on at the eleventh hour to find something appropriate. The piece that the town council had been promised did not turn up, so Mr Routley was forced to run through the streets with some replacement under his arm, cheered on by the enthusiastic crowds.

The *Chronicle* called the Queen Mother, a 'real mum' who 'put people before her tight schedule', and whose smile 'never wavered'.

Not quite so popular was an amusement arcade proposed for Mayors Avenue. It caused consternation in the town, and prompted a public inquiry at the Guildhall.

Countade, a company from Manchester, tried to challenge a decision by South Hams District Council to refuse planning permission.

The Dartmouth
Chronicle *welcomes the
Queen Mother to
the town.*
TOTNES IMAGE
BANK/ SOUTH HAMS
NEWSPAPERS

The main bone of contention seemed not to be the actual amusement centre itself – the town seemed to be universally against it – but that one correspondent in the letters page described 'bikers' as being the kind of undesirables that 'hung around' such places.

BIKERS ARE OK FOR DARTMOUTH

This prompted a surge of letters in defence of bikers; with one lady helpfully pointing out that the main problem was in fact 'drug pushers who prey on small children'.

More than 200 attended the public enquiry – and listened incredulously to the developer's argument that the arcade, featuring gaming machines and new 'space invader' type games, would be 'high class'.

The Department of the Environment ruled Dartmouth was a 'discreet town' and a 'settlement of unique attraction' and visitors were attracted by its 'history, architecture and small-scale character' and stopped the arcade, much to everyone's relief.

The same week that the final decision was made to stop the building of the arcade, September 18, another controversial establishment was proposed for the town: a sex shop.

Again people wearily lined up to speak out against the enterprise – though often concerned they did not seem prudish. The Mayor Don Webb said: 'I am by no means narrow minded but I have to say that a shop of this nature would be completely alien to the Dartmouth way of life.'

Town, District and County Cllr Les Savage said: 'My personal view is that it is quite wrong for this perfectly normal and natural part of our lives to be exploited in a shop.'

Also considered 'quite wrong' was Filthy McNasty's – both a bistro in Church Close and a snack bar/take away in Fairfax Place – and it was the subject of attacks from town councillors in July. The eateries sold such delicacies as 'mud pie' and 'sludge', which were both desserts, the *Chronicle* felt necessary to point out.

Deputy Mayor Fred Tremlett said: 'I honestly don't think the district council should allow it. The bistro is in Church Close and is right next to the church and it's also a conservation area. It's disgusting. It is an insult to the town and its good name.'

However the owner of the two businesses, Hal Lomax, said: 'They are just a bunch of parochial and childish people. If it was an insult to anybody, which it is not, it would be an insult to myself. The name is meant to be a bit of a gimmick. I thought of the name, I suppose you could call me Mr McNasty himself.'

A letter writer to the *Chronicle* commented that the name was 'mimicking the American way of life' and said 'wouldn't it be nice if we were all proud to be British and acted like Englishmen.'

The Farrell family celebrate the return of Carl from the Falklands.
TOTNES IMAGE BANK/ SOUTH HAMS NEWSPAPERS

The town also got thoroughly carried away – in a good way this time – by wedding fever on July 29; the wedding of Prince Charles and Lady Diana Spencer. The event prompted 'raves', 'parties' and 'raucous celebrations'.

The whole town turned out in a 'giant patriotic gesture' – with 400 watching the wedding ceremony on a single TV set in the Royal Avenue Gardens, and street parties organised all over the town which was lucky to be bathed in glorious sunshine for the occasion.

But there was sad news for Regatta in November – with the death of 'Mr Regatta' Rodney Tucker, aged 79.

He had been connected with the event since 1955 and was secretary of the committee from 1958 to 1976. He was also vice chairman from 1977 to 1978.

Not one to let himself become bored Mr Tucker was also secretary of the town's Young Men's Recreation Club, Stoke Fleming Horticultural and Sports Society, the Dartmouth Conservative Club, Dartmouth Rowing Club, Dartmouth Sailing Club and the Dartmouth Rugby Supporters' Club. He was a special constable, president of the Old Dartmothians Association and he restarted the district billiards league.

Mr Tucker had also been brave enough to become a reporter for the *Dartmouth Chronicle* during the national strike in 1926.

Rather better news came when Dartmouth's shops got an unexpected boost in November with the arrival on November 22 of the Bulgarian factory ships *Lorna* and *Melanita,* which were later joined by the Norwegian ship *Sea Crown* and later still by another Bulgarian vessel *Olusha,* all of whom were grading and freezing horse mackerel for overseas markets. The 'Rust Buckets' as the *Chronicle* dubbed them had more than 100 sailors onboard, who turned out to be big spenders.

Mr David Beamish, chairman and managing director of Ocean Resources, a London based firm which arranged for the ships to take the stock of local fishermen for processing, said: 'The men love Dartmouth and are overwhelmed at the welcome which they have been given. As far as local fishermen are concerned, they would normally be fishing for sprat and small mackerel at this time of year. The markets for both are very poor at the moment, what we have done is given them the chance to make more money.'

The sailors of all the ships visited the town regularly to buy products not available in their native lands. They would also sing for beer in the pubs and made a big, and positive, impression on many in the town.

The ship's 'rusted' appearance drew criticism from some, in the same way that the *Queen Frederica* had done in the 1970s, but Harbourmaster Colin Moore said: 'These are working ships. They haven't got time for making them pretty to look at. They are there to work and maintain standards of living.'

LT COL 'H' JONES VC OBE *Soldier*

(See year 1982)

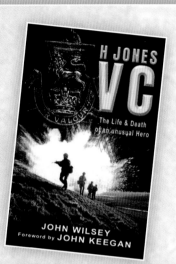

Lt Col 'H' Jones VC OBE, whose family home was in Kingswear, has become a legendary figure – and rightly so, after his sacrifice to defeat the Argentineans at Goose Green.

The charismatic, some would say 'devil-may-care' Lt Col was killed leading an attack on a machine gun nest during the Falklands War. It was one of the most significant engagements of the war, perhaps pivotal to the quick victory for Britain against the invading Argentineans. He was a strong, complex character who inspired loyalty and obedience from the soldiers under his command. He gave the ultimate sacrifice on May 28, 1982, and the village of Kingswear and town of Dartmouth shared in their grief.

He became the symbol of the bulldog British spirit during the Falklands War. We stood up to another country which thought it could take with force that which it could not with diplomacy.

He is and always will be an example held up by the armed forces as the quintessential British military man – brave, likeable and hard as nails.

In September 1982 the regimental journal of the Devon and Dorsets, Lt Col Jones VC OBE's regiment, held a poignant and honest tribute: 'He would have appreciated precisely the risks at Goose Green. He was extremely human and there lay his appeal, for had he been otherwise his brilliance, his determination and inner conviction, his bravery and his moral courage would have made him impossibly remote, whereas his human frailties ensured that he was someone with whom it was always easy to identify.'

(See page 239)

1982

The three factory ships, two Bulgarian and one Norwegian, pulled out of the harbour because they could not be kept stocked up with fish at the beginning of the year. Dwindling supplies forced the *Melanita* and *Lorna* to sail to Falmouth, which was nearer the fishing grounds. Harbourmaster Colin Moore vowed to bring more business similar to the ships back to the town, saying a temporary hiatus was 'part and parcel' of the fishing business and that 'up to eight' factory ships could moor in the river at once.

However, a plan to bring in another Norwegian ship in November proved a disaster, as catches of scad had to be dumped by fishermen because there was 'better fishing in Falmouth' and the ship stayed there rather than coming up to Dartmouth.

FALKLANDS WAR AFFECTS FAMILIES

In April two Dartmouth parents were celebrating their son's safe return from the Falkland Islands.

Doreen and Charles Evans of Above Town cracked open some bubbly to toast the luck of their son Graham, who was flown home with his wife and the rest of the Royal Marine garrison after they surrendered to the Argentine invaders. Graham was a driver in the Royal Marines, and met his wife Sheila during a one year posting there in 1979. He had just returned to the Islands with Sheila, when the invasion took place.

Mr Evans said: 'It was a ghastly moment when we heard the news. I went to pray for Graham and Sheila's safe return and, thank God, my prayer has been answered. Graham is now back in England on a short leave.'

Graham was soon back in the thick of the action, however, re-deployed on the *Canberra* troop ship.

As the conflict began many hopeful and nervous words were printed of families praying their boys would be safely returned.

The town seemed to have a huge amount of servicemen involved in the conflict, and many feared the worst for 'our boys' when the first engagements took place. When HMS *Ardent* was sunk during the first few days of conflict, the town mourned as it had been the Regatta Guardship in 1979. However, much worse was to come.

In early June, Kingswear was shaken by the death of one of their own – Lt Col Herbert 'H' Jones VC leading the 2nd Battalion, Parachute Regiment in the recapture of Darwin and Goose Green. Leading from the front Lt Col Jones was gunned down while trying to take an Argentine machine gun post. The *Chronicle* said: 'a national war hero who was born and brought up among them – died amid a hail of Argentine bullets, fighting for his country.'

His wife Sara, described him as 'a bit of an extrovert, who was a lot of fun'.

Lt Col Jones was reported to have been incredibly angry at the MoD after the BBC World Service broadcast at 1 pm 27th May that he was 5 miles from Darwin. Argentine reinforcements were flown in by helicopter the following morning, but, inspired by their leader's gallant death, 2 Para captured Darwin and 1200 Argentinians surrendered at Goose Green. However, the BBC said that the information given in its reports could not have been the reason for any troop movements because 'the timetable alleged is inconsistent with the facts'.

His funeral was carried on the front of the paper, with the headline 'THE SORROW – AND THE JOY' as it was above the story of Marine Commando Carl Farrell, who had been returned to his family after being injured.

When the ceasefire was announced in mid June special Thanksgiving services marked people's relief at the relatively short period of war. The following weeks and months saw the paper filled with happy stories of men returning from the conflict, to the birth of a child, or for their long planned wedding which had been put in jeopardy by the declaration of war.

In October 'H' as he was known was honoured again – with the country's highest award for gallantry, the Victoria Cross. Lt Col Jones VC was commended for his action of 'the utmost gallantry' by a 'commanding officer whose dashing leadership and courage throughout the battle were an inspiration'.

More prosaic, but also very important, was the need for new sewerage and flood systems in the town.

Lt Col 'H' Jones VC OBE. See Feature on page 143

South Devon pays tribute to two VC heroes. See Feature on page 239

Above left: *The new Fire station in College Way is ready for occupation.*
TOTNES IMAGE BANK/ SOUTH HAMS NEWSPAPERS

Above right: *The Fire Engine's move in to their new home.*
TOTNES IMAGE BANK/ SOUTH HAMS NEWSPAPERS

Left: *And who knew what lay in store for their old home behind the Flavel church?*
TOTNES IMAGE BANK/ SOUTH HAMS NEWSPAPERS

SEWERAGE SYSTEM A PRIORITY AT LAST

The town and district council's agreed to make a new flood-defence scheme and sewerage system 'a priority' and got agreement from South West Water to work on the plan.

The announcement was music to the ears of residents who had lived through warnings of typhoid infecting the town in the event of a flood, but work was slow on the sewerage system because of cost concerns.

The town, which could treble in population in high season, saw periods when raw sewerage could be seen along the riverbed at low tide, especially around Coronation Park and other areas, creating a noxious and unsightly reminder that the antiquated sewerage system was over worked. .

District Cllr Mary Laver Vincent dumped a bag with some excreta picked up along Victoria Road after a flood on the desk of a South West Water official, in an effort to illustrate the residents' fears.

It obviously did the trick; the official assured Mrs Laver Vincent that a team of surveyors would look at the problem within two weeks, and they did.

The various groups agreed to work together to find one final solution – and quick.

An extension to the Coronation Park outflow was agreed by the last few days of October, at a cost of £40,000, but a long-term solution would take much more time, as the existing sewers were so old and dilapidated.

MAN TELLS CHILDREN TO STOP HAVING FUN

Not at all as important, but illustrating how some people will go to any lengths to spoil another person's fun, a Strete man led a campaign against a children's play area next to his home because 'I came here to spend my retirement in peace and quiet'.

Mr Sidney Cook did not look *at all* like a mean spirited old curmudgeon when he objected to the planned play area, which the parish council had been trying to build for more than forty years.

He said he had a covenant on his land that said nothing could be built on the land adjoining that caused him 'annoyance or nuisance'.

The land next to the A379 had been donated by the County Council to the parish council and both were pushing forward to get children in the area.

Mr Cook collected 160 names on a petition against the area, and claimed it would be an 'eyesore' and would 'knock several thousand pounds off the value of my home'. But the validity of the petition was then called into question, with many accusing Mr Cook of not making it clear to those signing what they were in fact objecting to. He rejected this out of hand.

However, Parish Council Chairman Charles Reckitt said that any claim against the area to do with Mr Cook's covenant would be 'laughed out of court'.

In a situation reminiscent of the visit of the *Queen Frederica* in the 1970s – a visiting ship caused a furore in the pages of the paper.

The Greek ship *Captain Lemos* arrived in mid July, one of the longest ships ever to moor in the river. 480 feet long and more than 9,700 tons, the ship remained in the river awaiting its new cargo.

The fact that the mooring dues for the ship were £1,400 a week caused much discussion, with Harbourmaster Colin Moore saying the money would enable the harbour authority to 'improve' the port.

But after the 'wall of rust', as some christened it, had been in place a few weeks, many felt enough was enough and a solitary letter appeared one week saying: 'the harbour authority must have taken leave of its senses in giving space to such a disproportionate vessel at the height of the tourist and yachting season'.

It opened the flood gates and every man, woman and their dog with an opinion wrote in. Views were, as with the *Queen Frederica*, split down the middle.

Malcolm Hayter wrote that 'we have a working port so let's make it work. Every time we get anything which brings trade or work to this sheltered harbour up go the cries of dismay'.

On the other hand, D Ellis of Dartmouth wrote: 'It shows a disregard of the tourist interests in the town and a total insensitivity to the beauty of Dartmouth'.

The Lower Ferry also became the subject of controversy in November – as four members of its crew were dismissed and then reinstated after accusations of stealing.

The four men were sacked after district council officers sat and counted the amount of cars rolling on and off the ferry over a number of days, and then examined receipts for those days, and found many more cars were using the ferry than were being charged for the trip.

But the district council reinstated the men after an appeal supported by most local councillors, because the way the problem had been investigated seemed to owe more to the ideas of a dystopian fascist government than a rural district council.

On top of the secret observations of the ferry, the men were summoned to the district council offices in Totnes and kept in separate rooms for hours then 'interrogated' according to the men's spokesman Stan Davis. He didn't say whether rubber hosepipe or thumbscrews were used, but you feel reading the report that they might have been preferable.

'We feel we have been very badly treated by Follaton House,' he said. And many councillors agreed with him. The problem, said most, was that giving free rides on the ferry to your mates was part of the ferry culture, and it was the duty of the ferry's management to stop the practice and make sure the ferry returned a good profit. District Cllr Francis Hawke said: 'they used a sledgehammer to crack a nut.'

DAME NAOMI JAMES *Sailor*

(See year 1978)

Naomi James welcomed back from her amazing Round-the-World trip. Totnes Image Bank/South Hams Newspapers

The first record feat that both started and finished in Dartmouth was by Naomi James.

The beautiful and engaging wife of Rob – a sailor considered every bit as talented as both Chay Blyth and Robin Knox-Johnston – she decided to sail Round-the-World almost on a whim.

New Zealand-born Naomi met Rob when he was sailing *British Steel* in France in 1975.

She had never sailed and yet because of her attraction to Rob she carried on sailing with him up to five days a week, every week for months, despite suffering from terrible seasickness.

The couple moved to Kingswear in 1976, and soon after she began to harbour plans to go it alone on the kind of trip everyone expected her husband to undertake.

Plans for a trip Round-the-World in Chay Blyth's yacht *Cutty Sark,* as Rob and Naomi were friends with Blyth and his wife Maureen, looked to be dashed when no sponsor came on board.

Then a generous friend gave the much needed funds at the last minute. This meant that the trip was then on again, and in five weeks from the offer of money the yacht was ready to sail. Ironically after it became clear the trip was going ahead the sponsorship became easy to come by, and the *Cutty Sark* was re-named the *Express Crusader* before she left with great fanfare on September 8.

The trip was the subject of much speculation in the *Chronicle*.

The trip was rarely out of the headlines, sometimes featuring reports of good progress, and sometimes voicing fears as nothing had been heard of her in the southern oceans for days or even weeks.

She had to stop twice during her voyage, even though she had wanted to make a non-stop navigation, but was glad to make it back alive after capsizing in a 'monster' storm in the Pacific, just before rounding Cape Horn, the most feared landmark on any sailor's map. She overcame the elements to complete her voyage, and even though she had not managed to sail non-stop Round-the-World, she had managed to beat the record of Britain's Sir Francis Chichester by two days. She had spent 272 days on her own against the elements.

The reception she received was immense: tens of thousands came to see her arrive and travel around the town in an open top car. A park and ride was set up just for that day to allow all who wanted to see her to do so.

She wrote an autobiography, was made a Dame by the Queen, raced a few more times and then settled down to start a family and let Rob do the adventuring for a while.

His need to push his limits caught up with him, however, when he was drowned after falling off a yacht in stormy conditions off Salcombe in 1983, just ten days before the birth of the couple's daughter.

Naomi James never sailed again.

Scott McRoy

REGATTA 2010
★ ★ DARTMOUTH ★ ★
AUGUST 26th 27th 28th

PORT OF DARTMOUTH
ROYAL REGATTA
ESTABLISHED 1834

The Port of

Royal

A SELECTION OF PHOTOGRAPHS FROM SEVERAL RECE

Dartmouth
Regatta

PORT OF DARTMOUTH
ROYAL REGATTA

PAUL BARCLAY

1983

Ex-Kingswear yachtsman Rob James, husband to Round-the-World yachtswoman Naomi, died after falling overboard while sailing to Salcombe.

Mr James, a contemporary and friendly rival to Chay Blyth, the village's other world conquering yachtsman, had been competing in races for many years, and was described by one of the *Chronicle*'s interviewees as 'one of the best yachtsmen in the world.'

Mr James fell over board when the safety net he was on broke at around 5am on March 20. The boat was coming in to Salcombe to be prepared for a race to Bermuda.

Mr James spent nearly two hours in the water, much of which saw desperate attempts by his crew to save him. An inflatable dinghy onboard could not be launched due to the 'manpower' its launching required, and crew member Jeffrey Houlgrave finally jumped into the water with a rope tied round him in an attempt to pull Mr James to safety.

However, he lost his grip on Mr James who eventually disappeared from view. He died from drowning brought on through hypothermia; the water temperature was no higher than 7.5 degrees Celsius.

Mr James and his wife had moved from Kingswear at the beginning of the Seventies. After Naomi sailed Round-the-World in 1978, both completed various races, even against each other a couple of times, before beating Chay Blyth in a round Britain race in 1982, the race which marked Mrs James' retirement.

At the time of Mr James' death, his wife was expecting a baby. The paper described it as a 'terrible tragedy for Kingswear and the yachting world.'

GOODBYE MR MAWBY

The South Hams Conservative Association 'ousted' Ray Mawby MP as its candidate after twenty eight years, in favour of ex-youth worker and barrister Anthony Steen.

Mr Mawby came last in a vote for the association's nomination behind four younger men, all from outside of the area.

The 61 year old left the meeting 'by a side door' without waiting to hear who would replace him. He retired after the rejection, having also been turned down as candidate by the Teignbridge constituency.

Mr Steen was duly returned as MP for the area in the June election – using the press to constantly upstage his main competitor, Liberal Tony Rogers. He challenged him to a TV debate – helpfully avoiding the question of what TV company would feature a debate between two candidates from a not-particularly-marginal seat in the southwest – and then accused him of being 'scared stiff' of being 'shown up'. It was politics in the best tradition of 'Punch and Judy' attacks, and it worked like a dream.

In the solid and dependable building trade, far away from party politics, R.C. Pillar landed themselves in hot water by demolishing a wall in June.

A listed building in Anzac Street, the 'Palladium', was being renovated by the company, when residents called the district council and accused them of 'knocking it down'.

The council officers swiftly claimed the builders 'knew exactly' what they were doing and told the *Chronicle* without hesitation that the company could be taken to court and its owner 'sent to prison' for three months.

However, owner Christopher Pillar said that the complaints showed people involved in the decision to give planning permission to the project – to turn the building into a house – had not read the plans.

He said that the builders had not 'planned' to knock down an entire listed wall – the builders had found that the timbers supporting the wall were 'rotten' and had to be taken down.

'I took it down in good faith and started to rebuild,' he said. 'Then they came along and told me I had taken too much down. It's going to go back exactly as it was.'

However, the district council decided that Mr Pillar had meant to do what he did and knew it was the wrong thing, and took him to court.

But Mr Pillar won his case and the embarrassed council had to pay him costs. He was pictured on the front of the *Chronicle* with the brand new, and very well made building behind him, looking exactly like he had just said 'told you so.'

The newly elected Anthony Steen MP.
EXETER EXPRESS &
ECHO

OUR SUBMARINE IS MISSING

The letters pages of the *Chronicle* were filled throughout the year with a long and difficult debate – is there a submarine under Coronation Park?

The German First World War submarine had been brought into Coombe Mud – which is what Coronation Park had been before the park had been created by donations from Coal Lumpers and lots and lots of hard work.

Also buried was a Royal Navy motor torpedo boat from the early 1920s. 'The town was full of people who remembered the boat and submarine being filled with rubble and buried as part of the construction of Coronation Park.

Debate raged over whether the two boats were in a line or abreast, whether the submarine was in the middle of the park and the motor torpedo boat near the tennis courts and, most importantly, whether the park should be dug up to find the hulks.

The debate was perhaps best summed up by ex-Dartmouth resident, Cyril John Farr, 75. A 'son of the Dart' according to the paper, he wrote to the *Chronicle* from his new home in Plymouth pleading with the Mayor Beryl Calder to 'not allow' the excavation of the park.

In an attempt to make digging unnecessary, Mr Farr gave the full account of his time as a milkman in Dartmouth in the 1920s – confirming, once and for all, where the submarine was.

'The boat and the submarine were in line, not abreast,' Mr Farr said, and that he had often been on board the motor torpedo boat and that metallic traces near the tennis courts were actually 'corrugated iron from the roofing and old machinery from the demolished Ferris and Blank boatyard.'

Mr Farr appealed to the Mayor: 'Dartmouth is a place of great beauty, so please, Mr Mayor, do not let any outsiders come in to interfere with the park by digging it up.'

Much digging was to be needed just down the Embankment when the town looked to be getting its long-needed sewerage system – which surprisingly was to be linked with a total rebuilding of the Embankment.

For one of the first times in Dartmouth's long history it seems large organisations were working together for the greater good and making positive decisions.

The £1.5 million scheme was so big it would be the only capital project the district council took on during the 1984/85 financial year. The Embankment would have to be extended outwards to protect 'against flooding' and the cost

*The building of
Dartmouth's new
Embankment.*
DARTMOUTH MUSEUM

*The Best Laid Plans.
See Feature on
pages 102–103*

would be carried by the Ministry for Agriculture, the District and County Councils and South West Water. Dartmouth District Cllr Mary Laver Vincent summed up the problem and the imminent need for a solution when she said: 'This is an absolutely necessary scheme for Dartmouth. We have raw effluent going into the backs of restaurants and out of the fronts having gone through the kitchen and dining area.'

The *Chronicle* did not record whether said restaurants and hotels suffered a drop in customers following this wonderfully expressive remark. In fact town Cllr Les Savage took Mrs Laver Vincent to task the next time he had a chance – 'it is deplorable that remarks about sewage flowing through the doors of Dartmouth restaurants and in the streets should have been made and given publicity in the middle of tourist season,' he said whilst apparently brandishing a *Chronicle*.

However, the district councillor was unabashed: 'My words were quite deliberate. The facts I stated are purely facts. I did not name specific restaurants and streets affected by sewage for the simple reason that it is tourist season.' Meaning, of course, ANY Dartmouth street could be implicated, damaging the WHOLE town and its restaurants.

Rather more fragrant, however, was the town's Britain in Bloom appeal, which looked to be in danger in July when an 'epidemic' of plant thefts left the town looking 'decimated'.

Whole tubs, hanging baskets and window boxes of flowers disappeared during the crime spree, and Chairman of the Dartmouth in Bloom Committee, Capt Robert Franks said: 'I am angry because it just doesn't seem possible that people can act in this way. And I am desperately disappointed for the many people who have tried so hard to make Dartmouth even more beautiful and yet see their efforts ruined.'

The Royal Avenue Gardens also suffered vandalism on the day before judges arrived in the town in mid July.

However, they were distracted with a floral dance and a large effort from all involved got the town through and for the fifth year in a row the town won an award – the Sargent Cup for 'general outstanding effort'.

SAVE DARTMOUTH COMMUNITY COLLEGE

Dartmouth Community College also came under attack – and the local community fought back.

The county council received much communication after a small note on one of its agendas was noted by local people: 'local consultations to be held concerning the future of Dartmouth Community College'.

The Education Officer, Mr Joslyn Owen, said the school roll would shrink to less than 350 by 1991 and that the school had 'received favourable treatment in the past'.

He said that children from Stoke Fleming should go to Kingsbridge, from Blackawton to Totnes and from Dartmouth to Torbay.

Chairman of the school governors Harry Stewart refuted these claims however.

'The school roll is not falling,' he said 'about ninety pupils enter each year and the total numbers should therefore be around 450.'

Mr Stewart also said that plans to send children to three different areas were 'ridiculous' and that Dartmouth was a 'good school' with 'high standards'.

Temporary Headmaster Bruce Mackie called on parents to 'stand up and fight for your school' saying in October that local consultations had to produce a big response from the community to give the school a chance of surviving. He also advised everyone to write to the county council demanding not only the saving of the school, but also that people 'demand' investment, and bring about a one-site school, rather than being shared between two.

The county council officers came down for a public meeting and must have felt they were walking into the lions' den. The *Chronicle* described them as being 'marooned' on a platform surrounded by angry parents and governors. In fairness to them, they seem to have tackled the big issues head on.

Mr Owen said: '… the number of pupils will go down and the question in our mind is what will happen to the education of children in this school?' He said even when the new school had been built in the late Seventies the county council had been 'very concerned' at the viability of the school.

Rev John Butler seemed to speak for all Dartmothians when he said: 'We are concerned about the viability of a town. Dartmouth has a population of between 6,000 and 7,000. But the most important thing on my mind is that children who grow up in this town should be offered a whole field of education within the town.'

The paper kept up the pressure with front pages right up until the November county council meeting when the school was saved, but suffered staff cutbacks.

Mr Stewart said the decision was a call to arms for the school. 'It is now up to everyone in Dartmouth – not just the school staff – to give the fullest possible support towards the continued success of the school.'

*Flooding swamps
Dartmouth.
See Feature on
pages 164–165*

1984

Flooding was in people's minds in January – when it was warned a high tide in September would 'flood the town'.

The predicted tide, at 7.28pm on September 26, would be 5.5 metres, the limit of the town's flood defences, and would, if weather conditions were 'not perfect', flood the town. The front page headline about this prompted a high level of panic. This was not helped when the Harbourmaster pointed out that the tide would be over five metres four other times during the year, and that inclement weather on any one could result in flooding.

The public's fears were used to again put pressure on the three local councils and South West Water to move forward quickly on a new Embankment, sewerage and flood defence scheme.

The floods didn't actually materialise in the end – though there were some fears as weather systems deepened off Start Point, but the water just lapped over Bayards Cove and the town was left 'heaving a huge sigh of relief'.

But the needs of a new flood defence scheme were not forgotten and the £3.5 million – up thanks to inflation and a re-evaluation of the project's aims – Embankment and sewerage scheme, into which flood defence was included, began in October.

This being Dartmouth however, despite the fact that everyone had been calling for nearly three decades for a new system, the necessary reduction in parking spaces led some business owners to seek compensation for 'loss of trade'. These were, generally, completely ignored by the powers that be, which grimly got on with a complete re-working of the Embankment.

The Higher Ferry made the headlines across the county when it broke away from its wires to sail down the river Dart during high winds in February 'mowing down' yachts and leaving a seriously ill woman stranded in an ambulance on board.

The drama took place on Wednesday February 8, when a force ten gale ripped down the Dart valley and tore the 140 ton ferry from its guide wires, which then damaged twelve yachts berthed nearby.

Tribute needs to be paid to the ferry pilot Simon Deacon and fare collector John Leland, who both climbed over the side of the vessel to release the anchor.

Police Sgt Graham Bulford said: 'This was particularly dangerous because they had to stand outboard at the point which was smashing into the yachts, and they were fending them off as best they could. It was awful – all those beautiful yachts being crashed and smashed into. But the crew did a marvellous job in very difficult conditions.'

Less dramatic, but more devastating to some, was the news of education cutbacks which had already put the secondary school in Dartmouth in danger – causing job losses at Kingswear and Blackawton schools.

The announcement, which came at the beginning of March, resulted in both schools having their staff reduced by more than one full time member of staff, from just over three to two. This was a cut of more than a third of staff members, and was condemned by the Kingswear Headmaster Kenneth Irwin.

'I just feel that this is an extreme response,' he said 'I would have wished for a more gradual response – say losing a teacher for just half a week would have been a more logical solution. Although we are falling in terms of overall numbers, our problems will increase because the teachers left will now have to teach a larger class with an increased age range.'

The cuts resulted in a county-wide strike in March, but teachers in Dartmouth decided not to take part because 'it would not achieve anything' and that 'parent pressure' was much more important.

TAKE MY ADVICE, SON...

Pressure of a similar kind, but much less welcome, came when Dartmouth Town Council decided to give 'guidance' to some young and wayward men in the town, and completely got it wrong.

The old pontoon and walkway just before they were demolished.
DARTMOUTH MUSEUM

The ten youths, who were convicted of affray and assault after fighting with cadets of the Britannia Royal Naval College at a disco at the Guildhall – which turned into a 'running battle' in October 1983 – were not banned from the venue, as was the usual course of action.

Instead Dartmouth Town Council decided to invite them to a meeting with the Mayor and a number of other town councillors, to show them 'the error of their ways'.

Mr Don Webb said: 'If we meet with them face to face we may find out why they act this way.'

However, the 'youths', who blamed the Britannia Royal Naval College midshipmen for the fracas, were not enthusiastic about the meeting.

One of them said: 'I think it is unfair the way that we have been treated because we have been to court and been punished for what we have done. The fine was fair enough because we are guilty. But now the town council want to drag it up again when we want to forget it. I was surprised when none of the midshipmen got done. The councillors only want to be nosy.'

Pipe dreams were brought to the fore when Dartmouth was proposed in April as a ferry port by two companies. Channel Shipping from Jersey and Trathens from Plymouth both wanted to set up ferry services.

Channel Shipping proposed that ships caring 600 passengers and 150 cars would leave the town and sail to Cherbourg in France.

Michael White of Channel Shipping said: 'We are waiting for various bodies to make their minds up to see what can be provided. If suitable services are provided I would think it would go ahead. There has been a complete inertia about the whole thing from some Dartmouth companies. The Harbourmaster is the most enthusiastic person in the world but he has been poorly supported by other people.'

Mr White said he thought that Dartmouth was 'the best deep water port in the South'.

But the idea seemed to fall before it had even got going – the company announced it had 'cash flow' problems just a week after the first news of its proposals broke. It finally admitted defeat in July – at the same time that Trathens announced it would arrange passenger only, six-day pleasure cruises to Normandy first to see if the 'demand' was there. But these never actually materialised.

The Harbourmaster Colin Moore was despondent, saying: 'I hope it is not another example of Dartmouth missing the boat. The world's going to pass by Dartmouth again unless we stand up and fight for it.' He later described the two plans as 'pie in the sky'.

MYSTERY OF AMERICAN SAILORS' BODIES

More fanciful notions came up when the whereabouts of the American soldiers killed during the ill-fated Exercise Tiger on Slapton Sands in 1944 filled many *Chronicle* pages during the year – with local woman Dorothy Seekings, 64, saying she had 'seen' many bodies of American servicemen delivered to a field near Blackawton.

Ken Small and the Torcross Tank. See Feature on pages 156–157

Ken Small and the Torcross Tank

(See year 1984)

The tragedy of Exercise Tiger touched the people who lived around Slapton Ley. More than 600 American sailors and soldiers died preparing for D-day thanks to a mix of bad luck and stupid decisions from the chain of command.

The issue was swept under the carpet by both the American and British governments, desperate to keep the plans for D-Day a secret and maintain the two countries population's fragile morale.

But thirty nine years later a man from Slapton started on a campaign to make sure it was never forgotten. It would take his marriage and his health, but he achieved something remarkable which has meant Tiger was never forgotten.

Kenneth Small had moved to the area to run the hotel at Torcross in 1968, and knew nothing about Exercise Tiger.

He then found some ammunition from the exercise and this set him on the road to hero status, and a tragedy of his own.

He began to research the event, but found the going difficult. The 'cover up' was imposed as a number of officers with highly classified knowledge of the D-Day landings were missing and it was feared might have been taken to France for interrogation. However all of them were finally identified by the dog-tags on their bodies.

Mr Small found out that a flotilla of LSTs (Landing Ships Tank) had left Plymouth and Brixham on April 27, 1944, to rendezvous off Portland with an escorting destroyer and return to carry out a practice landing on Slapton Sands next morning. However the destroyer was damaged in a collision off Plymouth. The Portland MTB flotilla was warned to stand by, but had no American codebooks, so were not alerted to the exercise.

A group of fast German E-Boats based in Guernsey found the returning convoy south of Burton Bradstock, and attacked with torpedoes, sinking two LSTs and damaging two more. 638 American servicemen died, and next day many bodies were found floating in their self-inflating lifebelts. The bodies were recovered to Portland.

The damaged LST 281 limped into Dartmouth and was repaired at Noss yard, where the workers had to sign non-disclosure forms and kept their secret for decades. One of the attacking vessels, Schnellboot S-130, survived the war, and in February 2009 was being restored in Dartmouth for the Donington Grand Prix Museum.

One woman, who had two American soldiers billeted on her, could not get information about them when enquiring where to send their personal effects after their failure to return. She was told to throw the men's belongings out. The more Mr Small found out, the more he wanted to expose the 'cover up' and honour the men who lost their lives.

Ken Small's triumphant salute upon raising the Sherman Tank.

The tank sits proudly at Slapton as a memorial to the men who lost their lives in Exercise Tiger, and the sacrifice made by Ken Small to recover it from the sea bottom. PHIL SCOBLE

Mr Small became determined to make more people aware of the men who had died. His belief that the wartime cover-up had continued into peacetime stemmed from the lack of a memorial to the men. When a Sherman tank from the D-Day landing exercises was found by a fisherman he began to form an idea for a suitable memorial. He bought the tank from the American government for $50, and then spent a decade getting it raised from the deep and placing it as a permanent memorial to the men who died.

He called in the Royal Tank Regiment Association to help him raise the thirty two ton tank.

The national newspapers and especially the *Chronicle* loved him. He was a classic British underdog and eccentric, going to extraordinary lengths for the sake of preserving the sacrifice of the few for the many. The raising of the tank in 1984, into which he put thousands of his own money, was headline news nationally and his picture adorned many front pages: his Churchill-like Victory V sign as he stood atop the tank a fitting image to sum up his triumph at succeeding in a decade-long fight.

He even wrote a bestselling book about the tragedy and sold thousands of copies from the boot of his car, parked near the tank. He toured the world giving lectures on the tragedy and his achievement.

The fact that it was later revealed that the tragedy had not been covered up at all, in fact it had been listed in a number of publications after the war, did little to damage his reputation or his own fervour for the subject.

His dedication to telling the world about the events of the fateful two days did not come easy: he sunk thousands into the raising of the tank and printing the book and it also cost him his marriage.

When the book was published he became engaged in a bitter war of words with his ex-wife, in connection with his statements about her lack of support during his ten-year crusade.

During his last days, when he was battling cancer, he sat by the tank every day of the year, telling people its history and selling his book. A friend saw him there in his last days and asked him whether there was anything else he wanted to do, he replied: 'All I want to do is just sit here with the tank.'

He died in 2004.

Dartmouth Mayor Beryl Calder meets French President Francois Mitterrand in October 1984. Francois Mitterrand was paying an official visit to Dartmouth and Kingswear to mark the time he spent as a young Lieutenant on a Motor Torpedo Boat (MTB) in the river Dart awaiting his secret departure for Brittany in Occupied France in February 1944. Sub Lieutenant Philippe de Gaulle, the son of General Charles de Gaulle, was also stationed with the Free French Forces at Kingswear during the Second World War.

SOUTH HAMS NEWSPAPERS

Mrs Seekings said she had 'been given a lift by an American sergeant' in a truck which had turned out to contain 'dozens' of bodies. She said that she had seen 'great mounds of earth' in the field and said she had been 'told' that the bodies would be buried there.

This prompted salvage worker Dave Kimberley to propose using a 'specially adapted metal detector' to look for 'the buttons of the soldiers' uniforms'.

The story had broken all across the world and Mrs Seekings' story was backed up by soldiers and sailors who had been there at the time.

The farmer who owned the field refused any investigation, although he did say that there was 'no indication' that it had been used for graves.

The story continued until Ken Taylor, a paranormal investigator from the area, decided he was going to 'contact the spirit world' to find out where the bodies were buried.

The final result from this was the response from the Pentagon that the 638 men killed 'were taken home' after the war. The response confirmed only that the bodies had been repatriated and then re-buried in America.

A tank, which was left on the sea floor after the fateful Operation Tiger, and re-discovered when a fishing trawler got its net caught around it, was raised from the sea-bed in May.

Ken Small, a Torcross hotelier, had campaigned for a number of years to raise the tank and set it up as a memorial to the men who died. He had to spend two years negotiating with the American government to buy the tank for $50.

The tank did not rise from the depths without a fight, and took five days of failed attempts before finally breaking the surface for the first time in forty years.

When the great tank finally rose, a large crowd watched and cheered as Mr Small gave a 'Churchill style' salute.

After spending £3,000 on the project Mr Small said: 'I would have put a lot more into it if I had to. You can't give up on a thing like this. It was absolutely incredible it was in such good condition.'

The tank was dragged to a specially prepared plinth next to a car park on Slapton Ley ready for its permanent display.

The tank's re-emergence was timed to perfection, as Slapton was, just a week later, the focus of large celebrations of the fortieth anniversary of D-Day. The South Hams, an area which had been 'cleared' of its population before preparations for the great assault, was again invaded by American and British servicemen, who gathered to remember fallen comrades and exploits of heroism.

Slapton has the only memorial to the tragic night when German E-Boats discovered the LSTs of Exercise Tiger and killed men whose comrades later landed on Utah Beach. But sadly, some did not appreciate the sacrifice made by those men, and the Torcross war memorial was vandalised with 'No War' slogans just three days after the services of remembrance.

1985 In February the town was shocked by the death of one of its undisputed 'characters' – John Lewthwaite.

Mr Lewthwaite was killed when he lost control of his car on the way to his Stoke Fleming home. His car collided with a lamppost and a wall before turning onto its roof. He was 62 years old.

The former owner of the Gunfield Hotel – a remarkable and unique establishment – Mr Lewthwaite was a well known sailor who had also been commodore of the Royal Torbay Yacht club. He had won many Regatta sailing races in his Morecombe Bay Trawler *Ayesha*.

He and his sister Judy – known locally as the Pied Piper of Dartmouth for her amazing power to enchant children into performing plays and musicals at virtually every public event in Dartmouth – had bought the Gunfield in 1947, where they stayed until 1981. Mr Lewthwaite was due to join his sister for a holiday in Switzerland the day after his death.

His friend Victor Batey said: 'He was an incredibly kind and generous man. He would always help you if it was in his power and he took a great interest in everything which happened in Dartmouth. I simply cannot believe that he is no longer with us.'

TRAGEDY ON THE RIVER

Dartmouth and Kingswear were horrified by tragedy on March 30.

Douglas Coupland, 26, drowned after he and four others tried to row across the Dart after a party.

The four had been to a party on a Friday night. They had missed the last ferry and had tried to use a 12 foot boat to row across the river but were caught in a fast running current midstream.

Mr Coupland started 'fooling around' according to the inquest into the tragedy, allowing water into the boat. This caused the ladies to panic, and their movement caused the boat to overturn.

Nicola Edwards of Saltash, Elaine and Terry Finch of Newton Abbot, and James Mollaghan of Saltash were saved from the water by a Birmingham businessman who was sailing on the Dart.

Mr Coupland's body was not found for more than three weeks. His wife Lizzie could have been on the boat but had left the party early to relieve a babysitter who was looking after the couple's 3 year old son.

Flooding caused 'thousands' of pounds of damage on April 7. The forecast was for a tide of 5.2 metres, but a storm surge, low pressure and rain on Dartmoor all conspired to raise this by a few feet. Water 'cascaded' over the edge of the Boatfloat and along the Quay and Duke Street.

The floods were made all the more 'heartbreaking' by the fact that new flood defences were only a few months away from completion.

District council workers handed out more than 2,000 sandbags to homes and businesses that looked to be affected, but criticism still rained in on the council for not warning people soon enough.

The Embankment work, meanwhile, continued apace. The scheme was wrought with controversy from the start, when traders realised thirty three car parking spaces around the town would be lost. Then problems with the placement of the town jetty threatened the passenger ferry service.

After this the town pontoon hit the bottom of the river – after an accident in March.

Men working on the Embankment scheme escaped injury when the 70 x 40 foot floating pontoon structure capsized at midday on March 15.

The pontoon was being used by workmen to store debris and equipment and they overloaded it.

Debris was prevented from floating away by the quick action of the harbour authority and workmen managed to recover the equipment, including a 40 foot pile tower which had crashed into a crane when the pontoon went over. Harbourmaster Colin Moore said it was 'very fortunate' no one was hurt.

In April the town was in 'uproar' when they woke to see bulldozers ripping up trees planted as memorials to important individuals in the town by the Old Dartmothians Association.

1985 World Events
- Fire engulfs a wooden stand in the Valley Parade stadium in Bradford, England during a football match, killing fifty six
- Heysel Disaster: Thirty eight spectators are killed in rioting on the terraces during the European Cup final between Liverpool F.C. and Juventus at Heysel Stadium in Brussels, Belgium
- Live Aid pop concerts in London and Philadelphia raise over £50 million for famine relief in Ethiopia
- Riots are sparked with the shooting of Dorothy 'Cherry' Groce by the Metropolitan Police in Brixton

The ten-year anniversary of the Dartmouth Anglo-French Association is celebrated by its members in 1985.
SOUTH HAMS
NEWSPAPERS

Contractors had hoped to save the trees by placing piles where they would not compromise the root structure, but this soon proved impossible – so the trees had to go.

Tilbury Construction's Mike Tottle said that the decision had been taken 'late on' and that the trees, and their memorials, would all be replaced.

The War Memorial opposite the Royal Avenue Gardens also had to be removed, but it was kept 'carefully shrouded' in cotton wool and kept safely until it could be returned.

A hangover from local government re-organisation caused two crises in the town.

The long running dispute over the town's one cinema – the Royalty – was joined by a problem relating to the Ivy Lane Youth Centre.

Both had been owned by the borough council before re-organisation and were both on long-term leases. The district council – because it had no choice – had not raised the rents of the two buildings but when the leases came up for renewal the council followed its policy 'to charge fair market rents' for the properties.

This meant that the Royalty had a rent rise from £900 a year to £4,000. The youth club was facing similar rises, but also needed a new heating system and other major repairs. Town and District Cllr Francis Hawke, tried to get the town council to buy the youth club building for £10,000 and secure the future of the club. However, others on the town council disagreed with taking on this 'liability', and urged 'hard headedness'.

Tempers flared on the council as it referred the subject for more discussion at committee rather than making a decision. Cllr Hawke said that the town was known as 'Costa Geriatrica' and it was 'time we did something for the young people'. In the end the building was bought by the county council who paid for the repairs.

HANDS OF PEACE EXTENDED TO COMMUNIST RUSSIA

Stoke Fleming resident Pam Davies flew to Russia with a goodwill message for peace groups there.

Mrs Davies, who paid for the trip herself, went along with others on an expedition arranged by a journalist 'from Bath who is married to a Russian.'

The message Mrs Davies took to the Russians was composed by the Dartmouth CND group and included sentences such as: 'Dartmouth is a small picturesque town of about 5,000 people situated at the mouth of the river Dart on the southwest coast near Plymouth. It is an old port and is still the largest crab fishing port in Europe. The other major industry now is tourism. Dartmouth has the Britannia Royal Naval College where all naval officers are trained, including Prince Charles and Prince Andrew.

'Although Dartmouth is a very small place our group is very active with over seventy members who are all concerned that the dangers of nuclear weapons are not forgotten and that the waste of resources involved in their development is minimalised. We are opposed to the nuclear weapons of any country whether British, American or Russian.'

Slightly less international in scope, but just as important to many were the plans in Kingswear to knock down the railway station.

They brought condemnation, opposition and accusations of profiteering.

The Dart Valley Railway and Darthaven Marina wished to knock down the station to put up flats and holiday homes on the Quayside. They said that the railway would not be affected as the two companies could 'rebuild' the station 100 yards down the track.

The plan was fought and discussed and fought a bit more for eight months when in March 1986, owner of Darthaven Marina, John Holman, announced at a meeting of the Conservative Association in the village, that the two companies had decided to abandon the plan, securing the future of one of the few remaining Brunel-built stations in the country.

The 'Grand Old Gentleman' of Dartmouth died in August – at the age of 101.

Bertie Lavers – who had been four times Mayor during his life – died in Dartmouth and Kingswear Hospital.

Born in Southford Road, Mr Lavers was an apprentice at Noss Shipyard at the age of 14 and joined Devonport dockyard in Plymouth six years later. He married his wife Beatrice in 1908 and became a lay preacher in the same year. He worked for the Methodist Church in Dartmouth for twenty five years until it closed. At the end of the First World War he joined the Ministry of Fisheries as an inspector. Then in 1920 he took over his father-in-law's boat building business on Coombe Mud, which later became Coronation Park, forcing him to move to premises in South Town.

He retired in 1946 and went into local politics. In 1947 he became a member of the borough council and was a county councillor between 1961 and 1964. He was Mayor from 1947 to 1950 and between 1956 and 1957.

Plans to turn the Market Square car park into a bus terminal were scuppered by 'vested interests'.

County Cllr Marjorie Tomlinson fronted up the plan – which would have seen buses parked outside the Victorian Old Market as part of the inner relief road that was proposed during the year. She said that the protesters against it were scared of losing 'their' free car parking places. The plan had been put together after 'lengthy' negotiations with the Western National Bus Company.

The relief road was the subject of much debate, often bitter and divisive. It was planned to take a two lane road through from the Royalty Cinema to the Market Square to 'relieve the pressure' on Duke Street and the Butterwalk – allowing buses to use this rather than driving past the ancient landmark.

A public meeting was called after it was claimed that the plan would 'ultimately destroy the market and endanger the lives of the community' according to Town Cllr Len Manley.

Traders from the weekly market wrote to the county council appealing for the scheme to be scrapped as it would 'destroy' the market.

Mayor Les Savage, attacked the opponents of the scheme, saying that 'only thirty car parking spaces' would be lost, and that the listed Broadstone House 'would not in any way' be affected. He said that he was sure the road would not affect the market and that lost car park spaces would be compensated for by the North Embankment plan for a multi-storey car park. The scheme never happened despite much debate. It seemed the town's residents didn't want to see major disruption at huge cost for what would ultimately be a minimal benefit.

Her Royal Highness the Duchess of Kent on a walkabout around Dartmouth, delighting the crowds.
Totnes Image Bank/
South Hams Newspapers

Artists Andras Kaldor, Simon Drew, John Donaldson, John Gillo and Paul Riley before a joint exhibition. These artists formed the 'Dartmouth Artists Group' in 1986 and the 'Dartmouth Five' regularly exhibited together.

An economic crisis hit the town in November.

TTB Fabrications, the town's biggest private employer, put its workforce of eighty onto a 'Three-Day Week' due to lack of work. The decision was made after discussions with unions against the alternative plan of cutting a third of the workforce altogether. The problems seemed odd because this was the start of the economic boom times in Britain but a continuing downturn in engineering saw unemployment figures hit more than 3.5 million in 1986.

Work did start to come in but the plant's workers had been put through months of stress and anxiety.

Michael Boumfrey, General Manager, said: 'We are always on a knife edge because of the nature of our business.'

FIGHT THE POWER – TO REMOVE THE SMELL

Problems at the Old Mill Sewage works caused anger and uproar throughout the year. A terrible stench pervaded the area and many claimed that it had become so bad that they regularly felt ill.

South West Water had taken more than two years to fix the problem near the Archway Cottage part of the Townstal estate. More than 100 local residents crammed the Guildhall to the rafters for a public meeting and cheered when the water company admitted it had to do something.

It also admitted that the plant used at the treatment works had already been used at Totnes and found to be faulty there too. It was announced at the meeting that the works were to be replaced by a pumping station that would send sewage to the Coronation Park station.

After months of awful smells and a number of people feeling sick, anger actually got worse when they found out the equipment was known to be faulty *before* it was installed and many demanded their water rates back. Town and District Cllr Francis Hawke demanded that the Chief Executive of South West Water resign over the issue. Town Cllr Len Manley demanded 'public reprimands' for those responsible for the decision.

The water company also had to apologise to the town as well after sewage was transported in trucks from Old Mill to Coronation Park during the project to repair and upgrade the works.

1986 The Britannia Royal Naval College announced 134 job losses in the catering department at the end of January. All of the jobs were to go by the end of March and the workers were all made redundant at the same time. It was the biggest loss of employment in the town for years and perhaps the biggest ever.

Just a week after the initial announcement the new contractors, Compass Services, said it planned to take on 100 staff and pledged to consider all previous employees who wished to apply for the roles.

The company, who were London-based, were taking on their first Ministry of Defence contract at the Britannia Royal Naval College and said it 'looked forward to working with the College and Dartmouth.'

It looked forward to treating its workers considerably worse than the Ministry of Defence did – with the average wage being reduced to £80 from £135. It also announced that it did not provide sick pay, holiday pay or a pension.

Cecil Pippen, representative of the Transport and General Workers Union, said: 'It's blackmail, the company knows there are four million unemployed people trying to survive so there's not an awful lot the workers can do about it. This is a prime example of Mrs Thatcher's government saying our hardworking people are overpaid and that private enterprise is the answer to all our problems.'

The town continued to fixate on a project which it was hoped would cure all its economic woes. The Dart Port project – to put a new deep water quay at Noss had been touted and argued over for a number of years.

After it was seemingly rejected in 1985 when planners refused to support it – in fact they actively worked against it – DHNA released new plans for the scheme which showed three deep water berths and a large warehouse for unloaded and loadable goods north of Noss, with a container area and a road behind the Philip & Son Shipyard to the main road.

It also included a fishing quay with five berths, which it was hoped would save the dying fishing industry on the Dart. Trawlers were working out of Dartmouth less and less and Brixham was taking on the main trade.

The plan seemed to upset County Hall because it required substantial investment in the road system on the Kingswear side of the river.

The plan also received more opponents in January – with Torbay Borough Council formally objecting to it because of the traffic it would generate on the borough's roads and the fact that 'facilities would be duplicated' between Dartmouth and Brixham.

Two reports by county council officers sounded a disappointing note for those behind the plans. The officers, in a report on the deep port on the Kingswear side of the river, said a feasibility study of the Dart plan was 'optimistic'; it had failed to do any market research into whether there was a demand for the port; said its figures for construction were too small; said that the port could cost jobs at other southwest ports and said that road improvements needed for it would cost the taxpayer £800,000.

Perhaps wondering if this was enough to convince county councillors not to support the Dart project, the same officers, in the very same week, submitted a suspiciously positive report, said the *Chronicle*, on a Plymouth port project to create a container depot. This, said the officers, would be a very viable project, even though only twelve jobs would be created.

The evidence started to stack up – despite a surprise vote of support from Devon County Council in late September – with a *Sunday Times* article (assisted by sometime Dartmouth visitor David Bailey along with some of his pictures), which rubbished the plans and a pledge from the National Trust to fight the port plan 'to the end'.

The National Trust even threatened to take the fight to parliament as it was governed by an Act of Parliament which gave protection to the land around the Trust's Longwood land. It also claimed to own the foreshore where the deep water quay would be built, but this was disputed. The Countryside Commission also joined the fight and described the port plan as 'utter folly' and said there was 'no evidence' to support the need for a port at Dartmouth.

Despite continued attempts to get it off the ground until the end of the decade – millionaire Peter de Savary even had a look to see if it was viable – the project was never likely, especially with the town's proximity to Brixham, Plymouth and Falmouth, all with better facilities and existing road links.

1986 World Events
● Space Shuttle *Challenger* disintegrates seventy three seconds after launch, killing the crew of seven astronauts,
● President Ferdinand Marcos of the Philippines goes into exile in Hawaii after twenty years of rule
● A fire devastates Hampton Court Palace
● The Chernobyl disaster: A mishandled safety test at the Chernobyl Nuclear Power Plant in Pripyat, Ukrainian SSR, Soviet Union 'killed at least 4,056 people and damaged almost $7 billion of property'

Flooding swamps Dartmouth

(See year 1984)

Dartmouth is a town defined by its geography. The town originally sat atop the hill at Townstal. It was an easy to defend place and one with easy access to water from the streams and food from the woods.

But then ships came, and the need to be near the water became too strong. Buildings began to be built by the water, and soon a thriving community had built up with its own churches, markets and even civil engineering projects.

As the Victorian Era dawned the town was beginning to realise it needed more land, and reclaiming much of the tidal mud was undertaken with breathtaking speed and ingenuity.

But this left a legacy.

The lower town is built on a flood plain. This did not give the best base to build a good, large, strong and efficient sewerage system.

In a land-locked place where flat land is the norm, drains have to cope with a few thousand people doing the washing up, bathing and flushing the toilet regularly. Most places have sewer systems that can cope, no matter how old they might be.

Not so in Dartmouth.

Every time it rains in Dartmouth the rain funnels down the hills, mainly into sewers under Victoria Road and Duke Street, heading towards the Boatfloat.

A remarkable amount of water falls from the sky when it rains. Weather men use glib phrases such as 'ten centimetres in ten hours' with such dull regularity that they cease to have any meaning. One inch of rainfall means 65.78 million litres of water falling on every square mile. That's 1,012,000 washing machine loads.

The area around Dartmouth town centre is a square mile which all converges on Victoria Road.

It works, but only up to a point.

This resulted in some difficult and rather messy situations.

The flooding of Victoria Road became such a regular occurrence the paper only reported it at length if the problems featured some new never-before-seen element, such as a councillor being affected or a car being moved.

Less work had been done to repair and maintain the drainage system than many would have hoped in part because of the paper itself.

The keen eye of generations of reporters during the period since the Second World War meant every decision was scrutinised at great length. Many residents really did follow every twist and turn of the debates in the borough council chamber.

This had made local politicians scared of doing something unpopular like putting up taxes to pay for vital maintenance work.

Thanks to this, Dartmouth had had the lowest increase in the rates in the South Hams over the last twenty years by the time the sewer problem came to a head in the late 1960s.

It became clear, after a number of bad floods that something needed to be done.

Councillors boldly declared the sewer system needed revamping.

But they balked at the costs.

A cost of £380,000 was quoted in 1969 – it amounts to around £3 million in 2010 prices. To put that cost on to the rates of residents was simply not acceptable, and so began a long history of bodging and making do that resulted in slightly better systems, a bit less flooding, or flooding which was not as severe, but no solution.

The problems persisted and fears of disease spreading in the lower town were very real throughout the 1970s. The regular flooding, which brought with it unsavoury items from the sewers were not the best advert for the town and many felt that something had to be done, and soon.

The answer came to combine flood defences on the Embankment with improvements to the sewerage system.

It was a massive project and took more than a year to plan and put into action. The whole town was aware of the plan and its importance in the middle of the 1980s – but traders still complained that the loss of parking hurt their business.

It was impressive, expensive and changed the face of Dartmouth forever, but it was not entirely successful.

The fire brigade still kept an eye on the skies and came down to Victoria Road, pumps at the ready, if downpours started to look too heavy.

The debate then began to focus on climate change; with only a few feet to the top of the new Embankment the predicted rise in sea levels looked quite alarming.

Debates raged in the town council over whether to ask for an urgent review of the flood plan for Dartmouth.

In the end these battles were lost because the town is next to a tidal river. Short of raising the town by a metre or more, there will be increasing problems with flooding at very high tides.

Totnes Image Bank/South Hams Newspapers

However, the thought occurs that Dartmouth has been, for all of its history, working against the elements; trying to hold itself against the water from the sea and the water falling from above.

The list of areas in Dartmouth which were once part of the sea is longer than those that were always dry.

The town is a remarkable, unbelievable miracle created by men changing their environment to suit their needs and desires.

Perhaps a new generation will find a way to beat King Canute and hold back the tide. It will be interesting to see how the town changes yet again in the face of new environmental challenges.

Dartmouth Museum

ATTEMPTED MURDER AND SUICIDE SHOCK

A much more shocking story was featured on the *Chronicle*'s front page in the summer. A man hanged himself in Torquay Police Station in July after allegedly trying to murder his girlfriend.

Timothy Langton, 32, was found hanging from his own shoelaces in his cell on Monday July 14, three days after being taken into custody and charged with the attempted murder of Dartmouth chambermaid Carola Prehn. Mr Langton 'went berserk', said the *Chronicle*, and attacked Miss Prehn at the Sunnybank guest house in Vicarage Hill, trying to stab and strangle her. The Merseysider had only just arrived in Dartmouth at the time of the attack.

Miss Prehn stumbled into the street, hysterical and covered in blood after the 'frenzied' attack from her boyfriend.

A group of people, walking up the road after a boat trip, found her and tried to calm her down, when Mr Langton appeared.

A member of the group managed to restrain Mr Langton while someone else phoned the police. Mr Langton was taken into custody and remanded without bail on a charge of attempted murder. He took his own life three days later as his girlfriend was recovering from serious neck and head injuries.

The police had a busy summer.

A man smacked a police officer in the face in the town in July – just after the PC had saved his life.

The 22 year old man had just smashed two windows at the George and Dragon pub with his bare hands and severed the main artery in his wrist.

PC John Casson tried to restrain the man long enough to help him and got smacked for his trouble. In what was described by the man's mother as 'striking out of fear rather than anger', he continued to strike PC Casson while the PC ripped off his own shirt and staunched the flow of blood.

The man was taken to hospital, where he attacked the nurses trying to help him, but eventually received twenty two stitches. He then chose to attack another PC on the ride home after being arrested, and then, for good measure, ripped the stitches out of his arm and had to be urgently returned to hospital. He later claimed he had no recollection of the incident and apologised to all concerned personally.

PC Casson did not have a good summer. He followed his life saving and pretty painful experiences in July with being assaulted by a gang of 'youths' using bottles as weapons, turning Dartmouth into a 'battleground' in the town at the beginning of August.

A group of five young men 'marched into' the police station on a Wednesday night in early August. They became 'extremely aggressive and violent' towards PC Casson and his female colleague WPC Gail Bond. Both were assaulted and the group of youths stole a police radio from the station during the incident. They then ran out of the station and threw the radio through the window of a restaurant in Duke Street and assaulted the two owners who had run out to see what had happened.

Four men were charged in relation to the incident, two from Mutley in Plymouth.

These two were jailed for six months and two brothers from Dartmouth both received suspended custodial sentences.

WHO'S WITH ME? ANYONE?!

Another long contest ended in a defeat for a Dartmouth man early in the year.

Martin Cater of Hermitage Road, who had been fighting single-handedly against South West Water and a pong it had produced, finally gave in.

He had been refusing to pay a £333 water bill for more than a year after smell problems from a sewage treatment works had continued for too long.

Months after the water company had admitted there was a smell problem *and* promised to do something about it – the smell remained, said Mr Cater. He refused to pay and called on his neighbours to join him in the protest.

He got no support however and after being cut off and summoned to court he gave in and paid the bill in January. He said if more residents had joined his protest they could have forced a climb-down and action from South West Water. He also vowed to stage another protest if the smell remained.

Just a week after he threw in the towel South West Water announced that work on the new sewer and pumping station, which would end the problem, would be finished by May – and sent a letter to Mr Cater asking if they could dig up his garden and run the sewer through it.

Much more serious on the Townstal estate at the end of the winter was the death of an old man. The town was horrified when a pensioner froze to death in his Britannia Avenue house.

Francis Chapman was found dead by neighbours on March 1. He was found sitting in an armchair, wrapped in a sleeping bag in front of a one bar electric fire. The electricity had run out and the room was freezing. The *Chronicle* said: 'The grim discovery has shocked the whole town. It has left a host of unanswered questions as to how such a tragedy could happen in such a close-knit community.'

The same week South Hams Council started its horribly ironic 'Operation Old Folk' which proposed to 'check how old people in the South Hams are coping with the weather.'

Plans for the new open air heated swimming pool were put into jeopardy yet again after a change in design added £25,000 to the cost price.

Fundraising, due to frustration and apathy, had been low key the last few years, following heartbreak in the late Seventies when rocketing inflation made it impossible to raise the funds, plan and then build a swimming pool. But at the end of 1985 the project was reborn under a new committee which made a huge effort to raise £60,000, just £5,000 short of its target, to build a pool on the school grounds at Milton Lane.

The pool committee decided to spend extra money on better changing facilities, a stone surround and footings to make the proposed second phase of the pool – a roof – much cheaper and easier to install.

The building of the pool actually began at the end of October, but the committee was still £30,000 short of its target. A letter was sent round to 5,000 homes in the area asking for donations to help push on to the final target. It received just 200 replies in the first two months and although these brought in £3,000, they were still well short of the target.

The Royalty Cinema closed after sixty five years, with the loss of six jobs but it was immediately announced that the site would be used for a new £265,000 health centre.

The future of the cinema had been in doubt for two years – since the lease on the building off Mayors Avenue and Broadstone had expired. The Torbay Area Health Authority bought the site for £50,000 and aimed to have the new centre built and open by October the next year. The centre would be based across two floors and have 3,200 square feet of space.

The owners of the cinema, Charles Scott Cinemas said it was planning to build another cinema in Dartmouth 'by June 1988 at the latest' but the town did not get a permanent cinema again until February 2005 with the opening of the Flavel Centre.

Tindle Newspapers, owned by Ray Tindle, OBE, bought South Hams Newspapers in November.

Whether or not it had anything to do with the takeover, the paper experimented with new fangled technology at Christmas – with a colour photo on its front page of Santa Claus arriving at Kingswear Station. It looked absolutely lovely but it would be years before colour regularly appeared in the *Chronicle*.

Fundraiser David Kelland in the ball pool paid for by Children in Need cash – which he helped raise.

TOTNES IMAGE BANK/SOUTH HAMS NEWSPAPERS

Demolishing the old Royalty cinema for the new clinic in 1986.
TOTNES IMAGE BANK/SOUTH HAMS NEWSPAPERS?

1987

Dartmouth Primary School nearly brought many of the town's bus services to a halt by changing their bus service provider.

Western National Buses warned that it would 'cut services generally' because of the problems. The school had decided to change the buses they used because pupils were left standing at the side of the road, sometimes by as much as forty minutes as the Western National buses were often delayed due to a change in their route.

After a year of troubles and negotiations between the bus company and the school – during which Western National agreed to change its timetable to make sure buses were at the bus stop before the children and would wait for them – the school decided this was not good enough and hired Burton's Buses of Brixham instead.

Nick Smith of Western National said: 'Carrying the school children is part of a commercial service in the Dartmouth area and if we no longer carried the children it would lead to other less profitable services being withdrawn.'

The decision, made by the primary school governors, was backed by the group's Chairman Hilary Bastone.

'Until last term everything about the service was right,' he said 'then Western National started using buses coming from Newton Abbot and Plymouth to do the school pick-up, rather than local buses. By the time they got to Dartmouth they were very often late. Western National cannot complain. They had a whole term in which to sort something out and didn't.'

Dark events took place in Blackawton bringing with them stories of satanic rituals. A kennel in Blackawton found itself the target of a strange individual or individuals who killed a puppy and apparently drank its blood.

The *Chronicle* printed that the killing was down to 'black magic' showing Minilee Kennels owner Janet Stringer holding one of the incredibly cute and 'lucky' terrier puppies that had not been hurt in the attack in February – on Friday 13.

Someone had been hanging round the kennels for a number of nights and had been chased off once.

Then one night the padlocks were smashed on the gates and one of the Scottish Terriers was found dead and drained of blood. It had been stabbed in the stomach. Another terrier was found to have a two inch wound in its neck but had survived.

Back in the urban centre of Dartmouth, violence and aggression also allegedly reared both their heads.

A Dartmouth gallery owner called for cadets from Britannia Royal Naval College to be banned from the town after their 'drunken revelry' was described as a 'reign of terror'.

Norman Dilley, who owned Facets Gallery in Broadstone, said the cadets were making residents' lives a misery with shouting and other behaviour. He said they acted like 'animals'.

'I consider this to be a war,' he said. 'If things go on like this I will be forced to buy an airgun.'

However, Britannia Royal Naval College officials said: 'There is no hard evidence that it is people from the College.'

Mr Dilley continued, saying the cadets swore, shouted, pulled down displays on shops, climbed and pulled down drainpipes, destroyed flower baskets and vomited in doorways.

He said: 'This is a short cut from the town centre to the College. No one else would use it. They are always young men in their early 20s and smartly dressed. I have followed them back to the College gates and watched them go inside on numerous occasions.'

When he wasn't following drunken young men around the town late at night, Mr Dilley had come up with a plan for what he wanted to happen. He wanted a curfew on cadets, and if that did not work he called for them to be banned completely from the town centre. They weren't.

More upset took place when a 'temporary' car park on the corner of Coronation Park created a bit of an argument. In April the district council suggested spending £35,000 to turn a corner of the park into a car park with spaces for seventy cars.

The council believed that the park could be used to benefit the district council facilities on the park, the tennis courts and putting green.

A Dartmouth estate agent, Derek Scorer, came out fighting before the idea had even got to full council.

'There is a covenant on the park which says it should only be used for recreational purposes,' he said. 'The council is trying to get round it by saying the car park would be used by the people using the park. I cannot believe it will be just a temporary measure. You do not spend £35,000 on a temporary car park.'

Boat owners who used the corner of the park to house their boats were also rather upset.

Dartmouth Yacht Club Commodore Bryan Measures said: 'Not enough thought has gone into this. What happens when a dinghy owner comes off the river to find his space taken by a car?'

The Dartmouth & Kingswear Society got involved and said the plan was 'tantamount to theft' and they sent letters and put other pressure on the council at every opportunity.

It worked; just three weeks after the plan was front page news, the plans were shelved. The council said it was to allow a 'broader' consultation.

Left: *David Kelland with Mavis Kneil at the Seven Stars pub as he tries to raise funds for Children in Need by giving up smoking.*
TOTNES IMAGE BANK/SOUTH HAMS NEWSPAPERS

Right: *The* Dartmouth Chronicle *office decked out for the winning Britain in Bloom entry.*
TOTNES IMAGE BANK/SOUTH HAMS NEWSPAPERS

The Polaris –
*The first cruise
ship to visit
Dartmouth,
moored in the
river.*
DARTMOUTH MUSEUM

Yachtsmen in the town were generally unhappy with the district council yet again when it proclaimed in a leaflet sent to all residents in the district that it had 'significantly improved' the facilities in Dartmouth.

The new Embankment wall had been controversial – it made it 'impossible' for visiting yachtsmen to tie up alongside. Apart from the Embankment Mr Measures said the district council might have improved the facilities by installing 'perhaps a litter bin'. He said the claim the council had improved facilities was 'laughable'.

CRUISE SHIPS ARRIVE BRINGING PROSPERITY WITH THEM

The river attracted a far more positive story when the town welcomed its first cruise ship. The 2,214 ton *Polaris* caused a stir when it arrived in the harbour, carrying 100 passengers.

The visitors were welcomed by the Mayor Donald Webb and Town Crier Peter Randall. After a short tour of the town they were presented with a 'small gift' from the town, although the *Chronicle* failed to say what this gift was.

Also receiving something pleasant was Dartmouth Community College, which was found to be 'one of the top eighty one schools in the country'.

The College was awarded a School's Curriculum Award, for 'excellence in curriculum design and for the quality of teaching and learning in school'.

The report also said that the College's curriculum was 'more advanced than in any other Devon College'.

Only eighty one schools were given the award nationwide and marked the zenith for the College which had enhanced its reputation over the previous few years. It had won awards for its connections with local businesses, and Headteacher Ann Keast had travelled all over the country during the decade to give talks on how the school was run.

The College was then embroiled in controversy around results time when a less than stellar performance in some subjects led a number of parents to contact the *Chronicle* and say that the teaching 'left a lot to be desired'.

The College appealed against the results with the examining board but much discussion in the letters pages ensured that the problems rumbled on for many weeks.

*The children of
Dartmouth get
ready to take their
first plunge in the
new swimming
pool.*
TOTNES IMAGE
BANK/SOUTH HAMS
NEWSPAPERS

**The Long Road to a
Heated Swimming
Pool – and then
the Long Road to
a Heated, Covered
Swimming Pool.**
*See Feature on
pages 136–137*

POOL ARRIVES AFTER SHORT WAIT OF THIRTY SIX YEARS

More happily on the school site, after waiting nearly forty years, Dartmouth got
its first heated swimming pool.

The idea had first been proposed in 1949 when locals had banded together
to collect money for the idea.

Any number of new dawns had come and gone and many had given
up hope but a new initiative had come together a few years before with
secured funding and a site at Milton Lane which had inspired residents
enough to persevere.

A change to the plans, which added £40,000 to the build price, nearly brought
matters to a sorry conclusion at the 11th hour but a late fundraising campaign
and kind developers meant that the pool was built and opened on July 17.

£16,000 was given to the project by the Trustees of the original fund, along
with grants and other funding found within the business community plus
individual donations. The fund was still short by a few thousand pounds, with
no changing rooms having been built before the big opening, so people were
forced to use the school changing rooms.

The town was delighted to finally have its pool and it proved very popular.
Unfortunately as anyone who runs a swimming pool will tell you, running
costs are high, and even with generous grants from local councils, there has
never been anywhere near the cash to build a cover for the Milton Lane pool.
But no one stopped dreaming of a covered swimming pool in Dartmouth.

This did not stop ingenious ideas to raise the funds needed for the changing
rooms at the pool.

Elizabeth Cooper came up with a brainwave when she realised that the town
had a chemist called 'Killer', a bank manager called 'Price', a ferry operator
called 'Crews' and an artist called 'Drew'. She decided to create Dartmouth's
own *Happy Families* card-pack.

She convinced the town's notable artists – Simon Drew, John Gillo, Tony
Close, Marc Farrell and Andras Kaldor – to do some illustrations for free and
the packs proved a huge success.

Finally pressure put on the district council forced it to give an extra £7,500
to help get the changing rooms built.

It seemed at the end, in a vote won by only one councillor's decision to
support the grant, that the district council simply wanted to be rid of the pool
plan altogether.

*Mr Killer the
Chemist from the*
Happy Families
*card pack – see
endpapers.*

171

The Onedin Line Stars Peter Gilmore and Anne Stallybrass judge the best cake competition in 1988s Town Week fete.
TOTNES IMAGE BANK/SOUTH HAMS NEWSPAPERS

Another council drama unfolded in the papers as a town councillor opened the council to accusations of nepotism in July.

Melvyn Stone, who had been a town councillor since May, was one of ten applicants to take on a town centre flat.

After a discussion in council, which Cllr Stone took no part in, he was handed the tenancy for the flat, in which he would live with his wife and 12 year old son.

However, someone else who had wanted to apply, but had not, said he was 'furious' over the decision.

Mr John Foster had wanted to take on the tenancy, but said he had been told by Cllr Stone that children were not allowed. He was obviously surprised, he said, since Cllr Stone had a child, that he was handed the flat.

Cllr Stone said he had only said to Mr Foster that there had never been any children in the flat and that he had applied 'just like anyone else'. He said he was looking forward to moving in to the 'town where I was born and bred.'

DARTMOUTH IN BLOOM FINALLY GETS THE RECOGNITION IT DESERVES

Dartmouth Mayor Don Webb accepts the Westcountry Britain in Bloom cup from BIB representative Muriel Preece.
TOTNES IMAGE BANK/SOUTH HAMS NEWSPAPERS

For the first time, Dartmouth was named the outright best in its class and went through to the national 'Britain in Bloom' final.

It then proceeded to compete in the whole UK 'Britain in Bloom' competition, looking to be named the most florally beautiful town in the whole country.

'Dartmouth in Bloom' Committee Chairman John Craddock-Turnball said: 'I was stunned. Then I thought what a great day for Dartmouth.'

Mayor Don Webb said everyone should be very proud, but should continue to work hard to keep the town looking lovely for the next round of judging.

'That will be the critical time and the appearance of the town, including litter, will be a crucial factor' he said.

The weather is also a crucial factor it seems, for the judges came to Dartmouth in early September when it was pouring down with rain. Dartmouth was the last town to be seen by the judges and hopes were not high for a good result.

However, it seemed that the town had won against the odds when South Hams District Council put out a press release that the town had 'won'. The news was announced on local TV and many thought it was time to crack open the bubbly. Unfortunately it was a mistaken re-release of the previous win news.

Dartmouth had lost out to Stratford-upon-Avon in the final judging but did win the cup for outstanding community effort – otherwise known as the 'Sorry-you-didn't-win' Cup.

1988 Dartmouth Community College was shocked when its best exam results in years saw it 'at the bottom' of Devon's league tables.

However, the mystery was soon solved – the county council admitted it had input the wrong figure for the amount of students taking exams – resulting in a very different set of results. The new results gave a figure of a 56 per cent pass rate for O Levels – when in fact it was 92.7 per cent.

Headteacher Ann Keast, said: 'I was angry when I saw the figures because they were so unbelievable. We have never had such good examination results.'

The school also won an appeal against results given in July 1987 – as only six passes had been registered in Environmental Studies when the College said that there should have been twenty four. The county council wrote to the examination board on behalf of the school and got the decision overturned.

Miss Keast said: 'The examination board has been reconvened, which obviously took time, but eventually the right answer was arrived at. I'm delighted with the results. It has been a great deal of worry over the past few months.'

CAR PARK OR PLAY PARK?

South Hams District Council – yet again – courted controversy when it suggested not rebuilding a children's play area on Mayors Avenue – after the construction of a sewage treatment works – to create more car parking spaces.

The suggestion was one of those peculiarly local press stories – beginning with a tiny NIB (news in brief) piece, which then snowballs, resulting in a deluge of letters to the editor and a popular movement of local people uniting in a common fight.

A group of mothers threatened to march around the town protesting against the plans. The district council pointed out a play area already existed on Coronation Park, but that was dismissed as being 'too far' from the centre of the town.

Shirley Pepperell, organiser of the campaign and march, said: 'We were assured by the district council that once a sewage treatment works had been built at the end of Mayors Avenue car park the toddlers play area would be reinstated, but they have gone back on their word.

'All the mothers put on fund raising events so we could buy play equipment for the children. The Mayors Avenue play area is safer; it's in the middle of town, near the shops. We intend to fight all the way for what is rightfully ours.'

The thirteen extra parking spaces made no difference to the mothers.

The District Council Leisure and Recreation Committee Chairman Percy Moysey decided to carefully announce in March that it 'might' be possible to keep the play area and create more car parking spaces. The mothers took it as a victory and described themselves as 'delighted'.

However, the story was not over yet – in July the district council wrote to the town council stating there was 'no decision' on whether to reinstate the children's playground in Mayors Avenue. Funds were 'no longer available' in that year's budget and the existing equipment, paid for by public donation, was deemed not compliant with health and safety regulations, so could not be used.

Left: *Her Majesty the Queen chats to Britannia Beagles kennelman David Trinnick after naming one of the beagle puppies.*
TOTNES IMAGE BANK/ SOUTH HAMS NEWSPAPERS

Right: *Her Majesty the Queen inspects the Officer cadets at Lord High Admiral's divisions in April 1988.*
TOTNES IMAGE BANK/ SOUTH HAMS NEWSPAPERS

More supportive of the town's well-being was Dartmouth's new £350,000 health clinic. It was officially opened in February by Anthony Steen MP, although it had actually been open since December. The clinic was built on the site of the old Royalty Cinema. It replaced an antiquated wooden building in the Royal Avenue Gardens and offered such wide ranging services as chiropody, speech therapy, audiology, orthoptics, dietetics, child health, guidance and family planning. There would also be 'regular patient sessions in general surgery, gynaecology and oral surgery', but hopefully not all at the same time.

Less conducive to health, the town's streets were filled with 'yobbos' after a rugby match in March. A team from Plymouth were 'the cause' of a running battle through the town's streets involving 'more than 40' people. The Plymouth Captain asserted 'I expect it was the Dartmouth locals picking on our lads.'

However, the investigative journalism bug was not dead and the *Chronicle* found the trouble had been caused when the whole Plymouth team – who had lost 45 nil to the Dartmouth first team that afternoon – 'rolled in' to the Market House Pub and were refused service.

DRUNKENNESS CAUSES PROBLEMS SHOCKER

And that's when the trouble started. As with many problems such as this, only one person was actually prosecuted for 'threatening behaviour' and only one person was officially injured.

Rather more civilised was a Royal visit.

The Queen visited the Britannia Royal Naval College for the first time since 1974 in April. Her Majesty and Prince Philip's route and timetable were kept a closely guarded secret for security reasons.

Her visit 'bathed in sunshine' was 'a very happy one' for the Monarch according to the *Chronicle*.

The day was a long one – she spent five leisurely hours in the grounds of the Britannia Royal Naval College and seemed 'in no hurry to adhere to the planned departure'.

Townstal woman Lisa Chesswas caused a bit of a commotion when her ambulance brought the Royal cavalcade of limousines to a halt as she headed off to hospital to give birth to her daughter Claire. 'They had to stop the Queen to let us through,' said Lisa. 'I passed her at Norton Park and saw her from the ambulance.'

On 19 June Lt Col Richard Webb died. After a distinguished military career, including serving in Burma both during and after the Second World War, he had contributed much to the town in his retirement. He was co-founder of the Dartmouth & Kingswear Society and President of Dartmouth St.John Ambulance.

Dartmouth's Methodist Chapel became the subject of a bitter fight.

The district council decided to knock it down and build a block of flats, a pharmacy and cinema.

The Victorian Society decided to fight for the building to be listed and along with the Devon Buildings Group succeeded in getting the Department for the Environment to agree to do so.

This did not stop the district council continuing with its plan. They went to the department to ask for permission to knock down the building. The council's solicitor, a young man called David Incoll, said he was 'surprised' the Victorian Society was fighting to save the Chapel because 'above the façade of the Chapel it says it was rebuilt in 1935'.

The society's secretary, Dr Christopher Brook said that the Chapel originally dated from 1873 and was designed by John Wills from Kingsbridge who 'became a national figure, and the Dartmouth Chapel is significant in terms of architectural history.'

The Chapel was finally sold in September after two years of hopes, arguments and problems. A last minute petition to prevent the sale was dismissed as 'far too late' by district council officers.

The district council said it had failed to come up with a 'viable scheme' for the Chapel to be converted into a community centre because of the 'inherent problems' in the building. These included severe structural defects, planning requirements and the fact that the Victorian Society had succeeded in getting it listed.

Lieutenant Colonel Richard Webb, Royal Signals, Officer Brother of the Order of St. John and co-founder of the Dartmouth & Kingswear Society, died on 19 June 1988. Proud of his Fiennes family ancestry he was always described as a 'true gentleman'. He was married to Iris Webb (see page 213) and was the father of publisher Richard Webb.
RICHARD WEBB

I RESIGN! ER, CAN I CHANGE MY MIND?

The problems relating to the Chapel continued well into the autumn, when town Cllr Richard Rendle resigned after his proposal to call in the Ombudsman in connection with the sale was rejected. This decision – supported twelve – three by the full Town Council – was then rescinded in committee – without the public present.

Cllr Rendle tendered his resignation, criticising the way the decision had been made 'in secret' and said the council had a 'do-nothing' attitude.

A matter of hours later he tried to withdraw his resignation but he was told it was not possible. He was thanked for his 'forceful' arguing during debates by the Mayor.

Mr Rendle actually stood for the seat he had vacated and competed in the by-election with local fundraiser and stalwart of the amateur dramatics scene, David Kelland.

Mr Rendle won, by just fourteen votes out of several thousand.

A wreck got people excited during the year. The *Golden Hinde* sank in 1987 while being towed to Dartmouth for repairs. She then sat on a buoy until her continuing break up forced the company who salvaged her to use a floating salvage vessel, where, not surprisingly, she rotted a bit more for about six months.

The Harbourmaster Colin Moore threatened to send workmen in with chainsaws to cut the wreck up unless its owners moved it in July.

The boat was finally broken up at the end of August and she received a rather fitting end with the timbers cut off the hull and then burnt on the deck of the salvage barge.

The death of Kingswear District Cllr George South in July inadvertently caused a fight in October.

Mr South, who had been a long serving member of the Dartmouth Harbour Authority, and who had been awarded an MBE in 1944 for his service during the war in the Tank Regiment, died in July while visiting his son in Canada.

Top left: The Golden Hinde II *as it sailed into Dartmouth in 1974 – with no hint of its future woes.*
TOTNES IMAGE BANK/SOUTH HAMS NEWSPAPERS

Bottom left & right: The Golden Hinde II *languishes by the embankment, held up only by massive salvage floatation bags.*
TOTNES IMAGE BANK/SOUTH HAMS NEWSPAPERS

The Italian Navy's sail training ship the Amerigo
Vespucci *(launched in 1931) arrives for a goodwill visit
to the port of Dartmouth and to the Britannia Royal
Naval College in June 2005. Her tall masts (at 50, 54
and 43 metres high) dwarf Dartmouth Castle and St.
Petrox church at the mouth of the river Dart.*
GORDON THOMAS

Some traders of Foss Street with their cameras promoting a photo competition to publicise the street. Left to right are Cliff Mason, Simon Drew and Gilly White (now Webb).
SOUTH HAMS NEWSPAPERS

The district council, led by Trevor Pennington, thought it would be fitting to name the garden at the Priory in Kingswear after Mr South, who had taken a keen interest in its upkeep along with his wife Pamela. She was involved in the design of a new garden, and the district councillors decided that it would all in all be a lovely and popular gesture.

However, they had figured without the strong form of Liz Williams, who took it upon herself to remind the district council that the land on which the garden was had been donated to them by another Kingswear resident – Leonora Carlow. She had died eight years earlier and any garden in the area should be named after her.

She produced a petition signed by 200 residents and felt it necessary to point out 'nobody refused to sign'. She said that the naming of the garden after Mr South without any consultation with the local residents was 'insensitive'. She continued that after eight years without any recognition for Mrs Carlow 'now Mr South has died they want a memorial garden for him. It is high-handed to say the least.'

However, the garden was finally named after Mr South after Parish Council Chairman Dick Parkes pointed out that the £36,000 amount left by the good lady for works around the village had been eaten away by rampant inflation and that the works she had wanted done had in fact cost the district council an extra £65,000 on top of the £36,000 legacy and the decision to fund it had been 'pushed through' by Mr South. To placate the annoyed residents, Mr Parkes proposed the parish council ask the district council for the erection of a plaque to Mrs Carlow.

Dartmouth was shocked by a crime of breathtaking daring in which £10,000 worth of jewels were taken from W Lloyd Attree in Duke Street.

The 'professional' group of thieves cut telephone wires and then silenced the alarms before forcing their way into the shop through the front door. The group took a wide range of expensive jewels, including a 'particularly identifiable' group of pendants and charms in the shape of shackles, pulleys and block and tackle. They were unique to the shop, and were stamped with the initials WTA.

The thieves showed themselves to actually not be *that* professional at all by dropping a number of items as they made their getaway.

Mr Attree showed refreshing calm when he said that he was just relieved nothing 'put by for repairs for customers' was taken.

Army Landing Craft alongside in Dartmouth – to celebrate D-Day.
TOTNES IMAGE BANK/SOUTH HAMS NEWSPAPERS

1989
The year started off with another honest simple idea to help the town – which was mocked mercilessly by most of its residents and condemned by the rest.

Town Cllr Bryan Measures proposed selling the Butterwalk 'for £1 – 2 million' to raise funds for a new, 'proper' community centre.

Mr Measures, just to make sure he caused a big enough controversy, also suggested knocking down the Guildhall and 'developing the site'.

However, he had to admit that it was listed so suggested instead 'gutting it on the inside and starting again'.

Mr Measures even admitted that other town councillors were 'dumbfounded' by his idea. Someone pointed out any investor would expect to make 10 per cent of their investment back a year – which at a £1 million price tag would mean £100,000 for the Butterwalk.

The seven tenants did not like the idea of their rents going up by about 1,000 per cent. The long and the short of it is the Butterwalk wasn't sold.

Other money problems for those on low income caused an argument when a host of Dartmouth couples, trying desperately to get onto the property ladder, were dismayed when Dartmouth County Cllr Marjorie Tomlinson spoke out against 200 new homes in the town.

Cllr Tomlinson said the new homes – planned to be built before the end of the century – would 'destroy' the town and called for 'a massive 'No!' vote to these proposals for Dartmouth'

'If we have to accept another 200 houses we are going to destroy the environment of a beautiful small town which we have got at the moment.

To encroach further on to the green fields around Dartmouth would be a disaster.'

Four couples took exception to these comments – as they tried to buy their own home.

'We feel we have a right to be given a chance of housing in our area', they wrote. 'We are fed up with outsiders, with no cash limit, out-bidding us for homes, forcing up prices beyond our reach, and then having to listen to them deciding that no more houses should be built in case it spoils their adopted area.

1989 World Events
● Ayatollah Khomeini places a US $3 million bounty on the head of *The Satanic Verses* author Salman Rushdie
● The *Exxon Valdez* spills 240,000 barrels of oil in Alaska after running aground
● The Tiananmen Square massacre takes place in Beijing
● Germany opens checkpoints in the Berlin Wall, allowing its citizens to travel freely to West Germany for the first time in decades

HRH The Princess of Wales, accompanied by Captain Robin Shiffner (now Rear Admiral Robin Shiffner CB DL), astounds everyone with her striking red sailor's outfit whilst visiting BRNC for the Passing Out Parade in April 1989.
BRITANNIA MAGAZINE

Many young people who work in and around Dartmouth wish to live here and we believe that if they leave to find affordable homes elsewhere, then other youngsters filling jobs vacancies would soon end up in our situation.

We have no objection to outsiders living here, but let us have a chance to buy our own homes in the area.'

The Regatta Committee were forced to shell out for new whalers after the Britannia Royal Naval College decided to replace the heavy wooden whalers that it had traditionally loaned to the event for the local racing.

The Regatta agreed in February to pay £14,000 'when funds allowed' to buy seven fibreglass 21 foot boats. The town council came forward to pay £6,000 towards the boats and were 'delighted' to support the town's greatest annual event.

Or so it seemed, until the decision came for ratification at full council – when Cllr Melvyn Stone raised an objection that the council only gave out £4,000 each year in total in grants and to give just one organisation £6,000 was too much . He proposed that the council only pay £2000 for one boat, rather than for three. After much impassioned debate the council voted – just – to give the full grant.

Thanks to this and other donations, the seven boats were delivered on time before the Regatta and were named at the event.

SORRY FOR ATTACKING YOUR MEN, ADMIRAL!

The Regatta itself was hailed by many as a 'huge success' and Mayor Brian Measures thanked everyone for their sterling efforts in making it another brilliant event. Unfortunately the festivities got out of hand on the Saturday night with 'a running battle' between sailors from HMS *Cardiff* – the event's Guardship – fairground workers and 'local youths'. 'Around eighty' were reportedly involved in the 'fracas' – a word only used in newspapers, never in conversation – which spread from Victoria Road to the Royal Avenue Gardens.

A police sergeant stressed the sailors, who were apparently banned from shore leave after the incident, were not to blame for the trouble, but were attacked.

The Mayor sent a message to the navy that the town did not attach any blame to the sailors and said they 'entered fully into the spirit of the Regatta'. An MoD spokesman described the 'running battle' as a 'minor incident' and said confining the sailors to ship was for 'no other' reason than wanting to 'appear as conscientious as possible'.

A possible solution to the town's habitual parking problems was scuppered – because it was too ugly.

A car park was proposed by South Hams District Council to 'protrude' into the river from the Higher Ferry Slip for 150 feet, providing car parking for 290 cars.

The scheme would have cost £2 million but was not popular.

The 'wedge shaped' car park would also have featured a facility to lift boats in and out of the water but Cllr Beryl Calder said it would 'spoil the natural beauty that visitors come to see. Cars on the middle of the river would do nothing for Dartmouth.'

Other councillors did support the idea. Cllr Melvyn Stone said: 'people, cars and yachts are not going to go away and Dartmouth urgently needs an alternative car park. The town has to make up its mind in which direction it is heading or we will be left behind by other towns in the area.'

OUT OF PUFF

Dartmouth's railway station, the only one in Britain never to see a train, celebrated its centenary in 1989, and received its first ever train. Well, sort of.

A plan to celebrate the 100th year of the station and 125 years since trains first came to Kingswear included a scale model of a steam train puffing around the Royal Avenue Gardens, which is the nearest the station on the Embankment would ever get to a real one.

CELEBRATING THE 125TH ANNIVERSARY OF THE RAILWAY 1989

IMAGES COURTESY OF DARTMOUTH MUSEUM

Below: *Hilary Bastone and David Kelland prepare for the 125th anniversary of the arrival of the railway to Kingswear.*
TOTNES IMAGE BANK/SOUTH HAMS NEWSPAPERS

Prince Charles meets the Harbour Authority team, surprising Dartmouth with a quick visit
TOTNES IMAGE BANK/SOUTH HAMS NEWSPAPERS

The train, made and lovingly maintained by Dartmouth man Brian Brooks, was supposed to steam all along the Embankment to the old station, which was now a restaurant, transporting a load of happy children.

However, 'safety concerns' stopped the original plan from taking place – the first time 'elf and safety' had been mentioned in the *Chronicle*.

However, the train never got to carry anyone as it failed to progress even an inch during the day. It just sat there, refusing to move like an errant child no matter what the technical people did.

A different kind of fight saw Dartmouth go toe to toe with Tiverton for the right to have a new library – and lose.

The two towns both believed they had the strongest case for a new build library, with Tiverton claiming it deserved it as its library was much worse than Dartmouth's in relation to its size. Dartmouth claimed that not only did the town need a new library desperately, but the town had the perfect host for the library in the old fire station on Mayors Avenue.

Devon County Council did what all councils do before they spend lots of money – it spent lots of money on a feasibility study to see if it really should spend so much money on something.

The county council spent £50,000 on a study comparing the two cases and decided that indeed, Tiverton did have a stronger case and Dartmouth was left disappointed with no foreseeable situation where a new library would be built. It would have to wait a further fifteen years for one, when it was placed in a building no one thought would ever be built anyway.

THIS IS YOUR LIFE CAPTURES TOWN'S IMAGINATION

The town celebrated its notable celebrities with two 'This is Your Life' style events organised to raise funds for the swimming pool.

David Kelland acted as compere for the two evenings in the Guildhall, which has to be the best kept secret in the town's history, as they featured large audiences and the entire families of the two subjects' involvement.

In a small town over a number of months that is no mean feat.

HEROES & HEROINES
LISA CLAYTON *Sailor*

(See year 1995)

Lisa Clayton was the enigma of the Round-the-World sailors; she was barely in the public consciousness.

The former holiday company executive started working towards her dream when she was 35, and received funding for her 35 foot yacht *Spirit of Birmingham* from the city's university, which she attended.

The boat left Dartmouth on September 17, 1994, and she was determined to become the first British woman to sail single-handed, non-stop and un-aided Round-the-World. She also hoped to smash the record for the non-stop circumnavigation for a woman. She was only the second woman to attempt it.

Her feat was queried, but in her 285 days at sea she certainly earned the right to be described as a gutsy and brave lady; capsizing seven times and doubting on long stretches whether she would ever make it back to Dartmouth.

She sent long faxes back to her support team in Britain and they betrayed her desperate and frantic state of mind at times. There were many low points for Clayton as she managed to sail Round-the-World when no one believed she could.

Welcomed back to Dartmouth on the June 29, 1995 at the end of her voyage by a similar flotilla of boats to that which welcomed Naomi James in 1978, she had to undergo the ignominy of having her circumnavigation challenged in the national and international press, a challenge which ultimately failed.

But after her return, and despite an autobiography, she has managed to sail out of the limelight, and seems happy to remain there. She is now Lisa Lyttelton, Dowager Viscountess Cobham.

Lisa Clayton signs a copy of her book Mercy of the Sea *at Dartmouth's Harbour Bookshop for fan Rona Severns.* SOUTH HAMS NEWSPAPERS

Elizabeth Cooper was responsible for putting together the evenings, which were for Brian Riddalls of the famous Red Boats on the river, and Di and John Distin, who were treated to a couple's version.

The Distins almost destroyed the weeks of careful planning by arranging to go to Southampton on the special weekend – but their quick thinking son demanded John stay and help him knock down a wall in his garden. One can only hope that the wall actually needed knocking down.

Unfortunately the decade ended on a rather sad and discouraging note.

Thieves broke into Dartmouth's ambulance station in December and completely stripped the station's newest ambulance of life-saving equipment.

The perpetrators seemed to know what they were looking for, taking only the most modern and valuable equipment causing very little damage in the process. The value of the items was estimated at £13,500.

PC Mike Pope of Dartmouth police said he had 'never known' an ambulance or fire station being broken into before.

Irene Scawn of the Dartmouth Hospital League of Friends, which had donated the £6,000 defibrillator taken in the robbery, said: 'It is sickening to think there are people walking around who can do this sort of thing.'

Supt Chris Cole of the ambulance station said all the thieves had left were 'pillows and blankets'. Paramedic Ralph Woodward said the worst thing about the raid, on top of the loss of life saving equipment, was that it took the whole station off line for a morning, potentially putting lives at risk.

The decade had seen huge changes and huge economic shifts from the positive to the negative but the 'Nineties' were now arriving, and as all new decades do, seemed full of hope.

CHAPTER V

Dare to Dream
1990s

THE QUEST TO BRING NEW FACILITIES TO DARTMOUTH

The 1990s, following on from the 'decade of excess' had a lot to live up to – and it managed it. The town's residents were caught up in some of the world's most important and traumatic events in Iraq and Somalia, as well as achieving amazing things sailing the world and walking the length of Africa. The town also realised how powerful it could be if its residents worked together – especially when everyone started noticing exactly what facilities its neighbouring towns enjoyed. Everyone started to wonder why THEY had THAT and when WE could have one too?

This was a decade of dreaming, but also hard graft to get the things the town needed and desired. Discussed were a new sports centre and swimming pool; a water sports centre; an arts centre and a park and ride. The park and ride was achieved, but though the others weren't, people didn't give up.

They also decided the town wouldn't be dictated to, and threw out a number of plans from Devon County Council to bring in a residents parking system which would have included on street parking meters.

The main feeling you get throughout the ten years of the 1990s is that there were some amazing stories in the town – really interesting and fascinating stories which made the *Chronicle* a riveting read for the whole decade. It became imbued with more colour and verve in its style than ever before as desk top publishing techniques gave sub-editors more tools to make the *Chronicle* look as interesting as possible. This would be followed by the opportunities offered by new technology leading up to the new Millennium, which heralded the *Chronicle* and its sister titles embracing the digital age.

The world was suddenly full of opportunities: could the people of Dartmouth make the most of them?

Café Alf Resco's first opened on 1 April 1994 and quickly became a Dartmouth institution famous for its award-winning breakfasts.
Nigel Evans

1990

The Poll Tax was revealed in April but it barely registered a mention in the *Chronicle*, the town just seemed to accept it.

Much more important to many was what was being done with the taxes they paid – were the roads being maintained? It seemed not: businesses dependent on tourism were left fearing for their future after the A379 above Blackpool Sands was closed.

BORE-ING PROBLEM

The road was shut after a landslide in January and remained shut for months due to very real concerns about public safety as the entire road was considered dangerous. Further falls after the road was closed seemed to confirm everyone's worst fears and the use of a wartime Bailey bridge was even discussed to span the unstable section of road.

Geologists bored into the road and reported it could not take the weight of traffic safely. A whole section needed significant strengthening. Everyone involved scratched their chins and tried to decide what to do – as the Bed & Breakfast and pub owners in the area became increasingly perturbed. It was eventually repaired a number of months later after protracted negotiations with the landowners.

Another argument broke out due to Western National Buses failing to stop its buses.

The company refused to comply with a traffic experiment which pedestrianised Duke Street. The plan was designed to see if the long mooted, and extremely unpopular, inner relief road could actually work.

Devon County Council Highways Officer Geoff Downes warned the entire experiment would be put in jeopardy unless the company complied, and the police warned that it could put pedestrians, expecting a traffic-free street, in danger of 'injury or death'.

The move was far from popular with residents, who had just endured a number of weeks of disruptions due to the road being closed, thanks to South West Water flood protection works. The experiment went ahead in the spring, just in time for the May Day Bank holiday. It disrupted the routes of all the town's buses, twelve an hour at the time, and caused snarl ups around the whole town for its many tourist visitors.

The closure went ahead between 10am and 4pm each weekday during the summer and when it ended in October everyone heaved a huge sigh of relief because it had, seemingly, caused a lot of disruption and seemed to solve nothing at all.

One correspondent to the *Chronicle* summed it up when they said: 'What a huge waste of time, money and effort'.

DARTMOUTH REMEMBERS THE LITTLE BOATS OF DUNKIRK

The town marked the 50th anniversary of the 'Miracle' of Dunkirk with a large and impressive service on the South Embankment.

Three boats which had been part of the great Armada, which had crossed the Channel to rescue more than 330,000 troops of the British Expeditionary Force in May 1940, were alongside during the service.

Before the religious ceremony, led by Rev John Butler, there was a procession from the Royal Avenue Gardens of veterans, all of whom owed their lives to the use of hundreds of boats like *Gondolier Queen*, *Seymour Castle* and *Our Lizzie*, which had been called upon to make the perilous journey across the Channel to Dunkirk and back.

The state of the Royal Avenue Gardens was the topic of much discussion in December. Six lime trees were chopped down much to the chagrin of many residents who led a short campaign to save the beloved trees. The campaign was short because it appears that South Hams District Council, who as owners, were responsible for all the work done in the gardens, had managed to keep the scheme very quiet.

The story of the tree felling broke in one week's edition and the next featured the story of them actually being cut down.

Veronica Wood, Kingswear resident, said on the day the trees were felled: 'I was so angry this morning. I had just come across to do some shopping and actually saw the men cutting the trees down. I gave them a piece of my mind. There were only two trees left when I got there. They should have given us a chance to make our views known. I hate to think the council officials are sitting back comfortably as if this is an end to the matter.'

But Deputy Mayor Joan King, who was also tree warden for the town, dismissed the protests, saying 'only a few' people had complained.

Royal Avenue Gardens in all their splendour. The beauty of these gardens was under threat during 1990.
Nigel Evans

'If the trees were left the plans for the gardens would make it difficult for new plants to grow there. The trees (which were 40 years old and growing steadily) were getting bigger and bigger and apparently the grass was dying because of the gooey sap that oozes from lime trees. Sometimes changes are necessary.'

The lime trees were replaced by cherry trees, which were threatened by felling in 2006 because they were 'exactly the wrong sort of tree to plant there' according to the head gardener at that time – Les Barnes.

CASTING AROUND FOR SUCCESS

Kingswear man Reg Little made headlines across the world because he asked Prince Charles for his unwanted plaster cast.

Mr Little contacted the Prince after he broke his wrist in a fall during a polo match. He told the Prince that he thought it would make a good raffle prize to raise funds for Kingswear church roof. To his and everyone else's surprise, the Prince agreed.

The raffle attracted huge interest from the national press and tickets were sent all over the world and also raised £1,700 for the roof.

As well as helping achieve a much needed roof for St Thomas Church, it also helped bring the Little family closer together too.

Distant relatives of Reg in Australia read about the auction in *Tit Bits* magazine and got into contact with him. The family in Kingswear is now aware of and is in regular contact with a large new portion of their family and all thanks to what the *Chronicle* described, with punning fun, as 'a cast off' from a Prince.

Mayor Bryan Measures was 'ousted' from office at the annual Mayor-making Ceremony after losing a vote of no confidence.

Cllr Measures, who was also district councillor for the town, was up for a second term in office, but was rejected by his fellow councillors, who voted him out with the same majority with which they had voted him in.

His amazing fall from grace came after other councillors said they felt 'left out' of decisions, and said that the decisions that they were involved in were not then carried out.

The man who took ex-Cllr Measures' place, Brian Edgington, later said in defence of those involved in the 'ousting': 'Some members thought they had been subjected to a year of trickery and double dealing and these were not just a splinter-group of malcontents or disenchanted councillors but the majority of those legally appointed to represent the views of the people of Dartmouth. So, quite rightly, the Mayor was called upon to give an account of his actions. It could be clearly seen that the majority confidence in the Mayor had evaporated.'

Mr Measures was the most popular councillor at the parish council elections the next year with 200 more votes than his nearest competitor.

1991 British forces joined an international coalition when they rolled into Iraq on January 17, bringing the many forces' families around the town much concern along with a strong sense of pride. The war had been sparked by the invasion of Kuwait by Iraqi forces and there was a sense of justice for the actions of the international community.

Elspeth Harbord, Dartmouth representative of the Soldiers', Sailors' and Airmen's Association, said they had been preparing for the possibility of war for some time and were geared up to give full support to local families with relatives involved.

Mayor Brian Edgington made sure the men from Dartmouth involved in the conflict – Jason Hart, Glen Sunderland, Adrian and Barry Langmead and Simon Vickers – were kept informed of their home town by sending letters to them and also copies of the *Chronicle* every week. The conflict ended on the last day of February, and none of the town's 'boys' were injured during the brief and incredibly one-sided conflict.

The 'war' proved mainly a progression through Kuwait and then into Iraq. However, fearing a loss in the next Presidential election, George Bush (Senior) stopped the advance through Iraq as dictator Saddam Hussein prepared to flee. Bush lost the election to a man from the south of the USA known as Bill and it took Bush's simple son to go and finish the job, and nearly finish off the country more than a decade later.

BLOWN OUT OF PROPORTION?

Also in danger was the state of a much-loved landmark in the town.

The Methodist Chapel on the Market Square hit the national headlines when an explosion ripped through the building.

The police began their investigation by issuing a description of two men who had been working on the building just before it blew up at the end of February.

Their suspicions soon fixed upon the building's owner.

The building had been sold to developer Peter Denega of Torquay in the late Eighties after plans for a community centre and cinema complex in the empty chapel fell through.

Mr Denega had submitted plans for a number of sheltered accommodation units, but found his plans dashed when South Hams District Council, which itself had sold him the building after it failed to agree a scheme and funding for the conversion, refused him planning permission. Angry and in financial hardship, Mr Denega had caused a makeshift explosion within the Grade II listed building which he thought would free the site up and allow him to build whatever he wanted, after claiming a large sum in insurance.

What he didn't count on was being arrested and imprisoned for four months in April for illegally causing the explosion. He was convicted along with an accomplice, Steven Mann.

The Chapel, which had been the subject of long wrangles during the 1980s, with the Victorian Society fighting to make sure its façade was preserved, was demolished after it was found to be nearing collapse following the explosion.

Workmen were forced to scramble out of the ruin as the main body of it collapsed a few days after the blast. They had been trying to carefully bring the structure down without endangering the buildings close by the Chapel. Luckily no one was hurt and the other buildings remained standing.

Pictures of the building, with a smoking gaping hole in its front, adorned most of the national press after the explosion took place and it became clear it was not an accident.

Also explosive was the tirade Mayor Brian Edgington gave when he hit out at the press as he was re-elected to the office by his fellow councillors.

He said that the reporting of events at the council was biased and partial. He also accused the press – mainly meaning the *Chronicle* itself – of covering items of no importance and ignoring very important business indeed.

'Where is the coverage of notable events of wide interest compared to the wide coverage of trivial events with minimal appeal? There appears to be absolutely no notion of newsworthiness, or indeed any real desire to present the important issues fairly and in due proportion.'

Friday, April 10, 1992   Volume CXXXIX No.15   Registered as a Newspaper   Price 25p

CHAPEL OWNER GOES TO JAIL

12 months for lawyer's clerk

A HARD-UP property developer who hired a quarryman to blow a crack in Dartmouth's listed Methodist Chapel was this week jailed for four months.

His accomplice, who bungled the operation and caused an explosion which shook residents in their beds, was sentenced to 28 days in prison and given a three-month suspended sentence.

Plymouth Crown Court heard the plan was to damage the building to get round planning laws and build by developer Peter

Mr Andrew Chubb, prosecuting, said the chapel had been bought

Denega from South Hams Council in 1988.

Two years later he gained planning per-

Flashback to the explosion scene

mission to convert the grade two listed Wesleyan chapel pro-

these processes in pursuit of profit and the use of explosives to

A DARTMOUTH lawyer's clerk has been jailed for a year by Plymouth Crown Court.

Ronald Thorne, 58, a former Metropolitan Police sergeant with 30 years' service, was convicted by a jury on two counts of trying to pervert the course of justice and acquitted on two other charges.

Thorne had appeared before Exeter Crown Court in February where he was found guilty on two counts of attempting to pervert the course of justice.

He was sentenced to 12 months in prison on each count, to run concurrently.

The trial followed a police investigation started in January 1989 concerning allegations that while Thorne was employed as a clerk to Dartmouth solicitor Mr John Hansell, evidence was fabricated or dis-

course of justice, which was a serious offence.

In fact, no injustice had occurred, the judge was told.

One of the offences related to Thorne giving a youth a false story to mislead police following a stabbing incident.

A second indictment against Thorne containing 20 counts of forgery, deception and false accounting – which Thorne denied – will not be proceeded with following consultations with the Director of Public Prosecutions, Judge Taylor was told.

Crabber crew rescue

TWO Dartmouth crewmen were rescued from a liferaft in the English

This followed reporting of 'underhand tactics' during the parish council elections and various councillors taking swipes at each other through the pages of the *Chronicle*.

The sad remains of the chapel on the front page of the Chronicle *after its owner, Peter Denega is sentenced to four months in prison for blowing it up.*

WOE BETIDE THE POLITICIAN

It got so bad that the vicar Rev John Butler preached against the discord from the pulpit – on Mayor's Sunday no less, with the whole of the town council and the new Mayor in the congregation in front of him.

'The local people have been sickened by the methods used in our recent elections and subsequent events,' he said, 'the smear campaigns and vitriolic attacks and the corresponding ripostes. A community and its good citizens have no place for petty, puerile party politics, nor for reactionary response. Today's great Christian feast prays that pride, arrogance and folly might be no more and that they may be replaced with love, joy, peace, patience, kindness, goodness, trustfulness, gentleness and self-control. Self needs to be forgotten, self interest needs to be forgotten, past wrongs need to be forgotten and we need to work together for the good of all, for the good of our town.'

A Dartmouth man was killed after being caught up in the escalation of violence in Somalia – and his family heard it first on the national news.

Brian Bowden, 62, brother of Dartmouth Amateur Rowing Club stalwart and ex-Regatta chairman John, was killed when robbers broke into his home in the country's capital Mogadishu on Thursday May 16. He was shot. He was the only Briton left in the country having chosen to stay with his wife rather than abandon her.

He had moved to the capital in 1988 when the civil war there had forced him, his Somali wife and their children to move from the rural town of Hargeisa.

The country had been thrown into chaos when the president Siad Barre had been overthrown in the late Eighties and the British ambassador had been withdrawn from the country with all his staff. Mr Bowden, who had moved to Somaliland, as it then was, in 1958, took over management of the Embassy registry in late 1990 and had worked there tirelessly despite the terrible and very dangerous conditions.

Captain Colin Moore (third from right), the Harbourmaster, takes interested parties through South West Water's plan for a sewerage works and car park built out into the river.
Totnes Image Bank/South Hams Newspapers

He was given the option by the British authorities to leave the country with his children, but chose to stay on because he could not secure passage for his wife.

Mr Bowden, or Chas as he was known, was part of the famous four that won the Under 20s West of England rowing championship, and went on to be champions four times in the 1950s at senior level.

John told the *Chronicle* he had found out about his brother's death while watching the national news on television.

'I rang the Foreign Office to get details and they told me what had happened and that Brian had been buried out there by a Red Cross organisation. We are not sure what has happened to his wife and children.'

HOT RATS AND RUBBISH TO GO

Rubbish and rats got the town hot and bothered in May as businesses blamed inadequate collections for litter strewn in the streets.

Waste from restaurants in particular was left out to be spread by seagulls, which in turn attracted rats. There were calls for severe fines for those found to be leaving rubbish out at the wrong times or in the wrong places.

Restaurateurs hit back saying they were 'forced to leave their rubbish out in flimsy plastic bags overnight – which encourages rats and gulls'.

Roy Beardsmore, owner of the fantastically named Filthy McNasty's in Fairfax Place said: 'We can't win. I have very little storage room at the back of the property. People moan if we leave the bags out overnight but if we don't we could miss the collection which comes very early. We then have to keep the stuff back for another day. I think it would be better if a collection was made in the evenings.'

Janet Hill, of the Cherub pub and restaurant in Higher Street said: 'It's very unfair. People who don't have to pay are scattering their rubbish all along the streets and adding it to ours. We triple wrap our waste and only put it out overnight for the collection twice a week. This year I have paid out £1,000 on refuse collection and have also bought a special cupboard to keep the waste in until it's time to be collected. We do exactly as the law tells us to do.'

1992 The old secondary school in Victoria Road was knocked down to make way for 22 two-bedroomed flats.

The school, which had become an iconic building in the town, as most of the great and the good had been through its doors, was knocked down in the first week of July and old pupils were invited to 'help'.

The school had been bought by South Hams District Council in 1989 with a view to replacing it with a housing scheme. It had been used until the mid Eighties by the Community College in Milton Lane because the final completion of the school had been delayed by various problems. These were mostly to do with the local education authority not being prepared to pay for it. Since it had been empty, the debate had raged about how to use the buildings effectively.

The South Hams scheme – which was planned at £1.3 million – was delayed by the presence of a pair of nesting house martins.

South Hams District Council Chairman Jeanne Thomson said that it would be a 'pity to destroy their homes just to make way for ours'. It was not recorded what the twenty two couples due to move into the flats thought about the birds.

Dartmouth Regatta became the victor in a High Court battle over its annual fair.

FAIRGROUND FIGHTS DRAG ON

The implausibly named 'Showman's Guild' had fought the Regatta all the way to the top court in the land to allow Whitelegg and Sons to run a fair in the Mayors Avenue car park. Whitelegg's had run the fair until 1991 but the Regatta committee had 'sacked' them for 'irresponsible behaviour' although the *Chronicle* failed to say exactly what that behaviour was.

The guild tried to prove that the Regatta committee were being unreasonable and that Whitelegg's had a 'right' to put on a fair because, basically, it had in the past. The date was all set for a 'High Court showdown' between the committee and the guild, but an '11th hour climb down' according to the *Chronicle*, left the guild with a red face and all the costs to pay and the Regatta crowing. It was 'allowed' to install De Vey Fairgrounds as the 'official' provider of the Regatta fairground.

Chairman Richard Rendle said: 'It is a good conclusion. We will have a good quality fair, which will reflect well on the Regatta.'

The event's problems were not over as another ride owner David Rowland took the Regatta Committee to the High Court for the second time in four months and won.

The dodgem owner won the right to bring six rides to the Regatta, which would have to be accommodated alongside the De Vey's 'legitimate' fairground. Mr Rendle said: 'They will be unwelcome guests.'

The event itself featured the worst weather for sixty years, and many events, including the by now traditional Red Arrows air display, were cancelled.

1992 World Events
● Boris Yeltsin announces that Russia will stop targeting United States cities with nuclear weapons
● Betty Boothroyd becomes the first woman elected Speaker of the British House of Commons
● A jury acquits four LAPD police officers accused of excessive force in the videotaped beating of African American motorist Rodney King, causing the LA Riots – leading to 53 deaths and $1 billion in damage
● A fire breaks out in Windsor Castle, causing over £50 million worth of damage

The new archway for the Royal Avenue Gardens was installed in 1992, after being constructed by Dartmouth blacksmith Alan Middleton
South Hams Newspapers

*Richard and
Gilly Webb from
Dartmouth on
their wedding day
in Gibraltar on
February 25, 1992.*
RICHARD WEBB

Happier times, however, beckoned for Dartmouth publisher Richard Webb as he married his fiancée Gilly in Gibraltar in February. The couple had met at the popular *Good Food Guide* listed Billy Budd's Bistro in Foss Street which she owned in partnership with Keith Belt.

The Royal Avenue Gardens entrance got a new archway designed and paid for by a man who lived in Maidstone.

Jack Middleton decided to have the archway made by his nephew Alan, who ran the family blacksmiths in Zion Street, after South Hams District Council had the old arch removed during 'refurbishment'. In another move seemingly designed to anger people in the town, the district council then decided not to replace the structure.

The Old Dartmothians put out a call for someone to get an archway, so Old Darts member Mr Middleton, a former blacksmith himself, designed and paid for the arch. It came in seven pieces, weighed two-and-a-half tons and was dedicated in the middle of July in a large ceremony attended by the great and the good – though not by officers from the district council.

THAT'S NOT FINE, OFFICER

Ex-Kingswear hero sailor Chay Blyth tried to get out of a speeding ticket – and landed himself with a driving ban instead.

Mr Blyth, as he was before his knighthood, was clocked on the A38 doing 110 mph. When the police (finally) caught up with him he was reported as saying 'I'll call it 90 and take a fixed penalty'. The officers involved in stopping him had obviously not had the memo stating that national heroes get to decide their own punishment and booked him. A week later he was in Totnes magistrate's court getting banned for four weeks and being fined £200. A rather sheepish future knight apologised to the court saying he had no excuse.

Also not happy at a fall from an exalted position, the town of Dartmouth ended its remarkable run of thirteen straight awards in the Britain in Bloom competition.

The town lost out to Crediton in the category of a town with a population between 4,500 and 10,000. The town had really pulled out the stops with more than 200 hanging baskets and had raised £3,000 to put on the display. The disappointment was palpable in the quote from Committee Chairman Wilf Lye: 'A lot of hard work was put in by the committee and the people of Dartmouth. There were many more baskets put out this year.'

English cricket star Ian Botham walked into Dartmouth – backwards – and offended a lot of school children. He was walking 535 miles through the westcountry but was so eager to make his schedule he marched through many of the towns on his route and didn't slow down – in fact he seemed to go faster.

Stoke Fleming Headteacher Pam Eales said: 'The children were disappointed. They'd gone down there with their money to give and he came through so fast surrounded by his henchmen that they couldn't even see which was him.'

He then dumbfounded those watching by walking backwards up College Way to 'save his calves' according to his spokesman.

Also inexplicable was the behaviour of a man who nearly killed himself when he set fire to his flat when bailiffs turned up.

On Thursday November 13, Mr Chris Keanan, of Mayflower Close, doused his first floor flat with petrol and set light to it. The bailiffs had arrived at 11.30am to evict him, so he doused the place in petrol and lit a match. Mr Keanan was dragged semi-naked from the property suffering 30 per cent burns on his face, arms and legs. He was airlifted to Derriford Hospital at Plymouth by the Air Ambulance.

The man's landlord, South Hams District Council, confirmed he was being evicted after 'substantial non-payment of rent over a period of time' but said it hoped his injuries were 'not severe' and that he had a 'speedy recovery'. They also confirmed they had taken back the flat and would have it repaired and let out again as soon as possible.

STINK OVER A POTENTIAL STINK

The town reacted with 'fury' over plans from South West Water to build a sewerage works along the Embankment, next to a children's play area.

The project, which was set to begin building in 1995, left residents 'aghast' when it was revealed at a public consultation at the Guildhall.

Despite claims from the water company that the £30 million site

Ian Botham walks through Dartmouth – impressing very few people – before walking up College Way, backwards, and then out of the town.
SOUTH HAMS NEWSPAPERS

would be 'odourless', the main complaint of residents was the need to pick up sewage by tanker three times a day from the point where the Mayors Avenue car park joined the Embankment. The water authority had to defend itself against claims that it had misled people with a series of earlier presentations on the proposed scheme to groups such as the town council and the Dartmouth & Kingswear Society. These presentations had shown quite a small development with a modest building at its centre. The new models and drawings showed a 'more obtrusive' and less 'modest' building, which was 148 yards long and 21 yards wide.

Geoff Breckin, of South West Water remained 'unmoved' when pressed by councillors and members of the public at a large meeting. He was told the building was 'unacceptable' and the water authority should 'reconsider' the plans. He was told of other sites where a sewerage treatment works would be appropriate, but simply said it 'depends how much more you want to pay for sewerage treatment'. He said the site was the most affordable and comparatively the most desirable.

The letters pages were full for weeks. The publicity went on and on, and still South West Water insisted that the site was the best for Dartmouth and the rest of the area.

However, the pressure from the town was overwhelming and the scheme was shelved. South West Water went on looking for a site to solve its sewerage problems in Dartmouth.

November saw possibly the most dramatic event of the decade in Kingswear, when a school bus caught fire and burned so fiercely that it bent drainpipes through the heat it generated.

The bus was picking up children from Kingswear to go to St.Cuthbert Mayne School in Torquay around 8.30am on Friday November 20. Fire was spotted coming from the engine as it pulled up on the banjo turning area and only quick work from the driver and the prefects on board prevented a tragedy as all the children rapidly exited the bus. A lucky escape as within ten minutes the bus was an inferno.

The children had to shiver in the cold as firemen used breathing apparatus to fight the blaze, with toxic smoke pouring off the foam in the bus's seats.

A reconditioned engine had been put into the bus just weeks previously and an electrical fault in this engine was blamed for the blaze.

New moorings on the river caused controversy in December – as the town council claimed they would do nothing for Dartmouth.

The councillors said the 100 new moorings were 'of no benefit' to the town at all – and Cllr Richard Rendle said that he had tried to convince the Dart Harbour and Navigation Authority not to go ahead with the plan 'but to no avail'.

This brought a swift response from the DHNA Chairman Major Don Campbell who said that the objection was 'a bit late' as the moorings had been discussed for two years at public meetings. He also said that the Duchy of Cornwall would demand the maximising of the economic potential of the river, so would demand that moorings be laid where they were viable and useful.

The letters page was full of correspondence on the issue, all of it attacking the position taken by the town council. Many pointed out that the lifeblood of Dartmouth's businesses was tourists and visitors arriving by water, and to stop more moorings was to stop money coming in. The town council did not reply.

1993 World Events
● The European
Community (EC)
eliminates trade barriers
and creates a European
single market
● A 51 day stand-off at
the Branch Davidian
compound near Waco,
Texas, ends with a fire
that kills 76 people,
including David Koresh
● A large scale battle
erupts between U.S.
forces and local militia
in Mogadishu, Somalia;
18 Americans and over
1,000 Somalis are killed

1993

The year began with 'mayhem'. Just fifteen minutes into the New Year, a woman had been run over, six people had been injured and a drunk driver had to be taken into custody for his own protection.

The incident brought calls for the annual New Year's celebration to be curtailed.

'Thousands' gathered on the Quay to see in the New Year, many bussed in from other parts of the county and beyond.

After 1993 had been welcomed in, the volume of people was such that the Quay did not clear quickly and after fifteen minutes of blockage one impatient, and as it turned out drunk driver, tried to push his way through in his car. He pushed too hard and a woman fell beneath the wheels of the car. She was treated for bad cuts and bruises but released later in the night. Five other people received injuries as the car hit people in the crowd. When people around the car realised what had happened they began to attack it and the driver, smashing the windows and badly denting the vehicle. Quick thinking policemen got the man away from the vengeful crowd. They were then even more thoughtful and breathalysed him – and caught a drunk driver.

Two others were arrested in connection for their part in the attack on the car and a further two were arrested for drink related offences. South Hams District Council workmen cleared seven tons of rubbish off the streets following the celebrations – more than they would do after Regatta Saturday. Much of the rubbish was broken bottles that seemed to have been deliberately smashed by raucous revellers.

HOW MUCH IS TOO MUCH?

The incident at the end of one of the busiest nights in the history of the New Year celebrations in Dartmouth prompted calls for a plan to draw people away from the streets and into the Royal Avenue Gardens with lights and entertainment. Many businesses were fearful of losing what was one of the most profitable nights in the year, so were cautious of encouraging too much change.

It was obviously a bit of a raucous night, and one which Nigel Way owner of the Royal Castle Hotel would probably want to forget. He lost £1,500 worth of antique swords, taken in a daring robbery from right under his nose. The swords, made by Wilkinson between 1860 and 1900, were hung on the wall of the Galleon bar in the historic hotel, wired 'securely' to the wall, but some clever revellers brought wire cutters with them, used the cover of a packed bar to cut them down and then smuggle them out of the hotel without anyone, not the staff or even the doormen, noticing anything about it.

Mums from the Windward nursing home who all had babies within a year of each other: Gabbie Amos, Elizabeth Keddad, Moira Laidlaw and Laura Malley.
Totnes Image Bank/ South Hams Newspapers

Rolf Harris entertains the children during a Christmas Extravaganza in Dartmouth's Royal Avenue Gardens.
TOTNES IMAGE BANK/ SOUTH HAMS NEWSPAPERS

JOBS NEEDED TO PROTECT THE SCHOOLS

Dartmouth Community College Headteacher Ann Buckingham warned that unless more jobs were created in the Dartmouth area, the College would close.

Mrs Buckingham told the public enquiry into the Dartmouth Local Area Plan, being put together by South Hams District Council, that more industry was needed to attract people between 20 and 30 years of age whose young families could boost the flagging numbers at the small College, which had fallen by 150 in less than ten years. The low figures and the nature of education funding meant that this put a huge strain on the finances of the College: 'The school is part of the town but is taken for granted,' she told the enquiry. 'It is a facility which would be a huge loss if it went. We have to deliver the national curriculum under which science and technology require the use of expensive specialised equipment. In spite of our small size we have proved to be a successful school and we are really determined to continue to be successful.'

Mrs Buckingham claimed that if investment in the town could be encouraged so young families began moving there then the College could grow to be 500 strong again in 2000. Although she pointed out that this was smaller than the Whitehall model which said a school of between 600 and 800 pupils provided the best and most cost effective size for schools under new funding schemes now based on pupil numbers.

Keith Floyd made the headlines for breaking up with his wife on his birthday – but then getting back together again.

Floyd was one of the first chefs to be a celebrity in the modern sense of the word. Rather than a serious foodie only famous for what he concocted in the kitchen, he was famous for his all-smoking, all-drinking persona. He married Shaunagh Mullett of Dartmouth in 1991 and they were running the Maltster's Arms in Tuckenhay at the time of their break up.

Mr Floyd reportedly flung a huge hissy-fit when he thought Shaunagh had forgotten to buy him a birthday present in the last days of 1992.

However he was mistaken as he had forgotten that he had opened the birthday presents she had bought him at Christmas. Perhaps a bit too much wine had confused him. Floyd was onto his third marriage and was perhaps a little tired.

Dartmouth Celebrity Chefs – A Brief History. See Feature on pages 92–93

Above and below:
*The Russian
training ship*
Gangut *moored
at Dartmouth in
October 1993.*
SOUTH HAMS
NEWSPAPERS

Mr Floyd was so angry he 'kicked out' the 26 year old beauty, and put a slur on all women from the town, saying they were 'Vikings' and that 'they could make up an England rugby pack'.

But just days later the couple were seen enjoying a happy lunch down the road at the Waterman's Arms and seemed to be on fantastic terms. He then appeared back at the pub as Shaunagh arranged a party.

It turned out that the couple had in fact made up just forty eight hours after their row, but had decided not to tell the world because the press – dubbed 'vultures' by the couple – had turned up at the pub in their droves after Floyd had ranted in the national media that the marriage was over. Perhaps not surprisingly, Keith was promoting a new TV series and book at the time and the couple admitted that though they had not planned it, the 'split' had turned into a publicity stunt.

A group of women from Dartmouth decided they would get their own back on Floyd for his 'Vikings' comments and they got their chance in the summer at the carnival when a group of screaming Viking women cornered him and gave him a very good natured telling off. Floyd took it in his stride and laughed it off knowing that his TV series was currently being broadcast.

PICTURES OF ENGLAND

A Dartmouth man was imprisoned after repeatedly beating his own baby son and eventually breaking the boy's arm and ribs.

Robert Austin was convicted and sent to prison after pleading guilty, telling the court he had lost his temper on a number of occasions. His barrister actually managed to blame the boy who had been less than 6 months old when the assaults took place for his injuries.

The man said the family's home was cramped and the walls covered in damp.

'The arrival of a second child was in every way a disaster; [his son] was a fractious child who grizzled a lot.'

HEROES & HEROINES
Ffyona Campbell
(See year 1993)

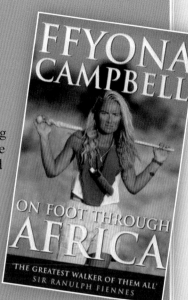

The story of the 1990s for the *Chronicle* was the world-record breaking efforts of Ffyona Campbell. Still in her 20s, she achieved remarkable things, 'walking the world' as it was dubbed, and her parents looked on proudly from their home in Stoke Fleming.

She walked out of Africa and into the record books on August 1, 1993 after walking 10,055 miles from Cape Town to Tangiers.

She had left home ten years earlier, at the age of just 16, with the aim of walking round the world. She had walked more than 17,000 miles across Britain, the USA and Australia before beginning in Africa in April 1991.

She planned to take a year to walk the length of the great continent – but civil war, robberies and assaults hampered her journey considerably.

Her family must have gone slowly mad as they heard about her exploits, which included being escorted out of Zaire by the French Foreign Legion during the civil war there in 1991, being robbed and having to push a hand cart carrying water supplies through hundreds of miles of parched desert.

She nearly didn't make it: just five days before reaching the Mediterranean Sea, she was the victim of an attempted rape in Morocco. She was grabbed by a 'beach bum' in the middle of a crowded market and subjected to an attack which left her battered and bruised.

But Ffyona was shocked when two squads of police failed to act when she described what had happened. She had scratched the man on the face and thought that would give them a good lead to follow – but to no avail. She called the British Ambassador who got onto the country's Interior Ministry. They had the local police pick the man up and ensured he received punishment.

She reached the beach in Tangiers on September 1 and was welcomed by a large group of friends and family.

She made a trip to Stoke Fleming and was taken aback by the lushness of the vegetation, and the cleanliness of the animals. She also demonstrated how driven she was, an observation made by nearly everyone who encountered her. Just days after completing her epic three-year trek, she went for a jog on Blackpool Sands.

'There is something so clean and fresh here that you don't get anywhere else,' she told the *Chronicle*.'Everything looked so plump, the hedgerows looked so vibrant after the desert and all the animals are clean. You just want to go and hug them.'

But there was soon to be a backlash. Her public image had already been tarnished by her 'difficult' nature which had resulted in many of her support team members refusing to work with her anymore, and she had famously fallen out with Janet Street Porter, who 'shadowed' her during her Africa walk for a BBC 2 documentary: the two had hated each other on sight.

And then in 1996, 'consumed by guilt' she released a new book *The Whole Story* in which she admitted taking lifts when crossing America.

On the crossing she had become pregnant by one of her support crew. She found it harder and harder to make the gruelling set of public engagements for her main sponsors. Realising the reason, she made a hard decision and had an abortion before getting back on track. However she had received lifts for the best part of 1,000 miles. She went back and re-walked the sections she had missed and asked the *'Guinness Book of Records'* to remove her entry. The book's administrators refused. This was partly because as she was pregnant, the rules allowed help to be given when the participant was in medical need, and partly because she still had the world record for the longest walk by a woman. She had walked more than 5,000 miles further than her nearest competitor for the record.

Despite this, the damage was done. Sales of the tell-all book were less than half of her earlier books, but libraries had waiting lists. People wanted to know 'the whole story' but didn't want Ffyona to profit.

She disappeared from public view and has seemingly found peace. In later interviews she revealed that she had become an art student. It seems she found what she was looking for when she stopped moving.

Russian sailors outside the popular Billy Budd's Bistro in Foss Street. It was owned and run by Keith Belt and Gilly White (now Webb) and, along with the Carved Angel, was one of the only two Good Food Guide *restaurants in Dartmouth at the time.*

Richard Webb

HIT AND RUN TRAGEDY

Cherub restaurant owner John Hill was sentenced to two months in prison after running over and killing a pensioner, and driving away with the man's dentures on his dashboard.

Leslie Harney, 61, died two weeks after smashing through the windscreen of Mr Hill's car on a rainy and foggy night in January. His windscreen had been so badly smashed a police officer refused to drive it to a garage when he was traced days after the incident, thanks to a wing mirror he left behind after the collision. He had driven home fourteen miles to Torquay with a smashed windscreen and having drunk a quantity of alcohol.

Mr Hill claimed that Mr Harney 'came out of nowhere' and walked in front of his Mercedes around 11.30pm on the evening in question. Mr Hill drove away leaving Mr Harney bleeding in the gutter. He never regained consciousness.

Mr Hill was told by the magistrate's Chairman Neville Craven: 'We consider this offence so serious that a non-custodial sentence cannot be justified. You left the scene knowing a man had been seriously injured particularly at this time of night.'

RUSSIAN INVASION

Sally Gillo shows off a hat she obtained from a Russian sailor from the visiting ship Gangut.

Totnes Image Bank/ South Hams Newspapers

Dartmouth suffered an 'invasion' in October – when the Russian ship *Gangut* arrived in the port.

The ship came to the town as part of a programme to improve relations between the British and Russian navies. The crew, many of whom were on their first visit to a western country cleared the shops of many goods, especially electrical items and clothes and many sold their uniforms and coats to do so. It became a common sight over the weekend of their visit to see British residents handing over cash in the street to Russian sailors for a belt buckle or a military cap, after which the sailor would dash into a business and buy something else to take home to his family.

The 'Ruskies' also failed to live up to the Cold War image of hard drinking, hard fighting communists.

Terry Pheeby, Chamber of Trade Chairman said: 'It has been a real breakthrough. They could go anywhere, do anything. We have been impressed by their good manners and behaviour. We certainly bent over backwards to help them. I just hope they don't think capitalism is that easy'.

When they left many were sad to see them go. It would be more than ten years before another Russian ship visited.

Members of Dartmouth Amateur Swimming Club on the bridge at Castle Cove.
DARTMOUTH MUSEUM

1994

Britannia Royal Naval College's MoD police dogs found themselves at the centre of an argument around military funding.

TOP DOGS DESERVE LUXURY

Labour MP David Jamieson of Devonport demanded to know how much the new kennels for the five German shepherds that patrolled the grounds of the College would cost. When he was informed the new block of kennels would cost £54,000 he hit the roof saying it was a disgusting waste of money at a time when military personnel were being cut. He said that 'luxury' accommodation was sheer extravagance and said the dogs could have had a brand new Wimpey home for the same price.

The College hit back by saying the main cost of the buildings were the levelling of the land and that the dogs were vital to the security of the College. They said the dogs new homes were in fact quite small though good quality and they had been living in sub-standard homes prior to this.

The College then got themselves in a bit more controversy when Mr Jamieson discovered that the establishment had spent £25,000 on a double garage for the Captain. He yet again described the building as 'luxurious' and said that the MoD was 'spending freely' on stupid items such as these when people were being made redundant and the navy losing training establishments. He said the garage was 'obscene' and said other service personnel were living in sub-standard accommodation which meant they feared for the health of their families. The Britannia Royal Naval College described the garage as being a necessary security feature for the Captain, who paid rent on the garage and said the high cost was down to the need for the garage to 'blend' with the Grade II listed College building.

Mr Jamieson then criticised the Britannia Royal Naval College because it gave a home to the Britannia Beagles 'At the nation's expense'. He said that the hunting dogs, which were first formed as a hunting pack BEFORE the College was built, were there solely for the leisure pursuits of high ranking officers, while 'thousands' of servicemen were being made redundant. The *Chronicle* was tired of his tirades by this time and described him, as 'hounding' the College on a personal vendetta. He even got the League Against Cruel Sports involved who claimed 80 per cent of the population was against hunting. It also said: 'tearing apart wild animals with hounds has absolutely nothing to do with the defence of the realm and the MoD should stop all funding for hunting now.'

The Britannia Royal Naval College wearily denied that the beagles cost the taxpayer anything, and pointed out they were completely self funding, but Mr Jamieson kept on shouting.

WEATHER SNOW JOKE FOR VALENTINE WALKABOUT MAN

Snow fell on Valentine's Day and brought chaos and blizzard conditions putting people's lives at risk.

Blackawton man John Nicholls, 57, walked out of his Higher Cotterbury farm wearing only a Barbour jacket and a boiler suit. He was missing overnight during the worst blizzards in living memory. A search by police and farmhands failed to turn up any trace of Mr Nicholls and his family feared the worst.

However, just after the search for him resumed at 8am the next morning he walked back into his home almost exactly twelve hours after he had left. He had sheltered out of the storm in a 'nearby copse' according to the police, and appeared none the worse for his ordeal. However they may have been optimistic as Mr Nicholls was later taken to Torbay hospital and spent the night there for observation.

Traders criticised the building of a large Plymco superstore in the town, describing it as a 'time bomb' that would destroy their businesses.

The traders fought tooth and nail against the store which would occupy the old bus depot site on Mayors Avenue. The main problem for the initial plan was that the company made no provision for parking.

The proposal also included plans for four shop units, which seemed excessive to traders struggling to survive in a town which had a number of empty shops as it was.

Jenny Rothery of the Market Square Fish Shop said: 'People don't realise the seriousness of this. It's like a bomb ticking away waiting to explode. To make the store viable they are going to have to get every half penny they can get and at the end of the day there is not the trade for them. We already have seven empty shops in Dartmouth.'

David Boswell, who ran the Deck of Cards, was angry over the four shop units saying:

'If those were not there, there would be room for about twenty cars. Dartmouth has a concentrated blend of retailers. Some could say the town is like a museum, but we need a working museum and we need to be different to survive. We cannot rely wholly on the panoramic views and picturesque setting. We must protect our independent retailers already providing service and goods which will surely be duplicated within this proposed complex. If we don't it could lead to further hardship for retailers and inevitable closures.'

The plans were recommended for refusal by the town council because, said councillors, the lack of parking and additional shop units would not be beneficial to the town.

The Co-op did not help itself by then asking to use fifty car parking spaces in the district council car park – infuriating traders even more.

However, the scheme was revised to include more parking and the plans went through before the end of the year.

HOUSING MONEY TO MAKE BIG DIFFERENCE

More than £8.7 million was earmarked for the development of Townstal and its 1,500 residents in April.

Despite being announced in the *Chronicle* on April Fool's day the decision was of the utmost importance for so many families, especially those living in the properties which needed to be completely rebuilt. The money came from central government, South Hams District Council, the Housing Association and some from private finance. The homes on Britannia Avenue, Davis Road, Faulkner Close and Townstal Road received the most attention.

There was also money allocated to improve open spaces in the area. It was the result of years of planning and those responsible wanted the readers of the *Chronicle* to know it. The estate had been built, again to great fanfare, in 1937, but many of the 600 houses were no longer suitable for habitation.

The plans had been put together with the Townstal Action Group, which gave the views of residents to the planners and to Midas Homes who would be carrying out the re-building work. Richard Rendle, district councillor and vice-chairman of the council's housing committee said: 'There have been many

problems due to the size of it, but I hope this scheme will put some character and community spirit back into the estate.' The scheme would also include 127 new homes and utilities to expand the industrial areas of the estate.

The area's most famous couple said they had 'split up for good this time' until it wasn't – and then really was. In April Shaunagh and Keith Floyd separated and told everyone they were 'still good friends'.

Shaunagh returned to work at the Clifton Road surgery where she had been an employee before being swept off her feet by the TV chef in 1991. They had split up once before and both given interviews to national press representatives. When they were seen having a cosy lunch together within days on that occasion the couple were accused of staging the break-up for a publicity stunt.

This time, however, there seemed little doubt the break was for good.

'I just want it to be over and done with,' Shaunagh told *Chronicle* reporter Avril Balharry. 'I don't want to speak to anybody about it anymore. I'm sick to death of it.'

Floyd himself told the *Chronicle*: 'You don't go messing about with people's lives and emotions for publicity stunts for heaven's sake. That's not how human beings live or work. We are all very sad about it and that's really it. It's just one of those things and we are doing our level best to make it all amicable.'

They were back together in August and took a 'second honeymoon' in Ireland.

But a week after returning they split and this time it really was for good.

Showing a bit more staying power was the town's premier event with the 150th Dartmouth Royal Regatta being celebrated in style.

Argentinean, Belgian and Royal Navy ships moored in the harbour for the event and Prince Andrew spent a happy visit walking around various events and went out on the river with Regatta Chairman Richard Rendle. He didn't get to the pavement drawing competition however because of a suspected gas leak by the Boatfloat, which turned out to be a smelly dustbin.

The Prince fired the starting cannon for the Open Whaler Race, which would reward the winners with the new Duke of York Trophy which was donated by Mr and Mrs Tommy Rowland and he climbed ashore to present it to the winners who were the Dartmouth Arms crew.

The Dartmouth Arms also won the LVA cup and the double victory earned them a year's free beer, though the *Chronicle* neglected to say from whom. This wouldn't be Dartmouth however, if there wasn't an argument, or, in this case, two.

Mayors Avenue in 1994 – Western National Bus depot before demolition, then a Plymco store, and now a Marks & Spencer's!
DARTMOUTH MUSEUM

Dartmouth Celebrity Chefs – A Brief History. See Feature on pages 92–93

Top: *Phil Geen, landlord of the Dartmouth Arms pub, receives the Open Whaler Trophy from the Duke of York, Prince Andrew.*
SOUTH HAMS NEWSPAPERS

Bottom left and middle: *The Duke of York enjoyed being out on the river, even starting one race.*
SOUTH HAMS NEWSPAPERS

Right: *Dartmouth Mayor Jack Cutter, South Hams District Council chairman John Squire enjoy a joke with the Prince.*
SOUTH HAMS NEWSPAPERS

The first was due to the 'snub' by the Royal Dart Yacht Club's Commodore John Clarke, who took the Prince to meet lone Round-the-World yachtswoman Lisa Clayton rather than Kingswear Parish Council Chairman Susanne Welsh Rollings, and members of the Regatta Committee from Kingswear. Mr Clarke asked on no less than three occasions prior to the move if he could take the Duke to meet Birmingham sailor Miss Clayton, and on three occasions had been told it was not appropriate. Regatta Secretary Wendy Rendle said: 'He was totally out of order.'

WE SHOULD BE DISGUSTED BUT DIDN'T NOTICE

Added to this was the fact that foreign visiting ships – especially the Argentinean one, just over a decade since the Falklands, were heavily criticised by some in the town for 'showing complete disrespect for Prince Andrew'. How did they do this? By flying the Union Jack at the wrong end of their ships, of course!

Harbourmaster Colin Moore expressed 'dismay' when a few pointed out – apparently in 'disgust' that the Argentinean ship flew the Union Jack on the bow and their own national flag on the stern. The Belgian ship did exactly the same but received suspiciously little criticism compared to the South American ship.

Capt Moore said that virtually every foreign vessel visiting Dartmouth made the same mistake.

'Who could blame them when faced with a complicated flag system such as ours,' he said. 'Despite the ardent efforts of a brainless few who were scrabbling around trying to cause trouble, the ship's visit was a great success as a gesture of peace and renewed friendship between our countries.'

Perhaps arguably more serious was an accident during the Saturday fireworks which left several people nursing burns and fifteen with medical problems or singed clothing. The problem was caused by a 'bombette' roman candle exploding at the wrong time as it descended, firing its spray of stars into the crowd.

1995 The clearing of advertising boards, not to mention fruit and vegetable stalls, caused uproar for traders in Dartmouth at the beginning of the year.

The town council, fed up at the cluttering of the streets with unauthorised advertising boards, called in Devon County Council who had responsibility to clear the public highways of unsightly and obstructive boards.

A 'crew' was sent down by Devon County Council, accompanied by a police officer, and they cleared the streets of all items except small flower tubs one February morning. Warning letters had been sent out to traders, but many weren't expecting the drastic action and were amazed to see their goods in many cases confiscated by the 'commando squad' as they were dubbed in the *Chronicle*.

The town council probably felt quite pleased with itself and must have been surprised to find shopkeepers camped in its council chamber at its next full meeting.

The traders handed in a petition of 813 signatures protesting at the move and demanded answers and a solution, as many said their businesses had been damaged by the lack of displays on the pavement.

Letters were handed into the *Chronicle* accusing the council of 'ripping the heart out of our town'. The councillors vainly pointed out there had been many complaints but faced continued heavy criticism. They hurriedly arranged a meeting with the traders to find a solution.

Co-operation was finally achieved when both the town and county councils took on the views of the Dartmouth traders and decided to allow modifications to the strict by-laws which had resulted in the conflict. Both councils agreed to turn a blind eye to displays on the pavement unless they caused a real and imminent danger to the public.

Peter Buckingham, husband of Dartmouth Community College's Principal Ann, who had been badly brain damaged in a severe head-on car crash in late 1993, appeared on the front page of the *Chronicle* in March. He had been awarded a Master's Degree in business administration. Although undoubtedly a happy and proud day for the family, with the picture featuring Peter, Ann, his son Spencer, aged 15 and daughter Fay, aged 12, it was a bitter-sweet occasion.

'Peter was doing a three-year, part-time post-graduate course and had completed 90 per cent of the course when the accident happened,' said Ann. 'Because of the high marks he had achieved during that time, it was decided to award him the degree. Sadly he can't remember doing the course or anything he learnt.'

Sailors on the
Libertad *stand on
the rigging as it
sails into port.*
SOUTH HAMS
NEWSPAPERS.

BRNC SAFE – FOR NOW...

The Britannia Royal Naval College was classed as 'safe' from closure after a MoD review, though the worrying words 'for now' were also included in the *Chronicle*'s front page story in March.

The historic establishment, on top of the hill overlooking the town since 1905 had been the centre of many rumours in the run up to the widely expected military spending review, which many said would include considerable cuts. As it was the town's biggest employer, the announcement from the First Sea Lord Admiral Sir Benjamin Bathhurst that it was safe for the 'foreseeable future' was pleasing news.

The chief naval officer in the country said the College was staying 'in recognition of the fact that it provides training to young officers joining the Royal Navy which is fundamental to the ethos and operational capability of the navy today.'

Drunken exploits left the town council with a bit of a tall order – and a headache.

Someone, though no one seemed entirely sure who, shinned 60 feet up the precarious Old Dartmothian's flagpole in the Royal Avenue Gardens one evening in March. The culprit then, to make sure everyone would know they had achieved this seemingly impossible feat, left a traffic cone on the top and shinned down again.

This left the town council with the dilemma of how to get the object down again. Mayor Jack Cutter said: 'I dread to think how much it bent with a person at the top' and his fellow councillors were not going to volunteer to climb up, so they called on the fire brigade to bring their large 'Bronto' platform engine which allowed two firemen to bring it back down. They also used the time to repair the pulley at the top of the town halyard which had been broken for a while. So the drunken daredevil could be said to have performed a public service.

Lisa Clayton sails into Dartmouth after her Round-the-World trip in the yacht Spirit of Birmingham.
SOUTH HAMS
NEWSPAPERS

*Lisa Clayton.
See Feature on
page 184*

Round-the-World yachtswoman Lisa Clayton sailed into Dartmouth in late June after a non-stop unassisted circumnavigation of the globe. She was greeted by huge crowds, though not as big as had greeted Naomi James more than a decade before.

Lisa had, by all accounts, had a frightening and frankly treacherous trip when her boat *Spirit of Birmingham* performed 360 degree rolls, during one of which she was knocked out for ten hours, and also encountered 100 foot waves. The triumphant nature of the entrance into the harbour was checked somewhat because of an accusation in the national press that she had accepted spares from a passing fishing vessel in the sea off Cape Town. Finally after nearly two months deliberation from the World Sailing Speed Record Council it was found she had done nothing wrong and her time of 285 days, 26 minutes and, in some unbelievably accurate measuring, 27 seconds at sea was accepted. She was the first woman to sail the 31,000 miles Round-the-World non-stop and unassisted.

Regatta courted controversy in more ways than one for the second year running. The organising committee was disappointed and concerned that the Royal Navy could not supply a Guardship due to NATO exercises in the north Atlantic. However Anthony Steen MP contacted the Defence Secretary Nicholas Soames and then told the *Chronicle*: 'I've pulled off a coup.' He modestly declared: 'Due to changes in the NATO exercises HMS *Orwell* can be pulled out and will be in Dartmouth for Regatta as its Guardship.'

REGATTA GETS CONTROVERSIAL

Mr Steen said Mr Soames had been convinced to make the change because he didn't want to break the years of tradition of having a Guardship in Dartmouth for Regatta.

However a week later a man appeared on the front page of the *Chronicle* accusing Mr Steen of fibbing over his involvement in the change of heart from the navy.

Charlie Pitts of Mayflower Close revealed he had written to the Prime Minister to ask if a Guardship could be provided. John Major replied saying he would 'look into the matter'.

Mr Pitts said: 'Okay Mr Steen has done his job and we appreciate it, but there were an awful lot of other people involved who helped to make it happen, not just him.' Regardless of who was responsible, a Guardship did indeed appear and Mr Steen joked that the Royal Navy did not want to be 'outdone by the French', because of the presence of the French Naval vessel *Aldébaran* during Regatta. This caused a large amount of concern for the Regatta committee because the newly formed Dartmouth branch of Greenpeace announced its intention to protest against its presence.

This was due to the French government's decision to carry out nuclear bomb testing on the Mururoa Atoll in French Polynesia. The move was hugely controversial and inexplicable to many and brought condemnation from countries across the world.

Dartmouth was rather surprised to find itself at the centre of a worldwide debate but then it suddenly didn't seem to matter, when it was revealed the 'ship' was in fact only twenty two metres long and not very impressive.

As it turned out there was a group protesting when the ship arrived and they gathered signatures for a petition against the French. There was then a small 'flotilla' of boats that went out to show their disagreement with the French nuclear tests, but all in all it turned out to be a bit of a storm in a teacup.

Regatta as a whole was a huge success and dubbed 'the friendly Regatta' by the *Chronicle* which said: 'There was not one ounce of trouble, just plenty of sunshine and lots of fun events.'

Almost as much fun was the saga of how Graham Pearce got two trees back which were stolen from outside his house.

SOME OF OUR FLOWERPOTS ARE MISSING, HERB...

Mr Pearce, a retired police officer, wrote to the *Chronicle* after two thieves took the trees from his property in Church Road just before midnight on a Friday in September. He had followed a trail of earth from his property after discovering the theft and then followed it as it weaved across the road into the top gate of the Britannia Royal Naval College.

He then contacted the Britannia Royal Naval College and asked to see their CCTV camera footage from the area and obtained pictures of the two men. He outlined exactly their actions in the letter to the *Chronicle*, even pointing out that the men carried the trees in bags in their left hands and walked one behind the other.

What was his reason for writing to the *Chronicle* and describing their passage? He made it very clear: 'I reported the theft on Saturday morning, but at this stage I have not yet made a statement of complaint. Here is what I propose doing. Although I am a retired police officer with years of experience of thief catching behind me I am a fair man. All I want is for you both to search your souls, think of what could happen if and when I report the theft – embarrassment when your doorbells ring and your collars are felt. A criminal record for the rest of your lives (although I suspect you already have records) and finally to court and maybe put your livelihoods in jeopardy! A lot to lose eh? All for the price of two miniature conifer trees worth £1.60 each! I will give you both forty eight hours from today, Friday October 6 to return my trees and that will be the end of the matter. If you fail to take advantage of my more than generous offer then on Monday October 9 I will put the matter in the hands of the local keepers of the law, accompanied by my statement of complaint and the said photographs.'

The trees appeared in bags the very next day – accompanied by a letter worthy quoting in full: 'On the alleged night my friend and I were returning from our Bible reading evening when we noticed two very peaky looking dwarf cypress trees. Being two keen arborists we took them home for some tender loving care. The last thing we want is to have our collars felt and possibly spend six months in the chokie.'

They signed it Conni Fer and Herb Acious-Border, and suggested those responsible for the theft should 'do three hours community service in the public house of their choice'.

Mr Pearce said he wanted to present the trees back to the men if they were to come round 'for a cup of tea'.

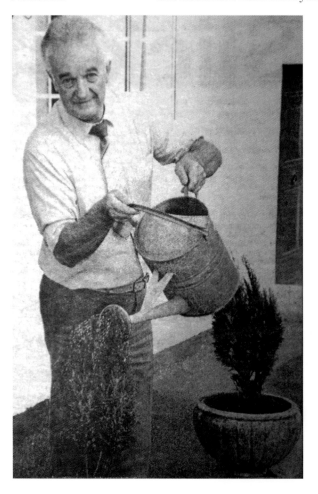

Retired police officer Graham Pearce celebrates the return of his trees from 'Herb Acious-Border' and 'Conni-Fer'.
SOUTH HAMS NEWSPAPERS

DON'T BREAK YOUR OWN RULES

1996 The Dartmouth & Kingswear Society won no friends at both Dartmouth Town and South Hams District Councils when it started a campaign against plans for the use of the Norton heliport site, which had caused such controversy the year before.

John and Bessie Holland had outbid the district council to buy the whole of the eighteen acre site, and then sold part of it on to the district council and in addition gained another plot of land in the town centre.

200 people turned up to a public meeting in the Guildhall where the town and district councils asked what would be best to put on the large site. The call was clearly made for a sports centre, including a swimming pool, as well as a park and ride and football and rugby pitches. These ideas were greeted with enthusiasm even though the district council admitted there was no actual money to build the proposals.

However, the deal to buy the land by the district council left the Hollands a significant chunk of the old heliport site and they put in a planning application for industrial units. They had sold the rest of the site to the district council on the proviso that they would build them.

But then the Dartmouth & Kingswear Society reported the move to the Secretary of State for the Environment, saying it went against the district council's own planning policy. The society asked for the planning consent on the site to be revoked, because it was designated as 'countryside' meaning any development was banned. The society were not of course against the proposed sports centre and park and ride, only against the 'secret' deal to allow industrial units to be built on the heliport site.

The society's Chairman, the first woman to hold the post, Elizabeth Jarrold said: 'There is still ample space on the industrial estate in Townstal and further land zoned for industrial development which is as yet untouched. We felt we had no option but to request the Secretary of State to revoke the planning consents. No justification on grounds of providing employment opportunities could be put forward.'

The society members obviously felt strongly as this was the first time that the society had taken such action.

The town council reacted with anger that the society could try to scupper a project which had such a lot of residents' support. The district council had only re-negotiated to buy the land because of a large public outcry when the Hollands bought it and now the society was trying to scupper the deal which allowed the majority of the heliport land to come into public ownership.

The Secretary of State refused to accede to the society's request. However, the four district councillors – Paul Darby, Richard Rendle, Peter Norton and Melvyn Stone, then wrote an open letter to the *Chronicle*, in which they lambasted the society for its actions: 'to make this request to the government, the society was obviously quite aware that such revocations can only be made in the most serious of cases. In other words the society must have been of the view that the council was grossly wrong in its actions. Perhaps it is too much to expect the

Fireman Dennis Abraham, Alan Middleton and Maxwell Perring with their long service medals.
SOUTH HAMS NEWSPAPERS

society to apologise but we hope the matter is not just brushed aside by them. The society accused the council of maladministration, misleading information and making decisions without public consultation, all of which is untrue. Is the Dartmouth & Kingswear Society going to be public spirited and gracious enough to drop their critical distance and join in with the majority of people and try to make this exciting opportunity work for the benefit of Dartmouth?'

THE DEATH OF A QUIET AND SERIOUS MAN

Society members had more sombre things on their minds in April when its co-founder Christopher Robin Milne died.

Mr Milne, 75, famous as the inspiration for the Christopher Robin character in the much loved 'Winnie the Pooh' series of books by his father AA Milne, moved to Dartmouth in 1951 and started the Harbour Bookshop, after trying, and failing to gain a job in London.

The shop proved successful and gave him the opportunity to develop his love for, and philosophical theories about, nature. He spent most of his life resenting his un-asked-for fame, and it took the writing of his autobiography, *The Enchanted Places*, for him to lay to rest many of his demons connected with a childhood and adult life haunted by a fictional representation of his early years.

He co-founded the Dartmouth & Kingswear Society with John Smith and Lt Col Richard Webb in 1959. The society was set up to conserve the unique beauty and character of Dartmouth. Its aims linked with Mr Milne's strong feelings on nature and the intricate 'web of life' that surrounds us. He was quoted in the *Chronicle* as saying 'It is a fairly fragile web, and if we are not careful we will destroy it.'

DEFINITELY NOT ALL-WHITE

Unwanted development again caused huge uproar around Dittisham during the year when plans for a new business park opposite the village were brought forward.

The idea, for a sixty two acre business park and a fourteen acre leisure complex including a cinema, was put forward by Sir Robert McAlpine. The plans, named White Rock, also included a special 'buffer' zone of more than 200 acres which would be landscaped to lessen the impact of the complex.

The £50 million scheme was planned to create up to 2,500 jobs, a claim from the developers perhaps to lessen the controversy of building in one of the southwest's most beautiful valleys, but it horrified many. Most horrified were Dittisham residents who would have had to look straight at the development if it were built.

Dittisham Parish Cllr Robert Smith spoke passionately against the scheme at a meeting of the Torbay Borough Council Policy, Planning and Transport Committee in May.

*Emmerdale
Farm star Sally
Knyvette showing
her disdain for
the White Rock
development.*
SOUTH HAMS
NEWSPAPERS

'Are all the members of this council satisfied that sufficient information and detail is available to make positive judgements about the environmental impact, pollution – air, water, noise, light – the impact of traffic both locally and the entries to Torbay, on services such as water, sewerage, schools, housing and tourism in the area as a whole? In these circumstances is it right to sacrifice and destroy a cherished part of the countryside? We respectfully submit that the Dart Valley is in the moral ownership of all and no council has the right to act in a way that will harm it.'

The developers then saw the planning restrictions which were to be placed on them – and hurriedly withdrew their application for the leisure side of the complex. They then suffered another set back when planners told them that no extra warehousing should be allowed unless it was linked to office or high-tech industries – effectively reducing the number of businesses that could be attracted to the site.

The story took a starry turn when Sally Knyvette, 'Kate Sugden' from long running soap *Emmerdale Farm*, who owned a holiday home in the village, weighed in.

'I'm absolutely horrified,' she told the *Chronicle*. 'This is a crazy idea. It will be a complete eyesore and destroy a beautiful part of the river Dart. I feel this whole thing has been rushed through so fast without taking any notice of local opposition or looking into the finer details.'

In a nice link with her alter ego, Kate Sugden was involved in a story line that very year that had her fighting, and winning, against a planned theme park near the fictional farm.

The plan was so unpopular that the Dartmouth & Kingswear Society and Dartmouth Town Council, who had spent most of the year at loggerheads over the Norton heliport site, decided to join forces to fight the proposal.

So vigorous was the opposition to the plans that a public enquiry was called the next year which looked to leave the chances for the scheme in the balance, before John Prescott, Environment Secretary, decided that the roads to the scheme were not good enough, that the building of such a site would damage high quality arable land and that there was no provision for such a scheme in the Torbay Local Plan.

Left: *Pupils of St
John the Baptist
primary school at
their desks where
they hoped their new
classroom would be
built.*
SOUTH HAMS NEWSPAPERS

Right: *Chairman
of the Dartmouth
Chamber of Trade,
Terrence Pheeby
points to the
disruption on the
town's embankment.*
SOUTH HAMS NEWSPAPERS

Team Philips – *the Goss Superyacht, sails out of the river Dart after its launch in February 2000 with crowds of well-wishers on the Embankment.* (*See year 2000*) GORDON THOMAS

Dart Marina owner Richard Seton looking at the plans for the extension to Dart Marina.
SOUTH HAMS NEWSPAPERS

GOING OUT IN A BLAZE OF GLORY

Also doomed to failure – but of a much more heroic kind, was Stoke Fleming's Green Dragon pub landlord. Peter Crowther nearly drowned when his beloved yacht went down in the Atlantic.

Mr Crowther was sailing in his yacht *Galway Blazer* – in which he had already crossed the Atlantic four times before on his own – in a transatlantic race in June when he was holed by floating debris, leaving a gaping tear in the side of the boat which promptly sank and nearly took the plucky 54 year old down with it.

'We were going along well when we were hit with what felt like a sledgehammer,' he said. 'A large hole appeared in the side and I knew the boat was gone. By the time I'd sent out a distress call the water was up to my knees. I grabbed the waterproofs and the portable VHF set and went up on deck and sat in the dinghy as the bows sank.'

He then realised the dinghy was caught up in the lifelines and would be dragged down with the sinking yacht.

'My only thoughts were to get off,' he said. 'The raft was filling up with water. Finally I managed to yank myself free and started to bale out the water.'

650 miles out of Plymouth he radioed for help and was picked up six hours later. The laid-back adventurer had not had a hard time of it, having been thoughtful enough to pack some salmon and a nice bottle of whisky in the dinghy – which he used to celebrate his rescue.

Left: Stoke Fleming pub The Green Dragon's landlord, Peter Crowther about to set off across the Atlantic single-handed upon his yacht Galway Blazer.
SOUTH HAMS NEWSPAPERS

The whole family mourned the loss of *Galway Blazer*, which had sailed Round-the-World before Peter and his wife Alix had bought it, and they even lived on it in the 1970s.

Parents had long been campaigning in Stoke Fleming for better facilities for the children and a plan was put forward for an all weather surface at the Harefield Drive public playing field allowing children to roller blade, skateboard, play basketball and netball.

Unfortunately the elderly residents of Harefield Drive itself were stiffly opposed to the scheme, stating that the hard surface area would mean increased noise and a loss of privacy.

Parent Linda Howard, who campaigned hard for the new area, said: 'There is an urgent need for a proper play area in Stoke Fleming. I just don't understand how these people can be so selfish. It is not as if we are asking for a skateboard park with concrete ramps. The very same people who are objecting now have complained about children playing in the street. They can't have it both ways.'

NO FUN HERE PLEASE, WE'RE RETIRED

The pensioners had got themselves a reputation for complaining for complaining's sake after making the council re-paint the swings in the existing play area for smaller children because the green chosen was too bright.

Pensioner George Main said: 'No one is against the kids having fun, but in the right place. We feel the playing field is unsuitable. It is not a large area and already has a football pitch and a toddlers' play area.'

Ruth Dennington, another objector said: 'It used to be a lovely cul-de-sac but now the peace has been shattered. Many of us had children of our own. All we want to do is live in peace.'

AN IRIS AND A ROSE

The town mourned one of its most respected characters when Mrs Iris Webb died at the age of 87 on October 5, 1996 having lived at Warfleet for over 40 years. Her father was Finch Portman Ingram, a local entrepreneur and benefactor, and her childhood home had been at Stoke Fleming. Later she accompanied her husband, Lt Col Richard Webb on his various postings at home and abroad – notably to Burma just after the Second World War.

She became President of the National Association of Flower Arrangement Societies (NAFAS) from 1974 to 1976 and she lectured, demonstrated, and judged all over the country. She was the series presenter of a BBC TV series with Pebble Mill and her book *The Complete Guide to Flower & Foliage Arrangement* became a bestseller on the subject.

Iris Webb, RHS Gold Medallist and past President of the National Association of Flower Arrangement Societies (NAFAS), in her Warfleet garden. Highly respected for her talent with flowers she died on October 5, 1996. She was married to Lt Col Richard Webb (see page 174) and was the mother of publisher Richard Webb.

DAVID BARWICK

Iris founded the Torbay, Dartmouth and Kingsbridge Flower Clubs and, being Founder President of the Devon & Cornwall Area, she designed and planned their NAFAS exhibits at the RHS Chelsea Shows in 1975 and 1976, both of which were awarded RHS Gold Medals.

She organized many Flower Festivals both locally and nationally, including those at Westminster Abbey and St Paul's Cathedral, and thereby raised hundreds of thousands of pounds for charity.

She was honoured in 1990 by having the *Iris Webb* rose named after her.

The town's Fatstock Show in December, not for the last time, attracted controversy because of its policy towards the 'fairer sex'.

The show's overwhelming winner, with ten of the available trophies, was Jill Rowden, who then couldn't collect them because women are banned from the annual dinner for farmers which follows the show. Secretary Nevil Pedrick said no-one could remember a woman winning so many prizes.

The reason women were excluded from the annual dinner, explained the secretary, was 'you could say we are the last bastion of male chauvinism. Some of the speeches are what you might call 'bluer than pink' and we wouldn't want to risk offending any ladies that might be present.'

Dartmouth was the only Fatstock Show in the South Hams to retain the male-only celebratory dinner, but no-one seemed to be worried, least of all Jill.

'I had a very enjoyable evening with the other ladies and didn't really want to listen to the men telling dirty jokes,' she said.

New houses built by Guinness Trust 1997.

DARTMOUTH MUSEUM

1997

The Chairman of the Chamber of Trade Terry Pheeby told the *Chronicle* out-of-town shopping centres were forcing many shopkeepers to consider shutting for winter making Dartmouth once and for all a tourist town rather than the market town it had always considered itself to be.

THINGS ARE TERRIBLE – OH NO THEY AREN'T!

'It's easier for people to shop out of town, especially those living in Townstal,' said Mr Pheeby. 'People seem prepared to travel further to places such as the Willows and the new Safeway store in Paignton. All the time they do this they are draining money out of the town.'

Mr Pheeby became the first person – as far as one can tell – to say the town could become 'another Salcombe', that dreaded phrase which appears more and more often as the new Millennium dawned.

Mr Pheeby was backed up by restaurant owner Janice Walker who claimed Christmas and New Year had been 'dismal' and said that without tourism '75 per cent' of traders would go under.

However, the next week another group of traders decided they didn't like the sound of Mr Pheeby's defeatist statements.

Woolworth's Manager Chris Harris said: 'We had an excellent December on top of an excellent year. There is now a major possibility our company will invest extra money in the town. We shouldn't blame local people for not shopping in our town, but look at ourselves to see what we can do to meet local needs.'

A meeting was organised to plan a 'marketing strategy' by trader David Gent, who said he would not invite the chamber to be involved because long term planning was not what it was best at.

The chamber seemed to decide that it would show exactly how good it was at long-term planning by backing a fatally flawed plan to bring the old Royal Yacht *Britannia* to be permanently moored in Dartmouth harbour to become a conference centre and tourist attraction.

It was, however, immensely expensive and also would have virtually blocked the harbour all year round.

It was described by Harbourmaster Colin Moore as 'a non starter' as it would prevent 'any large vessel' from visiting Dartmouth at all.

The new group decided the town needed Christmas lights done properly, not the single tree in the Royal Avenue Gardens which had been all the town had managed in recent years. They also suggested a new map showing where to go in the town.

A marketing man offered his services for free to the town of Dartmouth. Keith Davis then got himself in hot water by suggesting that the way to solve Dartmouth's problems was…to scrap the Lower Ferry.

Mr Davis said that the ferry was the 'cause' of most of the traffic 'snarl ups' in the town. An estimated 540,000 vehicles passed across the river at the time on the Lower Ferry alone – a figure more than double that of its Higher Ferry rival upstream.

Top left: *Children near new houses built by Guinness Trust 1997.*
DARTMOUTH MUSEUM

Top right: *Seymour Drive's new homes unveiled in 1997.*
DARTMOUTH MUSEUM

Left: *Traders united against Chamber of Trade chairman Terry Pheeby, who suggested most shoppers were happier to shop out of Dartmouth.*
SOUTH HAMS NEWSPAPERS

Mr Davis said that because the cars, vans and motorcycles were 'going elsewhere' Dartmouth was dealing with the traffic issues associated with them without gaining anything in return. He suggested that to get rid of the Lower Ferry, or perhaps to 're-position it so that it runs between Waterhead Creek and the proposed new roundabout at the junction of North Embankment and Mayors Avenue.'

The new roundabout was part of yet another parking and traffic plan, which had been proposed by Devon County Council. They were up for 'public consultation' later in the year. The plan would – said Mr Davis – 'pave the way for pedestrianisation, making it increasingly attractive to visitors'.

His ideas did not meet with universal acclaim and the Harbourmaster said scrapping the Lower Ferry was something he 'couldn't see' ever happening and as for moving it to link the North Embankment and Waterhead Creek? 'It isn't feasible'.

Former ferryman Kevin Pyne was more effusive in his criticism of the proposal: 'People need to have lived in Dartmouth a lot longer before having the audacity to presume they are in a position to speak for all of us. Mr Davis would be advised to exercise a little more tact.'

PARKING AND RIDING ARE ALL THE RAGE, DEAR

The town got a much needed boost with the opening of its park and ride on the site of the old heliport on Norton Fields in May – and although it wasn't all plain sailing it was still hailed as a success.

A detailed parking and traffic plan was released in August – outlining reserved spaces for 500 residents cars and 'all' tourists being required to use the park and ride. It also brought in, again, the possibility of pay and display on-street parking schemes along the Embankment.

Mr Pheeby, perhaps unsurprisingly after the onslaught he took in January following his 'negative' comments, stepped down as chamber chairman in September to be replaced by Mr Gent – and Mr Davis also washed his hands of the town, firing a final salvo as he went.

'Apathy is, without doubt, the biggest stumbling block to greater prosperity in Dartmouth,' he said, 'closely followed by an apparent disinterest in seeking consensus on just about anything. Why, I ask, should I waste my time trying to assist you if you will not help yourselves? I have come to the conclusion that a very large number of traders just can't be bothered to raise a finger to help improve the prosperity of this town – an attitude which I find both sad and depressing.'

*Dartmouth Mayor
Margaret Roberts
at the construction
site of the new
park and ride.*
SOUTH HAMS
NEWSPAPERS

WELCOME, MA'AM

The Queen was welcomed to the town when she visited the Britannia Royal Naval College for Lord High Admiral's Divisions in April, accompanied by Prince Philip.

She had last been in the town in 1988, somewhere she was always happy to visit, said the *Chronicle*, because it was where she met her husband in 1939. She was only 13 when she met the 'dashing Greek Prince'. She planted a Goldenrain tree which was chosen to mark the couple's impending Golden Wedding anniversary.

The town council were split over the religious persuasion of its Mayor.

The *Chronicle's* front page was dominated by five councillors' attempt to 'oust' Paul Darby before he had even taken up his post because he was an atheist.

Cllr Darby, a mechanic with his own business, had made it clear when he was elected what his beliefs were and that he would consider it 'hypocritical' to attend the traditional Mayor's Sunday church service. He opted instead to hold a 'civic Sunday' event instead.

This brought condemnation from a number of councillors who, in the month before the Mayor-making Ceremony decided to try and force Cllr Darby out of office before he got into it, so to speak. They said Cllr Darby should 'uphold Christian principles' as the representative of a public body in an officially Christian country.

Cllrs Margaret Roberts, Clive Bowerman, Melvyn Stone, Robert Hannaford and Iris Pritchard all voted against the new Mayor at the Mayor-making Ceremony. They failed by a recorded vote of eight to five, and then tried to stop Richard Rendle becoming deputy Mayor for good measure. They failed in that too.

The 'gang of five' as the *Chronicle* dubbed them took their own defeat on the chin, especially the outgoing Mayor Cllr Roberts, who said: 'Those of us who voted against Paul felt we had to because we had been inundated by concerned townspeople. But that is over and gone and the result stands. I am sure Paul will bring his own touch to the job, I wish him all the best.'

Cllr Bowerman made some pointed references to Cllr Roberts attendances at religious services as part of her role as Mayor and said they were 'worthwhile traditions' and that many townspeople felt the same way as he did. Cllr Darby was magnanimous in his response.

'I would like to thank my fellow councillors who elected me,' he said. 'For those who didn't I believe we should put personal differences behind us and work together for the good of Dartmouth.'

Carnival was the subject of much debate after it went 'off like a damp squib' according to the *Chronicle's* front page.

The carnival procession, at one time the crowning glory of the event in July, featured only a 'handful' of floats. Organisers blamed the high cost of insurance and the fact that the procession clashed with the more easily accessible carnivals at Ashburton and Ivybridge, but many of the residents in the town were not satisfied with the explanation and wrote to the *Chronicle* to describe the procession as 'embarrassing'.

Jean Kellond wrote and summed up the feelings of many: 'I felt rather sad and embarrassed for our visitors on Saturday at the demise of the carnival procession. Are we going to lose yet something else? Come on Dartmouth – get planning next year's entry. Other towns do it. We can be great again.'

CONNED TWICE OUT OF THOUSANDS

What wasn't great was the heartless targeting of an 88 year old partially sighted and deaf woman by conmen who convinced her to hand over £5,000 in cash.

The first attack took place in June when two 'roofers' convinced the lady to pay £800 for 'work they did on her roof'. She happily went with the men to the bank and withdrew the money while they waited in the car. The next trick was particularly cruel and drawn out.

Two men turned up at her house and said they were CID officers and needed to 'check' that the money in her bank account was not counterfeit. They drove with her on two consecutive days and withdrew a total of £4,200, which they took away for 'checks' and promised to return it in a week. They didn't.

The crimes, as well as being totally despicable, also seemed to have been committed by the same men. They knew what they were about and managed to avoid appearing on any CCTV footage during their trips to town with the old woman.

Also feeling robbed were the residents of Mayors Avenue who campaigned against the development of the old Dartmouth Motors site into three-storey flats. The owners had been trying to get planning permission for the development since May 1996 and had a number of application revisions thrown out by planners.

The developers finally pushed through permission for the building after taking just over a metre off the height of the building and re-designing the roof to be more 'in keeping'. Resident Dennis Veale however said the only reason permission had been granted was because South Hams District Council planners knew the developers were preparing to go to court. He said that the potential loss to the council, if a decision went against them, was too great and it 'caved in'.

'We are the people who will quite literally have to live in the shadow of this building for the rest of our lives,' he said. 'I am not so much angry, but amazed that this building has been approved.'

The developers started building within ten days of the planning approval.

Regatta was hailed as a great success and was featured on the BBC TV programme *Holiday*. Presenter Jayne Evans became very involved and was pictured taking part in the waiters and waitresses race, and chatting to Blackpool Sands owner Sir Geoffrey Newman (not at the same time).

The Red Arrows flew but didn't display thanks to heavy cloud. An outcry afterwards did not save the committee from having to pay out £4,500, one of the pitfalls of hiring the world's best aerobatic display team.

1998 The Townstal relief road, which was built at a cost of hundreds of thousands of pounds, was further delayed – by badgers.

DON'T STEP ON MY SETT

The road was finished but it opened three months late. South Hams District Council workers could not complete a fence which was designed to keep the badgers who lived in a sett above Old Mill Creek, one of the largest badger setts in Britain, off the road. The badgers had been built a £5,000 tunnel under the roadway but the fence was required to force them to use it.

The project had already been delayed by problems related to the installation of the lighting along the side of the road, and by a pumping station to protect against the build up of water. There had also been the tragic death of worker David Poole, crushed against his own digger by a runaway earth mover in November 1997.

The contractors needed the permission of Raleigh Estates to build the fence, although they had 'no legal requirement' to do so. The badger sett had nearly scuppered the whole enterprise, despite the fact it had received a £200,000 EU grant because it was believed it would increase road safety and promote employment by easing access to the employment estates in Townstal itself.

The opening was delayed to the end of February – three months over schedule – until the fence was built and the badgers safe.

Seemingly more straightforward but actually a complete nightmare was the running of a 'town poll'.

Local legislation was used to gain evidence that the people of Dartmouth overwhelmingly wanted a covered indoor swimming pool.

South Hams District Council had pledged to look in detail at the proposals if such a poll proved a significant majority wanted a pool.

Almost immediately the people of the town became suspicious because the organisation of the vote was, to say the least, shambolic. It was booked for February 19 – which had to be almost immediately changed to February 18 because the Guildhall, where the polling station was to be, was booked for that day. It was then revealed that the district council was adhering 'strictly' to the parish poll procedure and said that votes could only be registered between 4pm and 9pm. This excluded many who would find it difficult to come down into town on a cold winter's night. It also meant any shift workers would not have the opportunity to vote. It also transpired that the date of the vote had been set, rather conveniently, two days after the new electoral roll was sent out, meaning any new voters were unlikely to know they could vote.

Tony Carlson, the Mayor of Monkey Town, Peter Randall, the Dartmouth Town Crier and Father Chris Smith at the resurrected Monkey Town Regatta.
SOUTH HAMS
NEWSPAPERS

The poll asked two questions: 'Are you in agreement that Dartmouth needs a new indoor swimming pool?' and 'Will you be prepared to pay £3 per household adjusted in line with inflation through your council tax as a contribution towards the running costs of an indoor pool?'

The result was never really in doubt, but with only a quarter of the town's population turning out for the vote it was hardly a ringing endorsement.

More than 1,000 said yes to question 1 and just under 1,000 said yes to question 2. Twenty four people said they did not want a pool.

Attracting as much passion was the debate over Dartmouth's parking problems.

A public meeting, which would quickly pass into town folklore, had to be moved from the Guildhall after it had begun because too many people had turned up to discuss proposals made by the county council. The whole meeting – more than 200 people – marched down Victoria Road on a cold February evening and into St Saviours Church.

Once there, the discussion was wide, varied and very often, quite heated.

Don Campbell and Tim Freeman organised a public questionnaire, an astonishing achievement considering the work involved in getting the thing printed, delivered and the results collated and verified. It was sent to every house in the town – and 1,128 returned them, with an overwhelming 95 per cent against the proposal to put pay and display machines on the town's streets.

85 per cent were in favour of a scheme which favoured parking for residents and 'permits for people in the town'.

However, the County Council's Highways Chief John Halliday made it clear he did not necessarily agree with the way that the questionnaire had been worded.

'This survey does not question how the proposals should be amended. Mr Campbell and Mr Freeman should be congratulated on their achievement, but the value of what they have done is limited.'

Builders Dave Clarke and Geoff Sharam about to put a Dartmouth Chronicle *under the cobbles of the Old Market for future generations to find.*
SOUTH HAMS
NEWSPAPERS

WHAT HAVE YOU DONE WITH THE MONEY?

The district council faced a lot of criticism during the year, most of it from town councillor, and former District councillor, Richard Rendle.

He slammed them for 'misappropriation of funds' to do with millions obtained to 'revamp' Townstal, in which he opened a bitter war of words between himself and the District Council's Chief Executive, Michael Carpenter.

Cllr Rendle said that the money, which had come from central government, had been squandered away and not used to provide the vital things the estate needed, such as a doctor's surgery, community hall and more units to create businesses and jobs. Cllr Rendle said he had been instrumental in getting the funding of more than £8 million for the estate and had been dismayed to watch it being wasted and frittered away.

He said that 'poorly designed and poor quality homes' on the estate made life 'misery for residents'.

'There was no heart to the community or facilities for the residents,' he said, 'but from day one it started to go wrong. Old houses were demolished and replaced with high density housing and instead of putting Dartmouth families into those houses we have become a solution to the district council's housing problems. Only two Dartmouth families have been allocated houses with all the others being brought in from outside. We have had nothing but broken promises and South Hams District Council has let the Dartmouth people down. The money was meant for the residents already living in Townstal and has not been used as such.'

Mr Carpenter, however, hit back in the strongest of terms.

'I do not believe the council has misappropriated government money and I disagree with Cllr Rendle's figures. I do believe that Cllr Rendle has misunderstood the financial arrangements, which is surprising because I thought he was aware all along how it worked. The point he continually misses is that all housing allocation or nomination is against council policy set by members on a sophisticated points system.

It is true people from outside have been moved to Townstal, but that is equally the same in other towns. We have a long-term obligation to house people. It is my firm belief that Dartmouth people have done well. I would like to challenge Mr Rendle to be specific. How have we done this, give me chapter and verse. It is easy to make allegations but where is the evidence?'

Cllr Rendle said he would 'take the matter further' if enough residents signed a form asking him to do so, but no sooner had he made the pledge than another problem occurred on the estate and he was, again, quoted on the front page of the *Chronicle* criticising the district council.

YOU WANT HOW MUCH?!

The Townstal Community Hall project, which had been running for more than twenty years, had finally got the backing of not only the residents but also both the district and town councils. A bid was put in to the National Lottery for hundreds of thousands of pounds for the building. The district council submitted the proposals, and included in it the details of the sale of the land – which the district council owned – to the Townstal Community Hall Committee for £150,000. But the bid was unsuccessful.

Cllr Rendle slammed the district council for its 'sloppy' application and said that the project had been refused because it was too expensive, mainly down to the cost of the land, which he claimed could have been donated to the project.

'I am incensed about this,' he said. 'I hope that the council reconsiders its decision to charge for the land.'

Jill Sroka, Secretary of the Townstal Community Hall Association said that the group was 'extremely disappointed' to hear about the decision and said the committee felt that the district council could have 'been more generous' with the land.

She said the committee would go back to the drawing board and try and reduce the costs of the project and the head of the housing committee, Vera Harvey, said the council could 'look at the land costs again'.

Bandmaster Phil Watson enjoys conducting Her Majesty's Band of the Royal Marines onboard a pontoon in the Boatfloat, at the first Dartmouth Music Festival.
SOUTH HAMS NEWSPAPERS

Soloists had to be careful not to fall in.
SOUTH HAMS NEWSPAPERS

I CAN HEAR MUSIC, SWEET MUSIC

Dartmouth was the focus of a new music 'extravaganza' during the year. The Dart Music Festival was organised by a committee which came together, booked acts, venues and advertised the event in the space of five months. The event was a huge success and gave them the confidence to immediately start preparations for the next year's event.

For the second year in a row, and only in his second year, Mayor Paul Darby survived an attempt to 'oust' him by other members of the town council. Cllr Darby was threatened with a vote of no confidence after launching a stinging attack on his fellow councillors at a meeting.

He told them to 'put their house in order' and to 'sort themselves out'. He also said many councillors were not declaring an interest in many debates where they stood to gain from a particular decision.

The other councillors were not happy.

At a special meeting, in which standing orders, the rules of a meeting which stop certain types of behaviour, were suspended, many councillors took their chance to attack Cllr Darby.

Cllr Clive Bowerman told Cllr Darby 'I have been asked to move a vote of no confidence in you tonight' a vote which never materialised, because town council standing orders 'did not allow' such an action to take place even though they had, apparently, been suspended. He then asked Cllr Darby to withdraw his comments officially.

Owners Hugh and Mary Heywood celebrate the twenty first anniversary of their shop the Dartmouth Vintners with employee Ed Capper on trumpet.
South Hams Newspapers

Former Mayor Jack Cutter said that if an organisation is failing, as Cllr Darby had suggested, perhaps the Mayor could look in the mirror before pointing the finger of blame: 'Any organisation is only as effective as its leader.'

Another ex-Mayor, Margaret Roberts, said she took Cllr Darby's comments as a personal slight.

Cllr Darby did not apologise, or withdraw his comments and left the meeting refusing to give a statement to the *Chronicle*.

HE'S JUST NOT AT ALL BOUNCY

The antics caused uproar in the letters pages of the *Chronicle*, with many asking what the town council were hoping to achieve. One even suggested scrapping the town council to 'save money' because 'What is the point of the town council? They have no power, always fight among themselves and whenever they do make a decision, the district and county council ignore them'. However, Cllr Darby did lose out a few weeks later when he ended up 'in a minority of one' on the issue of bouncy castles in the Royal Avenue Gardens.

He had tried to get bouncy castles banned from the beautifully well-tended gardens because they were 'too tacky'. He seemed quite bemused the suggestion attracted such controversy. 350 people signed a petition to keep the bouncy castles in the gardens, and a group of parents and children packed the gallery during a committee meeting which discussed the subject.

Cllr Darby won no friends when he told the protestors that a bouncy castle was more appropriate for 'the Mayor's Avenue car park'.

Councillor after councillor stood up to speak in defence of the vinyl inflatable wonders, with Cllr Robert Hannaford summing up what many felt when he said: 'It shows how out if touch this council is and how it misjudged the situation completely. The bouncy castle is no more tacky than many other things in the gardens.'

In the end public pressure won and the placards could be put away.

Despite the huge negative coverage for the town council throughout the year, they did get something right in November, when they decided to give £8,000 a year for three years to the outdoor swimming pool in the town. It had been closed for the year because it was in need of urgent repairs but the volunteer committee did not have the means to do them.

Sir Geoffrey Newman, Chairman of the Committee said: 'We are extremely pleased the town council has decided to back us. We were also very pleased with the words of support from the members. It has encouraged us enormously.'

1999

In May a tragedy which shook the town occurred. Toddler Jordan Deacon drowned after his mother was 'momentarily distracted' whilst onboard his family's floating restaurant the *Res Nova*. Jordan 'moved out of sight in a matter of seconds' and fell into the river. His body was retrieved less than an hour later under the hull of the vessel in eight or nine metres of water.

His parents Jean-Paul and Suzette Deacon, who had owned the restaurant for a number of years, were devastated by the loss of their 15 month old boy.

Their grief can't have been made any easier by the testimony of a diver who said if health and safety regulations hadn't been in place he felt he could have saved the child.

Chris Reeves, a retired diving instructor, said the enforcement of safety regulations, requiring more than one diver to be on a dive of any sort meant he delayed crucially before going into the water by 'ten minutes', or the difference between life and death.

He said he had been warned by the Harbourmaster not to go into the water alone previously and agonised before going in. He discovered Jordan's body and brought him to the surface.

He was then in receipt of a letter from the Harbourmaster informing him of the legislation and saying he could only enter the water with his permission.

The Mayor of Dartmouth, Paul Darby, again caused controversy when he decided to vote for a parking plan which had been thrown out by the town council.

Cllr Darby was accused of betraying the people of Dartmouth after voting for a proposal to continue developing a plan for parking in Dartmouth which included a residents' parking scheme. This had proved very unpopular with the people of Townstal, who would not be counted as residents of Dartmouth and would be treated the same as any other visitor in the eyes of the proposed scheme.

BETRAYAL?

Cllr Darby attended a special meeting of a partnership committee aimed at bringing together the district and county councils. The town's County Cllr, John Mills spoke passionately about the problem and was highly critical of the town council's decision.

He said many councillors voted 'without declaring interests' which was the very accusation which had got Cllr Darby into so much trouble the year before and he also criticised a petition signed by 700 Townstal residents by saying: 'I don't actually feel it does the people who signed it any good. It was an ill-founded concept by those who organised it.'

Cllr Darby told the meeting that the people who had voted against the proposals on the town council had 'no cars' and 'maybe that says something'. He also said the fact that the plan was defeated 9-5 did not show an 'overwhelming majority'.

The meeting ended with the ominous statement from Sir Simon Day of the committee saying 'we will decide for them'.

Cllr Robert Hannaford, one of the people who had organised the petition described by Cllr Mills as 'ill-founded' said afterwards: 'The Mayor of Dartmouth has betrayed the people of Townstal. He is not listening to the local people who are fed up with parking schemes.'

The argument seemed to be the final straw for Cllr Darby, who did not stand for re-election in the town council elections in May. His wife, Irene, who was also a town councillor, decided to step down as well.

He gave a parting shot as he went: 'I have had a bellyful' he said. The *Chronicle* went even further, summing up the town council's reputation thus: 'The council goes to the polls still surrounded by the controversy and in-fighting that has dogged it for years. It is infamous for not making decisions.'

Philip & Son, Dartmouth's historic shipbuilders, established in 1858, finally closes in 1999.
DARTMOUTH MUSEUM
See Feature on pages 54–55

A Dream Too Far?
The *Team Philips* Goss Superyacht

(See year 2000)

The new Millennium was marked with the 'revolutionary' *Team Philips* Goss super catamaran, built at Totnes under the guidance and leadership of superyachtsman Pete Goss.

GORDON THOMAS

Mr Peter Goss MBE, an ex-Royal Marine, who claimed to have clocked up 250,000 nautical miles, came up with the project to build the world's biggest catamaran to set new records for speed on the open seas.

The project's subtitle was 'Dare to Dream' and many did.

It was hoped the yacht would smash world records in sailing thanks to its radical 'wave piercing' design. The unique boat, it was said, would penetrate huge waves and thanks to its double sails, cruise through large seas faster than any other sailing vessel in history.

Sir Robin Knox-Johnston, and if anyone could judge its potential, he could, estimated it could, if it worked as it was planned, take ten days off the circumnavigation record of the globe by a yacht 'easily'.

The papers all over the world were writing hundreds of column inches about the design, so the *Chronicle* wasn't going to miss out on few lists of facts: the yacht, it informed its readers, cost £4 million to build and was the largest carbon-fibre structure in the world, and weighed only as much as 'three small elephants'. 80 cars could be parked between her hulls and each

mast was taller than 10 double-decker buses.

Worryingly however, the boat's designer Adrian Thompson said getting the balance between strength and lightness was tricky: 'Simply, a boat that is impossible to break will never win' he said.

The first challenge, however, was getting the huge vessel around the bends in the river from Totnes to Dartmouth in February 2000. This was no easy task because the 120 foot long, 70 foot wide boat only had a couple of feet either side to spare at points down the river.

The first effort, watched by 5,000 people, was a failure due to the hostile weather conditions.

A week later they had better luck, and the publicity from the first, failed launch, meant many more came out to see the huge structure launched: 100,000 lined the banks of the Dart to see the unique boat sail by.

Team Philips only just made its Royal appointment with Her Majesty the Queen in London for its naming ceremony. However, cruising at 23 knots in very light winds she hinted at how fast she could go. One crew member commented she 'felt like a Rolls Royce in second gear, she's so smooth'.

However, the team hit a huge setback after two days of sea trials – when 40 foot of port bow tore away from the boat. It happened in small seas which should have been nothing if the design was sound.

Goss tried to remain upbeat: 'It's a real disaster, you haven't got to be a sailor to realise that,' he said. 'But, you know, life goes on, doesn't it. We're not going to give up, we are in there fighting and the whole team is behind it.'

Designer Thompson said: 'It's like an albatross with a broken wing and we just have to repair it and nurse it through.'

The need for the repair meant that the first challenge the boat was supposed to undertake – the Jules Verne Round-the-World challenge had to be dropped.

In September 2000 the boat was unveiled to the world for the second time, and before going on sea trials Pete Goss said: 'If I wasn't confident in her I wouldn't go to sea in her.'

His confidence was misplaced.

The first sea trials in October saw a hasty return to harbour after mast troubles, and the next was even worse.

A 'perfect storm', the combination of a number of smaller storms to create one, terrifyingly strong one, caught the catamaran during its next sea trials in December and when a ten-metre wave smashed the steering mechanism in the middle of the Atlantic, it left the yacht and its crew at the mercy of the waves.

Pete Goss put out a 'Mayday'.

The crew were picked up by a German tanker and the multi million pound boat was left to the elements. Pete Goss was praised for his seamanship in bringing the yacht towards the tanker and bringing her head to wind to stop her, allowing a line to be thrown to the yacht.

Managing Director of Team Philips *Mark Orr, Pete Goss and crew member Makie Calvin.*
SOUTH HAMS NEWSPAPERS

'The decision is always based on life, not on the boat,' Pete Goss said at a press conference, 'I felt the risks were too high for the crew to take.'

The failure was a huge blow for the South Hams, which had taken the project to its heart. Less than a year later the two main companies owned and run by Goss went bankrupt, with the loss of forty jobs.

Goss himself had taken a huge beating in the press over the failure of the project. He seemed a broken man, the former Royal Marine and sailing hero famed for his skill and bravery, was forced to defend himself against huge criticism in numerous press conferences. He backed a bid to row the Atlantic and was mocked by journalists for backing 'another *Titanic*-like disaster'.

But he did, eventually come through.

He took nearly eight years to bounce back fully, launching the Cornish Lugger *Spirit of Mystery* and sailing to Australia without any electronic aids.

The huge catamaran awaits its mast at Totnes. SOUTH HAMS NEWSPAPERS

People take precautions to watch the solar eclipse.
SOUTH HAMS NEWSPAPERS

MR CAWTHORNE BOWS OUT

Everyone associated with Dartmouth Museum was saddened by the death of Ralph Cawthorne, 70, who died after a two year battle with lung cancer.

Mr Cawthorne had been a stalwart of the community ever since he moved to the town after the Second World War but it was for his association with the Dartmouth museum that he will be best remembered.

He took the reins as curator at the museum in 1975 and his passion for the history of his adopted home town inspired many and helped develop the Butterwalk based collection as a centre of knowledge and research on the town.

However, his obituary in the *Chronicle* revealed a man of discerning tastes and wide ranging talents; he had been Commodore of the Dartmouth Yacht Club; raised money for Cancer Research UK and Macmillan Cancer Relief among others; was a member of the Dartmouth Players and the Chamber of Trade; taught evening classes in Cordon Bleu cookery, French and navigation, made models as a hobby and was a keen bridge player.

The town mourned the death of John Smith, the final co-founder of the Dartmouth & Kingswear Society to die.

John Smith, Dartmouth & Kingswear Society co-founder, dies.
MICHAEL SMITH

The Duke of Edinburgh visits the Britannia Royal Naval College.
SOUTH HAMS NEWSPAPERS

Mr Smith had moved to Dartmouth in 1957 when he obtained a job at the Britannia Royal Naval College teaching mathematics. He co-founded the Dartmouth & Kingswear Society in 1959 along with Christopher Milne and Lt Col Richard Webb. The society quickly came to have influence over the development of the town and was seen to protect Dartmouth's heritage. His influence showed clearly at the 1961 town council elections when he had topped the poll.

He was also an examiner for the Cambridge Board in mathematics, served as deputy Mayor in 1991 and ended up being deputy director of studies at the Britannia Royal Naval College before his retirement due to poor health. He found time and energy, despite this, to become chairman of Dartmouth United Charities. He was also church warden at St Saviours and oversaw renovation

work which secured its beauty for future generations, but unfortunately he died before seeing it completed.

His son Michael said: 'He always felt drawn to offer his services and talents to supporting the community and town of Dartmouth. He truly loved Dartmouth, the people, the architecture and the character. He truly admired St Saviours Church and wanted it preserved for future generations.'

The eclipse of the sun that was supposed to be a bonanza for hoteliers and the tourist industry in general came and went with little ceremony.

The 'great event' as it was dubbed was ruined by cloud cover and a number of festivals organised to mark the occasion fizzled out.

Dartmouth saw a huge influx of visitors, for one night only, and then the circus left town leaving very little behind.

*The South Hams
District Council's
'Historic' Lower
Ferry crossing the
river Dart.*
WIKIPEDIA

FERRY FIASCO

The sale of the Lower Ferry, which had been ongoing since February 1998 – was cancelled. Many were disgusted that the costly, lengthy, and for the families of the ferrymen, stressful eighteen months ended up being a complete waste of time.

The ferry, which has been running in its tug and float form since 1865, was considered for sale because, despite investment from the council of more than £1 million since it inherited it in the local government shake-up of 1974, it claimed the service only just 'broke even'.

The District Council's Finance Chief Paul West told councillors a good 'housekeeping' exercise would be to look at options to 'release capital' for the council and selling the ferry would do that.

'One way could be to tender it out, but we want to look across the board at all opportunities,' he said.

The ferrymen who worked long shifts to move hundreds of thousands of people across the Dart looked into buying out the ferry – but Philip & Son Ltd. who ran the Higher Ferry also expressed an interest.

It then went very quiet, as negotiations were carried out and many careful sums were done by all concerned parties. More than seventeen months later the wives of the ferrymen broke their silence angrily, They had taken legal advice, spent thousands of pounds of their own money and put their livelihoods on the line to form their own company to take on the ferry.

Mandy Abraham, wife of ferryman Mark said: 'The consortium was formed to take over the ferry so that the men could be in control of their own futures free from council meddling. The district auditor has told us that the council does not have to put the ferry out to tender, but the council insists it must.'

Well, less than a month later it turned out they didn't. The district council decided to keep hold of the ferry.

Chairman of the Economy and Employment Committee, Cllr Trevor Pennington, said: 'We gave the employees' bid to run the ferry very serious consideration.'

Dave Coysh, spokesman for the ferrymen said: 'We were warned three weeks ago by a member of the council that the decision had been made. Although we would have preferred to run it ourselves it is far better for the council to keep it than to put it out to tender to outsiders.'

District Cllr Robert Hannaford said that the families of the ferrymen had been treated disgracefully and said: 'It has been a fiasco from start to finish.'

Flavel protestors put their point across at South Hams District Council.

JOHN MITCHELL

GIVE US THE MONEY SO WE CAN SPEND IT WISELY

Hundreds of people supporting the Flavel Centre project marched on Follaton House and proved that people power does work as they left with a promise for £100,000 towards a new arts centre.

The Flavel Project committee (including John Mitchell, Anne Peaker, Marjorie Tomlinson & Ray Bridges) which had been lobbying for an arts centre on the site of the old fire station and the Flavel Church Hall, organised the march on the head quarters of South Hams District Council after it looked as though it would turn down the group's application for funding for the project.

The decision was described by the *Chronicle* as 'astonishing' because no one expected the council to say anything but no. It showed what organising hundreds of people to walk into council offices can do to the mind of councillors – people who by their very nature usually try to look good in front of a crowd.

The decision was made thanks to the 'militant Dartmothians' who marched on Follaton House to demand financial support from the District Council towards the £1.9million building costs of the Flavel in the Council's future Capital Expenditure budget. The possibility of funding the Flavel had not even been put on the agenda.

The four district councillors for Dartmouth then stood up and began to bring up the Flavel project – sensing this could be their moment. All of them used a theme: 'When is it Dartmouth's turn?' they asked, with some justification after the district council had turned down proposals for a new sports centre, a water sports centre and refused to give the land to the Townstal Community Hall Association, which would have allowed them to get the funding they needed to build the hall the estate had been dreaming of for twenty five years.

The list of failures obviously shamed the council – as they did much more than agree to give £100,000 to the Flavel – they also promised to look again at the sports centre proposals, make sure Dartmouth residents were getting the best use of South Hams District Council provided facilities and safeguard the future of the open-air swimming pool with funding support.

The good natured crowd outside, consisting of members of all the area's major arts and social groups, sang, danced and whooped throughout a good natured show of support which absolutely made its point.

Cllr Jonathan Hawkins said: 'We would never have done it without the unanimous support of everyone sticking together. We in Dartmouth are tired of waiting, tired of hearing the promises, tired of hearing the pledges of good intent, tired of the disgraceful lack of facilities we have – or should I say do not have.'

The Rev Roger Flower, who ensured his notoriety forever by 'running off with the Bishop's wife' in 1999.
South Hams
Newspapers

However the long fight was only just beginning – with many pitfalls along the way making the fight for the Flavel a seven year battle, rather than a four year one which many felt was the case in 1999.

In late September Dartmouth hit the headlines in a way unprecedented in modern times – when its vicar ran off with the bishop's wife.

TOWN SCANDALISED BY A MAN OF THE CLOTH

Rev Roger Flower, 54, disappeared immensely quickly when his long term relationship with Jill Frith, 42, the wife of Rt Rev Richard Frith, the Bishop of Hull, was revealed.

The first anyone heard of the scandal was when Mr Flower announced his immediate resignation from his duties because of 'personal issues'. The *Chronicle* did not pry but then it was splashed all over the Sunday tabloids that he had been in a relationship with mother-of-four Mrs Frith for some time and was, at that moment in a house somewhere near Taunton. Mrs Frith had been estranged from her husband for more than a year.

The people of the town's thoughts were with Mr Flower's wife Liz and children Becky and Daniel, who remained in the town's vicarage for some time as they came to terms with the revelations and the unwanted media attention.

The official announcement was made to the congregations of St Saviours and St Clements by the Bishop of Plymouth the Rt Rev John Gorton.

The couple had met when Mr Flower, 54, was Archdeacon of Taunton seven years previously. He spent fifteen years of his ministry in the Taunton area before moving to Dartmouth in 1996. He had been priest in charge at Taunton in 1982, vicar in 1984, rural Dean in 1990 and Prebendary in 1992.

The Archbishop of York, Dr David Hope said: 'Stresses and strains are never far from many marriages, and we need to do all we can to support any couple experiencing problems and dilemmas in their relationships.'

MR POCKETT MOURNED BY ALL

The year ended with a sudden and shocking death when Town Sergeant John Pockett, 70, died of a heart attack at the annual Mayoral Ball.

Born and bred in the town, the 'much loved and popular man' as the *Chronicle* described him, had been town sergeant for eleven years and was considered part of the town's fabric, such was his dedication to the role.

The Mayor, Melvyn Stone, who was welcoming the guests to his first Mayoral Ball at the time of Mr Pockett's heart attack, described how many felt about the man.

*Blackawton
Primary School
pupils jump for
joy at their new
playing field.*
SOUTH HAMS
NEWSPAPERS

'John was a person who was so devoted to his work as Town Sergeant. He treated all the Mayors with the greatest respect,' he said. 'He was very particular about the Mayor's appearance and very helpful with advice which was a great advantage. I will always remember his sense of humour and his favourite comment 'Let's get this show on the road' as it sums up how proud he was to guide us into the finest role possible. He will be sadly missed by Dartmouth Town Council.'

Ex three-time Mayor Margaret Roberts said: 'You couldn't fault him at his job – he will be difficult to replace. His job was to protect the chain and I remember one time putting him to the test. I was coming off HMS *Northumberland* and onto the floating pontoon when I slipped. John immediately grabbed the chain, which is, of course, what he should have done.'

Mr Pockett left school at 14 years of age to become a coffin maker in Anzac Street with the town's undertaker WG Row and he joined the staff at the Britannia Royal Naval College in 1953 as a cleaner and progressed to become head of civilian security. He lived in the College grounds with his family for thirty years and was awarded the Imperial Service medal in 1989 and the Long Service medal from the police for his role as a special constable and later special sergeant.

As the Millennium drew near the town began to get excited about the celebrations in the town.

People had been talking about the party for years in the run up to the dawning of the year 2000. In the end it was a well orchestrated, fun and raucous welcome for the New Year, decade, century and Millennium. Dartmouth certainly did party like it was 1999.

PHIL SCOBLE

CHAPTER VI

A New Millennium
2000s

A NEW HOPE?

The 'Noughties' – as they have since come to be known – were viewed with great optimism and excitement due to the 'New Millennium' tag which greeted them. The dark years of the recession in the early Nineties were a distant memory – here was a time when wonderful things could be achieved.

The economy as a whole was on the up and as the new decade dawned three years of continuous growth were giving people extra confidence.

This was demonstrated in the way that Dartmouth looked to the future. The Flavel, Dartmouth Leisure Centre and the Townstal Community Hall, all of which looked to be extremely unlikely just a few years before, gained new momentum and were all achieved, thanks to the determination of bands of volunteers who never gave up their dreams.

The continuing fight for a swimming pool was kicked-started again after a long hiatus mainly thanks to the example set by these projects. Socially the town began again to look at itself and ask questions about how it was structured. Many were on low incomes, much employment was seasonal and the Townstal estate had a high proportion of social housing. This seemed a strange mix in a town with many properties worth more than a million pounds – some just a stone's throw from the estate.

The need for housing, or at least 'affordable' housing, dominated the political agenda for much of the decade. The social problems caused by a lack of homes for young families loomed in many debates. This meant the town lost many of its brightest young people who moved away for better opportunities or simply to find a house.

However, it was not all doom and gloom – the Community College was marked down for a three-quarter re-build and if you add into this the prospects for the indoor heated swimming pool, there were many reasons to be optimistic towards the end of the 21st century's first decade.

Celebrating the opening of the Flavel
PHIL SCOBLE

231

TROOPER BRETT HALL *Soldier*

(See year 2009)

Trooper Brett Hall was a hero who never expected to be one: the first South Hams soldier to fall in the Iraq/Afghanistan conflicts of the new Millennium.

21 year old Brett had joined the Army in November 2006, aged 18.

He served with the 2nd Royal Tank Regiment and shone as a mechanic and driver of tanks and armored vehicles. Nicknamed 'Albert' for obvious reasons, the Army did, in the old fashioned way, make a man of him, and he clearly loved his job.

He died on September 16 at the Royal Centre for Defence Medicine, Selly Oak, from injuries sustained when an explosion hit his Combat Logistic Patrol in rural north-west Helmand province on September 12. He was driving a Viking vehicle when it was attacked by an improvised explosive device.

The town reacted to his death with shock and deep sadness. Shops shut and hundreds lined the streets as his coffin made its way first to St Saviour's Church and then after his funeral service the cortege wound its way to Longcross Cemetery. He was buried with full military honours.

His commanding officer gave a eulogy of such power and honesty that none could doubt his sincerity or his own emotions on the loss of his young charge: a man he had placed in control of one of the command vehicles after so little time within the regiment.

Major Charles Burbridge had been in the vehicle in front of the one Brett was driving when their convoy was attacked.

He compared losing 'Albert' to 'losing a nephew'.

'It is impossible to replace Albert, as he was known, because he was such an exceptional soldier,' he said. 'He was an extremely talented tank driver and an extremely talented 'grease monkey'. He was a tremendous young man who always wore a smile on his face and had a cigar in his mouth.

In each regiment you would expect to find two exceptional tank drivers, and Albert was one of them. Anyone can drive a tank, but Albert had a gift. His skill was such he was chosen to drive one of the command vehicles in the combat patrol.

The bonds between tank crews are particularly close because of the way you have to work together and anyone who worked with him could see he was an unusually gifted soldier of conspicuous ability.

He was in charge of making sure his vehicles were in top condition for combat theatre. It's said you need to make sure your vehicles never break down, but it's easier said than done with the tank's two engines weighing seventeen tonnes. Albert's never broke down.

I always said that you could dress him in a Savile Row suit and he'd still be covered in grease. He lived to do the job well.'

Respect for a fallen comrade. PHIL SCOBLE

2000 Dart Marina's parent company proposed building a £5 million development at its Sandquay site – and stirred up a hornets' nest.

The Philip Leisure Group proposed to build forty five homes, a new water frontage and improved marina facilities along with a two-storey car park behind.

Residents living in Sandquay Road were particularly horrified because the three-storey housing blocks would obliterate their view.

CONSULTING CAN TAKE A LONG TIME

An 'open consultation' provided the first opportunity for a demonstration, and many residents turned out with placards and a petition against the scheme.

David Heather, who lived directly above the site, said: 'I feel very strongly that the proposed development is unsympathetic to the Dart Valley and will take away Dartmouth's heritage forever. If planning permission is granted it will open up a Pandora's box because if they can do this in an Area of Outstanding Natural Beauty then South Hams District Council will have no defence to stop similar developments along the whole river.'

Eric Preston, the Chairman and planning officer of the Dartmouth & Kingswear Society said: 'I accept that we can't say no to any development whatsoever, but it needs to be broken up with gaps, set back from the river and not built up so high.'

The operations director for the Philip's Group, Paul Bonnet, tried to put a brave face on the situation.

'We set out to let the public see the plans for themselves and to give them the opportunity to understand the scheme,' he said. 'A number of people living in the South Hams who came expressed an interest in buying an apartment. The proposals fall within the development area of the Local Plan and we hope our plans will encourage more people to come and explore Dartmouth. People understand that there is nothing standing in our way. Clearly the issue facing us is the style of the development. We have taken on board and listened very carefully to what people have had to say about the proposed development.'

400 objections poured into the South Hams District Council Planning Office within two weeks of the consultation. A further 300 were received in the week after that.

Less than a week later, Philips announced it would 're-think' the plans, and form a 'design think-tank' with planners from South Hams District Council to 'look again' at the proposals.

District councillors for the town, Jonathan Hawkins and Elizabeth Jarrold said in a joint statement: 'All in the community, we believe, share the belief that the application was one that was totally unacceptable.'

The scheme was clearly designed to attract second-home owners, and despite the other issues surrounding the designs, this caused probably the most comments. The prices of the properties reflected what local people had dubbed the scheme all along – it was millionaires' row.

Two attempted re-designs failed to bring smiles to the faces of protestors.

After the second was released, showing the line of dwellings moved back 5 feet and the number of houses reduced by four to forty one; people really began to think there was no solution. The two storey car park was still in place and that was too much for protestors.

Phil Liberson, who had been co-ordinating many of the protests, said: 'Our whole issue is about the loss of view, the number of buildings needs to be dramatically reduced and moved back to be in line with the hotel.'

The completed Dart Marina development.
Dart Marina

Left: *Anthony Steen MP debates the proposed building works at Dart Marina with protestors including their organiser Phil Liberson and District Cllr Elizabeth Jarrold.*
SOUTH HAMS NEWSPAPERS

Right: *The Dartmouth in Bloom committee, Jane Joy, Les Barnes, Wilf Lye, Carol Forsyth, Mary Catton, Kathleen Heeley celebrate winning yet another trophy.*
SOUTH HAMS NEWSPAPERS

A Dream Too Far? The Team Philips Goss Superyacht. See Feature on pages 224–225

Former Firestation Commander Albert French who was made OBE.
SOUTH HAMS NEWSPAPERS

Mr Bonnet said: 'I feel we have met many of the views and points made at the three public meetings we have held and we think we now have a proposal that balances the views of the various organisations although we recognise we can't meet everyone's aspirations.'

In the year that the Goss superyacht *Team Philips* sailed past the Marina, focussing the world's media attention on the town, it highlighted that Dartmouth's waterfront was its biggest asset and the arguments went back and forth between those who thought the development would 'ruin' Dartmouth and those who felt it would improve it and attract more people to the area.

The Philip's Group faced further accusations: this time of trying to add a 'sweetener' to get the plans through.

It was announced that £369,000 was to be shared around community groups, including £100,000 for the Flavel project, £250,000 for affordable housing for the town and £19,000 to the Community College for new classrooms.

The newly revised plans in September were recommended for refusal by the town council, who received a standing ovation from the packed public gallery, and passions were running high.

The debate and argument ran into the next year, in fact only a public enquiry could resolve the issue – and did so in controversial circumstances yet again.

A third re-design was also rejected in February 2001. After two years of claim and counter claim, the public enquiry was called and everyone got into gear, gathering arguments for and against.

Government Inspector Martin Andrews did not delight residents with his decision.

'The design is compatible with its location,' he decided. 'On balance the visual impact is acceptable. In the views from the river and its eastern bank, including Kingswear the scheme would enhance the Area of Outstanding Natural Beauty. It would be an improvement to the somewhat featureless quay with its extensive area of tarmac.'

Dartmouth Town Cllr Roger Kempton said: 'It will be just another bunch of holiday homes. For short term greedy gain they have completely spoiled the use of the river as it is the last place here that people can store their boats in the winter.'

WHO'S A GOOD MAYOR, THEN?

The annual Mayor-making in Dartmouth had gained a reputation for double dealing and back-stabbing, after several 'nights of the long-knives' in recent years. But this year the backstabbing and recriminations happened after the ceremony itself.

Melvyn Stone, who had been Mayor for the last year, was ousted in a single round of voting by Richard Rendle. The year before Cllr Rendle had stood aside to allow Cllr Stone to stand unopposed.

Virtually no comment was made on the night – but it was a different story once the paper reported it.

Council staff Les Wright and Brian Halsey chat to county Cllrs Jonathan Hawkins and Elizabeth Jarrold about the reopening of Castle Cove.
SOUTH HAMS
NEWSPAPERS

A letter appeared in the paper questioning why Cllr Stone had been 'ousted' in the vote when he had been 'such a good Mayor'. This prompted many town councillors to point out the election of the Mayor was just that: a democratic vote, but to no avail.

A poster campaign started around the town – anonymously claiming Cllr Stone was the 'rightful' Mayor.

A petition was handed in to the town council signed by sixty people calling for Cllr Stone to stay on in the role.

However, at the town's annual meeting, where any objectors would have had the chance to voice their grievances, they failed to materialise.

There were a number of front page stories following the saga. After a while it ended up with a story quoting Cllr Rendle and Irene Scawn OBE, former Mayor and president of the Hospital League of Friends saying Cllr Stone should be ashamed of himself and could 'put a stop to it all now'.

Cllr Stone said he would not comment before speaking to his lawyer, and ended up not, in fact, commenting at all. The argument fizzled out.

Ironically one of the new Mayor's first roles was attending the carnival, which itself had pulled itself apart that year with in-fighting. In the chaos that ensued at the gathering for the procession Cllr Rendle proved saviour for the event's Queen and Princesses, who had no float. Cllr Rendle got hold of an open top car and drove them around the procession, hopefully making their day a bit special, amidst the pandemonium.

The carnival, which actually disbanded its committee and then re-formed after in-fighting in the few months before the event, was such a shambles its chairman was seen 'crying like a baby' at the park and ride where the annual procession was supposed to start, with no prizes, no majorettes to lead them and hardly any floats anyway. It had the feeling of the beginning of the end, and it was. The carnival staggered on for a few more years, but the writing was on the wall.

Don Collinson author of The Chronicles of Dartmouth Volume 1 1854 – 1954
GORDON THOMAS

A LABOUR OF LOVE

Dartmouth's book publisher, Richard Webb, published a volume fifteen years in the making, a definitive local history which was universally greeted with delight: the first *Chronicles of Dartmouth*.

Don Collinson, the book's author, had become interested in the history of Kingswear, his adopted village, and Dartmouth, before finding himself on 'a crusade' to write the history of the town from the very first edition of the *Chronicle* in 1854 through to 1954, a century later.

Mr Collinson said: 'The book has sprung from a love of the area where I am spending my twilight years. I am elated to have this book published in my old age and to be able to leave behind something useful.'

Mr Webb said: 'It has been a labour of love. I wanted to become involved in the book because I am a third generation Dartmothian and it was something I felt I wanted to do.'

Top left and right:
The damage to the Slapton Line Road by January storms.
SOUTH HAMS
NEWSPAPERS

2001 Storms at the start of the year caused chaos and headaches galore – mainly through the loss of the Slapton road for many months.

The Slapton line, which separates the sea from the fresh water ley, was battered by force-nine gales, which closed the road and left car-sized boulders littering the line itself. The county council sent engineers and workers down on the morning of the storm and moved more than 4,000 tons of rocks to the sea-side of the road to shore it up.

Unfortunately for them more storms that night undid all their work.

Their job was made all the more difficult by Second World War debris, including large mortars and explosives, left over from the preparations for D-Day. Bomb disposal experts had to be on hand to make sure a difficult situation for the area didn't turn into a tragedy. The American War Memorial, dedicated to the 638 victims of the Exercise Tiger catastrophe, had to be dismantled after its foundations were severely undermined by the storms.

Emergency meetings between the Environment Agency, South Hams District Council, the County Council, the Slapton Ley Field Centre and the Whitely Wildlife Conservation Trust were held to decide what to do. To reinstate the road with sea defences which would stop such destruction happening again would cost an estimated £20 million, said district council engineers. But this was highly unlikely to happen, because a link road inland would be much cheaper.

The problem in the debate lay in the fact that shifting shingle banks in front of the ley had been removed in the late 19th century to provide material for the Plymouth Docks project.

STORMY TIMES FOR SLAPTON AND BUSINESSES AHEAD

This had left a whole swathe of the coast unprotected from the sea and had directly caused the Hallsands disaster when a whole village was essentially abandoned to the waves during a storm in January 1917. Without the shingle and gravel, laid down in the ice age, there was little protection for Slapton, and there was a strong feeling among local people that the 'authorities' should make up for the mistakes of their predecessors. However the 'experts' and the authorities, linked together and made a call for 'nature to take its course' – or let the sea wash the line away bit by bit until repairing the road was no longer possible.

This caused huge consternation among residents of Torcross especially, as it would have been a death knell to many of their businesses. They would have been at the end of a very long road, as opposed to a part of a link road between a number of villages and towns. However, the costs involved and the support of the conservationists, meant the official position became one of 'managed retreat' whereby the authorities would repair the road and install temporary sea defences, but allow the road to come 'out of use' within the next fifty years.

The re-opening was rushed through, mostly to help businesses which claimed their trade would be 'cut in half' by a permanent closure.

Joan Mason, Chairman of the Coleridge Association of Local Councils, said: 'The economic effect of this closure is obvious for all to see. Many of our local businesses rely heavily on passing trade to survive. The closure of the A379 above Blackpool Sands several years ago was the start of the decline of several businesses which have closed since.'

Many responses from residents illustrated how frustrated they were at being 'abandoned' by the authorities – but to no avail.

The road re-opened in April, with a new 'kink' away from the most badly eroded part of the line by Strete Gate, but it was too late for some.

Andrew Pound of Strete Post Office, said: 'Those who have applied for business rate relief may have to wait till 2003 and they have also been affected by the Foot and Mouth crisis. Many people are staying away from the area and we are still losing trade. The re-opening of the road has definitely been a saviour for us but obviously it is still a desperate situation and I predict some businesses will go to the wall.'

District Cllr Jonathan Hawkins next to the damaged public slipway.
SOUTH HAMS NEWSPAPERS

The storms at the start of the year also damaged the town's public slipway on the North Embankment, and South Hams District Council faced scorn from councillors and residents alike as it simply repaired the damage and did not initiate a rebuild with a larger launching area for the good of the town's water based clubs, such as the gig and amateur rowing clubs. Paul 'Bungy' Williams, Chairman of Dartmouth Amateur Rowing Club said: 'We have been fighting for improvements to the slipway for quite a while and it's disappointing nothing is being done again. During Regatta there are about fifteen crews on the water all waiting to come ashore at the same time and it all gets very hurried and panicky because they have to go out again straight away for the next race.'

Panicking was very understandable after the Foot and Mouth Crisis.

The outbreak, detected first in Essex, quickly spread throughout the country and brought agricultural life to a standstill. The response of the UK Government was described as 'laughable' by many industry experts – though few in the South Hams were smiling. Similar outbreaks on the continent brought little disruption. However, the British shot and burnt thousands of animals in response to the disease and many businesses faced closure.

A number of shows and events throughout the southwest were cancelled, including the famous Worm Charming Festival in Blackawton.

STEEN WINS HIS BATTLE TO REMAIN MP

The election, called to reinstate the authority of the government and Prime Minister Tony Blair in particular, resulted in no change in the area's representation, but it was a dirty fight to keep the status quo.

Anthony Steen, the incumbent, had his majority cut to a mere 800 in the 1997 election, and his opponent, Lib Dem Rachel Oliver, smelled blood.

She went on the attack, describing Steen as a 'white-haired, burnt out old man' and challenged him to a race up Totnes High Street. Steen came home with an increased majority of 3,500. A jubilant Mr Steen said afterwards: 'They weren't straight and I saw red. Their campaign was repugnant, they were trading on dishonesty. Rachel Oliver was dishonest and the public saw through it. I hope Mrs Oliver will now realise she will never win while I am in the Totnes seat – I shall continue until I am burnt out.'

The town was saddened by the death of Marjorie Tomlinson, for many years the town's county and town councillor. Mrs Tomlinson died after falling down steps at her home, aged 76. Moving to the town in 1983 with her husband Jeffrey, she quickly became involved in local politics. She was instrumental in the beginnings of the Flavel Arts Centre Project – one she never saw come to fruition – and was a governor of both Dartmouth Community College and Primary Schools and was vice-chairman and Alderman of Devon County Council.

A brave attempt to row the Atlantic ended in failure – and a family feud.

Cousins David and Jason Hart had signed up to the Ward Evans Atlantic Rowing Challenge and planned to row the North Atlantic through November. Soon after leaving however, David started to feel the stress of being out at sea and began to suffer hallucinations, such as hearing children's voices in the wind. After six days David demanded to get off the boat.

*Atlantic rowers
David and Jason
Hart before their
attempted crossing.*
SOUTH HAMS
NEWSPAPERS

After three years fundraising and training, David's decision must have been tough on both of them. Jason decided to row on alone. Two days later the organisers decided to try and persuade him to stop, rowing alone in a boat designed for two being too much effort, they felt, in seas regularly going above a 20 foot swell. They eventually succeeded in coaxing Jason to give up, and then, in a final action perhaps very symbolic for the two rowers, he burnt their boat, the *Dartmothian*. The end of a dream created huge emotions for the two, and they did not speak initially after their return.

'It was David's decision and maybe in time I will come to understand it,' said Jason. 'He requested to go off the boat and he was adamant about it. Psychologically it was a very hard thing but I'm a lot more used to it having been in the army and it was what we tried to prepare ourselves for. It was not a hard decision for me to carry on rowing on my own, but it was really hard to call it a day because of my selfish ambition to get to the end because I did not want to let anyone down.

To say I am disappointed is an understatement. There are three things I do not like doing and they are failing, not finishing something and giving up. It was very emotional and I was crying some of the time.'

David said: 'Jason has not spoken to me. It's up to him at the end of the day but we both have to get on with the fact that we have not fulfilled our dreams. It could have worked the other way around and Jason could have dropped out first. I was sea sick for the first three days and didn't eat because it was really rough, both night and day with swell up to twenty feet. It was strange at night because you didn't know where the next wave was coming from and on the third night the moon didn't come up until late and you couldn't see a thing. One minute we were up on a wave and the next down in a bowl surrounded by water. It was very scary and freaked me out. I didn't talk to Jason about how I was feeling because he is very quiet and keeps himself to himself. We lost sight of every other boat after the first night. The turning point came on Thursday night – I was suffering from heartburn and did not want to eat. I knew I was beaten and didn't see the point of staying on any longer.'

Jason said: 'I regarded the boat as part of my family. Seeing it burnt was like having a dog die. I want to do it again at some point because it's like an unfinished chapter in my life.'

VICTORIA CROSS CEREMONIES BOTH SIDES OF THE RIVER

*Lt Col 'H' Jones VC
OBE.
See Feature on
page 144*

A plaque recognising the sacrifice and achievement of Dartmouth's sole recipient of the Victoria Cross was unveiled after the publisher and author of the first *Chronicles of Dartmouth* realised how little public recognition Corporal Theodore Veale VC had received in his home town. Cpl Veale had received the Victoria Cross for saving a wounded officer in no man's land during the battle of the Somme in 1916. He later fell on hard times, and was forced to sell all his medals including the Victoria Cross during the depression.

Publisher Richard Webb and Don Collinson, author of the first *Chronicles of Dartmouth*, with the help of *Chronicle* owner Sir Ray Tindle, proposed that a blue plaque should be erected in the Royal Avenue Gardens.

Mr Webb said: 'A Victoria Cross is rare enough and this is the only one Dartmouth has ever had. It is incredible that no local memorial exists to his bravery.'

Sir Ray, who had served in the Devonshire and Dorset Regiment, the same as Cpl Veale, said: 'I am delighted to have been given the opportunity by Richard Webb and Don Collinson to mark, in some public way, the Victoria Cross awarded to Corporal Theodore Veale. He was a very brave man and I am extremely pleased as a Second World War Devonshire Regiment soldier to be able to join in the move to erect this plaque to him.'

The following is how events were described in the *Journal of the Victoria Cross Society*:

Sir Ray Tindle.
TINDLE NEWSPAPERS

SOUTH DEVON PAYS TRIBUTE TO TWO VC HEROES

Two Victoria Cross recipients from the neighbouring riverside communities of Dartmouth and Kingswear were honoured in two ceremonies that took place, appropriately, on Remembrance Sunday, 10 November and Armistice Day, 11 November 2002. In what may be a unique event in the recent honouring of Victoria Cross holders, two such ceremonies were held within 24 hours of each other in the communities which face each other across the River Dart.

Local publisher Richard Webb and author Don Collinson discovered that there were no memorials to Corporal Theodore Veale of Dartmouth or Lt Col H. Jones of Kingswear.

It was rather poignant that, in a traditional Royal Navy community, both VCs were awarded to soldiers, albeit members of the Devonshire – later the Devonshire and Dorset – Regiment. The next two years were spent searching, organising and seeking funds for the memorials.

DARTMOUTH – CORPORAL TWH VEALE VC

Sir Ray Tindle, the owner of the *Dartmouth Chronicle*, as well as a former member of the Regiment, helped to make the event possible. Similarly, the Jones family donated funds for the memorial to the Falkland's hero.

Sunday 10 November 2002 was a wet and blustery day that did little to dampen the spirit of those who witnessed the ceremony in one of Britain's most picturesque towns. In a moving ceremony at Royal Avenue Gardens. Sir Ray Tindle paid tribute to Corporal Veale: 'Teddy Veale served his country as did many in that war in which a million and a quarter British men and women were lost.

'We remember them all today, but Teddy Veale risked his life over and over again to save another. His bravery was beyond the call of duty. That is why we are placing this plaque here in this public place. He will never be forgotten by his town or his regiment.'

KINGSWEAR – LIEUTENANT COLONEL 'H' JONES VC

The following day, another ceremony took place on the opposite bank at Kingswear. About 100 onlookers, dignitaries and representatives of the Parachute Regiment and the Devonshire and Dorset Regiment joined Mrs Sara Jones and her family in the unveiling of a memorial plaque on the ferry slipway. H.Jones's brother, retired Royal Navy Commander Timothy Jones, delivered a eulogy in which he preferred not to dwell on his brother's sacrifice, but rather about his love of Kingswear.

Mrs Jones said that the Kingswear tribute meant a great deal to the family as, 'Of all the things that have been done over the years to commemorate my husband's bravery, this is possibly the most wonderful. There is already a memorial in the church, but I think this is particularly poignant and will be a reminder to all of us whenever we board the ferry. This was a part of the world that my husband loved and he hoped to retire here.'

Left: *Mrs Theodora Grindell, Corporal Veale's daughter*
Right: *Mrs Sara Jones CBE and Commander Timothy Jones, Lt Col Jones's widow and brother. (See page 143)*

COURTESY OF THE JOURNAL OF THE VICTORIA CROSS SOCIETY

2002 World Events
● The ex-currencies of all euro-using nations cease to be legal tender in the European Union
● The funeral of Queen Elizabeth, the Queen Mother takes place in Westminster Abbey, London
● The Party in the Palace takes place at Buckingham Palace for Queen Elizabeth II's Golden Jubilee celebrations

2002 Homes were on the minds of residents at the start of the year – thanks to a near 50 per cent increase in the price of houses in the South Hams in twelve months.

Many homes were beyond the grasp of the common man – and second home owners were the focus of much ire in the letters pages as the frustration of the situation began to tell.

A plan to secure affordable homes in the town for 'local residents' was one response from South Hams District Council – but town Mayor Richard Rendle said it was not worth getting excited over.

'We need to do all we can for genuinely local people,' he said. 'But to do that we need to change the housing policy which has, in the past, filled houses at Townstal with people from all over the district.'

He was responding to a proposal in the new Local Plan which was being thrashed out for the area. This would set the blueprint for development for Dartmouth for the next five-to-ten years. It would set which areas could be developed and those which needed to be protected, and a high level of public involvement was invited to ensure the plan reflected the desires and aspirations of the town's residents.

Cllr Rendle said that the danger was that land would be snapped up by big developers with no incentive to build homes which were affordable, because they weren't profitable.

The Local Plan was not well received by the town council, and its opposition put the district council under a huge amount of pressure, as without an approved Local Plan new development would be stifled. The town council demanded 'more infrastructure' be installed in the town before new development was permitted.

The main problem was the 170 new houses proposed for Townstal.

Town councillors said in their official response: 'Until an integrated and sustainable infrastructure is provided for Townstal, the council will vehemently oppose any further increase in dwellings. The district and county councils have failed in spending money elsewhere which should have been used to address these issues.'

The council received warnings that without the chance to 'breathe and expand' it would 'simply die' by District Cllrs Jonathan Hawkins and Griselda Guthrie.

DEATH OF A TRUE HERO

The town lost a true character in February – and a true hero too.

Capt Trevor Hampton AFC, who died at the age of 89, was a pioneer of the use of the aqualung in Britain after its invention by Jacques Cousteau. He opened the British Underwater Centre at Warfleet and taught thousands to dive.

Captain Trevor Hampton AFC, a brave test pilot and world-famous diving instructor.
Dr Peter Glanville

But 'Skipper', as he was known, had much more to him than that. He joined the RAF just before the Second World War. His quick reflexes and calmness under pressure saw him become a test pilot, and his 3,000 flying hours through the war aided the development of the Spitfires, Lancasters Wellingtons, Beaufighters and many more. He was awarded the Air Force Cross.

He then became a marine surveyor, through which he gained his interest in diving. He set up his diving centre at Warfleet Creek in the early 1950s and by the end of his career he had trained 3,000 divers to go into the world's most hazardous diving situations, especially in the mining and oil industries.

He wrote a number of books, including his autobiography, entitled *Wheels, Wings, Water* in which he gave the perfect illustration of his personality: 'I've had a wonderful life, and been lucky beyond my expectations. I wouldn't have my life one bit different and only wish I could do it all again.'

Princess Anne visited the Britannia Royal Naval College just two days after the funeral of her grandmother, the Queen Mother. She said 'I cannot think of anywhere more appropriate to be after my grandmother's funeral,' said the Princess Royal. 'To be unveiling a statue of her beloved husband is even more appropriate.' She unveiled a bronze statue of her grandfather, King George VI, a casting of which the Queen Mother had seen before her death and with which she had declared herself 'very satisfied'.

Above: *Peter Slaney, publisher, novelist and owner of the Dartmouth Pottery.*
Richard Webb

The Dartmouth Pottery closed down after more than half a century of trading, putting twenty five people out of work. The pottery had been created in the 1950s and had built itself a good reputation, mainly through the famous 'Gurgling Jugs', which obtained a world-wide recognition. But the collapse of British manufacturing, caused by cheaper foreign products had put the business under huge pressure.

Magazine publisher Peter Slaney bought the business in 1999 and had poured more than a million pounds into the business, restoring its Warfleet factory and opening a restaurant to boost business.

But he had lost a considerable sum over a three year spell, and realised it was not sustainable.

He put the business on the market and thought he had found a buyer in Mintscene, a London-based investment company. However, Mintscene did a detailed analysis of the accounts and trading situation of the factory – probably more detailed than was necessary seeing as the enterprise had never actually made a profit – and decided it would turn the building into luxury flats.

'I had no choice but to sell it because we are losing a lot of money,' said Mr Slaney. 'It's very upsetting. My wife and I have put three years of hard slog into it and I invested a lot of money, but I am losing £1,000 a week and I cannot afford to lose money on this scale. The staff are taking it well because they know we have tried very hard to try and find a buyer willing to do business. But I have to say hand-on-heart, unless someone is prepared to work very hard, it is questionable whether the business will make money, and even then there are no guarantees that it will succeed.'

Left: *The famous Dartmouth Pottery 'Gurgling Jug' and other products. Image from the cover of* Dartmouth and the South Devon Potteries *by Matt White (Crowood Press).*

CRABBING UNDER PRESSURE

Cramped and badly maintained facilities on both sides of the Dart put the town's crabbing fleet at risk.

The harbour had the largest crabbing fleet in the UK, but landing the catch had become a headache because the Embankment was incapable of taking the weight of large lorries. The trucks coming to collect catches were causing large holes in the surface of the Embankment and there were fears for the structure of the promenade. A three-and-a-half tonne limit was imposed after the sand used to backfill the Embankment in 1985 was found to be leaking.

'Part of the Quay was supposed to be reinforced by South Hams District Council but their engineers advised it can only support three and a half tonnes,' said Harbourmaster Simon Dowden. 'But it's my belief it was constructed to take large lorries and we are going through our old files to try and find the building specifications. We are duty bound to encourage the best use of the port and as we are the biggest crab fishing port in the country we should be doing everything we can to support that.'

Rick Mitchelmore, who owned the crabbing vessel *Keristum*, the biggest in the Dartmouth fleet, said: 'The council went from no weight restrictions to a ridiculous one. Three-and-a-half tonnes is useless and no good for us at all.

Britannia Royal Naval College under Threat

In October 2010 the whole country was bracing itself for swingeing cuts from the coalition government. There was a comprehensive review of ALL spending, including education, health and the military.

As part of the rumours about what would be cut and by how much, a nasty 'Whitehall' source told a newspaper that the Britannia Royal Naval College would be closed.

Although there have been many rumours of the College being closed in the past, considering the political backdrop, this time it caused panic in the town.

In an atmosphere when anything was being considered to bring down the biggest budget deficit in history, the clout of the navy command in London could not be counted on to save it. Many Britannia Royal Naval College lecturers had already been made redundant earlier in the year. For some time there had been talk of a joint training establishment for all the armed services to cut costs and increase co-operation between the different services.

Business leaders and the community as a whole considered what just a couple of years before had been unthinkable – what would Dartmouth be like without the College?

The biggest and most noticeable change would be economic – the College employed nearly 100 people in various roles, all taking home salaries and spending their money in Dartmouth and the surrounding area. Even if every single one of them was on minimum

Prince Andrew gives a speech at the BRNC's Centenary Celebrations. PHIL SCOBLE

wage it would have meant £1,000,000 instantly disappearing from the Dartmouth economy – and in reality there was much more than that.

The College also used countless companies to supply services, from the Sandquay Boatyard looking after its fleet of small boats – which employed more than twenty people – to the suppliers of food for the cadets and guests, to the companies that maintained the grounds and houses, provided one-off services for special events, even the cobbler who maintains a huge number of shoes for the College. If the College had been closed, this alone would have meant millions of pounds would have been sucked out of the Dartmouth area.

However, it didn't end there.

Cadets march around the Parade Ground as they prepare to 'Pass Out' of the College. PHIL SCOBLE

Top: *The Naval College and the town are inextricably linked.* Nigel Evans

Without the College, the pubs and restaurants in town would have suffered as 350 cadets drink and eat a lot and their 'run ashore' brought the cash they had 'burning a hole in their pockets' out into the community. The families of cadets 'Passing Out' stay in local Bed & Breakfast establishments and hotels, the cadets have huge celebratory dinners for their big day – all in Dartmouth, all costing a pretty penny.

In short the loss of the Britannia Royal Naval College would have been an economic disaster.

But this loss, in many ways easy to work out, would have been only one side of the story.

Naval officers have been making their homes in Dartmouth ever since the ships *Britannia* and *Hindostan* were first moored opposite Old Mill Creek in 1863. Since the construction of the College above the town in 1905, this has become even more prevalent. The young officers often meet girls from the town and do what young people have always done: fall in love and decide to settle down.

Throughout Dartmouth there are people who marched up the steps to 'Pass Out' and then became an integral part of the town's community. To lose that connection, as the town lost Her Majesty's Band of the Royal Marines which was stationed there until 2009, would rip out its naval heart, leaving very little in its place.

The speculation about the future of the College led to questions of what would become of the Aston-Webb designed buildings which dominate the town. For 105 years the College had looked down benevolently over Dartmouth, symbolising the close bond between town and navy, but what would it represent if its role were to change?

Her Majesty's Band of the Royal Marines, Dartmouth, with the Scroll declaring their Freedom of the Town. South Hams Newspapers

The two main ideas for the site seemed to be either apartments or a 'Five Star Hotel'. The first would have represented for many in Dartmouth its continued and accelerating slide towards a town of second homes, with the heart ripped out of its community. A hotel would again bring money and employment, but it would show that Dartmouth was even less of a 'working town' than it was when the Britannia Royal Naval College was there. Dartmouth would irretrievably be a tourist driven, seasonal town.

The day of decision in Dartmouth came and when the Chancellor George Osborne stood up to announce the results of the Comprehensive Spending Review, the Britannia Royal Naval College wasn't mentioned, though the combined training facility for all services planned in Wales was scrapped. Those two facts meant that the town could breathe again but in the years following the credit crunch the future is surely darker than before, and the threat of the College's closure was left stronger than it had ever been.

I was using the Quay for eighteen months with lorries up to forty tonnes but now we have to try and spread our catch around and land in Weymouth or Plymouth half-way through the trip to lighten the load. I have suggested using steel tracks to support the weight of the lorries and I was even prepared to donate money to strengthen it, but the council did not want to know. The council should strengthen the fish quay and bring it back to what it used to be. If it can't let a local person land their catch it's a sorry state of affairs.'

Bill Lawrence, the district council's principal engineer, said: 'Unfortunately, the area was never intended to accommodate forty tonne articulated lorries. Such vehicles increase the risk of subsidence of the Embankment surface and a weight restriction is therefore necessary to reduce the chance of dangerous accidents.'

The Queen's Golden Jubilee was celebrated across the South Hams in June – parties featured in all the towns and villages. Combined with a forthcoming football world cup, the whole area was gripped in national pride and people festooned themselves, their cars and their houses with flags of St George and Union Jacks.

DEATHS SHOCK TOWN

The town was distressed by two motorcycle deaths within weeks.

Philip Riseley, 23, died on College Way in a collision with another motorbike – he was declared dead at the scene. He left a 'large extended family' and a large group of friends and was described as a man who 'enjoyed life' and always had a 'wave and big smile'.

Then a month later Mark Coxon, owner of the 'Hooked' fish restaurant in Higher Street, was killed on the Kingsbridge to Malborough road while riding his 250cc Piaggio with his wife Lyn riding pillion. The father of four was declared dead at the scene, and his wife was taken to Derriford Hospital.

Nigel Way, owner of the Royal Castle Hotel, said: 'It is horribly tragic – he was a lovely guy with a nice well-adjusted family who was committed to the community. He was incredibly hard-working and had the interests of the whole town at heart.'

Linda Wotton, a family friend said: 'He was a lovely man. He was great fun and lived life to the full. He was a great family man. He loved his family and was a great dad.'

Dartmouth Tourist Information Centre admitted to allowing its former treasurer and secretary embezzle £32,400.

John Kingham was 'given virtually free rein' with the centre's accounts and took the money over six years. His impropriety only came to light after his death in 2002.

He committed the fraud by simply adding a nought to his expenses cheque for £33 after it was signed by another Tourist Information Centre (TIC) director every single month for six years. As he was the man in control of the accounts he simply didn't show the discrepancy and no one was any the wiser.

The then TIC Chairman Colin Campbell said: 'I hold my hand up and say 'sorry guys we lost you a whole lot of money".

The problem was there wasn't enough money in Mr Kingham's estate to pay back what he had taken. There the matter rested.

2003 The argument over the new Local Plan put the town council in hot water during the very cold winter months.

South Hams District Cllrs Jonathan Hawkins, Griselda Guthrie, Melvyn Stone and Elizabeth Jarrold told the town council its opposition to 170 new homes proposed in the Local Plan 'threatened the economic viability of Dartmouth'.

The councillors stated that if the opposition to the houses from the town council, because of the lack of services and amenities available in the Dartmouth area, continued, it would result in the town becoming 'like Salcombe'.

'We need young people to stay in Dartmouth so that the community can develop and have a future, but we are concerned about where they are going to live,' said Cllr Hawkins. 'If they leave the schools will go under, the playgroups and service shops will be lost and Dartmouth will die. The town council's objection to the new houses is threatening the town.'

Cllr Jarrold said the town would become a second home owner's paradise.

The Chairman of the Town Council's Planning Committee, Peter Norton, said: 'We do not trust or believe South Hams District Council's highest hope that it would be able to restrict the allocation and sale of these houses to local people. The reason we objected is because there is already an enormous amount of affordable and local authority housing on the Townstal estate and, unless the council provides the infrastructure and the jobs, we don't believe there should be more houses. There is a shortage of jobs in Dartmouth and those that are here are largely in the tourist industry and very often seasonal. As such, the people who come down to fill them settle here, and then they get laid off and become a charge on the local authority because they are unemployed.'

The debate on housing continued with criticism of 'greedy landowners' by South Hams District Council's Housing Officer Andrew Fisk.

He also said that the town should look to promote business in the town, rather than where to house the workers for jobs that didn't exist.

ALL HANDS TO THE CALCULATORS!

Panic stations were called over the long-gestating Dartmouth Leisure Centre, when an increase in build costs meant there was suddenly a £615,000 shortfall in funds.

A delay in the project was caused by disagreement over where it would be sited: either on the Community College site in Milton Lane, or on the more community-centred Norton fields site where the Britannia Royal Naval College heliport was sited.

Dartmouth's contribution tripled to £150,000, Devon's increased from £250,000 to £500,000 and South Hams' from £410,000 to £725,000.

However, this was only part of the deal, as the centre had to have a root and branch re-evaluation of its equipment and specification.

An agreement was thrashed out to make the building secure, though smaller and much more modest than originally planned.

2003 World Events
● The Space Shuttle *Columbia* disintegrates during re-entry over Texas, killing all seven astronauts onboard
● The second Iraq War begins with the invasion of Iraq by the U.S. and Allied Forces
● The body of David Kelly, a scientist at the Ministry of Defence, is found a few miles from his home, leading to the Hutton inquiry

Dartmouth Primary School Headteacher Philip Medway and pupils celebrate a refitted and refurbished school.
South Hams Newspapers

The new centre was a much slimmed-down affair. Toilets were got rid of, along with office space, but the council made sure the all the exercise equipment was saved.

Deputy leader of South Hams District Council John Tucker said: 'The changes are beyond our control because building inflation is spiralling but there will be no loss of facilities. Officers are working with Sport England, the county council and Dartmouth Community College to put together a package for Sport England to make a decision on. We have a commitment to Dartmouth because the people are deprived of sport and leisure facilities.'

A Chilean ship on its way to Dartmouth sparked an international protest and a 'victory' for Amnesty International.

The Chilean ship *Esmeralda* was a training vessel for cadets in the country's navy in 2003, but was used to as a floating torture centre during the terrible rule of dictator General Pinochet.

Hundreds were tortured, raped and killed on her decks during the 1970s, including the British priest Michael Woodward in 1973.

The Chilean Navy refused to acknowledge the ship had been involved in such unsavoury events and simply said that its young officers were looking forward to being ambassadors for the country.

However, Amnesty International said it was going to subject the ship to protests until the navy admitted its past.

'The thousands who survived torture under Pinochet have still not been acknowledged and their torturers have not been brought to justice,' said Kate Allen, UK Director of Amnesty. 'The Chilean Navy must acknowledge the dark history of the *Esmeralda* and the authorities must launch a full investigation into allegations of widespread torture under Pinochet's rule.'

TORTURE IS REGRETTABLE

Dartmouth Mayor Richard Rendle said the charity's stance was 'regrettable'.

'I think the Chilean Government should take great credit for its part in changing the ship from its unsavoury past and to a purposeful ship for naval training purposes,' He said. 'Amnesty International should give the government credit for how it has imposed change, and for enabling its young recruits to take their next step of activity on board the *Esmeralda*. I shall be glad to welcome it to Dartmouth.'

However, he never did welcome it to Dartmouth.

The week of its visit the Chilean Navy changed its mind – it released a statement saying that the ship had been damaged in Germany and could not sail – but Amnesty claimed victory anyway.

'We're pleased that the vessel on which hundreds of people were tortured will not be coming to the UK as a ghoulish goodwill ambassador,' they said in a statement. 'Cancelling the *Esmeralda's* visit means that this affront to human rights will not take place. The Chilean Navy will only face further protests unless it acknowledges that the ship was used for torture.'

A spokesman for the Chilean government said that although the ship WAS damaged, it was probably a 'good thing' to avoid the controversy.

Richard Rendle also revealed the Vosper Thornycroft Shipyard he ran at Sandquay had been asked to repair the ship when it did visit, but the damage had mysteriously got worse as the media storm grew.

*Town Crier Peter
Randall who died
in July 2003.*
SOUTH HAMS
NEWSPAPERS

Dartmouth mourned one of its larger-than-life characters, after the death of town-crier Peter Randall.

Mr Randall had been the town's 'crier' since 1973 and had travelled all over the world in his bright red uniform, but was most loved in the town for his complete dedication to Dartmouth. He went along happily and, of course, loudly to all events in the town to which he was invited. He took part in, and won many prizes at town crier competitions up and down the land and internationally as well. He was asked to be an ambassador of Britishness by British Airways on exotic tours and was even employed to portray Santa at Hamley's in London.

He was a family man and performed on stage with his daughter Helen many times, the last time at the Dartmouth Proms at Regatta in 2002.

Regatta Chairman Wendy Rendle said: 'He was a great help on the Regatta committee, particularly with the fun events on Friday morning. It wasn't just his colourful costume, it was his whole character that was colourful. He was great fun with the children. This year's Regatta will go ahead as planned but there will be something lost without Peter. He will be sorely and noticeably missed.'

THE END OF THE AMAZING LT COL KITCAT

Also passing on that year, after a particularly full life, was Lt Col Terence Kitcat, at the grand old age of 95.

Lt Col Kitcat joined the navy when he was just 13 and came to Dartmouth to train at the Britannia Royal Naval College.

He spent time on ships and then moved onto submarines as a navigator. The times were simpler then – to achieve communications submarines had to fly a kite behind the boat to act as the aerial.

He decided this was not for him and transferred to the army – one of his famous stories was when he led the funeral cortege for King George V with a broken collarbone after a fall from his frisky horse. He rode that horse for the whole way keeping his sabre upright and his horse under complete control.

He was then sent to North Africa to command an artillery battery during the Second World War.

They were attacked by a German force with tanks and mounted machine guns not long after he took up the post.

Outgunned, he ordered a retreat. The artillery took up positions six times on their twelve mile journey to safety, inflicting sufficient damage on their opponents that even when the British ran out of ammunition, the Germans could not press home the advantage and the majority of men made it home safe. For his calmness in the heat of battle he was awarded the Military Cross.

In January 2004 four men conquered the elements, world records and their own demons to row the Atlantic in **Queensgate** *in just thirty six days. See Feature on pages 260–261*

In 1943 he was taken into the Special Operations Executive working with the local Resistance across Europe. He was stationed with his colleague and close friend Capt Paul Pike in Bulgaria, fighting a Guerrilla war. Capt Pike was shot in the leg and taken prisoner. A few days later the Greek washerwoman of his cell handed him a note written by Kitcat: 'Am within five minutes of you, arrange contact, expect me any time in any guise, yours till hell freezes over, Sailor.'

Capt Pike scribbled back to tell him not to bother as his injury meant he couldn't travel. Kitcat turned up the next day with the cleaner and bundled him into a car he had stolen, and they got away.

After being selected for the British Winter Olympic ski-jumping team following the war, he found himself unable to attend the event after breaking his leg in training. So instead he went to the Arctic to test cold weather equipment and clothing in temperatures as low as -50 Celsius.

He was seconded to the American Secret Service and carried out operations in Iraq, Singapore, Hong Kong, Turkey, Malaya and Korea during the war there.

He retired from the army and became a skiing instructor and travelled all over Europe, always returning to the Torbay dry ski slope.

He was always a keen sailor, crossing the Atlantic many times. Once, after a particularly hairy crossing he came into Dartmouth as the sun broke through the clouds, and decided on the spot to settle there. He bought a house on Horn Hill steps and became famous for his stories and generosity, his wit and sense of fun. He was once observed running up and down the steps and when asked why he said because he had a pain in his chest, so if he didn't drop dead he'd know it was indigestion.

Thanks to his time in hot climates he suffered late in life from skin cancer and had his ear removed. It was replaced with a prosthetic one. As he got older, and deafer, he was prone to taking it off, holding it up to whomever he was speaking to and saying 'Speak up please!'

He was a true, endearing character you couldn't make up. He could only have lived in Dartmouth.

ARGUMENT FLARES UP

The year ended with an amazing emergency – which brought thirty armed police to the town's Embankment.

On December 19 a man and woman were heard arguing on the North Embankment and things appeared to be turning ugly. The police were called and after a series of not-easy-to-understand incidents the man was in a boat on the river in a stand off with police.

He then fired two flares at them, and a house on the Embankment was set alight by one of them which had gone off target. The flare burnt through its roof setting fire to an attic room.

As the fire service battled the blaze from within the building, police with guns and a trained negotiator concentrated their attention on the river.

A nine-hour siege ensued, until finally the man came ashore escorted by a number of officers. He was charged with arson, assaults on police officers and assault on a 24 year old Dartmouth woman.

Left: Pat Callard performs the 'turf breaking' ceremony for the new Townstal Community Hall as Dartmouth Deputy Mayor Iris Pritchard and South Hams Council chairman Bill Hitchins look on, in November 2003.
SOUTH HAMS NEWSPAPERS

Right: Pat Callard and Roger Hern celebrate the completion of the new Townstal Community Hall 2004.
SOUTH HAMS NEWSPAPERS

2004

Townstal celebrated the end of a forty year fight in 2004, with the building of its new community hall.

The £270,000 building was paid for thanks to money from the National Lottery, Dartmouth Town Council along with Tor Homes, the William Sutton Trust and Devon County Council. South Hams District Council donated the land in Davis Road, which had just been waste ground, but contributed nothing to the build costs. However, they did allocate an officer to the task of attaining the Lottery grant!

Many arguments had categorised the long campaign to get the building constructed, with numerous sites and schemes suggested over the years.

The Davis Road site had been the focus of efforts since 1992, when a new committee was formed. However, problems arose mainly because the district council wouldn't give up the land and allow the centre to be built.

Group Treasurer Pat Callard said: 'It's very difficult to raise money in Dartmouth because there are lots of organisations trying to do it. We are a small committee and we have worked really hard for this since 1992, we had quite a few setbacks but, with help from other people, we overcame them.'

The new hall was opened in November by Mayor Richard Rendle.

'The hall is a brilliant facility,' he said. 'A lot of people have been very patient for many years to get this building. Townstal needed a heart of the community and I hope this is the start of it.'

MAYOR FOR FIVE YEARS STRAIGHT

Cllr Rendle became the town's longest-standing elected Mayor since the Victorian era as he was sworn in for the fifth consecutive year.

Cllr Rendle was only beaten by William Row, who had had a seven-year unbroken term spanning the years of the Second World War, but there had been no elections during the period. The only other man with five, Thomas Wilton, was Mayor during the First World War when again there were no elections. Cllr Rendle, who was made MBE for his services to the navy through his management of the Vosper Thornycroft shipyard at Sandquay, said he was delighted to take the helm of the council for another year.

The town granted the Freedom of the Town to Her Majesty's Band of the Royal Marines, Dartmouth. The decision was made to mark the town's proud association with the band since it first moved to the 'ship on the hill' in 1956. The whole town it seemed braved the clouds and impending torrential rain to see the band march through the streets, led by a man bearing the new Freedom Scroll, designed and decorated on the best Vellum paper by Dartmouth Town Cllr and 'Devon Scribe' Melvyn Stone. The rain paused during the band's march and the civic service showed the regard in which they were held.

Canon Gordon Martin told the crowd: 'They add colour and music to the town's events. They take a full and active part in the Royal Marine Band service both nationally and internationally. It is appropriate that their connection with Dartmouth for so many years should be honoured.'

Captain Mike Dowerick accepted the scroll on behalf of the band.

'I'm extremely proud,' he said. 'It's the first time a Marine band has been honoured in such a way. The band has strong links with the town with members joining the various sports clubs and taking an active part in the community.'

Mayor Richard Rendle, Town Sergeant Rob Trowbridge and Mayoress Wendy Rendle prepare to present Her Majesty's Band of the Royal Marines, Dartmouth, with the Scroll declaring their Freedom of the Town. SOUTH HAMS NEWSPAPERS

The Flavel: A Long, Hard Road to Build the Arts Centre that Dartmouth Deserved – Thanks to People Power

(See year 2005)

The 1999 march on Follaton House which yielded a promise of £100,000 from South Hams District Council.

In 1997 a group in Dartmouth decided to fight for something impossible – to build a multi-million pound arts centre.

The Dartmouth & Kingswear Society probably didn't know what it was letting itself in for when it decided to form a committee to try and achieve it.

The recently unseated County Councillor Marjorie Tomlinson suggested the old fire station site in Flavel Place and the church hall alongside it also became available.

It seemed a good idea – to the D&K anyway. The fight began.

But nearly three years into the campaign the project seemed to have been dealt a devastating blow: despite securing some funding, South Hams District Council failed to list it on its proposed capital budget in 1999 for the coming financial year.

Many said it spelt the end of the dream.

Not so said the committee, and they decided it was time to stop being nice. It was time for a show of strength.

One hundred supporters sailed from Dartmouth to Totnes, where they go off the boat, met more than sixty others, and got out placards and banners and marched up to Follaton House, the home of the district council.

This wonderfully choreographed show of strength brought an amazing thing: the district council pledged to support the project to the tune of £100,000.

It was an amazing near-miracle, but it was only the beginning.

Twenty seven fund raising events took place in the first year and more the next; the ideas went on and on, hundreds of events over three years, all organised by volunteers.

The project kept making steady progress through the year in 2000, securing much of the needed £1.98 million budget.

The town council then announced in December 2000 it would sell the Guildhall – its home for 98 years, and move to the Flavel when it was built. A great show of support.

But then in 2001 the town council pulled out of the project, citing a lack of confidence in the figures for its turnover. Its decision cost the committee £30,000 in architects' fees.

Then South Hams District Council, which had given a pledge of £100,000 towards the project demanded 'more evidence' that the Flavel's business plan would work – because there was no feasibility study for the building. An officers' report on the project was submitted to the district council which elicited more protests from campaigners.

Campaigners thought they had won the day when the district council decided to definitely give the £100,000 to the project in November – but then it changed the goalposts again.

It demanded that to receive the £100,000, the Flavel Trust had to raise £365,000 on its own by the end of the year. This was the gap between the funds acquired up to that point and what was actually needed to build the centre, which the committee was of course still working towards, but not on such a tight time scale.

After frantic fundraising and with £332,692 still to find, Jim Murray, an experienced businessman who had in the past brought together large funding for commercial projects, got eleven wealthy Dartmothians into a room, and spent less than an hour describing the situation, and asked each one to in turn go into a room and pledge an amount to the project, in strictest confidence.

He emerged with pledges for the entire amount – if you included Gift Aid. Those eleven people pledged more than £259,000. This amazing story seemed to have finally secured the needed funds from South Hams Council, the final part of the funding jigsaw needed to build the centre.

But more was to come.

The district council then decided to dispute the projected VAT the project would cost, and demanded someone to underwrite an extra £60,000 to prove it had 'secured' its funding. Step forward committee member and stalwart fundraiser John Mitchell, who agreed to pay the full amount if the VAT ended up being more. He also joined with group chairman Ray Bridges and John Stephenson to underwrite the 'pledges' by town's people for £149,000 which could not be counted on by the Government office for the southwest. Every single pledge was honoured in the end.

Then the Town Council decided in May that its funding offer had run out, and threatened to withdraw its pledge of £100,000

Ray Bridges went ballistic.

He accused the council of damaging its own credibility by withdrawing the funding, pointed out the councillor who had claimed the funding was no longer valid had a prejudicial interest because she owned a café in the town centre, in direct competition with the café at the Flavel, and that the council was going against the wishes of the residents it was supposed to represent by withdrawing funding.

The Mayor eventually stated the council would honour its pledge. Finally everything was in place and the bulldozers moved in at the end of 2004 and knocked down the old fire station and Flavel Church Hall.

On February 25, 2005 on a bitterly cold evening, the countdown was over and the Flavel finally opened its doors to the public as an arts centre. People poured into the impressive building, which used design references from the area but also infused its lines and spaces with a distinct modernity, looking to the future.

It is a living testament to the dedication of people who decided they would fight for a facility they truly believed the town wanted and needed, and wouldn't take no for an answer.

The achievement of the Flavel project was summed up in the words of the remarkable Sheila Anscombe, a Dartmouth resident who was development engineer for Frank Whittle on the Jet engine project in the Second World War.

She said at the Flavel's opening ceremony: 'In my life I've had two main missions, the jet engine and the Flavel.'

Top right: *The old Fire Station and Flavel Hall prior to demolition.* John Mitchel
Above: *The completed Flavel with Ray Bridges, far right, celebrates new cinema facilities for the visually impaired and hard of hearing with campaigners who raised funds for them to be installed.* Phil Scoble

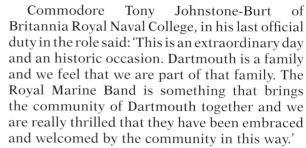

*This decorated
Scroll, with its
beautiful calligraphy
by the talented local
scribe Melvyn Stone,
proclaimed the
Freedom of the Town
to Her Majesty's
Band of the Royal
Marines, Dartmouth.*
RICHARD WEBB

Commodore Tony Johnstone-Burt of Britannia Royal Naval College, in his last official duty in the role said: 'This is an extraordinary day and an historic occasion. Dartmouth is a family and we feel that we are part of that family. The Royal Marine Band is something that brings the community of Dartmouth together and we are really thrilled that they have been embraced and welcomed by the community in this way.'

Maoris invaded Dartmouth, performing frightening dances which looked like an invitation to war – and received an invitation in friendship back whenever they liked.

The group from James Cook High School in New Zealand visited Dartmouth as part of a long visit to Britain and loved it so much they performed the Haka at the College's annual Town Day. Their performances made a huge impression on the crowds.

Principal Keith Grey, just installed permanently as replacement for Ann Buckingham at the Community College, said: 'I think the Maoris brought a touch of the South Seas with them. Hearing them sing, well, if it doesn't touch your heart, nothing will. It's very powerful. What has been really great is the amount of interaction between the schools. We've played rugby against them, sung with them and they've taught us dancing. It's been lovely.'

SEWERAGE WORKS PROPOSAL CAUSES STINK

Below: *The last
Kon Tiki race at
Dartmouth.Regatta
2004.*
SOUTH HAMS NEWSPAPERS

Bottom: *Dartmouth
Primary School year's
three and four with
teacher Hilary Hudson
after performing
for the Dart Music
Festival.*
SOUTH HAMS NEWSPAPERS

Less lovely was the argument over where to place Stoke Fleming's new sewerage works. It wasn't an easy problem; people definitely agreed they wanted a new sewerage works, just not in the one place South West Water seemed to want to put it, at Redlap Cross on Weeke Hill, near one of the area's most beautiful spots on the South West Coastal Path. The site was just off a well-used public footpath, near a car park for National Trust land, and would require the widening of a small lane to allow large vehicular access.

Ruth Piper who lived just down the road said: 'There has been no consultation with residents and there are hundreds of people that use the path and car park in the summer and it will look awful. Everyone coming off the cliff path will have the full overview of the sewerage works.'

Rosemary Shiffner said: 'It's great news for Stoke Fleming and I'm all in favour of sewerage works for the village but it's a great pity that it will damage farmland and we will lose the beautiful little lane which will have to be widened for industrial vehicle access. Although South West Water is doing all it can to disguise the site it will actually be visible to visitors using the car park.'

The site bordered Dartmouth parish and in fact as many people were unhappy in Dartmouth as in Stoke Fleming. A public meeting showed the strength of feeling when sixty people turned out to voice their displeasure. They did so in the same week that Stoke Fleming Parish Council voiced their support – with conditions.

Parish Council Chairman Barry Morris said: 'At the site meeting the parish council recommended that the entrance to the sewage treatment site should be from the B3205 at Redlap Cross and not from the little lane proposed. We don't want to spoil the bank of that lane. I have lived here for fifty five years and was born in Dartmouth. I am not trying to wreck the place. That's the last thing I want to do. We wanted to pipe the sewage to Old Mill where the Dartmouth treatment site is, but we have a budget of £3 million and that would be too expensive. It's going to be a good thing as at the moment the sewage is still going into the sea.'

In fact sewage poured into the sea from three locations in Stoke Fleming parish, and the plant was planned to replace all of them.

Criticism of South West Water rained down: such as they hadn't investigated other sites and it wanted to steamroll the community into saying yes by giving incomplete information and playing a 'take it or leave it' scenario.

South West Water contested this and put on presentations outlining the seven separate sites which had been considered around the village, and the reasons they were not being used. These included two landowners, one of which was the local district councillor refusing to sell the land to the company. It made little difference.

Then Anthony Steen MP got involved. He revealed that the sewerage plant would only treat 'solids' which would be carted away by lorry, and that 'liquids' would still be discharged into the sea, right next to Blackpool Sands which was a Blue Flag beach. He said that the sewerage works was a 'smoke screen' hiding South West Water's actual plans.

'Our Band': Dartmouth's 53 year association with Her Majesty's Band of the Royal Marines. See Feature on pages 24–25

COVE NOT FOR SALE

Mr Steen had a busy year. He also offered to buy Castle Cove which had been closed to the public for five years after cliff falls damaged the pathway to the site.

He said in a letter to South Hams District Council: 'I presume it has little value as the council takes the view it is too dangerous for public use. The council's role is clearly not to be landlord and to obstruct the community from enjoying an activity that had previously existed for 100 years. I would therefore be interested in purchasing the path and giving it to the community so they can enjoy it once again.'

It wasn't sold to the vocal MP.

The town celebrated more investment in its facilities with the building of its new leisure centre.

More than 2,000 people poured through its doors in its first two days in October to sample its 'state of the art' gym, along with myriad facilities and sets of equipment. The £2.35 million centre was nearly scuppered by the mid-Noughties building inflation boom: which saw the build cost rise from £1.8 million to the final build cost in a year. This necessitated the cutting of meeting rooms and toilets from the facility. All three councils, Dartmouth Town, South Hams District and Devon County had to significantly raise their contributions – the town council's tripled to £150,000 – to get the place built, but after years of wrangling it would have been a huge PR own-goal to back out, and the place was opened with much fanfare in the second weekend of October.

Fighting for Castle Cove. See Feature on pages 74–75

SKI HARRISON

Dartmouth's resident poet, Kevin Pyne's first book, Further up the River *was published by Richard Webb. David Dimbleby said 'Kevin Pyne's poems are powerful and original, his images unexpected and perceptive. He evokes with equal tenderness his love for his dead wife and his love of the river and the sea. I believe anyone who reads them will be both touched and profoundly moved by his passion'.*

150 YEARS AND STILL GOING STRONG

Another commemoration took place – at the *Chronicle* itself.

The *Dartmouth Chronicle* celebrated its 150th anniversary with the visit of HRH Duke of York and a flood.

The long-planned visit of the Prince to the *Chronicle* office and the head office in Kingsbridge of South Hams Newspapers Group coincided with torrential rain, which flooded the whole of Victoria Road and the Over 60s Restroom which had been designated for the visit's displays of pictures and old papers. The water left staff scrabbling to dry the carpets and even ironing pictures on display.

The visit went like clockwork and crowds filled the Market Square to greet the Prince with cheering and flag waving. Deputy Lieutenant of Devon Sir Nigel Essenhigh introduced dignitaries to the Prince after he flew in to the Britannia Royal Naval College.

The Prince told employees: 'I want to say how important you are to the fabric of the community and I want you to realise how important the service you provide is. Often the national newspapers give a jaundiced view of reporting – but regional and local papers really are the bread and butter of journalism and you should be congratulated on what you do.

I sincerely hope you continue to provide this service and the wonderful investigative journalism in this part of the world. I love local newspapers – you get the best stories from them. I wish you well in the future. Good Luck.'

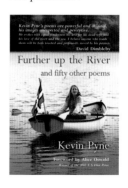

Top left:
Prince Andrew looks through Dartmouth Chronicles *at the* Chronicle *office in The Old Market on the paper's 150th anniversary.*
SOUTH HAMS NEWSPAPERS

Top right: *Reporter Victoria Vaughan takes Prince Andrew through what she does in the community of Dartmouth.*
SOUTH HAMS NEWSPAPERS

Prince Andrew and Sir Ray Tindle celebrate the Dartmouth Chronicle's *150th anniversary.*
SOUTH HAMS NEWSPAPERS

The Flavel – arts centre opens in 2005.
WIKIPEDIA

See Feature on pages 250–251

2005 The Higher Ferry sailed down the river Dart, after a combination of high tides and high winds caused the 45 year old ferry to become detached from its cables.

The ferry floated downstream with thirty four people and fifteen cars on board. Sixteen boats were damaged during the crisis, which saw stranded passengers taken to shore by the Torbay lifeboat. A number of cars were left on the stricken vessel until it could be returned to its wires. The drama was documented on television, as scared passengers used their mobile phones to contact loved-ones, and word quickly spread.

The ferry was back, safely on its cables and running again, just two days later.

FLAVEL ARTS CENTRE OPENS
AFTER EPIC JOURNEY TO CONSTRUCTION

The Flavel Arts centre opened its doors on a fun-filled evening. The centre had been a dream of many in Dartmouth, and a dedicated group had been fundraising and lobbying Dartmouth Town Council and South Hams District Council for funding for more than seven years. Its construction was nothing short of a miracle brought about by the fortitude and determination of a large group, who remained largely un-thanked for their efforts, but were glad to have contributed to the cause in which they all believed so strongly.

John Burton-Race's new television programme caused a boom in interest in Dartmouth and caused an upturn in tourist activity.

The Return of the Chef marked the irascible gourmet's return to take on the once famous Carved Angel restaurant on Dartmouth's South Embankment. He had already seen success in his previous series *French Leave* when he went to the south of France for a year to re-discover his love of cooking again following hard years in London. He, his wife and their five children became celebrity figures around the town and his prime-time series on Channel Four gave the town six weeks of free advertising. It brought in huge amounts of interest and clearly brought a lot of people to the town.

A spokesman for Dartmouth's Tourist Information Centre said: 'Every other phone call we take someone says they've seen the New Angel programme.'

Mr Burton-Race was rarely out of the headlines after he arrived, often for good things, but also for bad, such as when he and his wife separated following revelations of his love-child with a woman from Strete.

The end of an era was marked as Dartmouth's Swimming Club folded after nearly 100 years. The club blamed restrictive rules and regulations and a drop in the number of swimmers. Although the yearly Regatta swimming gala, always the responsibility of the swimming club, continued with some success, the folding of the club was a dark day for Dartmouth. A lack of an indoor swimming pool was blamed by some because it meant the club had no permanent home.

Dartmouth's Norton Park was plunged into darkness when its then owners disappeared, owing more than £25,000 to Southern Electric. David Lamb, who was leasing the main house and entertainment complex, disappeared just before the lights went out. The park remained in darkness for four days before the power was turned back on, with chalet owners asked to pay £40 to cover power costs by land owners Wykeham Land.

Left: *Staff and potential customers celebrate the arrival of the equipment at the soon-to-open Dartmouth Leisure Centre 2004.*
SOUTH HAMS NEWSPAPERS

The park had always struggled to make ends meet since the advent of cheap foreign holidays with owners finding it particularly tough since the turn of the century and after Mr Lamb ran for the hills, the site went through three more owners in just five years.

BRITANNIA ROYAL NAVAL COLLEGE CELEBRATES 100 YEARS

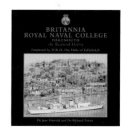

The Britannia Royal Naval College celebrated 100 fine years. As part of the centenary celebrations, the College welcomed a Royal visit. HRH the Duke of York Prince Andrew visited Britannia Royal Naval College and placed a letter to the future inside a time capsule, into which was also placed a copy of the *Dartmouth Chronicle*.

The time capsule had been arranged after the College's original time capsule had been found and opened, very carefully, by Drs Jane Harrold and Richard Porter.

Above: Britannia Royal Naval College – An Illustrated History *is published.*

The Duke said: 'I won't tell you the subject of the letter, but if you bear in mind the fact that it is 2005, then that might give you a clue.'

A lavishly illustrated new book outlining the history of the Britannia Royal Naval College was launched to coincide with its centenary year. Written by the College's resident historians Dr Richard Porter and Dr Jane Harrold, and with a foreword by Prince Philip, the book flew off the shelves, selling over 1,000 in its first week. Richard Webb, the book's publisher, said: 'Everyone's been really positive and likes the look of the book.'

Below: *HRH The Duke of York prepares to place his own contribution, in a sealed envelope, into the new time capsule, on 20th July.*
BRNC

Dartmouth's longest serving post-war Mayor, Richard Rendle, found himself in an unpopular position immediately after being replaced in the Mayoral role by Peter Norton. He took a major part in the new parking plan for Dartmouth, and whatever he tried to say to the contrary, the plans would be known forever as 'Dick Rendle's Parking Plan'. The new plans to solve the parking crisis went in front of the public in July and caused instant controversy. The plans suggested turning part of Coronation Park into a 157 space car park, and the park and ride, it was suggested, should become free to use, encouraging visitors to keep their cars out of the town centre.

A survey revealed high support for the new plans for parking in Dartmouth. The survey, completed by 394 participants, discovered that 62 per cent found the plans acceptable, and 96 per cent agreed that Dartmouth had a parking problem.

Left: *Carlos Edwards, who was an officer at the Britannia Royal Naval College, is recognised for his commitment to the College and the town with a Town Plaque presented by Town Mayor Peter Norton.*
PHIL SCOBLE

Right: *Dartmouth Community College students learn about science using CSI type techniques, inspired by the American TV Show.*
PHIL SCOBLE

However, the use of Coronation Park, reclaimed from the Coombe Mud in the 1930s thanks to donations from local people for 'recreational use', meant that opposition was incredibly fierce. Letters deluged the *Chronicle*, people threatened to lie in front of the bulldozers when they appeared to convert the park and people lined up to tell the paper why it shouldn't be allowed.

The plan faltered. The authorities that would have to implement the plan, Devon County Council and South Hams District Council looked carefully at the integrated plan involving parking meters, new park and ride facilities and bus stations, and then balked when the group behind it demanded it all be implemented at the same time, 'or else it won't work'. They told the group, as politely as possible, that changes in town planning don't happen like that and each part of the plan would have to be considered separately.

SCOBLE STARTS

Phil Scoble, the author of this book.
PHIL SCOBLE

The staff of the Lower Ferry donate a Christmas hamper to the residents of the Churchill Court sheltered accommodation.
PHIL SCOBLE

A youngish reporter started at the *Chronicle* in June – thrust into a world of journalism he barely understood. Phil Scoble found his work hard but enjoyable.

Dartmouth Community College celebrated being awarded specialist arts status, meaning it would benefit from an extra £210,000 over the next four years to promote its arts activities. The College had raised its own funds in sponsorship which allowed a bid for arts status to be considered. Principal Keith Grey said: 'This is a real step forward and we are thrilled to be able to realise all the plans we've made.'

Dartmouth was shocked as a series of vandalism attacks in the Royal Avenue Gardens took place. Three attacks took place in one week alone. The public outcry against the attacks in the well-loved gardens resulted in a series of meetings between police and local community leaders.

'Every day of the week it seems my team and I are having to clear up damage caused by vandals,' said Les Barnes, manager of Dartmouth's Operations team, who handled street cleaning for the District Council. 'It's not just an upsetting thing for us; it's a huge waste of taxpayer's money.'

After this spate of attacks anger grew in the town towards not only the vandals, but also towards the owners of the gardens, South Hams District Council, for not investing in CCTV to protect the gardens, and the police, for not having enough foot patrols to combat the crime. The vandals damaged the gardens while standing less than 150 yards from the town's police station.

Both groups also received harsh criticism when they revealed that their plans to combat anti-social behaviour in the Royal Avenue Gardens did not involve CCTV. The plans involved cutting back the trees and other foliage in the gardens to improve visibility and thereby discourage anti-social behaviour. This was met

A boat sunk by its owner to prove to his estranged wife he cared more about her than the boat. The gesture did not succeed.
KEVIN PYNE

with universal derision because people thought it wouldn't work and because it was felt that to cut back the gardens would mean the vandals had 'won' because the gardens would be less beautiful, all in the name of public safety. Later in the year vandals attacked the community orchard, causing nearly £800 worth of damage to a wooden fence. Dartmouth Mayor Peter Norton said: 'The orchard is such a haven for the town, its depressing to see such wanton destruction.'

If, after a year of high-profile vandalism attacks, any proof was needed the town had a problem, in December there were statistics to confirm it.

Dartmouth was shown to have the highest rates of criminal damage in the South Hams, with more crimes than towns with three times the population.

I SUNK THE BOAT FOR YOU

The yacht *Rebel* was sunk by a man who wanted to save his marriage, but ended up costing his family thousands of pounds.

Mark Bridgewood sunk the boat, worth over £60,000, after an argument with his estranged wife Tracey. The couple had put the yacht up for sale together, but after an altercation, Mr Bridgewood sunk the boat in the middle of the Dart to prove to Tracey he only loved her and didn't care about the boat they had bought and lived aboard together. This however created a headache for harbour workers and a large salvage bill that Mrs Bridgewood picked up. The boat was brought up off the bottom of the river and cleaned up, before Mrs Bridgewood sold it, losing much of its value on the £10,000 salvage bill.

The town reacted with horror at the death of a young teenager after a party took a tragic turn.

Teenager Karl Turnstill died after falling from the window of a third floor flat overlooking The Quay during a party to mark the end of the summer holidays.

Dartmouth teenager James Plant was also hurt after falling, but recovered from serious head injuries. Karl seems to have fallen from the window in a moment of 'high spirits'. James fell after apparently trying to save the young man.

Karl's parents paid tribute to their son: 'He will be sadly missed as he was a lad with a brilliant sense of humour and was always in high spirits.'

A new supermarket was proposed in Townstal which could create 100 jobs. The developer, Location 3, was preparing a planning application for a supermarket, rumoured to be Waitrose, which would have a 227 space car park. If plans went well, the site's developer said, the new store could open at Easter in 2007.

An 87 year old man was arrested and charged with the murder of his 86 year old wife in Strete. Local people expressed shock at the death, as details emerged. The man had killed his wife using a kitchen knife, stabbing her many times while she lay on their bed. He then stabbed their cat to death also.

'They always seemed such a lovely old couple,' said villager Pam Wills.

The man was convicted but released less than a year later, after a judge decided he 'posed no threat to the community'. He went back to live quietly in the house where he had killed his wife: he was officially the oldest murderer in Britain.

Gigs from the Dartmouth Gig Club returns to the town triumphant after rowing the channel from near Roscoff in twenty four hours in aid of Clic Sergeant, a cancer charity.

PHIL SCOBLE

2006 World Events

● Russia cuts natural gas to Ukraine over a price dispute

● Israeli troops invade Lebanon in response to Hezbollah kidnapping two Israeli soldiers and killing three. Hezbollah declares open war against Israel two days later

● North Korea claims to have conducted its first-ever nuclear test

● Former President of Iraq Saddam Hussein is sentenced to death by hanging by the Iraqi Special Tribunal

2006 Dartmouth Community College was slammed by town councillors for driving students a few yards to receive sports lessons.

The students were being bussed from the College to Dartmouth Leisure Centre due to health and safety fears, at the cost of £20,000 a year.

The 250 yard-walk to the centre meant it stood outside the boundary which national legislation allowed students to walk to lessons. The county council pointed out that if the leisure centre had been built within the grounds of the Community College, which the town council opposed, then the buses would not be needed. This did not sway the councillors.

Cllr Roger Kempton said the buses showed how students were 'mollycoddled'.

However Devon County Council said the only way to avoid using the buses was to build a pathway to the leisure centre, at a cost of £500,000 because landowners had decided to make the land between the centre and the College a 'ransom strip'. The price represented twenty five years of bussing students to and from the centre, and the buses remained.

RENTS DOUBLE THANKS TO LARGE SHOPS PAYING PREMIUMS

An argument erupted in Dartmouth over rents for commercial properties after a town centre business ended up paying double after a rent review.

Jamie Horton, owner of Café Cache with his wife Dawn said that the rise was 'ridiculous' and that he was very annoyed. But David Mallinson, the agent who brokered the new rent deal, said he followed a strict code of ethics, and that his 'heart went out' to the owners. The problem highlighted an issue which would rear its head many times in the next few years: large shops had come to Dartmouth and paid premium, some would say exorbitant, sums for well-placed shops. This pushed up rents around them until many businesses in the town, including Café Cache, which although it won its case still saw its rent hiked a huge amount proportionately, go out of business because they couldn't maintain enough trade year-round to pay the bills.

One of Dartmouth's chartered surveyors claimed the town faced ever-increasing rents. David Freeborn said that rents had doubled in Dartmouth in the previous three years, with some traders in the town paying 'over £50 per square foot' for their premises. He said rents would increase, despite some landlords 'being reasonable and charging less'.

Shop owner Nick Crosley claimed that unless estate agents and landlords stopped the trend for charging more and more, many independent shops would go out of business.

In slightly better financial shape was Dartmouth Hospital, but its rude health hid a more wide-spread malaise in the health service. The hospital revealed that it would balance its books for the year 2005/06 despite monetary chaos around the country for other NHS trusts. The NHS had been dismayed by the second major re-organisation of trusts in ten years under new government plans. The smaller Primary Care Trusts set up by the Labour Government were being replaced by much larger ones for larger areas, a very similar structure to how the NHS was organised before the reforms of the 1980s.

Dignitaries from both sides of the argument on stage for a public meeting discussing the fate of the Dartmouth passenger ferry.
PHIL SCOBLE

Dartmouth Hospital Administrator Birgit Morrison said the ability of the trust to avoid money troubles was partly down to being 'very careful' and having 'wonderfully supportive staff'.

However, the re-organisation was so expensive it swallowed up the £12 million which had been allocated by the old South Hams Primary Care Trust to build a new Dartmouth Hospital in Townstal to replace the ageing cottage hospital on the Embankment. Dartmouth feared it would never get such a good chance of a new hospital again.

LEAVE OUR TREES ALONE!

Dartmouth residents protested in the streets after it was revealed South Hams District Council planned to cut down eight trees in the Royal Avenue Gardens.

The plans were suggested to help curb anti-social behaviour in the popular tourist attraction. Nearly 200 people packed the gardens to protest at the plans, led by the district council's own volunteer tree warden Roger Kempton. The public display of defiance complete with banners and speeches shocked South Hams District Council and meant they shelved the plans. Some of the trees were going to be taken down and replaced with others which would be better for the long-term health of the gardens, but after the protests all plans to change the trees were indefinitely put on hold.

Anti-social behaviour, especially by young people, became a real hot potato this year and the public reaction to vandalism attacks prompted action.

Residents filled the Guildhall for a meeting about policing levels in the town twice in six months. The second meeting, chaired by Anthony Steen MP, featured the police revealing figures showing crime had fallen by nearly 10 per cent from a similar period last year according to Inspector Paul Morgan.

Jonathan Hawkins, South Hams District and Devon County councillor for Dartmouth, who called the meeting, said that the figures seemed to suggest that the policing in Dartmouth was improving, but that visible policing still needed to be improved in the town He said: 'It was a very positive meeting, and the statistics showed perhaps we are moving in the right direction. However, high visibility policing is still an issue, but we need to ensure the town works together with the police to make sure things continue to improve.'

However it didn't improve enough to stop nine tyres on three marked police vehicles being slashed during a spate of vandalism outside Dartmouth police station. The damage was estimated at £630. An alarming aspect of the midnight incident was the fact that the town had no cover from emergency response vehicles for three to four hours. Inspector Morgan condemned the attack and said it was fortunate that there was no major emergency during that period.

Those calling for better policing were pleased to see Dartmouth's first Anti-Social Behaviour Order (ASBO) awarded to a teenager from Townstal. The order, part of a new move by authorities to target specific behaviours of offenders was given for repeated offences and one 'sickening' assault on two middle-aged couples in Dartmouth in summer 2005. The ASBO banned James Plant, 19, from all the town's pubs, and from being in the town centre between 6pm and 6am. He was also sentenced to 150 days in prison.

First Four to Row an Ocean – Dartmouth's *Queensgate* Crew

(See year 2004)

In January 2004 four men conquered the elements, world records and their own demons to row the Atlantic in just thirty six days.

For one it would be the culmination and triumph over more than five years of hard graft and personal disappointment, and the key to moving on in his life.

For two of them it would be just the start of the physical challenges they would set themselves.

The Dartmouth Four of Phil Langman, Iain 'Yorkie' Lomas, Sean Barker and Jason Hart rowed in the Ocean Rowing Society's John Fairfax Regatta from the Canary Islands to Barbados.

The crew were the first 'four' ever to row an ocean and their time was an astounding thirty six days – only a crew of eleven French Navy cadets had done it faster in 1992, and that team followed a course more than 100 miles shorter.

The group had been tantalisingly close to the record after leaping into the lead in the race in its early stages, and the *Chronicle* had weekly updates giving the readers a glimpse of how the 'boys' were doing. Boys undertaking a feat many 'men' would have run from.

When they rowed their boat *Queensgate* into Barbados, after thirty six days and fifty nine and a half minutes, they had broken the previous record for that route by four clear days, won the race and were the first four to row an ocean.

The bearded men were shown smiling in the Barbados sunshine, though they were more emotional than that the night before as they crossed the finishing line.

The 'boys' had got their victory the hard way. They had paid for their boat by instalments and had fitted it out themselves after their evening training sessions. They had all worked long

and hard and done it their own way – deciding collectively what equipment to take and which to leave behind to reduce weight, ignoring safety advice from the race organisers to gain minutes a day over their rivals.

The crossing was in no way easy, with the boat being swamped and a couple of them nearly getting washed overboard more than once.

For Jason Hart it was probably sweeter than for his colleagues, as he had failed in an attempt to row the Atlantic two years before.

He had been forced to burn his boat after being left mid-ocean by his rowing partner – who was also his cousin. The two had sunk thousands into the row and it caused a bad family rift after their return. Jason said burning the boat – not something he chose to do; it was in the rules of the race that anyone abandoning the row had to burn their boat – was like 'the death of a family dog'.

Shaun said he had enjoyed the row.

'*Queensgate* performed really well and we didn't have to put our capsize drill into operation although the cabins and deck were swamped on occasions,' he said.

The congratulations poured in.

Ken Crutchlow of the Ocean Rowing Society said: 'These four rowers join an exclusive club. A total of 1,672 people have climbed Everest, but in 100 years of rowing only 117 people have made this journey. I am sure this record time is due to the total dedication of a crew working together under what must have been, at the very best, uncomfortable conditions.'

Mayor Richard Rendle said: 'We congratulate them and want them to know that the town is very proud of them.'

The Queensgate *crew with another team from the historic fishing village of Beer on the Jurassic coast of East Devon. All Relative – who are in fact all related – were about to attempt the same crossing. The Dartmouth boys gave them advice on nutrition, dealing with heavy seas and expert advice on how to scowl at the camera. Thanks, perhaps in part to the* Queensgate *advice, they completed the crossing in January 2006. Left to right: Jason Hart, Justin Adkin, Phil Langman, Martin Adkin, Iain 'Yorkie' Lomas, Robert Adkin, Shaun Barker, James Green.* PHIL SCOBLE

Chairman of South Hams District Council Bill Hitchins invited them as guests of honour to his civic dinner and telephoned their families individually to congratulate them.

Chairman of the Dartmouth Regatta, Basil Williams said: 'Congratulations to the boys, the Regatta committee is very proud of them. I sent them an email telling them to save themselves a bit because they are the chairman's crew in the invitation whaler race this year.'

The crew returned and spent the next year talking about their experiences – they lectured and chatted and even released a book.

And then they went their separate ways.

But Phil and Yorkie still wanted to challenge themselves in the most extreme ways possible.

They first decided they wanted to take on an 'extreme marathon'.

Using the dreaded Google, they searched and found the 'Au Grabies' extreme marathon running six marathons in seven days through the Kalahari carrying 40 pounds of weight, including water and food to be consumed on the way. They both finished in the top five out of more than fifty competitors.

For some people this would have been enough excitement and adventure for a lifetime, or at least a few years.

But not Phil and Yorkie.

They next – in fact they started training less than two months later – took on a feat never before attempted.

They ran the Paris Marathon, then ran from Paris to London on tarmac roads over the next six days and then ran the London Marathon: the equivalent of 8.3 marathons in seven days. They nearly got on national radio, but were bumped off it when a one legged man was found by reporters.

The boys didn't mind, they just got down to planning their next adventure.

With a couple of other local men, they then decided to cycle from John O'Groats to Land's End. But this is something lots of people have done. So they decided to run up the three highest peaks in Britain on the way – Ben Nevis, Scarfell and Snowdon, and canoe across the three biggest lakes. All this and they were aiming for the record for this – yes, one other team had been mad enough to do it – of ten days.

They completed the challenge in under nine. And to judge by their expressions at the finish line, they hardly broke a sweat.

The amazing things is that they have done it with the minimum of fuss; point out what they have done is mind-blowingly difficult and impressive, they respond with a resigned happy shrug of the shoulders. They won't tell you what they've done, but it's worth buying them a drink and finding out, because it will amaze and astound you.

WORLD'S LARGEST YACHT *EOS* FOCUSES MEDIA EYE ON DARTMOUTH

In happier news, the world's most expensive sailing yacht chose to visit Dartmouth on its maiden voyage.

The town received national recognition with the visit of *Eos* – the world's most expensive and biggest privately owned sailing yacht.

Eos attracted crowds to see it in all its majesty. The £120 million sailing vessel stayed in port for more than ten days due to bad weather allowing thousands to have a good gawp at such excessive luxury.

The boat was owned by billionaire Barry Diller, producer of the movies *Raiders of the Lost Ark, Grease* and *Beverly Hills Cop*. At the time Mr Diller was chief executive of the Fox Broadcasting Corporation, on the board of the Coca Cola Company and was the chairman of the Expedia travel website network.

With a length of ninety metres and a permanent staff of seventeen, the *Eos* was a lesson in luxury and comfort.

However, Mr Diller obviously wanted to push the boundaries of what 'luxury afloat' meant, as it was rumoured he was having a sister ship built – longer and sleeker – at the Bremen shipyard where *Eos* was constructed the year before.

The world's largest privately owned sailing yacht Eos, *owned by movie and media billionaire Barry Diller, moored in Dartmouth.* Eos *can also be seen on page 2 of this book sailing out of Dartmouth.*
PHIL SCOBLE

Hands up if you are one of the most improved primary schools in Britain – well done Dartmouth Primary School.
PHIL SCOBLE

The Dart Music Festival went down a storm in its ninth year.

The festival saw a wide variety of performances, including a set from jazz legend George Melly with Digby Fairweather's Half Dozen.

Rob Lyon, Chairman of the Festival, said he had received a huge amount of positive feedback about the quality of the acts during the festival

He said: 'It's been a great festival. Many people have commented on how good the musicians have been this year. Some of the performances have just been awesome; it's great to see in a festival like this.'

The Music Festival was nearly charged a huge sum for the policing of the event, but was reprieved at the eleventh hour, when the police waived the charge, mainly due to the public outcry.

Devon and Cornwall Police then showed they hadn't learnt at all by trying to charge Regatta as well. Residents were again up in arms when it was revealed the event could be charged £13,000 for policing.

Regatta Chairman Basil Williams claimed the police were becoming 'mercenary'. However, police Inspector Paul Morgan asked the town to have a 'sensible, rational' debate over the cost of events like the Regatta to taxpayers. The police eventually backed down and dropped all charges for policing the Dartmouth Regatta after intervention from the police authority member Sir Simon Day. Acting Chief Constable Nigel Arnold called Mr Williams just before the

Regatta was about to start informing him no charges would be brought and wished the Regatta Committee a fantastic event – which they duly did.

2006s Regatta was hailed as 'the finest we've seen up to now' according to Mr Williams.

The town was absolutely packed on Regatta Saturday for the fly past by the Red Arrows and the RAF Typhoon and a record number of people used the park and ride set up by South Hams District Council. Estimates ranged from 30,000 to 100,000 people in the town during the day. Figures were so high, however, that concerns were raised about the events during Regatta getting too big.

'RAIN' OF SUPERMARKETS BEGINS

Lidl announced it would be putting in a planning application for a new store in Townstal, getting in ahead of an announcement on the nearby Nelson Road site which had been the basis of much debate. The development would create thirty jobs with a new low cost food and homeware store.

Dartmouth was dubbed the 'town where it rains supermarkets' in the national press after Marks and Spencer also announced it would open in the town, and then the biggest announcement of the lot came along.

Sainsbury's announced that it would be building a 22,000 foot store in Townstal. More than this it would be a 'flagship' project for the massive company, and would be the most environmentally friendly store in the country, if not the world.

The site on Nelson Road had been at the centre of much speculation for more than a year, but this was the first concrete announcement about the site's future. The news was welcomed by many in the town, mainly due to the creation of 150 jobs.

Less positive however, was the reaction to the use of one word by one of the town's elected representatives.

Town Cllr Roger Kempton caused controversy by describing visitors to the town as 'dross' and saying Dartmouth needed to move upmarket. The comments caused public outrage and brought the council to crisis after Cllr Brian Boughton demanded Cllr Kempton apologise, which he refused to do. The comments created national comment, as visitors asked themselves 'am I dross?' and many, it was assumed, decided not to come again.

Dartmouth Town Council asked Dartmouth's Fatstock Show to allow women to attend its annual dinner.

The show normally invites the Mayor or their deputy to its dinner, but it does not allow women to attend. The problem was both Mayor and deputy Mayor were women, which left the show to invite 'a male member of the council'. The council demanded that the group review its policy and said it would not send a representative until it did. Although Richard Rendle did offer to go along in a dress.

Anne Stallybrass and Peter Gilmore, who first came to Dartmouth in 1971 with The Onedin Line, *bid a fond farewell in 2006.*
PHIL SCOBLE

Dartmouth as a Film and TV Location. See Feature on pages 64–65

Turkeys trussed up for Christmas at the annual Fatstock Show.
PHIL SCOBLE

2007The year began with fears that Dartmouth Regatta could be a much smaller event in 2007.

New Chairman of the event Robin Leask revealed that the marquee on Coronation Park had been dropped from plans because of the large capital outlay, thought to be more than £40,000 for its hire. The marquee housed three of the Regatta's biggest events: the Regatta Rock, the Picnic in the Park black tie event and the Shopping Village.

However a compromise was soon reached by bringing in an outside company which would take the rights for the shopping village and allow the Regatta Committee to hold the Regatta Rock and the Picnic in the Park free of charge. This was one of the 'big questions' the event had to answer to allow it to continue, as finances began to look ever tighter.

DEATH OF REGATTA CHAIRMAN

The year was also a traumatic one for the venerable event.

Its chairman Robin Leask passed away after a short fight with cancer. Mr Leask was described by his wife as 'a real gentleman'. Many paid tribute to his no-nonsense, old style work-ethic and honesty. His daughter Alex came to Dartmouth for Regatta and represented Mr Leask's family at all of the large scale events.

The weather was perfect throughout the week, and the dates on which the Regatta fell, after the bank holiday helped create a relaxed atmosphere and a fine mood throughout the town.

New Regatta Chairman David Kelland said: 'There was a terrific atmosphere throughout. The great weather meant that very few events were cancelled. I am very pleased at how everything went, with no trouble and a lot of people have a great deal of fun.

'Robin Leask's daughter Alex was a great support throughout the Regatta and it helped us to feel that this year was all for Robin.'

The whole town watched as Kittery Court, one of Kingswear's most memorable buildings, almost burned down in the space of an afternoon. The historic building was owned by the owner of the Hallmark card company and garnered national interest. This interest was piqued even more when it was revealed that a 16 year old apprentice had started the fire: many jokes were made about what card would be chosen to hold the young man's P45. Considering the millions the owner had put into renovating and developing the site, the fire was enough to make anyone wince.

BLAIR MAKES HISTORY BEFORE HE LEAVES OFFICE

Security was tight when Tony Blair became the first serving Prime Minister to visit Dartmouth's Britannia Royal Naval College.

Mr Blair met staff and officers at the College, but a tight schedule meant he had no time to speak to the press, so it is unclear what he thought about his visit.

The College's Commodore Tim Harris said that he was 'delighted' and 'excited' to welcome Mr Blair. Winston Churchill did visit the historic College in 1940, but months before he took the top job in British politics.

The visit, only announced the day before for security reasons, was part of a day of visits around the southwest, as Mr Blair began his final few months in office. Many saw the visit as a positive sign for the Britannia Royal Naval College as current talk of naval cutbacks left a question mark hanging over the College's future.

Security was immensely tight: all cars were searched before entry and all visitors escorted around the grounds by MoD and police personnel.

The town lost 'one of its last true characters' with the death of Judy Lewthwaite, aged 88.

Ms Lewthwaite founded the Strolling Playhouse in the town which was one of the best known ways for children to start acting in and around Dartmouth during the 1970s. Ms Lewthwaite was famously good at getting on with children, and was named locally as 'the Pied Piper of Dartmouth'.

*Prime Minister
Tony Blair arrives
at the Britannia
Royal Naval College
with Commodore
Tim Harris and
Commander Richard
King.*
PHIL SCOBLE

Ms Lewthwaite was famous for her 'live' Punch and Judy show, in which she and others would perform for crowds of adoring children at Regatta, Town Week and other events. She was well known for walking around in her costumes before performances, but was so well known no-one thought it was out of the ordinary.

Another death brought shock, anger and violence.

The people of Townstal reacted with disbelief at the death of a local man from a suspected drug overdose in Windsor Road. George King was discovered in the early hours of the morning and another man was arrested on suspicion of drugs offences.

The death of Mr King raised tensions on the Townstal estate, where many residents for some time had been concerned about drug taking, drug related crime and anti-social behaviour. Police mounted extra patrols after a group of men had an altercation in the area around Windsor Road.

Rumours abounded about the real reasons behind Mr King's death, and vandalism and threats against anyone connected with the incident threatened to spill over into much more serious crime and violence.

STOKE FLEMING FIGHTS TO SAVE ITS LIBRARY – AND WINS

Campaigners at Stoke Fleming library were celebrating when they heard their library had been saved from closure.

It was put at risk after a report in 2006 by Devon Libraries Service recommended its closure. At the same time Kingswear library was also put at risk, but no one stood up to fight for the dilapidated and badly-stocked library and many actually welcomed the replacement mobile service in the village.

In Stoke Fleming, however, a group was formed to increase usage of the library and prove there was a need for it.

They contacted every household in the village and encouraged them to use the service and even started taking books around to those who couldn't get out.

In the middle of this campaign Devon County Council were forced to admit the library was succeeding at bringing in new readers – after it had quoted its own figures incorrectly.

The libraries' service released a statement saying that while membership had gone up at Stoke Fleming's library since it was put under threat, book issues had not.

However, after the library's user group protested that its own figures showed a huge jump in membership AND issues, Devon County Council had to check – and found it was wrong. The county council expressed 'regret' about the 'upset and confusion' this has caused.

The library service then decided the Stoke Fleming Library could stay open. John Lewis, the Chairman of the Stoke Fleming Library Users Group said: 'We have been working long and hard for this so we are very pleased indeed. The library is now actively used by over half the households in the village. It is increasingly recognised as a major community resource.'

The police in Dartmouth called for witnesses to come forward after a rampage of vandalism around the town.

It was revealed that four youths, aged 14 and 15, were responsible for the trail of vandalism, including turning over a car because the police 'tipped away their vodka'.

The attacks came after a week of trouble with anti-social behaviour around the town. The four also threw nine flower holders into the Boatfloat – each worth more than a hundred pounds – partially destroyed a memorial bench in the Royal Avenue Gardens and attacked one of the kiosks on the Embankment, nearly rocking it off its foundations. The group caused £4,000 worth of damage.

Dartmouth's neighbourhood beat manager, Sgt Iain Simons, said he was glad that the four had admitted their guilt.

'These youths had been spoken to earlier in the day for riding their bikes illegally around the town, and had their bikes confiscated,' he said. 'They got hold of some vodka, and had been drinking in the street. They were spoken to again and had their vodka taken away. They told us later that they had decided that because we had 'tipped' their vodka away, they would 'tip' over a car. That is a frightening mentality.'

DART LIFEBOAT STATION OPENS
FOLLOWING CONTROVERSY

The crew of Dartmouth's new Inshore Lifeboat – which became operational after much controversy in 2007.
Phil Scoble

Dartmouth finally saw the opening of its new Lifeboat Station on Coronation Park. The station, the first in Dartmouth for more than 111 years, was fraught with problems during its planning stages.

Protestors claimed the station should be built on the north end of the park, nearer to the slipway the lifeboat was to use. Instead it was to be built on the site of the derelict tennis pavilion because the site already had all the amenities it needed, and this would allow quick installation of a station. Nevertheless, many felt it would herald further development of the park.

Flavel Trustees Chairman Ray Bridges said: 'I think a lot of people will be quite upset. The RNLI, of course, is everybody's favourite charity. I am a member myself and I have made donations to the local lifeboat appeal, but it shook me when I looked up the South Hams website and saw the whole thing. The proposed building with its felt roof looks awful and should have been sited at the other end of Coronation Park.'

An RNLI spokesman, however, suggested there was no alternative to the proposed site at present and that it was not for the want of trying that the site had been selected.

Despite the protests the station received planning permission during the summer, and construction on the station began as soon as Regatta finished.

The station, with its twenty three strong crew of volunteers, was declared 'On Service' during October. A massive fundraising campaign around the area had managed to collect more than £200,000 in under a year to pay for the building of the station.

Less impressive was Dartmouth's Celebrity Chef. John Burton-Race did not have a good month in December.

He went on the reality TV show *I'm a Celebrity…Get Me Out of Here!* living on scraps of food in a rainforest and undertaking the infamous 'Bush Tucker Trials' – and got news on his mobile that his wife had closed his New Angel restaurant in the town.

Mrs Burton-Race was estranged from her husband after he left her for his friend Suzi Ward in Strete, with whom he had a son. More than twenty staff were left out of work three weeks before Christmas, and a number of suppliers were still owed money.

Mr Burton-Race returned to Britain and claimed he had a number of offers to buy and re-open the New Angel, two of these offers were with him as head chef. However, he also stated that he was 'not good at going backwards'. He was back very soon, however, backed by internet millionaire Clive Jacobs, who bought all the New Angel businesses and installed Mr Burton-Race as his chef in the restaurant.

Getting up close and personal with the seafood at the annual Dartmouth Food Festival.
PHIL SCOBLE

John Burton-Race.
WIKIPEDIA

Dartmouth Celebrity Chefs – A Brief History. See Feature on pages 92–93

ONE OF THE MOST IMPROVED PRIMARY SCHOOLS IN THE COUNTRY

Dartmouth Primary School was named as one of the best improved primary schools in the country over the previous three years.

The school was named 33rd most improved school nationally in figures released by the Department for Children, Schools and Education. Dartmouth was the only school named in the top 100 from the whole of Devon, and the school ranked above both the Devon and national average for key Stage two results.

The good news came in the same year that the school agreed to 'federate' under one group of governors with the Community College, creating a 'Learning Campus'.

The school was scored out of 300 for its results at year six for science, maths and English. In 2004 it got 153, but raised itself to 253 in the last set of results, a rise of 100 points or 65 per cent. The English national average is 245, and the Devon average is 249.

Headteacher Rik Meek said: 'I am so proud of everyone here. The staff were delighted as they have worked really hard over the last few years, and this is a great recognition of this. It's giving the children some real pride in their school, to know it is one of the most improved in the country. We tell them they can do anything and this helps to prove it.'

2008 World Events
● The price of petroleum hits $100 per barrel for the first time
● Stock markets around the world plunge amid growing fears of a U.S. recession, fuelled by the 2007 subprime mortgage crisis
● The British government introduces emergency legislation temporarily to nationalize Northern Rock, the 5th largest mortgage bank in the UK, due to the bank's financial crisis

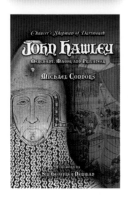

Michael Connor's book on John Hawley was published by Richard Webb to mark the 600th Anniversary of Dartmouth's famous merchant, mayor and privateer. He was also the inspiration for Chaucers 'Shipman of Dartmouth' in the Canterbury Tales.

Artist Simon Drew opens the new Ladbrokes at the corner of Foss Street and Duke Street with manager Dave Wild.
PHIL SCOBLE

2008

Twelve Stoke Fleming school children narrowly avoided disaster when the back wheels of their school coach sheared off along a narrow high road above Blackpool Sands on February 5.

The school bus was carrying twelve children from Strete to Stoke Fleming Primary School around 8.30am, when its rear axle snapped, and both near-side rear wheels came off the coach.

The driver – who was hailed as 'a hero' by the school and police – fought with the controls of the bus to bring it to a safe stop with no brakes and on a steep incline. The bus was travelling towards the small bridge above Blackpool Sands on the Strete side of the picturesque holiday destination.

PC Becky Sutton was one of the first on the scene and said the driver of the bus had done well.

'She did an incredible job,' she said. 'She stayed calm and brought the bus under control, which took more than fifty yards. I shudder to think what could have happened if the problem had occurred just 200 yards further back, the bus could have gone over the edge on a hairpin bend. It was clearly a situation where children could have been killed.'

CCTV NOT INFRINGING CRIMINALS' HUMAN RIGHTS

South Hams District Council attracted ire and national coverage after saying it could not install CCTV in the Royal Avenue Gardens because of the Human Rights Act.

The district council was responding to heavy criticism for not installing a new CCTV system to stop vandalism in the much-loved gardens.

Nick Hodgson, head of property services for the district council, said that its position 'had not changed' despite recent vandalism to the memorial fountain in the gardens. He said that the council had been 'advised' any system could be in contravention of the Human Rights Act, which had been controversial since it was brought onto the statute books in 1998.

But the advice turned out to be wrong and the council were forced to admit that no such legal problem existed. However this was not before headlines were splashed across most of the national newspapers.

Ladbrokes caused a ruckus in Dartmouth when they proposed moving to the town's most photographed street. The national chain put in an application to change the building at the corner of Foss and Duke Street, one of the town's most photographed and popular shopping streets.

Traders and residents reacted negatively to the plans and organised a petition which attracted more than 700 signatures. The planning office at South Hams District Council was inundated with letters of objection and more than thirty residents turned up to the meeting where the planning application was decided – and all to no avail – Ladbrokes opened in October.

COUNCILLORS IN NEED OF TRAINING

Members of Dartmouth Town Council were entered for 'training' by the Standards Board of England.

The order to South Hams District Council's monitoring officer took the council into the local government version of counselling to help resolve its ongoing disputes.

The order to get members of the council and the Town Clerk Chris Horan into 'mentoring, training and conflict management' was sent to Deputy Standards Officer Delyth Jenkins Evans at South Hams District Council. Dartmouth Town Council had

Left: *Dartmouth Leisure Centre's Junior Football team get a new kit thanks to the Yorkshire Building Society.*
PHIL SCOBLE

Below left: *Bad weather shuts the Lower Ferry.*
PHIL SCOBLE

Below right: *Heavy rain and high spring tides left the owner of this scooter a bit short.*
PHIL SCOBLE

been the subject of nine complaints to the standards board over different councillors' behaviour in the past three years. Most of the complaints have been made by councillors themselves, complaining about their colleagues. The majority of town and parish councils in the South Hams have not even had one in the same period.

A man died after deliberately driving his car off Kingswear Fish Quay.

Nigel Keen, 47, from the Ellacombe area of Torquay drove his silver BMW into the Dart on Wednesday May 14, in front of tens of witnesses, around 6pm. The Dart Inshore Lifeboat and Coastguard were called to the scene before police divers brought Mr Keen's body to the surface nearly three hours later. Reports indicated that Mr Keen clearly meant to drive over the edge.

The car was brought to the surface the next day after the police divers conducted a detailed forensic examination of the car when it was on the bottom.

Prince William visited Dartmouth and messed about in boats for the cameras as he began his short naval training. Prince William spent two months with the Royal Navy, following the completion of his training with the Royal Air Force.

HRH Prince William (as Sub-Lieutenant W Wales) during his short period of training at the Britannia Royal Naval College in June 2008.
GETTY IMAGES

The attachment was designed to familiarize Prince William with the structures, capabilities and working conditions of the Royal Navy. He 'shared the working lives of sailors, as he has already done with airmen, and to make comparisons with his own experience to date as an Army officer' according to his spokesman.

The Prince showed his prowess at boat handling on the river Dart in a Picket Boat, one of the fifteen metre twin-engine launches used by the Britannia Royal Naval College for teaching the principles of ship handling. The press loved seeing him working the boat in the specially arranged press call – especially when he failed to knock the slip off the anchor chain first time – meaning he had to buy drinks for his entire crew according to tradition.

Firefighters risk their lives trying to control the fire as it raged in the centuries old building in Higher Street in May 2010.
(See year 2010) Phil Scoble

Captain Robert Franks CBE DSO DSC *died on March 5, 2008, aged 95, after a distinguished naval career followed by a busy retirement in which he supported many local organisations. He was an audacious destroyer captain in World War II and was involved in action across the world at Dunkirk and then Burma and also the D-Day landings. In 1959 he was given command of the Royal Navy's first commando carrier HMS* Bulwark. *In Dartmouth he enjoyed family life, work in the community and cruising from the harbour in his yacht* Matawa *to both local and foreign destinations (see page 73).*

Top right: *Students and staff celebrate the new sculpture studio at Dartmouth Community College 2008.*
PHIL SCOBLE

COLLEGE NOT THREATENED WITH CLOSURE (AGAIN)

Dartmouth Community College acting Principal Julie Stuchbery-Ullah reassured parents the College was not threatened with closure.

The College was named among schools which needed 'transformation' to improve GCSE results by Education Minister Ed Balls. The minister singled-out schools which did not achieve a target of 30 per cent of students achieving five or more A* – C GCSE grades.

Mrs Stuchbery-Ullah said that the figures were based on 2007 results and that the school was listed as 'failing' because just five students got a D rather than C grade in Maths. She said the school was so small each student represented 'one percentage point' in these figures, and that the school was on track to make the target this year.

'We have obviously been aware of these figures since August last year,' she said. 'Our expectation is that we will exceed this target in this year's GCSEs. This is due to the hard work of our teachers and students. This list penalises Dartmouth as a small school because just five students attaining a C rather than a D would have taken us off this list.' In August's GCSE results the College achieved some of its best-ever results with 60 per cent gaining at least five A* to C grades.

British Gas apologised to a Dartmouth café after trying to charge it £12,000 for gas – when it didn't have any.

The Old Market Café, run and owned by Rob and Collette Smith, had been receiving bills from the gas company for nearly a year in September – even though they didn't use gas in the cafe. The bills varied in size, but had always been thousands of pounds – and the last came in at £11,278.

Mr Smith said he tried to sort the problem a number of times.

'We have called so many times, and have even had the town council, our landlords, call up, but we never got a solution,' he said. 'We were promised repeatedly it had been wiped and we would not be charged, but then would receive another bill. It became very frustrating. They even threatened to cut us off and send round the bailiffs!'

At their wit's end, Mr and Mrs Smith popped into the *Chronicle* office and asked if it could help. A quick phone call to the company and Mr Smith was talking to a very apologetic customer service manager, who waived the bill and even cancelled charges incurred as the café has a gas meter on site, even though they were liable to pay maintenance on it.

*Young sailor
Henry Bomby
starts his
preparations for a
daunting Round
Britain sail – he
gave himself two
years to be ready
to do the trip
single-handed.*
PHIL SCOBLE

ALLO, ALLO, WHAT'S GOING ON HERE THEN?
I'M WHAT? OPENING THE STORE?!

PC Paul Marels was shocked but delighted to be invited to open the town's new multi- million pound Sainsbury's store on August 16.

PC Marels, known locally as 'Molly', has been a police officer for more than thirty years, and for twenty seven of those has been based in the South Hams.

He had been a Dartmouth-based PC for nineteen years and would soon retire. He was asked to go to the opening by Community Sergeant Iain Simons on the pretext that a police presence was needed, even though PC Marels was on holiday. As he arrived PC Marels was surprised to be marched into the store and informed he was to be given the honour of opening the most expensive building in Dartmouth's history – and the 'Greenest Store in Britain' according to the retailer.

'I didn't know anything about it but began to have my suspicions as I arrived,' said PC Marels. 'I have loved being a policeman in Dartmouth and was delighted to be asked to cut the ribbon. My wife and family were here, which was great, along with a number of my current and ex-colleagues. I am totally bowled over!'

Sergeant Simons said: 'Molly is well liked, and a very respected officer whose policing style has always been community led. It was great to arrange this wonderful surprise for a PC who has dedicated his life to the community in the South Hams and particularly to Dartmouth.'

Town Cllr Brian Boughton was allowed to join council committees after a six month ban but almost immediately got into disagreement with his fellow councillors based on his own misunderstanding of the conditions of his re-admission. He had been removed from council committees for 'unreasonable behaviour' six months before. He defended his earlier actions by saying he would never apologise for 'fighting for what I believe in'. He said that the council 'does not have the infrastructure' to deal with councillors who 'fundamentally disagree' with council policy.

The vote to bring Cllr Boughton back into the 'committee system' was unanimous and a number of councillors said they were 'glad' to welcome Cllr Boughton 'back into the fold'. Although this was before Cllr Boughton spoke on the subject. He believed that he was only going to be allowed to join one committee. All councillors are entitled to join the planning committee and are expected to join one other, with some councillors allowed to join two.

Cllr Boughton had not understood that he would be able to join planning and one other committee, and claimed it was 'undemocratic'.

NIGEL EVANS

Reflections of Dartmouth *by Nigel Evans, a collection of beautiful photos of the town and river, was published by Richard Webb in July 2008. The book was launched in style at the Royal Dart Yacht Club.*

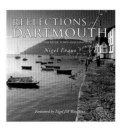

Opposite page
– bottom left:
Community College Headteacher Chris Long takes Anthony Steen MP around for a look at the College's improving facilities.
PHIL SCOBLE

The familiar smile of David Hawke, a much loved Dartmothian and local chef who died on his 58th birthday, 26 February 2009.
Exeter Express & Echo

Dartmouth's 53 year association with Her Majesty's Band of the Royal Marines ended in May 2009. See Feature on pages 24–25

Dartmouth's new Higher Ferry arrived on June 15, 2009. See Feature on pages 36–37

2009
Mayor-making was made to look laughable when more than half of the council members were nominated for the role.

SO, WHO WANTS TO BE MAYOR THEN?

The council used a Mayoral election system which has been in place for decades, and is still very similar to the way it was conducted in the 14th century.

Councillors were asked to nominate someone they thought should be Mayor and they can nominate themselves. Those nominated were asked to confirm whether they were standing or not before the election. No one on the council knew who was standing until the election itself.

The councillor's voted in a series of rounds, with the least popular candidate being eliminated in each round, until one councillor gained a majority vote. Nine councillors out of sixteen were nominated for the role of Mayor. Seven eventually stood, with the incumbent Mayor Debbie Morris winning after a series of rounds against new councillor Paul Reach.

Some councillors called for a public vote, and others said that the system needed to be changed so that the public had a say in the election of the Mayor; still others claimed that the rules needed to be changed so that councillors cannot nominate themselves.

Cllr Bill Wills said: 'I nominated myself for the council and consider it a protest vote. There needs to be changes on the council; the old guard who want no change to anything can happily block any efforts to do anything. Something new and good for the town should not be stopped.'

Mayor Debbie Morris said: 'In the past the system has worked well. The system does not need to be changed, but thanks to people trying to cause problems, we have this sad situation with so many standing.'

DEATH OF 'BON VIVEUR'

The town mourned the sudden death of David Hawke – one of its best loved characters. Mr Hawke died while on holiday in St Lucia on his 58th birthday. He died in his sleep from meningitis. Friends and colleagues paid tribute to his love of life and charismatic personality. He was famous for his welcoming and friendly nature and could talk to anyone, no matter what their background or creed.

Mr Hawke was general manager at the Royal Castle Hotel, but had owned and been chef at a succession of eateries in the town, and had also been chef on a number of superyachts – allowing him to indulge his love of travelling.

'It's horrendous, such a shock,' said one of his oldest friends Elwyn Horrell. 'David was a wonderful man. He was loyal and loved people. I've never known anyone have a bad word to say about him. Once he made a friend he kept them. I've been contacted and am contacting people all over the world to let them know – because David made friends wherever he travelled. He was such a positive and charismatic man – he got on with everyone he met no matter where they came from or what their views. I will miss him terribly; you had more fun when he was around.'

Students at the town's Community College got a huge shock when eleven police officers with sniffer dogs swooped on the College on a Wednesday morning.

A student was interviewed in relation to drugs offences after the 'raid'.

The dramatic operation was conducted after intelligence from several sources was received by police and school authorities. Four students were searched after being taken out of lessons during the school day and a small amount of a suspected banned substance was found. The school was thoroughly searched using the police dogs, including the school playing fields.

The actions were fully supported by the school and its management team, Principal Chris Long told the *Chronicle*.

The action was unprecedented in the South Hams said police Inspector Paul Morgan: 'The intention was to combat problems of this sort with swift and high profile operations that will send out a clear message that illegal substances being brought onto school premises is not acceptable,' he said.

DEATH ON THE EMBANKMENT

A man was killed in a mysterious and horribly tragic way.

John Ford was killed when he was run over on Dartmouth's South Embankment on June 30.

Mr Ford had been out drinking with his wife Lyn, and then stayed on to have a few on his own and she went home.

Details were difficult to come by, as there were few people around on the night the tragedy happened, but it seems that Mr Ford was involved in a fight with two other men, and either left in the road unconscious or collapsed there following the altercation.

Children staff and councillors line up to take part in the first public consultation about Dartmouth federation becoming an academy.
PHIL SCOBLE

The teenage driver of the Renault Clio that then ran him over did not see Mr Ford in the road and drove straight over him, inflicting the injuries that killed him a few minutes later.

Lyn Ford said that John had loved Dartmouth, his adopted town, so much and said he was proud to live here.

She spoke of her own grief at losing the man 'who loved me more than anyone else could' and said he 'didn't have a bad bone in his body'.

Mr Ford was born in Woking in Surrey and was a trained horticulturalist – and was linked with the Dartmouth in Bloom committee. He worked around the South East for most of his working life before moving to Devon with Lyn three years before his death.

Lyn described Mr Ford, who had been working at Sainsbury's as a baker since the winter, as a free spirit who had her best interests always in the forefront of his mind.

An inquest the following year returned an open verdict on Mr Ford's death because of the lack of evidence.

For the first time Westcountry Ambulance Trust asked one of its paramedics to publicly talk about an assault made on them whilst they were on duty. The paramedic came from Dartmouth, as did his attacker.

The unprecedented move was taken due to the severity and inexplicable nature of the attack.

Haydn Glanvill, 45, was attacked by a 64 year old woman in Thurlestone Gardens on July 26 when he answered a 999 call to help the woman's husband, an 83 year old man who had suffered cardiac arrest.

The attack could have caused his death as she lay across him trying to stop the paramedics getting access to her husband and even climbed into the ambulance and ripped off the oxygen mask and ECG cables which had been attached to aid his recovery.

Dartmouth Paramedic Hayden Glanvill with Police Sergeant Iain Simons and a colleague.
PHIL SCOBLE

Mr Glanvill told the *Chronicle* how he had now faced his attacker in a 'restorative justice' style procedure and received both a verbal and written apology. He said nothing would stop him doing his job, but attacks on paramedics and members of the emergency services were not acceptable.

Police Sergeant Iain Simons, who witnessed the woman's behaviour himself first hand, said any attacks on ambulance staff would not be

Dr Sarah Wollaston (right) meets Alvin Smith (left), the Dartmouth inventor of the 'Searaser' wave energy device. She was selected at the first ever 'Primary' in 2009, prior to being elected Conservative MP for the Totnes constituency in May 2010. She polled nearly 22,000 votes (46%) with a majority of nearly 5000.

RICHARD WEBB

Artist Simon Drew decided to throw his hat – briefly – into the political ring in protest at the behaviour of MPs, and especially local Anthony Steen MP.

PHIL SCOBLE

tolerated. He said the face to face meeting between victim and assailant was a good way of bringing back 'old fashioned' values of crime and consequence, as perpetrators of crime and violence were forced to consider the results of their bad-behaviour.

Extravagant TV chef and former Tuckenhay resident, Keith Floyd died of a heart attack at the age of 65.

Floyd was the first of the TV chefs to record 'on location'. He was famous for his bow tie, glass of wine and easy charm in front of the camera. He was famously as bad a businessman as he was a talented chef. He sank £1 million into the Maltsters Arms at Tuckenhay, only to lose everything, according to legend when he accepted a cheque for a drinks order of £36,000 which then bounced.

GOODBYE BRIAN, AND THANKS FOR ALL THE FIGHTS

Brian Boughton was disqualified from being a councillor for three years after being found guilty of bullying and bringing the office of councillor into disrepute.

Dr Boughton, who had been a town councillor since 2001, was found guilty of multiple breaches of the councillors' code of conduct by an independent Adjudication Panel at Torquay's Grand Hotel. Dr Boughton claimed that without him on the council there would be 'mayhem' and said he wasn't 'the devil incarnate' but a councillor that had been hard working and said he maintained that the council was in a 'shameful' condition.

The hearing was the culmination of a year-long investigation into Dr Boughton's behaviour towards Clerk to the Council Chris Horan. Mr Horan told the hearing that Dr Boughton's bullying and intimidating behaviour towards him had 'destroyed' him and taken away his confidence and enjoyment of a 'job he loved'.

Mr Horan had a number of absences due to stress which he attributed in the main to Dr Boughton – who would visit Mr Horan in the Dartmouth Town Council offices on an 'almost daily' basis. Dr Boughton would often begin his visit with the words 'The question for today is…' and would sometimes stay for more than half an hour. During these exchanges the hearing heard from various witnesses that Dr Boughton could become loud, aggressive and abusive, getting very close to Mr Horan in an intimidating and frightening manner.

Dr Boughton had rarely been out of the headlines in the preceding few years – he was thrown off all committees for 'unreasonable behaviour' and then started a long-running battle to have prayers before meetings stopped, which he started by listening to an iPod at council and humming over the prayer read out by Council Chaplain Simon Wright.

It was a shame that this was the way Dr Boughton left local politics – as he had been actively involved in many positive schemes, especially during his time as a district councillor, helping to get the Townstal Community Hall built and also working towards the building of the planned heated indoor swimming pool. Dr Boughton also fought for affordable housing alongside sustainable economic development though employment, and spoke strongly in favour of Sainsbury's, Lidl and the leisure centre in Townstal.

Also in trouble was the town's MP Anthony Steen, who was forced to stand down amid the national outcry over MP's expenses.

Mr Steen resigned and caused huge national outrage when he claimed people angry at the expenses he had claimed for the upkeep of his million-pound home near Totnes were simply 'jealous' because the house looked like 'Balmoral'.

After nearly thirty five years in parliament, Mr Steen ensured the only reputation he would take with him would be that of the man who summed up why the whole of Britain was angry at the House of Commons.

His expense claims, of £88,000 over three years on the house, including tree inspections and general maintenance, were by no means the worst in Parliament. But his outburst on national radio that, essentially, the general public would have done the same in his position was perhaps the most suicidal comment anyone could have made in the circumstances. His party leader David Cameron threatened to remove the whip from Mr Steen if he made any more comments, and the Totnes MP almost immediately disappeared from public view. The Conservative party decided to hold an open, public vote to choose the next parliamentary candidate for the area. The people, in the first ever such American-style 'Primary' election, chose GP Dr Sarah Wollaston, who seemed everything Mr Steen wasn't: young, personable and approachable. The press loved her and she made a concerted campaign to make up for the anger at Mr Steen's departure.

The loss of Her Majesty's Band of the Royal Marines does not mean the music stops – a new volunteer band was born and supported by the Canvas Factory in Dartmouth, which made the band's music holders.
PHIL SCOBLE

BRETT HALL DIES A HERO

Dartmouth and the South Hams mourned its first serviceman to be killed in Afghanistan.

Dartmouth born-and-bred Brett Hall, 21, of the 2nd Royal Tank Regiment died on Wednesday September 16 at the Royal Centre for Defence Medicine, Selly Oak, due to injuries sustained when an explosion hit his Combat Logistic Patrol in rural northwest Helmand province on Saturday September 12. He was driving a Viking vehicle when it was attacked by an improvised explosive device.

Brett, who was just 21, was brought up in Townstal and attended both Dartmouth Primary School and Dartmouth Community College. He joined the Army in November 2006, aged 18.

Brett was the oldest of four siblings, two of whom were still students at Dartmouth Community College.

The town came to a standstill for his full military funeral.

Trooper Brett Hall.
See Feature on
page 232

Top left: *Brett Hall's coffin is taken from St Saviours Church.*
PHIL SCOBLE

Top right: *Crowds listen respectfully to the funeral service of Corporal Brett Hall.*
PHIL SCOBLE

Bottom left:
A town mourned.
PHIL SCOBLE

Bottom right: *The funeral cortege slowly makes its way around the town.*
PHIL SCOBLE

2010

In the first few months of the year Dartmouth Community College's bid to become an Academy began to draw attention from those unsure it was a positive move for education in Dartmouth. Academies were a controversial bone of contention at the time, being a flagship idea from the incumbent Labour Government. The Anti-Academies Alliance, a group headed by the National Union of Teachers which was totally opposed to Academies, organised a meeting at the Flavel in March, and capitalised on parents' growing apprehension about the change. The *Chronicle* was contacted by a number of parents who felt that the proposed changes would make the school an experiment, one their children could ill-afford to go wrong.

At the same time the school was celebrating the announcement that £8 million would be spent on rebuilding it. The school pleaded with the community to wait before consultation events were held in May about the shift to Academy status. This would take the school out of control of the Local Education Authority and place it in the hands of its governors and a 'partner' organisation. In Dartmouth's case this was education charity E-Act. Parents already felt as if the decision had already been made – seemingly confirmed when the new academy uniform was ordered before the consultation had finished.

The defeat of the Labour Government in May – replaced by the strange Conservative/Liberal Democrat Coalition – seemed to do nothing to change the race towards the new Academy. Then in the Summer Headteacher Chris Long, who had only been in post a year, was passed over for the top job in the new Academy – and in fact was unsuccessful in gaining any role at the new establishment. A new 'Interim' Academy Principal was appointed. Shelagh Potter paid tribute to Mr Long for 'Stepping aside so graciously'. It was soon revealed that E-Act had never allowed the head of a school it had taken on remain in post – no matter what their track record. The Academy opened in September, and the new-look uniforms, with old-fashioned blazers did seem to create a new atmosphere for students. People decided to wait and see.

HELLO AGAIN

Dartmouth Town Council again chose Richard Rendle to be its Mayor – his sixth time in the role. Cllr Rendle's first act, before he had even donned the chain of office, was to write to every town councillor and plead with them to leave the arguments of the previous five years behind. He outlined in detail the proper behaviour expected of a councillor in all situations. He asked them all to get behind the decisions of the council, whatever they were, and work together, in peace and understanding, for the good of the town. He then attacked South Hams District Council for its policy on the Royal Avenue Gardens.

Vandalism again reared its head as an issue in the town, with a primary school getting its playground smashed up, and a number of properties in Townstal attacked.

St John the Baptist Primary School's £30,000 safe play area for its youngest pupils was attacked by young vandals who turned a CCTV camera to the wall before attacking flowerbeds, plant pots and the area's Wendy House. Teachers and police were left bewildered by the attack and concluded it was simply young teenagers interested in wanton destruction.

Later in the year a Dartmouth man was angered after his car had its windscreen smashed for seemingly no reason in April. However, what made him even angrier was being told by police they wouldn't come and look at the damage because there were no witnesses. Steven Westwood's wife told the officer she believed that a Neighbourhood Watch should be started in their road, and was promptly told an officer would pop up the next day to his house with the paperwork for starting a watch.

Angela White and Brian Langworthy celebrate the opening of Dartmouth Museum's new King's Room displays.
PHIL SCOBLE

WORST FIRE IN DARTMOUTH'S HISTORY

The town was rocked by a sudden and devastating fire in the ancient set of buildings between Fairfax Place and Higher Street.

The Tudor-beamed and wooden façade-covered building at 5 Higher Street had seen many crises in Dartmouth's history pass by its impassive face, but just a few hours were enough to nearly destroy it after an electrical fault.

The trauma of the fire, the results of which were clear as the smoke cleared and the ravaged building appeared, managed to affect many areas of life in the town.

One of the more surprising ones was in managing to dent the impact of the Regatta.

The Mayor made what seemed like a strange statement saying that the Red Arrows might not perform at the ever-popular event that year because the fragility of the fire-wracked building was such powerful planes flying over might cause it to collapse. He said a 'health and safety check' had to be done to check if the buildings were safe.

It started, as such headlines often do, instant belief around the country that the Red Arrows were not coming to Dartmouth this year.

There was no health and safety check and the Red Arrows never even considered not coming.

However, it meant that the Regatta committee had to fight a rear-guard action to get the crowds to the town:

'I am furious,' said Regatta Chairman Jim Brent. 'We are a small town which has had a kick in the backside with the fire anyway. We have recovered and we are all looking towards going forward and this is appalling. It's spin on spin.

'Everybody here is anxious to impress on people that it is the whole of the South Devon that is involved with the Regatta.'

The council also got itself in hot water over the conversion of its 19th century enclosed market – by announcing tenants would be 'evicted' in the *Chronicle* before actually telling the tenants themselves.

The row appeared over plans to spend £200,000 on the conversion of the whole square into shop units, to follow the £116,000 it had spent on revamping the toilets.

However, a potentially positive story about a regeneration of a town-centre area in the middle of a recession was ruined because the council discussed what would happen to the existing tenants in open council with a journalist present. Subsequent meetings with the business owners were icy and difficult, and all the existing tenants were consulting lawyers regarding their tenancies. Reassurances were needed from Mayor Richard Rendle to calm many fears.

Smoke billows over Dartmouth ...firemen approach the fire.
Phil Scoble
See Feature on pages 280–281

Dartmouth town Cllr Dave Cawley and the town Mayor Debbie Morris open the new Market Square toilets, which cost more than £110,000.
Phil Scoble

The Great Fire of Dartmouth

(See year 2010)

The most dramatic events in a town's history are often the most traumatic.
The collective memories of the residents are often united by the events which upset and shock
them. So it proved in late May 2010 when the block of buildings between
Higher Street and Fairfax Place were completely gutted by a fire.

The electrical fire started in the late morning and seems to have smouldered for a long time before suddenly sweeping through the centuries old wooden structures, resulting in business people spilling out onto the streets to get away from the fire and smoke billowing across the town and river Dart.

Fire engines poured into the town – eight appliances filled the streets as fire service personnel desperately tried to tackle the blaze on numerous fronts. High winds channelled into the central courtyard of the building and fed the fire creating a furnace quickly breaking through the roof and spreading throughout the whole building.

The thick choking smoke generated by the ancient beams of one of the town's oldest buildings was all the more upsetting as it represented the destruction of a real and tangible part of the town's heritage. The building

Phil Scoble

had changed its function throughout the centuries, reflecting the changing times and fortunes of a town dependent on the sea and later the navy. It had been the Labour Exchange throughout the tough times of the mid Sixties, then became the home for restaurants at the start of Dartmouth's shift into a holiday destination in the 1980s.

In many ways the set of buildings WERE Dartmouth. As well as a base for businesses which reflected the face of the town, they were homes – at the time of the fire all fifteen of the flats in it were occupied. This living symbol of all Dartmouth had been was being destroyed as the town watched in a matter of hours.

The fire took hold and the desperate attempts to stop its spread became the much sadder job of damage limitation and worry for many hours waiting to see if it would spread to other buildings. Forced to use water from the Dart the fire service valiantly stopped the spread of the fire but by using salt water it condemned the ancient building to even more devastation as the salt crystals damaged the wooden beams even more.

The 17 century building before the fire.

Nigel Evans

People thronged the streets, searching out friends and sharing their amazement and shock at such a dramatic turn of events. Everyone had a memory of the buildings, and through the fire found affection for the buildings which was more than just familiarity.

As in all tragedy, it brought the best out in many with the residents and businesses who had been displaced finding offers of new premises or homes coming in from all sides. It was a day when many found out more about their town's history too, it increased the appreciation for the remaining buildings of historic significance. An appeal for funds to support the families who had lost everything was overwhelmed. More than £10,000 was collected in less than four days, buying clothes and supplies for the families who had seen their possessions go up in smoke.

However, there were other less positive results.

Disputes about ownership, responsibility and insurance delayed the work which was needed to repair and restore the buildings. For nearly five months the structure remained uncovered because of these problems, each time it rained more damage was done.

The temporary scaffolding and 'Road Closed' signs made things more difficult for businesses not damaged by the fire in the area and the ravaged buildings remained a constant reminder not only of the tragedy, but also of the fragility of the town's historic buildings. Hundreds of property owners, especially those with wooden buildings obtained electrical checks.

The rebuild was estimated at three years and millions of pounds – which left huge gaps between what the buildings owners were insured for and what it would cost to restore the beautiful buildings.

The rebuild began in 2011. It was a relief for many: though it would take a long time, they could see that the work would one day be complete, and a majestic old block would be returned to its former glory.

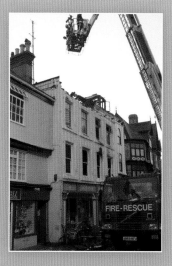

Water was pumped from the river to allow the fire teams to keep dowsing the flames. PHIL SCOBLE

The devastation. PHIL SCOBLE

Left: *Gordon D'Silva talks to HRH The Earl of Wessex Prince Edward before a tour of the Dartmouth Apprentice.*
PHIL SCOBLE

Right: *Prince Edward chats to restaurant manager Nina Stanesby.*
PHIL SCOBLE

Artist Simon Drew, in his 29th year in Dartmouth was sick of the many stories of MP corruption and deviousness, not least from Totnes MP Anthony Steen, who accused the public of being jealous that he had a house 'like Balmoral' following the MP Expenses Scandal. He decided to stand as an independent at the May elections for the Totnes constituency. He said that he wanted to 'encourage more independents to stand' because that was the only way to ensure that democracy worked for everyone.

He fought a brave campaign against a well-funded and impressive Conservative onslaught from Sarah Wollaston, but polled only 390 votes. He said he was 'pleased to have done it, but I wouldn't do it again'.

PARKING PROBLEMS COME ROUND AGAIN

Fears of parking chaos were again raised in the town after it was announced Dartmouth would finally get on street parking meters, after a decision by Devon County Council. The town claimed the fire meant that it should receive special treatment and avoid the roll-out of the dreaded meters that was due to take place in all Devon's market towns.

County Cllr Jonathan Hawkins said: 'I understand we are in a period of consultation regarding parking meters.

'I had a meeting last week with John Hart to re-emphasise how important a delay in the implementation of these measures would be.'

'It is totally insensitive to implement these measures at this time.

'Dartmouth's economy is under threat and I would hope that Devon County Council would delay action until after the fire damage has been resolved.'

However, a massive public meeting in December heard that the County Council, despite extending the period in which representations could be received, had in fact already ordered the parking meters. Things did not look good.

Despite heavy signs that the parking meters installation was inevitable, the town refused to back down. Suggestions of a 'local referendum', tireless lobbying by protestors to Devon County councillors and even Sarah Wollaston MP asking a question in parliament (the first mention of Dartmouth's parking problems in the highest legislature in the land) all added pressure to the decision makers. They were victorious, an announcement that the plan to install meters in a number of towns, including Dartmouth, was put on hold indefinitely at the end of the year. With the bitterly cold weather, it was an announcement to warm the cockles of all who heard it.

Late in the year the town lost one of its true characters. Beryl Calder, only the fourth female Mayor in Dartmouth's history, died in late November. As well as being a successful local politician, she was also a multi-talented performer and artist. She raised thousands for the Flavel through art shows and her own, famous, one-woman performances, which she also wrote herself sometimes. She was a proper old fashioned lady who treated others with respect, but could speak her mind in a devastating way when she wanted to. She was much mourned.

Mrs Beryl Calder as Mayor (1983 – 1985)
DARTMOUTH TOWN COUNCIL

EPILOGUE

DARTMOUTH HAS COME A LONG WAY IN FIFTY FIVE YEARS – OR HAS IT?

In the five and a half decades this book covers, the town has acquired a new link road, three new schools, a leisure centre, community hall, arts centre, a new larger Embankment, huge improvements to its hospital, a lifeboat, two brand new supermarkets at the top of town and many improvements to its infrastructure – not to mention the extra houses at Townstal, two new Higher Ferries and many new businesses in town.

It has also seen many businesses go to the wall or change beyond all recognition – such as Philip and Son's closure of both its Sandquay and Noss Yards and its development of the Dart Marina Complex.

Anyone who had a detailed knowledge of Dartmouth in the 1950s and had not seen it since would be flabbergasted by the changes all around.

Yet it still retains a certain something which is eternally Dartmouth. The need to be home for Regatta, the pride in the Royal Navy and the town's close association with it, a love for the sea and the men and women who risk their lives on it are just some of these traits.

I have come to love Dartmouth and its people. I feel a strong link to the stories that have shaped the town, both through those I have written as reporter, and also through those written by countless predecessors' of mine. Many of them were left unnamed because of the infrequency of by-lines in the 1950s and 1960s. They are the unsung heroes of their community, for they reported the ups and downs of Dartmouth going through huge upheavals – probably with terrible pay and a lot of hassle.

I have come to appreciate the need a town like Dartmouth has for its local paper; it is both a leader of opinion and a reflector of the public mood. It brings out the best and worst from a community and holds it up to the light, good or bad. It helps a place define itself through the views and experiences of its people.

People in Dartmouth will always fight for their beliefs: their love for the town fuelling their passion which stimulates the animated debates detailed in the pages of the paper on so many subjects.

I think as long as the people of Dartmouth retain that passion; that strength; that love, there will always be a town anyone would be proud to call home.

As I come to write the last few lines of this, a modern history of Dartmouth, I feel the need to look ahead and see where I think the town will be in the next fifty years.

I could mischievously predict a bridge across the Dart, or the filling in of the Boatfloat or the knocking down of the Butterwalk to make way for luxury flats for second home owners; but that would just be looking to make the headlines rather than report on them.

I do think that Dartmouth's community will find its future dictated by the development of the land around Townstal; the area which has in years since the new Millennium seen the building of two new supermarkets, a leisure centre and an industrial estate. If the permission and funding can be found for development to take place, I expect to see, at the very least, 400 houses built along or near the A3122 out of town in the next thirty years. If planners want to build a sustainable community there, it will also feature shops, a new hospital, retirement home, pharmacy and doctors' surgery. Hopefully there will be a pub or two and nice areas for people to walk and sit, admiring the view down to Old Mill Creek.

Dartmouth's population is steadily falling, second home owners and a lack of employment opportunities mean that if it is to remain a population centre then new homes are required, and quickly.

It has been a four year journey to complete this book for me – and a steeper learning curve would be difficult to find. I have learnt more about the town of Dartmouth than I thought it possible for one person to know, but it has left me with a deep sense of pride at a town which has constantly achieved more than could have been expected of it. I have been lucky to be that town's reporter – and then by being the author of this book – to have had the opportunity to explore its recent history.

DARTMOUTH'S ANNUAL CALENDAR OF EVENTS

February
DARTMOUTH COMEDY FESTIVAL – STARTED 2007

April
DART GIG CLUB REGATTA

May
DART MUSIC FESTIVAL – STARTED 1998

GALLERIES WEEK – STARTED 1988

June
CARNIVAL – STARTED PRE 1955, ENDED 2002

ART FESTIVAL – STARTED 2003,

CHANGED TO DARTMOUTH ART AND CRAFT WEEKEND IN 2009

TALL SHIPS – 1956 FIRST RACE LEFT FROM DARTMOUTH, STILL RETURNS PERIODICALLY

July
TOWN WEEK – STARTED 1971 ENDED 2001

August
DARTMOUTH SHAKESPEARE WEEK – STARTED 2002

THE PORT OF DARTMOUTH ROYAL REGATTA – ESTABLISHED 1834

MONKEY TOWN REGATTA, BAYARDS COVE, ENDED 1956,

REVIVED 2000 FOR THREE YEARS

September
AGATHA CHRISTIE WEEK

SOUTH DEVON WALKING FESTIVAL

October
FISHING FESTIVAL

FOOD FESTIVAL – STARTED 2004

November
DART DRAMA FESTIVAL – STARTED 2007

December
CANDLELIT DARTMOUTH – STARTED 2008

DARTMOUTH'S MAYORS 1954 – 2012

1954 – 1956	Dorothy Holwill (First Lady Mayor)		1976 – 1977	Brian Goss
			1977 – 1978	Richard Hoare
1956 – 1957	Bertie Lavers		1978 – 1980	Dennis Woods
1957 – 1958	Norman Hewson		1980 – 1981	Irene Scawn
1958 – 1960	Harold Lloyd		1981 – 1983	Donald Webb
1960 – 1961	James Lee-Palin		1983 – 1985	Beryl Calder
1961 – 1962	Richard Hoare		1985 – 1986	Leslie Savage
1962 – 1963	Dorothy Holwill		1986 – 1989	Donald Webb
1963 – 1965	Eric Rimmer		1989 – 1990	Bryan Measures
1965 – 1966	Margaret Keane		1990 – 1993	Brian Edgington
1966 – 1967	Harold White		1993 – 1995	Jack Cutter
1967 – 1968	Robert Middleton		1995 – 1997	Margaret Roberts
1968 – 1969	Eric Cook		1997 – 1999	Paul Darby
1969 – 1970	Albert Mashford		1999 – 2000	Melvyn Stone
1970 – 1971	Eric Cook		2000 – 2005	Richard Rendle
1971 – 1973	Frank Mullett		2005 – 2006	Peter Norton
1973 – 1974	Irene Scawn (Final Borough Mayor)		2006 – 2008	Iris Pritchard
			2008 – 2010	Debbie Morris
1974 – 1975	Albert Mashford		2010 – 2011	Richard Rendle
1975 – 1976	Brenda Breakwell		2011 – 2012	Paul Allen

DARTMOUTH'S FERRIES AND RIVERBOATS 2010

LOWER FERRY

South Hams District Council

The South Hams District Council-owned Lower Ferry uses a simple but tried-and-tested system of an independent, un-powered platform, hooked up to a tug boat by rope. It crosses the river between lower Kingswear and Dartmouth. A number of tugs and platforms are used in rotation, and its hard-working crew are all trained MCA Skippers. A much-loved and traditional way to cross one of England's most beautiful harbours.

The 'Historic' Lower Ferry.

DARTMOUTH STEAM RAILWAY AND RIVERBOAT COMPANY

In 2010, the Dartmouth Riverboat company operated seven vessels – and added the *Dartmouth Castle* – which was built in 1948 at Noss on the Dart by Philip and Son and had originally sailed on the Dart – to her fleet in this year as well.

Cardiff Castle
The largest vessel in the fleet carrying 400 passengers. Built in 1964 for the river Dart Steamboat Company. From 1977 operated for the Millbrook Steamboat and Trading Company out of Plymouth, but returned to the Dart in 1985.

Dart Explorer
A catamaran, carrying 300 passengers and built for the company in 1991 as *Devonair Belle*. She is mainly used on the one hour harbour cruise, and also operates most of the charters and evening disco cruises.

Dart Explorer, *owned by the Dartmouth Steam Railway and Riverboat Company*

Dart Venturer
Originally built as *Plymouth Venturer* for Plymouth Boat Cruises in 1982, this 300 passenger vessel ran for them until 2002, when it was 'swapped' with Dart Pleasure Craft's smaller *Plymouth Belle*. Used on all services.

Dittisham Princess
Built as the flagship of G.H. Riddall's fleet in 1995, this 181 passenger vessel was bought in 2000.

Dartmouth Princess
Built as the *Devon Belle II* in 1990, she joined the G.H Riddall fleet in 1995. Since being taken over by Dart Pleasure craft in 2000 she has become the main ferry on the short Dartmouth-Kingswear route.

Kingswear Belle
Originally built in 1972 for service in the Channel Islands as *Herm Trident II*, she was bought by Dart Pleasure Craft in 1989 for use on the Kingswear Ferry, where she can carry 23 passengers. She had a major fire in 2006.

Edgecumbe Belle
One of two built in 1957 for British Rail as *Humphrey Gilbert* (her sister was *Adrian Gilbert*) for use on the Dartmouth-Kingswear ferry service. When the Paignton-Kingswear branch line was closed by British rail, the two ferries were sold to St Mawes Ferry, followed by a sale back to BR for use on the Tilbury-Gravesend ferry, but they were deemed unsuitable for use on either of these two routes. The *Adrian Gilbert* returned to the Kingswear ferry in 1977. The *Humphrey Gilbert* was sold to Millbrook Steamboat and Trading Company, renamed *Edgecumbe Belle* and used on their Plymouth – Drake's Island ferry. She returned to the Dart in 1985, when she partnered her sister on the Kingswear Ferry until 1996, when *Adrian Gilbert* was sold.

HIGHER FERRY

The new Dart Higher Ferry started operating in July 2009 – the £3.5 million vessel was constructed in Holland and fitted out at the Pendennis Shipyard in Cornwall. Its arrival was greeted by huge crowds on its arrival on June 15, 2009 and it was seen as a massive improvement on its nearly 50 year old predecessor. It is owned and operated by the Dartmouth – Kingswear Floating Bridge Company (DKFBC Ltd).

The new Higher Ferry.

GREENWAY FERRIES

Greenway Belle

Greenway Belle, a local traditional clinker passenger launch, was built by J Hinks & Son in Appledore, North Devon. Previously know as *Puffin* and *Pathfinder*, she was used as a hire launch from Dartmouth for some time then was sold and left the river. She returned in 2005 when Greenway Ferries purchased her for use on the Greenway to Dittisham Ferry.

Dartmouth Belle

Dartmouth Belle a traditional clinker passenger boat was built in 1966 in Felixstowe, Suffolk. She was a purpose built passenger carrying vessel formerly known as *Fredrick William*.

She moved to Allington, was renamed *The Swan* and became famous as a passenger vessel on Allington Lock operating from the Malta Inn, Waterman's Park and Maidstone's town centre. Greenway Ferries purchased her in April 2005 when she became the Dartmouth to Greenway Ferry, carrying passengers to Agatha Christie's Greenway House and Gardens.

Dittisham Belle

A local traditional varnished clinker passenger launch was built by Clifford Adams of East Looe, Cornwall. She was a purpose-built passenger launch formerly known as *Sara* used between Looe and Looe Island in Cornwall for several years. Greenway Ferries purchased her in January 2006.

Herm Clipper

Herm Clipper was built in 1973 and ran at Guernsey to Herm up to 2007. She joined Greenway from Jamieson, Torquay, in 2009 and was renamed *Clipper*.

Christie Belle

Christie Belle was the *Dan II* at Pembroke Dock where she was used on liberty work. Arrived in the Greenway fleet in 2008 and was refitted over the winter for passenger service in 2009.

Riviera Belle

Originally built by HM Customs at Bideford for patrol around the Falmouth area under her old name *Guardwell*. She was sold and worked on Loch Lomond for some time before returning to Devon. Greenway Ferries purchased her in 2006 and renamed her *Riviera Belle* after she underwent an extensive refit.

The Fairmile

The Fairmile was a Fairmile B Rescue Motor Launch (RML) built by Southampton Steam Joinery Ltd. in 1941 and commissioned as RML497 in July 1942. Stationed with 62nd ML Flotillas at Portland between 1942 and 1944, she was then transferred to Kirkwall in January 1944 on anti-submarine target towing duties until August. She joined the 69th Flotilla based at Felixstowe until entering service with the Western Lady Ferry's service between Brixham and Torquay in that same year as *Western Lady III*. Returned to service from Swanage for Fairmile Classic Cruises in August 2007. Services ran again in 2008, but the company ran into financial problems in September 2008 and she also had certificate issues with the MCA. In June 2009 *Western Lady III* was bought by the Greenway Ferries and entered service later in the summer of 2009 as *The Fairmile* between Torbay, Dartmouth and Greenway, after a very substantial refit.

INDEX

Page numbers in *italic* show an illustration. Sub-headings are arranged in page number order.

ACKNOWLEDGEMENTS

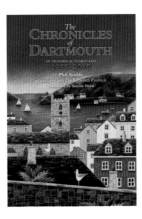

There are people who need to be thanked for this book: not least publisher Richard Webb, for taking the chance on an untrained, untested writer to put together his next book; my family and friends for their help, support and not hitting me over the head whenever I said something like 'did you know, in Dartmouth in 1975...' which I did a lot; Lesley, my wonderful and hugely supportive partner in life, who's fortitude, love and amazing willingness to be a proof-reader have made it possible for me to finally finish this book; to Barry and all at the Totnes Image Bank for going through thousands of negatives to find a few hundred images I had selected; to Greg Taylor for his help and support in photography, some of which is on view in the pages of this book, and his allowing me to rummage through the *Dartmouth Chronicle's* own archive; to Jackie Smith for letting me take on this task and have full access to the newspaper archive in Kingsbridge; Mark Hughes for finding the pictures Lesley and I failed to see; to Brian Langworthy for his generous help in sourcing *Dartmouth Chronicle's* from the 1960s, and letting me borrow them for months, and in his help accessing the images in Dartmouth Museum; Laurence Daeche for his design skills; Gareth Powell-Evans for his proof-reading skills and general ace-ness; and lastly all my work colleagues in the *Dartmouth Chronicle* office who put up with me going on and on and on about 'my book' without doing something silly to themselves or something violent to me.

Phil Scoble   www.PhilScoble.co.uk

BIBLIOGRAPHY

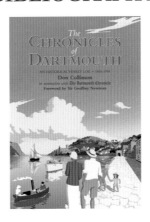

Don Collinson *The Chronicles of Dartmouth Volume 1 1854 – 1954* Richard Webb 2000
Ray Freeman *Dartmouth and its Neighbours* Richard Webb 2002
Dr Jane Harrold and Dr Richard Porter *Britannia Royal Naval College Dartmouth* Richard Webb 2005
The Dartmouth Chronicle South Hams Newspapers 1954 – 2011

COMPANION VOLUME 1854 – 1954

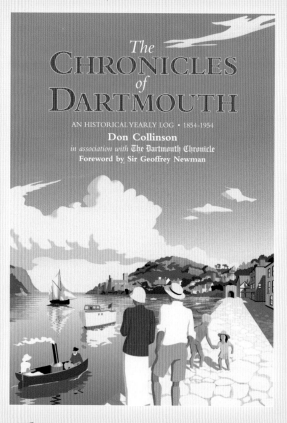

The CHRONICLES of DARTMOUTH

DEVON BOOK OF THE YEAR AWARD 2000 THE DEVON HISTORY SOCIETY

❮A book that no lover of the town and its past should be without.❯
Jan Barwick DEVON LIFE

❮A meticulously researched piece of local history of interest to all Devonians.❯
Peter Cave DEVON TODAY

❮It is well presented, the quality is good...and is overall a very stylish publication.❯
Ian Maxted DEVON COUNTY LOCAL STUDIES LIBRARIAN

❮For anybody who loves the Dart, this book is a 'must'. It is not only a book to read,
it is a book to which you will want to keep handy to refer to from time to time.❯
Dick Parkes HERALD EXPRESS

❮A fascinating read for anyone with even the slightest interest in the river Dart and its history...
The excellent illustrations and photographs will bring the reader back to the book again and again.❯
Ray Humphries TIDELINES, DART ESTUARY ENVIRONMENTAL MANAGEMENT NEWSLETTER

❮What must surely be the definitive book of Dartmouth and Kingswear during the period 1854-1954.❯
Gina Coles DARTMOUTH CHRONICLE

❮The ideal gift for the man or woman who has everything except THE CHRONICLES OF DARTMOUTH.❯
Clive Hulls SILVER RIVER, DYC MAGAZINE

❮An outstanding contribution to the history of the town, a book to be treasured by Dartmothians everywhere.❯
John Pike HERALD EXPRESS

❮This book is aimed at those who have visited Dartmouth and fallen in love with the place; they will not be disappointed.❯
David Bailey SOUTHWEST SOUNDINGS

Published by Richard Webb, Dartmouth   www.dartmouthbooks.co.uk

DARTMOUTH

DARTMOUTH HAPPY FAMILIES

Familiae Felices

HAPPY FAMILIES

DARTMOUTH'S OWN
HAPPY FAMILIES
Card Game
Devised and Sold
in aid of
DARTMOUTH'S
SWIMMING POOL
FUND
Illustrated by local
artists including:
SIMON DREW
MARK FARRELL
JOHN GILLO
ANDRAS KALDOR

Printed by Tozer & Co.
Dartmouth

MR. BLEWITT

The Bookie

MRS. BLEWITT
The Bookie's Wife

MASTER BLEWITT

The Bookie's Son

MISS BLEWITT
The Bookie's Daughter

MR. CREWS

The Boatman

MRS. CREWS

The Boatman's Wife

MASTER CREWS

The Boatman's Son

MISS CREWS

The Boatman's Daughter

MR. CRISP
The Greengrocer

MRS. CRISP

The Greengrocer's wife

MR. DREW

The Artist

MRS. DREW

The Artist's Wife

MASTER DREW

The Artist's Son

MISS DREW

The Artist's Daughter

MR. HAIR
The Vet

MRS. HAIR

The Vet's Wife

MR. KILLER

The Chemist

MRS. KILLER

The Chemist's Wife

MASTER KILLER

The Chemist's Son

MISS KILLER

The Chemist's Daughter

MR. LEGGE
The Athlete

MRS. LEGGE

The Athlete's Wife

MR. NASH
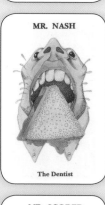
The Dentist

MRS. NASH

The Dentist's Wife

MASTER NASH

The Dentist's Son

MISS NASH

The Dentist's Daughter

MR. PILLAR

The Builder

MRS. PILLAR

The Builder's Wife

MR. SCORER

The Auctioneer

MRS. SCORER

The Auctioneer's Wife

MASTER SCORER

The Auctioneer's Son

MISS SCORER

The Auctioneer's Daughter

MR. SLEEP

The B & B Lady's Husband

MRS. SLEEP

The B & B Lady